Sources for the History of Cyprus

Volume XI

Enosis and the British:

British Official Documents

1878–1950

Sources for the History of Cyprus

Edited by
Paul W. Wallace and Andreas G. Orphanides

Volume XI
Enosis and the British:
British Official Documents
1878-1950

Selected and Edited by
REED COUGHLAN
(Empire State College, State University of new York)

Greece and Cyprus Research Center
2004

ISBN: 1-931226-11-3

ISBN set: 0-9651704-0-3

Table of Contents

Introduction

The organization of the documents in this volume into chapters reflects five phases of the Enosis agitation. Uncertainty and ambivalence on the part of the British administration marked the first phase. High Commissioner Sendall's plea for guidance in 1893 exemplifies the lack of clarity. It is remarkable that as early as 1902 (CO 67/132) the High Commissioner warned his superiors in London that the plea for union with Greece was accompanied by threats of violence. The assertion made by Haynes-Smith in 1902, namely that the movement for Enosis was motivated and led by foreign agitators and had no popular support, is one that is frequently repeated over the following half century.

The second phase was introduced when Winston Churchill visited the Island in 1907. Both the Memorial which the Enosists presented to him, and the response he returned to them, gave shape and definition to both sides in the struggle.

The memorials and London's responses over the next two decades anticipate the opening of the third phase in 1929, where we see the exchange of views and debate among Colonial Office officials about how best to respond to the flurry of deputations and memorials. The Memorial reproduced in CO 67/227/6 is annotated with detailed commentary. His Majesty's Government in December 1929 published the memorial along with the response by the Secretary of State for the Colonies as a White Paper. This was the first and last time the British Government publicly acknowledged the claims of the Greek Enosis movement and responded to the particular complaints laid out by them.

The riots of 1931 mark a definitive watershed in British policy on the Island and ushered in the fourth phase, a period of "benevolent autocracy." The documents in chapter four relate some of the immediate responses of the British to the uprising.

The final chapter in this book contains documents that show Enosis agitation to have been erratic but virulent before and during World War II. The documents referring to the plebiscite of 1950 reflect the level of British concern, as the final chapter in Enosis agitation was about to open.

Official British Documents reveal two different matters of interest and concern to Island administrators. The first was the daily concerns of trade, commerce and social administration. The Annual Reports sent to London typically dealt with all of these matters. Legislation for the year was summarized, the administration of justice and criminal statistics were presented, trade and agriculture were discussed, revenue and expenditures were presented, forests and public works were reported upon, and the current state of schools, prisons and public health was evaluated. District Commissioners sometimes included in their reports individual assessments of developments in their districts. All in all, things seemed to be running along smoothly, except that on fairly frequent occasions political agitation would occur, and the attention of officials on Cyprus and in London would be turned from administration to the vexing problem of how to deal with the political situation.

The documents assembled in this book show very clearly that Enosis was a pervasive and recurrent concern for administrators on the Island as well as for their superiors back in London. Enosis was most often presented as an unconditional demand, although in fact it was sometimes modified to incorporate more modest demands. In 1927, for example, the British made a major accommodation on the payment of the tribute, partly as a result of the protests and demands of the Enosists. In 1929, similarly, when the memorialists became convinced that there was no hope of achieving their ultimate objective, they modified the Memorial and included other demands and grievances.

There are various explanations for the ebb and flow of the demands for Enosis, for although the Greek elected members of the Legislative Council along with the church leadership kept up a persistent demand, it did tend to reflect the impact of external forces from time to time. For example, conflict between Greece and Turkey tended to exacerbate tensions between the two communities on the Island, and these tensions, in turn, encouraged the Greek Cypriots to agitate for Enosis. The Greek war of independence in 1821 and Cypriot support for the Greek nationalist movement led to a general massacre of leading Cypriot citizens by the Ottoman authorities. This was probably the most significant boost to the Enosist movement in the 19th century. The outbreak of war between Greece and Turkey in 1897 was another example. The Balkan war of 1912 resulted in riots in Cyprus. Although the British authorities seemed relatively unconcerned, the inter-ethnic violence left five dead and more than a hundred wounded.

Along with the animosity developing between the two communities by events in the larger arena, Greek dissatisfaction with economic opportunities and with the burdens imposed by high taxes, especially the burden of the so-called Tribute, was a constant theme of Enosis memorials until 1931. In 1927 the British eased the burden of the Tribute and the Legislative Council expressed its appreciation, but the memorial of 1929 continued to express unhappiness with the past effects of the payment of the Tribute. The riots of 1931 have frequently been attributed to economic factors. It is true that the Greek elected members of the legislature refused to support increased taxation and the reorganization of the tariff, but Storrs' account of political events leading up to the riots suggest that his home (Government House) was targeted because he had changed the laws governing education on the island, and the Enosists, who had for many years manipulated the system of education and the Greek schoolmasters in order to advance their cause, turned their wrath on the now notorious "Imperialistic Dictator . . . who had assassinated Hellenic education." (CO 67/247/10). No other High Commissioner or Governor was so vilified and despised in Cyprus and on the mainland, despite the fact that Storrs had been responsible for having abolished the Tribute.

If British administrators are to be believed, the elected members of the legislature were also motivated in their Enosis campaign by their resentment of British-inspired legislation that had the effect of cutting back on legal work available to lawyers among them. While this claim is difficult to verify, certainly the introduction of cooperative credit unions by the British in an effort to curtail usury must have cut into the business of money lenders, of whom several served on the Legislative Council over the years.

There is substantial indirect evidence of the effects of what we might call British cultural imperialism to suggest that the Enosis movement was partly nurtured by the simmering resentments of Greek Cypriots, who were systematically snubbed and humiliated in their own cultural milieu. In his remarkably candid and perceptive history of Cyprus in the British period, Captain C. J. W. Orr, who had served as a district commissioner and then as 'Officer Administering the Government,' admits,

> The English officials in the island hold aloof from the rest of the community, partly owing to their ignorance of the language, partly by reason of

the difference in social standards and customs. It must be admitted that there is amongst the majority of English officials . . . a kind of contemptuous arrogance, which forms a barrier greatly resented by the educated Cypriots, from whom the elected members of the Legislative Council are drawn. This attitude is by no means unknown in other parts of the British Empire, and is no less deplorable because it is for the most part unconscious. The Englishman is incorrigibly insular, and the characteristic is more apparent when he leaves his island than when he remains in it. The educated Cypriot when he visits England is treated with deference, courtesy, and sympathy, and is received everywhere on terms of complete social equality; it is not surprising that when he returns to Cyprus and experiences once more the barrier which exists between the English community there and his fellow-Cypriots he is filled with angry resentment and joins whole-heartedly in the cry for union with Greece. (Orr, 1918:171)

This disdain is in a great deal of the correspondence coming from British administrators on the island. As Orr says, the resentments these attitudes created must have contributed to the Enosis movement in no small measure. In 1902 Haynes-Smith (CO 67/132) explicitly acknowledged the social isolation experienced by Greek Cypriots and even proposed government expenditure for entertainment designed to counteract its effects.

Enosists were also encouraged by concrete evidence that Britain could be convinced to yield her interests in the Mediterranean. She had turned the Ionian Islands over to Greece in 1864, and Enosist agitators were fond of reminding the British of this precedent. Further, both Lloyd George and Churchill had expressed sympathy for the Enosists aspirations, and the British government had actually gone so far as to offer Cyprus to Greece as an inducement to enter World War I on the side of the Allies. These documents also illustrate the impact that events on Crete had at the turn of the century and again in the period 1910–1912. Haynes-Smith's letter to the Secretary of State on 30th August, 1902 makes a point of saying that "Crete is an unpleasant neighbour to Cyprus" and that agitators were hard at work trying to create parallel conditions on Cyprus.

Although the British Government resisted the demands for union with Greece over the entire period of British rule, the Greek Cypriots showed remarkable persistence and patience in pressing their claims. The British for their part alternately demonstrated ambivalent encouragement for Enosis and a dogged determination flatly to reject it. Their ambivalence is illustrated in CO 67/79, where several Colonial office staffers exchange views on whether the elected members of the Cypriot legislature should be permitted to debate the merits of Enosis. British impatience on the other hand, is personified by Storrs, who judged the Enosists petition in 1929 "no less absurd than pathetic" (CO 67 /227/6: extract on 11 September 1929).

In general, these documents show that the British attitude before 1914 was that Enosis was not within British authority. Over the next seventeen years, as Professor Arnold Toynbee states, "the Great Power says: 'What I have I hold, and that is that. The Cyprus Question is closed'—or rather, 'no Cyprus Question exists.'"(1932). Then, after the 1931 riots, they exercised what they themselves called "benevolent autocracy," although their resolve softened when Greece joined World War II on the side of the Allies. The

British attitude toward Enosis agitation, and there was a good deal of it during the war, was very much more ambivalent than in earlier times.

The documents shed a good deal of light on the role played by the system of education in Cyprus in the perpetuation of Enosis agitation. The special report solicited by the High Commissioner in 1902 spelled this out in some detail, though it was not until 25 years later that Governor Storrs did anything about it. The documents also highlight the prominence of the church leadership in advancing the cause on Union with Greece. Enosis, so conspicuous in the Correspondence, is rarely mentioned in the Annual Reports over the decades of British rule. It may be that the administration took Enosis agitation as a kind of constant element in the political scene on the island, one to which they had become so accustomed over the years that they thought it not worth commenting upon in the annual recounting of events. Even in 1912, following inter-communal rioting, the High Commissioner failed to comment on the political climate.

A note on Sources for the British period:

There are three sources for official documents on the history of Cyprus during the British period. The first is the Public Record Office at Kew Gardens, London. The second is the State Archive of the Republic of Cyprus in Nicosia. The third is the Archive maintained by the Turkish Cypriots in Kyrenia.

The Public Record Office in London, described below, is an outstanding source, meticulously maintained and easily accessed. The archive in Nicosia is also a rich source of original documents and contains details of the British period in Cyprus unavailable elsewhere, as with court records that would not have been forwarded to London. On the other hand, the archival materials are more difficult to access than those in the Public Record Office, because they have been organized in two different indexes, and their catalog is not on the web.

Finally, while the staff of the Archive in Kyrenia is congenial and helpful, the most valuable records held there are mostly in Turkish and deal with the Ottoman period. The archive and its organization are discussed in an article by Mustafa Hasim Altan, James A. McHenry, Jr., and Ronald C. Jennings, "Archival Materials and Research Facilities in the Cyprus Turkish Federated State: Ottoman Empire, British Empire, Cyprus Republic," *International Journal of Middle East Studies*, 8 (1977) 29–42.

Most of the documents in this volume come from the Public Record Office at Kew, London. The Public Record Office catalog can be accessed via the web site: http://www.open.gov.uk/pro/prohome.htm. At the Public Record Office there is a printed index to the archival holdings available in the reference room on the second floor. CO 67, "Original Correspondence," contains correspondence from 1878 to 1951. The index to this Class is 150 pages long and lists 373 files; some of the files contain more than 24 items. Topics covered by these files include railways, prisons, politics, newspapers, criminal codes, famine relief, child labor problems, the constitution, salaries of Cypriot judges, reorganization of veterinarian services, invisible exports, and so on. Correspondence about the agitation for Union of Cyprus with Greece appears in the same file as a petition from J. C. Peristianes about the computation of his pension and gratuity. Debate over the island's constitution is likely to be found along side a report of the activities of the Imperial Chemical Industries, the Troodos public health law or the Famagusta Harbour extension.

CO 67 is a rich source of information on the history of Cyprus. The documents included in this book that come from the Public Record Office were all found in CO 67.

Reed Coughlan
Empire State College
Utica, New York

A Further Note

This volume has been some years in preparation. In 1997 Professor Reed Coughlan approached me with the suggestion that we publish a volume in our series that would contain the most important British official documents. Professor Coughlan had visited archives in Cyprus, both in Nicosia and in Kyrenia, as well as in England, and had already collected many documents of great interest.

As we looked over these documents it soon became clear to us that the most important subject for the history of Cyprus in these documents was the Greek Cypriots' desire for Enosis and the British response to that desire. The Enosis documents that Professor Coughlan collected were mostly photocopies of documents in the Public Records Office, written by hand, or typewritten, on 12 in. by 16 ½ in. sheets. Transferring these documents into a readable format has not been an easy task. Professor Coughlan provided me with many of them by computer-scanning, and others have been typed by my daughter-in-law, Michele L. Wallace, to whom I give my warmest thanks. I am also grateful to David W. Martin for his help in proofreading.

The resulting collection of documents was arranged by Professor Coughlan into the chapters of this volume as he describes in the Introduction above. The arrangement within each chapter was mostly done by me. Most of these documents appear in Dispatches, which contain a cover-letter referring to the other documents included in the dispatch. The order of these documents in the file can be completely out of order and without sequence. In this volume I have arranged the documents in the order in which I hope they will make the most sense.

When the documents from Cyprus reached England, they were often commented on by officials in the Colonial Office. Some of their comments (often in nearly illegible handwriting) reveal very clearly the attitude of the government in England about the affairs in Cyprus. A number of these comments, though sometimes anonymous, we thought should be included, since they clearly showed the official view in England at the time.

We have attempted to reproduce all the documents exactly as they were written. Spelling, grammar, and formatting preferences (except in a few cases of obvious slips) are left as they appear in the originals. We have occasionally made a few small changes, such as in the use of upper or lower case letters and in the centering or listing of texts, in order to give some uniformity to the book, and provide, we hope, for easier reading.

Paul W. Wallace
University at Albany
Albany, New York

High Commissioners and Governors of Cyprus

High Commissioners		**Governors**	
1878-1879	Garnet Joseph Wolseley	1925-1926	Malcolm Stevenson
1879-1886	Robert Biddulph	1926-1932	Ronald Storrs
1886-1892	Henry Ernest Gascoyne Bulwer	1932-1933	Reginald Edward Stubbs
1892-1898	Walter Joseph Sendall	1933-1939	Herbert Richmond Palmer
1898-1904	William Frederick Haynes Smith	1939-1941	William Denis Battershill
1904-1911	Charles Anthony King-Harman	1941-1946	Charles Campbell Woolley
1911-1915	Hamilton John Goold-Adams	1946-1949	Reginald Thomas Herbert Fletcher, Baron Winster
1915-1920	John Eugene Clauson	1949-1953	Andrew Barkworth Wright
1920-1925	Malcolm Stevenson	1953-1955	Robert Perceval Armitage
		1955-1958	John Harding
		1958-1960	Hugh Mackintosh Foot

Bibliography

Alastos, Doros. *Cyprus in History*. London: Zeno, 1955.

Anderson, David, and David Killingray, ed. *Policing and Decolonization. Politics, Nationalism and the Police, 1917–65*. Manchester: Manchester University Press, 1992.

Attalides, Michael, ed. *Cyprus Reviewed.* Nicosia, Cyprus: Jus Cypri Association, 1977.

Crawshaw, Nancy. *The Cyprus Revolt*. London: Allen and Unwin, 1978.

Denktash, Rauf R. *The Cyprus Triangle*. 2 ed. New York: The Office of the Turkish Republic of Northern Cyprus, 1988.

Dodd, Clement. *The Cyprus Embroglio*. Huntington: Eothen Press, 1998.

Durrell, Lawrence. *Bitter Lemons*. London: Viking Penguin, 1973.

Ertekun, Necati. *The Cyprus Dispute and the Birth of the Turkish Republic of Northern Cyprus*. 2 ed. Oxford: K. Rustem & Brother, 1984.

Foley, Charles. *Island in Revolt*. London: Longmans, 1963.

Georghallides, G. S. *Cyprus and The Governorship of Sir Ronald Storrs: The Causes of the 1931 Crisis*. Nicosia: The Cyprus Research Center, 1985.

Georghallides, G. S. *A Political and Administrative History of Cyprus 1918–1926*. Nicosia: Cyprus Research Center, 1979.

Hill, Sir George. *A History of Cyprus*. Vol. IV. *The Ottoman Province and the British Colony, 1571–1948* Cambridge: Cambridge University Press, 1952.

Kelling, George Horton. *Countdown to Rebellion—British Policy in Cyprus, 1939–1955. Contributions in Comparative Colonial Studies*. New York: Greenwood Press, 1990.

Koumoulides, John T. A., ed. *Cyprus in Transition 1960-1985*. London: Trigraph, 1986.

Loizos, Peter. *The Greek Gift: Politics in a changing Cypriot Village*. London: Blackwell, 1975.

McHenry, James A. *The Uneasy Partnership on Cyprus, 1919–1939*. Edited by William McNeill, *Modern European History*. New York: Garland Publishing, 1987.

Necategil, Ziam. *The Cyprus Question and the Turkish Position in International Law*. Oxford: Oxford University Press, 1989.

Oberling, Pierre. *Negotiating for Survival. The Turkish Cypriot quest for a solution to the Cyprus Problem*. Princeton, N.J.: Aldington Press, 1991.

Orr, Captain C. W. *Cyprus Under British Rule*. London: Zeno Publishers, 1918.

Reddaway, John. *Burdened with Cyprus*. London: Weidenfeld & Nicholson, 1986.

Salih, Halil Ibrahim. *Cyprus: The Impact of Diverse Nationalism on a State*. Birmingham, AL: University of Alabama Press, 1978.

Storrs, Sir Ronald. *The Memoirs of Sir Ronald Storrs*. New York: G.P. Putman's Sons, 1937.

Toynbee, Arnold. "Cyprus, The British Empire and Greece." In *Survey of International Affairs, 1931*, edited by Arnold Toynbee. London: Oxford University Press, 1932.

Volkan, Vamik, and Norman Itkowitz. *Turks and Greeks. Neighbors in Conflict*. Huntington, England: Eothen Press, 1994.

Chapter 1
British Vacillation: 1878–1907

The earliest British official document to address the issue of Enosis dates to 1893 when the High Commissioner sought advice and guidance with regard to an appropriate response to the heightened agitation for Enosis. The Colonial office minutes generated by his request reflects the level of concern in London over the Enosis agitation. Correspondence in 1895 shows that inter-ethnic relations were strained when the Greeks agitated for Enosis, even at this early date. The war between Greece and Turkey in 1897 aggravated the hostility between Greeks and Turks on Cyprus and led the government to issue a proclamation banning public assemblies. The proclamation notwithstanding, Enosis agitation proceeded apace. The Colonial Office in London did not know how to react, other than to say, "It is no use trying to kill an agitation of this nature either with tea and cake or with specially devised flags and banners" (see below, IV.C.).

It is remarkable that the British noted as early as 1902 the role of Enosist propaganda in the elementary schools. As we will see in Chapter Four, it was Storrs' effort to deal with this issue that eventually led to the burning of his residence more than thirty years later.

I.   Dispatch of Walter Sendall, 29 January 1893, and Enclosures (CO 67/79)
    A. Letter of Walter Sendall, 29 January 1893
    B. Letters
    C. Newspaper Extracts
    D. British Commentary

II.   Dispatch of Walter Sendall, 23 April 1895, to the Marquis of Ripon, and Enclosures (CO 67/91)
    A. Letter of Walter Sendall, 23 April 1895 (pp. 1-18)
    B. Minutes
    C. Notes of Interview, 22 April 1895
    D. Letter of the Moslems, 17 April 1895
    E. Newspaper Extract, 15 April 1895
    F. Newspaper Extract, 31 March 1895
    G. Letter of M. B. Seager, 17 April 1895
    H. Newspaper Extract, 10 April 1895

III.   Letter of Walter Sendall, 23 April 1895, to J. Chamberlain (CO 67/105)

IV.   Dispatch of W. F. Haynes-Smith, 28 November 1901, and Enclosures (CO 67/128)
    A. Letter of W. F. Haynes-Smith, 28 November 1901
    B. Newspaper Extract, October 11/24, 1901
    C. British Commentary
    D. Chamberlain's Reply

V.   Dispatch of W. F. Haynes-Smith, 30 August, 1902 (CO 67/132)
    A. Letter of W. F. Haynes-Smith, 30 August 1902
    B. Report on the Schools, August 4, 1902
    C. Newspaper Extracts
    D. Political Matters
    E. Extract from the Times, August 5, 1902

I. Dispatch of Walter Sendall, 29 January 1893, and Enclosures (CO 67/79)
A. Letter of Walter Sendall, January 29, 1893

Cyprus
Confidential

The Most Honourable
The Marquis of Ripon, K.G.
etc., etc., etc.
Downing Street

Government House
Cyprus 29 January 1893.

My Lord,

A deputation of Turkish gentlemen, headed by the Mufti of Cyprus, waited upon me yesterday, to complain of the publication, in a Greek newspaper, the 'Phone tis Kyprou,' of certain letters written by two English members of Parliament bearing upon the political future of Cyprus.

2. The correspondence in question consist, (1) of letters which have passed between Sir Charles Dilke and Mr. George Shakalli, a member of the Legislative Council of Cyprus, and (2) letters purporting to have been addressed by Mr. Labouchere, M. P., to a correspondent in Ireland of the name of Harvey.

3. In these letters it appears (amongst other things) to be suggested, that, as England cannot relieve Cyprus of the payment of the annual tribute to Turkey which is secured to the latter under the Convention of 1878, except by reworking this instrument, and restoring Cyprus to the Turks, the best course for the Greek Community of Cyprus will be to work in the direction of a cession of the island by Turkey to Greece, in return for a payment in ready money; and that England might possibly be willing to guarantee a loan for this purpose.

4. I cannot say whether the above represents correctly the original meaning of the writers of the letters, as it is only in a Greek version that the latter have appeared in this country; but it is the meaning which is put upon them by the Greek press, and it is this which, according to the deputation, has aroused the susceptibilities of the Turkish community.

5. The members of the deputation disavowed for themselves the belief that any political significance was to be attached to these letters, which they seemed to think were perhaps not genuine; but they said that the mere publication of speculations of this nature under the alleged authority of well known members of the British House of Commons, were calculated to disturb the minds of the ignorant; that they (the Turks) were quite content with the present administration of Cyprus by England, under which the Island remains an integral part of the Ottoman Empire; but that they repudiated with the utmost energy the idea of being transferred to another Power.

6. They concluded by urging that the law (i.e., the Turkish press law, which is very stringent) should be put in force for the purpose of preventing the publication of such speculative and (from their point of view) inflammatory matter.

7. I could not tell the deputation that I saw any reason myself to doubt the genuineness of the letters, but I thought I might assure them that they were without political significance; that in England, and in all countries under British rule, both law and opinion

were in favour of allowing complete freedom of discussion on political matters, and that unless some very strong reason could be shown to the contrary, I thought that it would be wisest to follow a similar policy in Cyprus. At the same time I would bear in mind what they had said, and would take action, should action be found to be necessary. With this reply they appeared to be satisfied.

8. I have considered it right to inform your Lordship of this incident, but I do not think that much importance is to be attached to it. Whatever irritation may have been caused by the publication of these letters, and by the comments indulged in by the Greek papers, it is not likely to have any serious consequences; and for the future, a hint privately given would probably be sufficient to repress any tendency on the part of the Greek press to persist in publishing matter calculated to give just offence to the Turkish community.

9. But it is very likely that during the next session of the Legislative Council an attempt will be made to bring forward some of the questions suggested by this correspondence; and it may become necessary to consider whether a discussion could be permitted to take place on such a topic as, say, the cession of Cyprus to Greece. I mention this, in case Your Lordship should desire to give me any instructions beforehand, in anticipation of such a contingency. The opening of Council has been fixed for the 1st of March.

10. Enclosed are copies of the letters which are subject of this dispatch, retranslated from the Greek; together with articles on the same subject from the Greek and Turkish papers.

I have the honour to be\
My Lord\
Your Lordships most obedient\
Humble servant\
Walter Sendall\
High Commissioner

B. Letters

To Mr. G. Shakallis   London 10th October 1892

My dear Sir,

Here is the difficulty. Cyprus being altogether of no use to the English taxpayer, it is difficult for me, so thinking, to oblige him to pay for her. If I thought Cyprus useful, as she is, I suppose, considered by those who have occupied her, I would think it mean to make her people starve. As the case stands, I can but hope that they will come to themselves, and untying the unwilling knot of the Island with Turkey, will cede her, some day or other, to Greece, if such be the wish of the majority of the people.

Your arguments, however, for the diminution of the tribute, are invincible, and the best course for your would be to persuade some members to propose the reduction of the amount as you point out.

Can you give me the dates and names of the members of Parliament who have made questions on this subject?

Yours sincerely\
Charles Dilke

To Sir Charles Dilke

Nicosia Cyprus
14th November 1892

My dear Sir,

It is with great pleasure that I answer your favour of the 10th ultimo, and request you to accept my warm thanks for the interest you take in the interests of the Island.

Certainly the best solution for the Cyprus question is the cession of the Island to Greece, and such a solution would satisfy the wishes of the majority of the Islanders. Since out of the 209,000 people 165,000 are Greeks, the only desire of whom is to see their country form a part of the Greek Kingdom. But is such solution practicable under the present circumstances? And what may we do in order to attain that happy solution?

Amongst the members who have made questions about Cyprus, I can name Messrs Edmund Robertson, Stanley Leighton and Sommers.

The last question on the subject was made by Mr. Leighton on the 20th May 1892, and you will see from the newspaper, which I am sending you today, what has been said when the question was put by the Honorable Member.

If the payment of the tribute by the English taxpayer be not regarded as a correct solution of the question, can you point out to me another solution of the same? There is no doubt that the sum of the tribute, paid now away by the Island to Turkey, as representing the surplus in the time of Turkish Authority, is very much larger then the actual one; because the difference between specie and kaümé had not been taken into consideration when the sum was fixed by the British Deputy and the Turkish Government, and that, should the difference be taken into consideration, the sum of the tribute will not exceed the sum of £50,000 per annum. Is it not possible for the British Government to raise the question, and rid the Islanders from a portion of the burden which they are unable to bear?

It is with confidence that we expect to get rid, in either way, of this burden by the Liberals, and I hope that these lines will be taken into consideration by you whom we regard as one of their eminent leaders.

Yours sincerely
Georgios Shakallis

To Mr. G. Shakallis

Toulon, France 1st December 1892

Dear Sir,

I advise you to persist in the course you follow. Persuade the members who agree with you to propose the diminution of the tribute, but do not ask us to do this ourselves. As to me, I insist upon saying that no solution is right or wise, except the union (distant, I am afraid) of the Island to Greece, and that deriving no profit from the occupation of Cyprus, we cannot charge our people with the payment of the tribute.

Most sincerely yours
Charles Dilke

To Mr. E. Harvey, Ireland   Toulon 6th December 1892

Dear Sir,

I have said to Mr. Shakallis that I would, no doubt, speak of Cyprus when I shall be in the Parliament, since I have taken up the question, but that I could not undertake to support his views. He thinks that the British taxpayer must pay the tribute to Turkey. I do not think so.

It seems to me that it is very late that we should, after the lapse of 14 years, reduce the payment to Turkey, and any one doing so in a private subject would not be regarded as behaving rightly.

Therefore I entirely repel the proposal of the Council, and will speak and vote against it. But I shall continue to support, as I have always done so, the cession of the Island to Greece, according to the desire of the people, and on condition that the payment of the tribute to Turkey—a payment which weakens us—will be made by the Island.

I do not approve of the inquiries through Committees and Commissions. It is a gentle manner to lull asleep the affairs.

Yours sincerely
Charles Dilke

To Mr. E. Harvey, Ireland   London 1st December 1892

Dear Sir,

I do not think the assertion of Mr. Shakallis, as regards the reduction of the value of kaümé should be admitted. The opinion of Radicals is that it was not our business to occupy the Island, and that we should give her back to the Turks.

We hold her merely by rent, and she still forms, technically, a part of the Turkish Dominion.

But since we have delivered her from the Turks, it would be cruel for the Cypriots that we should place her again under the Turkish Sovereignty. As the case stands, the Island costs us annually a good deal, and this is equivalent to our paying a part of the revenues.

The following plan would be preferable for the Radicals: To cede the Island to Greece which to pay away £50,000 per annum, and a loan of £1,000,000 to be made by us in order to buy her from the Turks instead of paying tribute.

After this loan being made, the sum of £50,000 Pounds will serve for amortization and interests for its payment in full.

For this purpose, however, the Sultan's consent is required.

Yours sincerely
H. Labouchere

C. Newspaper Extracts

Extract from "Phoni tes Kyprou" of the 6/18 January, 1893.

We publish herein below some very remarkable letters addressed by English members of Parliament to Mr. G. Shakalli, a lawyer and member of our Legislative Council. As our readers will see, the Cyprus question thanks to the incessant endeavours of a man who works not ostentatiously and ineffectually, but in secret and effectually— Mr. G. Shakalli—that is, has begun to occupy seriously many of the leading personages in England and it is expected that at the next session of the British Parliament a great discussion will take place on this question.

And now, what do you Cypriots say? Sir Charles Dilke the man, that is, who ere long, will be called upon to steer the British vessel, does not think it fair that the English taxpayer should pay the tribute, because Cyprus is entirely useless to England and considers as the only possible solution of the Cypriot question the cession of the Island to Greece, if such is also the wish of the majority of its inhabitants.

This idea is shared also by another leading politician, the leader of the radicals, Mr. Labouchere, as well as by many other politicians who write to Mr. Shakalli recommending that the time has came when the Cypriot people ought to take the necessary steps and endeavour by all lawful means to persuade the English Government to take some generous steps in favour of the Island.

The Turkish tribute cannot be abolished. This is the opinion even of those English who are dear to the Cypriots and who openly declare, with a conscientiousness and candour that does them honour, that even if a resolution be moved in Parliament, they will both speak and vote against it. No other hope is, then, left to us than the purchase of Cyprus, and to this we must turn all our attention. Every town, every townlet, every village and every individual must stir on this occasion. There are in England persons working for us whose opinion has a great strength. Shall we, fellow countrymen, leave them alone on this occasion? Shall we keep quiet? Shall we not rise from the lethargy that has overtaken us? What do we wait for? Let us turn our eyes and see in what condition we all are. Let us look at the agricultural population, which is almost ruined, at commerce which has come to a deadlock, let us look round and see that there is no motion, no life, that a little more we will all become bankrupt, a little more we will all be hungry.

We must all, then, rise as one man. We must work. We must hold meetings, we must encourage the noble hearts, that show such a great interest for us and support their steps.

What do we wait for? Things have changed. Nowadays, the conditions of the existence or non-existence of Cyprus have changed and, if we will not profit by this occasion, more so because on the ministerial benches is now sitting as a prime minister a man who wishes a great and respected Greece, we will in vain look for a similar occasion in future. We must understand this well. Every other thought, every other idea must be expelled, must be silenced at this, so to say, holy moment. And ought we to think, when they propose to us our union with those for whose sake we have despised every thing and for whom we have survived so many misfortunes? Yes, Sir Charles Dilke. Such is the wish of the whole Cyprus, such is its ardent expectation. We are Greeks. Our history proclaims it, our customs and usages, our traditions, our origin and our language, which is pure and limpid as the springs of our pine-covered Olympus and which alien conquerors have often tried—but without effect—to alter, attest the truth of it.

And here is, then, that very same convention, which we have been blaming hitherto, facilitating, instead of hindering, our union with Greece. And here we are bound, instead of complaining and calling that Angloturkish convention a nightmare, to consider it on the contrary, as a saving angel and be grateful to the mistress of the seas, who for the sake of a political object of hers has seized us from the mouth of the wolves and made us fly more easily to the arms of our mother.

It is not of course necessary to say more on this question, for perhaps the heart of the reader of these few lines is already leaping for joy, hoping that the day will at last come when the blue and white flag will be hoisted on the bloodstained ramparts of Cyprus. But in order that our wish should be effected, it is necessary that we should work and for that reason we appeal to all and ask them to take up this question in earnest, since we have been shown the path we must follow.

In conclusion, we cannot omit to bestow due praise on Mr. G. Shakalli, who by his correspondence with distinguished English politicians has been the cause that we should learn the true dispositions of our rulers and to pray him to continue his noble exertions either by keeping a correspondence or writing in the English press—as he has often done—important articles on Cyprus, assuring him at the same time that his compatriots will never forget his noble and patriotic strife.

We think, then, that our present position allows that we should consider it as certain that, if we work, "next day will be better."

Extract from "Phoni tes Kyprou" of the 13/25th January 1893.

A short Reply

If our last article and the letters addressed to Mr. G. Shacalli by Sir Charles Dilke and Labouchere were better understood by "Yeni Zeman," we do not believe "Yeni Zeman" would get so angry as to feel bound to write a long and incoherent article in order to refute ours by unsound argument.

We wrote that in the opinion of those politicians the tribute, which paralyses not only all the forces of the country but also the kind dispositions of the Cyprus government for the country, cannot possibly be abolished and that the said gentlemen see, as the only means, the purchase, by loan, of Cyprus, which England should one day cede to Greece. This idea having been thrown out by persons whose influence is unquestionable, we urged our fellow-countrymen to support by meetings and all other lawful means, just as "Zeman" would do in case it would learn that there is a disposition on the part of England to return the island to Turkey. When, then, all ownership on the Island is estranged from Turkey, does "Yeni Zeman" think that England will not be entitled to continue its noble work as with regard to the Ionian Islands, then fulfilling what the Christian inhabitants of the Island have asked for, both officially and privately, ten thousand times and adding one more glorious page to her history?

By what we wrote it was not our intention in the least to stir up the minds of our fellow countrymen, and much less to seek the union with the mother-Greece by means of blood or sacrifices. The said contemporary by its arguments against us, by courageously acquainting its readers that only by blood can the island be given over to others, supports just what, in its ignorance it disapproves. We for one confess that we feel an aversion to an uncalled for slaughter of innocent victims and, having wished what we have wished, have done so as we feel confident in the liberal feelings of the British Government on the will of which and of which alone does depend our future and fate. We do not deny what as true Greeks we cherish and ardently desire the union with the mother-Greece and the realization of our wish we have always sought by lawful means and not by such others as are dreamed of by our contemporary.

Extract from the "Phoni tes Kyprou" of the 6/18th January 1893.

It is, then, time to act. It is necessary to shew by all lawful means that such is the wish of the majority of the inhabitants, more so because many Philocypriots in England write to Mr. Shacalli exposing this idea. Thus, the Irish philocypriot Mr. E. H., who has ever shewn a great interest for the Cypriot questions—and we, therefore, deem it our duty to express to him our warm thanks—writes to Mr. Shacalli what follows:-" So long as no action is taken in the Island, you must not hope any improvement from the English des-pots. But if you act, you will improve your position. Therefore, I say take what steps you can for the question, both in Cyprus and elsewhere."

Another gentleman writes: "This proposal of Sir Charles Dilke (about the cession of Cyprus to Greece) is worth while being given flesh and bones (through the efforts of course of the Cypriots) because it admits the principle, which all oppressed communities ought to endeavour to make a common one, that the status quo that is, must be in accor-dance with the wish of the inhabitants."

While expressing the wish that we should find ourselves quite soon in the pleasant position of being able to announce the action of our fellow countrymen, we cannot pass over without thanking Mr. Shakalli, who was pleased to allow us to take and publish cop-ies of these most important letters, which render clear the questions of our beloved father-land.

Copy translation of extract from the Turkish newspaper "Yeni Zeman" 23 Jan 1893

We roaringly laugh at this correspondence, and moreover, wonder at the belief and idea of the partisans of Greece, famous in and habituated to marauding the treasures of fancy in the world of visions, that they will be able to achieve any thing with such sophistries. Alas! Mr. Shakalli and those sharing his views are, most probably, likening the Convention concluded between the two great powers to the title-deeds of the lands of the village of Athiaenou and are, consequently, falling into the passion of selling or pur-chasing the Island!

We say that the administration of the Island of Cyprus, which forms an integral part of the Sultan's territories, has under the provisions of a convention made in conse-quence of the requirements of circumstances, been temporarily ceded to the great British Government, and that, whereas it is manifest that in case of the solution and settlement of any important question concerning the Island becoming necessary, every branch should naturally revert to its root, so also there is no doubt that, in case of its becoming necessary to change the Government of our Island, which was conquered and taken possession of by the blood of the Osmanlis 332 years ago, it will be given over to the Imperial Ottoman Government, in whose affectionate and equitable embrace we have been brought up; and that in case of any change taking place against the wish of that Exalted Government, the same will again cause the shedding of Ottoman blood.

The principal point which causes our astonishment and surprise is such an action, against civilization, on the part of persons like Sir Charles Dilke and Mr. Labouchere, the advice emanating from whose precious brains and sacred pens is, in this instance, subjected to disapprobation and abuse.

What an endeavour to work in the dark! What a nonsensical enterprise! What a strange state of things!

It is pretended that these publications are meant to convince the British Government that the wish of the majority of the population is in favour of the Island being ceded to Greece.

We are unable to form an idea as to the view with which persons, who promulgate to the civilized world that the British Government are in the habit of doing work by scraps of paper, should be regarded.

It is stated that agriculture and commerce have been annihilated in the Island: were we to confirm this statement, we would say that no one can now-a-days acquire riches in the way in which a good many of our Christian compatriots became possessors of wealth in a short space of time under the auspices of the affectionate patronage of the Government during Ottoman administration.

With regard to the proposal that no opportunity should be lost in taking urgent steps while the persons whose leaning is towards Greece is, great and respected, at the head of the Government in England, we must say Bravo!, so as to have afforded some consolation to the inventor and writer of that article.

The line of action has, indeed, been drawn in imagination, but we deem it expedient to warn those whom it may concern to conform their actions to the rules of geometry so as not to lose that way later on.

Though the merits of the case are as explained, i.e. the question deserves neither any importance nor anxiety, and we consequently do not make it any business of ours, the convenience of the present Government at such inane publications and at the occurrence of such a state of things causes, indeed, much regret and astonishment to us. Consequently, considering that the Ottoman Press Law is still in force in the Island, we particularly ask and pray the local Government to apply the provisions of that law in this matter, and thereby prevent the anticipated occurrence of evil consequences.

Oh! countryman—in the name of Osmanliship we place before you the example of those various nations which, owing to their exertions and endeavours in favour of reconciliation and harmony, by having in view the accomplishments and feelings of humanity promoted by present civilization, are leading a life of prosperity and ease of the highest degree, were we to inquire into the views and conduct of those found in that state, we would see that they all live in unanimity and concord, and it is owing to this that the inhabitants of the countries which we look at and hear of with admiration and appreciation, have gradually attained, and are still attaining to the summit of progress. Let us also act in like manner, and endeavour to advance in every thing that is conducive to prosperity and well being. And O! Phoni-tis-Kyprou, our colleague, we content ourselves with stating sincerely that it would be more advantageous and proper that we should abstain from such conduct which, as explained above, is irreconcilable with good dispositions that we should exert ourselves for the progress of public discipline, education etc., in our country, and that we should not engage in such futilities, beyond the bounds of moderation and duty, the press, which has acquired the fame of serving public instruction.

D. British Commentary

Mr Fairfield-

I would reply that Lord Ripon does not think it necessary to give him any special instructions in the event of the subject being discussed in the Leg. Council as the Greek inhabitants are evidently well aware of the fact that this country could not if it wished, cede Cyprus to Greece, and that therefore the consent of Turkey as well as Greece would be required for such an arrangement.

WAM 11/2/93

Mr. Fairfield-

I venture to suggest a doubt as to this ruling. No doubt it may be said that Legislative Assemblies can only debate things with which the body has to deal, but this does not help much—for the question remains what those things are. You contend that the Cyprus Legislative Council can only discuss those papers as to which it can make laws, and the point is whether this restriction (unknown as far as I am aware elsewhere) exists in the case of that body.

It is true that the only power specifically given to the Council is that of making "all such laws." But it is another "fundamental rule" that all rights and powers which are reasonably necessary for such a large purpose are given by implication; and the extent of such rights is really determined by general practice. Thus although the elective members could not propose a bill involving a new expenditure, they could move a resolution on the subject—as a private member of the House of Commons can.

These implied powers of the elective members in Cyprus are recognised in Lord Kimberley's despatch printed C-3211, in which it is said that "the elected members will have the right to <u>interrogate</u> the members of the Govt. in Council <u>on public matters,</u> to propose laws <u>and resolutions.</u>"

I do not think we can safely draw any line so as to exclude any resolution on a public matter: and, apart from any technical considerations, surely it would be better to allow a debate in Council under the eyes of the High Commissioner and the Govt. members than to leave it to the Greek press?

WAM 20/2/93

II. Dispatch of Walter Sendall, 23 April 1895, to the Marquis of Ripon, and Enclosures (CO 67/91)

A. Letter of Walter Sendall, 23 April 1895

The Most Honourable
The Marguis of Ripon, K.G.
etc.   etc.   etc.
Downing Street

Cyprus -- Government House
Cyprus, 23 April 1895

My Lord,
    I have today telegraphed to your Lordship for permission to repeat the assurance which was conveyed to me in September last that Her Majesty's Government has no intention of relinquishing the administration of Cyprus.

    2. My reason for this was that the feeling excited by the recent debate in Parliament, to which I have drawn attention in my confidential despatches of the 7th and 8th of April, still continues; and the attitude taken by prominent persons amongst the Christian population is causing much disquiet amongst the Moslems.

    3. Invitations and addresses are being circulated throughout the country, summoning the Greeks to public meetings to be held simultaneously at Nicosia and at Limassol on Sunday next (April 28th) with the avowed object of advocating the union of Cyprus to Greece, as being the only alternative to British rule, to which the people of the country would submit.

    4. A deputation of leading Moslems waited upon me yesterday to urge that these meetings should not be allowed to be held; and statements were made to the effect that insulting and menacing language and acts on the part of the Christians towards the Turks had already taken place. A copy of the notes taken at this interview is annexed.

    5. An assurance, coming direct from Your Lordship, that the language used by influential members of the House of Commons, which has been made the occasion of the present agitation, does not indicate any change of intention on the part of Her Majesty's Government respecting the continued occupation of the Island, would deprive the promoters of the agitation of any pretext for disturbing the public mind with the discussion of these questions, and at the same time would free the Moslems from any apprehension that they are in danger of being handed over to another power.

    6. I shall, of course, take measures to prevent any breach of the peace, but I have not as yet decided that it is necessary to prevent the holding of the proposed meetings. I shall make it my business to let the leaders of the movement understand the responsibility which they will be incurring should any disturbances arise out of their actions, and I shall take such other steps as the occasion may seem to require.

    7. In the meantime, as the mail is on the point of leaving, I send your Lordship these details for information.

    8. I also think it necessary to draw Your Lordship's attention to certain proceedings on the part of Mr. Philemon, the recently appointed Consul for Greece. This gentlemen visited the town of Limassol on the day on which the anniversary of Greek independence is celebrated, and allowed himself to be publicly received and fêted as the representative of what the Cypriot newspapers describe as "our King." Addresses and replies were interchanged, in which the Cypriote Greeks were represented as looking forward

through centuries of tribulation to union with their Mother Greece, and on the other hand Greece was described as longing for the restoration of her children.

9. I have no desire to exaggerate the importance of these demonstrations. The ultimate union of Cyprus to Greece, as the only practicable alternative to the continuance of the British occupation, may or may not be held to be an open question, which the Cypriote Greeks are at liberty to discuss without restraint, either in speech or in writing. But I hardly think that it can be consistent with his duties for the Greek Consul to take a prominent part in such discussions. And I am informed that Mr. Philemon has accepted engagements to renew this kind of patriotic demonstration on the occasion of the name day of the Heir Apparent to the Hellenic Throne, which occurs I believe in June next.

10. I should be sorry to make these comments upon Mr. Philemon's conduct without adding that I am quite sure that he is guiltless of any design of giving trouble to the Government. As your Lordship is aware the foreign consuls all reside in Larnaca, and it is only occasionally that I see any of them. If I have an opportunity, I shall myself speak to Mr. Philemon upon what appears to me to evince a lack of discretion on his part in giving countenance to political speculations which, whether or not they pass the bounds of permissible discussion, are certainly unfriendly to the Ottoman Government, and are likely to give legitimate cause of offence to the Ottoman population of the country to which he is accredited.

11. Mr. Philemon is an educated and cultured gentleman, and he is especially friendly to England and the English. But I cannot help thinking that in giving encouragement to what he probably regards as the patriotic aspirations of the Cypriote Greeks he is acting without due reflection, and it will be for your Lordship to judge whether it might not be well to bring this subject to the notice of his Government through the Foreign Office. At the same time, I desire to repeat that I do not wish to be understood as bringing any complaint against Mr. Philemon.

12. The following papers are annexed to this despatch.
1. Extract from minutes of Executive Council.
2. Notes of interview with Moslem deputation.
3. Letter addressed to the Chief Secretary by the Chief Cadi and the Mufti.
4. Extract from contents of the Turkish newspaper "Kybris."
5. Extract from the Greek paper "Evagóras." Election of a committee to organize meetings.
6. Confidential communication from Major Seager—President of the District Court, Nicosia.
7. Report, taken from the "Aletheia" newspaper, of Mr. Philemon's visit to Limassol.

I have the honour to be
My Lord
Your Lordship's most obedient
humble servant
Walter Sendall
High Commissioner

B. Minutes

Extract from the minutes of the proceedings of the Executive Council at a meeting held on the 22nd April 1895.

His Excellency communicated to Council confidential despatches he had sent by last mail to the Secretary of State on the subject of the feeling aroused here by debates in Parliament respecting the Cyprus grant-in-aid; and thereafter articles from the Greek newspapers summoning people to assemble at the various chief towns in the Island on Sunday April 28th, for the purpose of advocating union with Greece were read and considered at some length. Mr. Cade, local Commandant of Police Nicosia was summoned, and various questions put to him by members of Council as to the feeling in Nicosia and the steps he would propose to take in order to prevent a breach of the peace, should these meetings take place.

His Excellency also requested the Chief Justice and the Puisne Judge to attend while this matter was under discussion. An account of an address delivered at Limassol, on the anniversary of Hellenic Independence, by Mr. Philemon, Consul for Greece, was also read.

Finally, a deputation of leading Moslems of Nicosia and other places headed by the Mufti was introduced, and had an interview in connection with the feeling aroused in their community by the proceedings on the part of the Christians, and begged His Excellency to take some steps to prevent these meetings being held.

C. Notes of Interview

The following gentlemen interviewed His Excellency on the 22nd April 1895. The members of the Executive Council were present at the interview—

Mr. Utidjian acted as Interpreter—
Hadji Ali Rifki Eff: Mufti of Cyprus
Hadji Deroish Pasha. Proprietor of paper 'Zeman.'
Hadji Mehmet Raif Eff: Mufti's scribe.
Hadji Miazi Eff: -do-
Hadji Vehid Eff: -do-
Baroutgiade Ahmed Vassif Eff: M.L.C.
Ahmed Rashid Eff: M.L.C.
Zuchti Eff: M.L.C.

The Mufti on behalf of the deputation stated that Mr. Liassides has been visiting the district, rousing the villages and collecting signatures to a petition to the effect that Cyprus is not to be handed back to Turkey, but if given up at all it must be given to Greece, and if not given up by the English the tribute must be abolished; this is absurd and will not be listened to by intelligent people, but there is to be a meeting held on Sunday the 28th and these matters will probably lead to disturbances. One of the Christian schoolmasters has composed a song which has been sung publicly, and the following words end each verse "Let us kill the Turks with a soft sword and have our revenge."

Christians are insulting the Moslem women and also notable Turks, using the word "boom, boom" to imply that they will be shot.

The Turks are loyal and wish to live in peace but there are illiterate Mohammedans who may be excited at such sayings, and as there is every probability that such sayings and doings will lead to disturbances they ask His Excellency to take the proper measures to prevent them.

Mr. Liassides' arrangements and preparations are most certainly attempts to disturb the public peace, and they rely on His Excellency to take every precaution to prevent this and to punish anyone attempting to disturb it.

At Jochni on the road to Limassol there was a disturbance lately between Moslems and Christians; this bad feeling between the two races has spread to the women of the two creeds; they are insulting one another showing that race feeling runs high, and is being talked about in private houses.

Hadji Mehmet Raif Eff: states he was reading in his house the day before yesterday and was disturbed by Moslem school children passing near shouting and gesticulating. It appears that some Christian boys had thrown stones into a Moslem school, the boys of the latter ran out to chastise the offenders; he spoke to the master who stated that the boys were exasperated and beyond his control; eventually, he persuaded the boys to return but he quoted this instance to show the feeling in the town.

The Mufti continuing stated that he had exhorted the Moslems not to be present at the Christian meeting on the 28th instant; he had persuaded many but probably some will go and he anticipated a disturbance, but hopes that His Excellency will forbid the meeting to take place.

The Archbishop he hears deprecated the course being followed, but Mr. Liassides is doing his best to create disturbances.

From various districts he, the Mufti, has received letters concerning proposed meetings but has replied that no notice is to be taken of such meetings.

If England gives back Cyprus to Turkey, it is a matter between the two Governments and has nothing to do with the inhabitants; the inhabitants were not consulted when Turkey consented to England occupying Cyprus.

Public houses and brothels are open until the morning and are the cause, in a great measure, of disturbances.

Greeks in the market place are calling Moslems "Dogs and Donkeys" but the Moslems have not to the present retaliated.

At Larnaca, the police have been assaulted.

There is no use taking measures after disturbances have taken place and they ask His Excellency again to take the necessary steps to prevent breaches of the peace.

His Excellency stated that he was glad to hear that the Mufti in his high position had acted as he had done and as he would have expected him to do.

Proper notice would be taken of what had been said, and the deputation might rest assured that no disturbance of the peace would be permitted to arise.

D. Letter of the Moslems

The Honorable   17 April 1895
The Chief Secretary

Sir,

On the occasion of the Easter holiday of our Greek compatriots, certain ill-thinking and bad character Greeks having in their private gatherings, and in the streets uttered and used against the Moslems such indecent words as to cause precipitancy and boiling anger, and having displayed demonstration with impertinent remarks and besides this Mr. Liassides, member of the Legislative Council having posted up notices notifying his intention to deliver a speech on the 28th instant at the Square of the Newgate, and inviting the whole Christians to be present on that day, we hereby beg to inform you that the above-mentioned facts have created great excitement and distrust among the Moslem inhabitants.

Yesterday a great number of the Moslems have attended, first at the Mufti's residence and afterwards at the Mufti's residence and afterwards at the Mekkemé Sherié, and requested us to bring their complaints to the notice of the Government, and to ask the adoption of the necessary steps; although these are things which came forth from the improper acts of certain thoughtless and insensible people, and there is nothing to cause anxiety, but as we succeeded in dispersing the people by promising them that we will inform the Government of all these things, and will ask the adoption of the necessary steps, and as it is probable that the repetition of such things will produce a fearful consequence, we therefore pray in the name of all the Moslem inhabitants that the Government may take such measures as to prevent the occurrence of things causing the excitement of the Moslems.

(Seal) Mustafa Ferzi, Chief Cadi
Ali Rifki, Mufti

E. Newspaper Extract

Contents of the Turkish Paper "Kypris" of 15 April 1895

When the ant is winged its decline is near at hand.

This proverb with its simplicity insinuates and conveys in certain matters so important and advantageous truth that in our opinion no better comparison than this can be applied to the following events and circumstances we are now going to explain:

In our Island, there are occurring such events that if no importance is attached to them there is no doubt that they will in future produce a great anxiety.

Our Christian compatriots, who, for centuries have been living under the blessed protection of the great sovereign who having the glorious name of Osmanli and enjoying many favours and graces of the Padishah, were feeling proud to own the Osmanli name, and who were offering prayers for the longevity of our absolute protector, and gracious Sultan, and showing affection and loyalty to His Imperial Majesty, have during several years that is to say since the change of the administration, gradually and without any reason changed their tongues and manners, and commenced to show strange and surprising manners.

As long as the indifference and apathy of the Government and the patience and mildness of the Moslems are continuing, our Christian compatriots taking advantage of every opportunity do not abstain from showing demonstrations which are considered to be an insult to the Moslems, they carry it on in such degree that in their places of worship, in their meetings and in the streets, they are openly making such speeches and showing such demonstration which no conscience can bear and which causes great excitement and anger.

Although the motives which allow such things to continue are not unknown to us, yet we astonish at the short-sightedness of those who think that the Osmanlis are sleeping in neglectful heedlessness.

We regret that the Government while seeing clearly every day all these events, is instead of preventing such events that will produce some trouble and evil, regarding them as a fighting of blind men, and is paying no attention.

The Moslem inhabitants are registering with iron pens on the page of their conscience the events of the past 16 years.

But when that page is filled up and there is left no space or extent to register more events then they will be in the necessity of practically putting a stop to the events of daily occurrence.

Therefore, the first course the Moslems should take in such matters is to invite the attention of the Authorities concerned, and their second and principal duty is that they should be always watchful, and friendly and in harmony with each other.

At present, these are the recommendations we can give to them.

F. Newspaper Extract

Extract from "Evagoras" 31 March 1895
A Meeting of the Townspeople
Election of a Committee

Because of the discussions in the English Parliament concerning Cyprus, a great uneasiness prevails among our fellow-citizens with regard to the future of the Island. His Beatitude the Archbishop complying with the unanimous wish of the people sent last Sunday for the leading citizens, who went to the Archbishopric at the time appointed for the purpose. After a long exchange of views, the persons present, recognizing the critical state of the affairs, elected a committee consisting of twenty-four members and drew up a minute which was forthwith signed by all those who were present and next day by all our fellow-citizens without exception. The object of appointing a Committee was to come to an understanding, through it, with the other towns and places of the Island and take such steps as would be appropriate to the circumstances. The Committee met next day and resolved to take steps for the purpose of having a Pan-Cypriot meeting held, so that the mind of the Cypriot people, both with regard to the question of the future of the Island and also with regard to the tribute may be expressed in a public and solemn manner.

We are glad to see that things have proved again that our opinion, the opinion we expressed three years ago and we have since, on various occasions formulated, is correct.

As the day for the Pan-Cypriot meetings the 16/28 April has been fines and we do not doubt that the Cypriot people will on this critical occasion also, as always, come in great numbers to the meeting, on the appointed day, in order to declare for a thousandth time that they stick to their wishes and traditions and that they consent to no other solution than the union of their fatherland with mother Greece. Let the Cypriot people also declare to the English Government that, if the present circumstances do not allow an immediate fulfillment of their eternal wishes, that they can for a long time yet, acquiesce in the English occupation, but on conditions that the tribute to which they have been condemned by the English interests and the English Government should be paid by the English people. The Cypriot people, by adopting this policy and this course of action can be sure that the fulfillment of their wishes will not delay long and that they will be able to prepare themselves and their own children for a happier future.

Let us all then, on Sunday, the 28th April, assemble, those of us who belong to the District of Nicosia, at the Nicosia meeting and those who belong to District of Limassol, at the meeting of Limassol and so forth.

G. Letter of M. B. Seager

District Court
Nicosia 17 April 1895

Chief Secretary,

For three days past, I have heard what I thought to be idle gossip, relative to the feeling—religious in a sense, now existing in this town, between Greek and Turk—from what I can gather this hostile feeling has risen through the torchlight procession which paraded the town on the night of the anniversary of the declaration of Greek independence. This procession happened to go through the Tati Khele quarter of Nicosia, a quarter most inhabited by Turks; whilst parading through this quarter, the Greeks—school children for the most part—had the bad taste to sing songs which referred to the slaughter of the hated Moslems. This has given serious offense to the Turks and also alarm, beyond that a meeting had been held by the Turks to consider this and steps taken by some influential persons to stay the alarm. I know nothing more. But this evening, a gentleman has called upon me who is conversant with both creeds, and he tells me there is a large meeting called by Messrs. Liassides M.L.C. and Theodotou (advocate) persons called from all parts of the Island to meet together at Nicosia to protest against the version they have in view to put forward of the late speeches in Parliament on the subject of Cyprus. I am told that the Turks will most probably misunderstand this meeting and may very likely oppose it in their old way.

As magistrate of Nicosia, I formally call the attention of the Government to this proposed meeting; I cannot say in these days of liberty that persons have not a perfect right to meet and discuss questions of the kind, at the same time unless the real intention of the meeting is ascertained and clearly expressed to the Moslem residents of the town it may be, and very likely will be, misunderstood, and if misunderstood may very likely, and in all probability would, give rise to riot if not bloodshed.

I would also suggest to the Government that should such a riot occur, it would be on religious lines; it is suggested to me that we have a force of Zaptiehs of mixed creeds, so far nothing has arisen to test this force, and grave doubt is expressed that the discipline of this force would stand the test of religious strife, it might be that we may see Moslem Zaptiehs fighting with Greek Zaptiehs or the police force divided and taking each the side of their co-religionists.

The date fixed for this largely called meeting is the 28th of April. With all deference to His Excellency's present advisors, I would suggest first of all enquiry of the leaders of this movement, their objects in calling this meeting, if merely political it would not be against reason to require from the leaders some security, as to the proper conduct of such a meeting and it would relieve the minds of the peaceable inhabitants if, irrespective of this the Government would order up to Nicosia for a month's change (as a show of force) the remnant of the troops left in the Island.

As Magistrate of Nicosia, I have, after due consideration, considered it my duty to give this note of warning to the Government to act as it deems best.

M. B. Seager
P.D.C. and Magistrate of Nicosia

H. Newspaper Extract

Extract from the "Aletheia" 29/10 April 1895
The Eve
The Arrival of Mr. Philemon

Last Friday, as soon as it was made known that the Consul of Greece was to arrive here from Larnaca, the establishment of the corporations of our town as well as the churches were draped with flags. A great number of persons, among whom the Mayor, the Director of the Greek School, the School Managers, the Church Commissioners and many others went out to meet Mr. Philemon and drove as far as the river of Yermasoyia. Mr. Philemon arrived at about 5 p.m. and entered the town accompanied by all the carriages that went out to meet him. On the borders of the town, he was met by a great crowd which was waiting for him there and among which the female sex was sufficiently represented. Upon his arrival, the usual salute firing took place and the white and blue flag of the Gymnasium [The Sporting Club] was lowered. There, the Mayor Mr. Hadjiprastou addressed the Council . . .

III. Letter of Walter Sendall, 23 April 1895, to J. Chamberlain (CO 67/105)

The Right Honourable
J. Chamberlain, M.P.
etc.   etc.   etc.
Downing Street

Government House
Cyprus, 23 April 1897

Sir,

Referring to my confidential despatch of the 2nd, 7th, and 16th April on the subject of Greece and Cyprus, the outbreak of hostilities on the Graeco-Turkish frontier has considerably changed the aspect of affairs.

2. Telegrams, often contradictory, arrive daily from the seat of war, and their contents are eagerly discussed in every town and village in the Island. Strong excitement undoubtedly prevails, the two races withdrawing into separate camps, and refusing, in some places, to meet each other in the same café.

3. Without presenting any serious causes for alarm, there is ground for anxiety, and this partly arising from the composition of the police force. I cannot myself feel perfect confidence that in any disturbances that might arise out of a national quarrel of this magnitude, the Turkish Zaptieh would, without hesitation, take effective action against his compatriots if required to do so and on behalf of the national enemy. Precisely the same consideration applies to the Greek members of the force, who are now pretty numerous. Upon this subject I have made a general order, a copy of which is annexed.

4. Outside the police force the only means of preserving order in Cyprus is to be looked for in the forces of the Crown. The military force in the Island consisting of a single company of a line regiment, quartered at a distance of three days (routine) march from the seat of Government. This force is officered by a captain and two subalterns of whom the captain and the senior subaltern are at present on the sick-list, the former, I regret to say, with a serious fracture of the elbow (sustained at polo) which is likely to incapacitate him for some weeks. The Naval Squadron has not lately been in this part of the Mediterranean; and no British man-of-war has visited Cyprus for twelve months.

5. I only mention these details in order to put Her Majesty's Government in possession of the exact state of affairs. The population, while thoroughly well disposed to the existing government, is divided in itself; is in a fever of excitement about the present, and is apprehensive about the future; the local machinery for the maintenance of order, which would otherwise be quite sufficient, is now perhaps not wholly to be depended upon; and our immediate resources, outside the local police force, are as indicated.

6. I am about to leave Nicosia for Limassol and before returning I shall visit Larnaca. These three towns are the centres of movement and of agitation; and I shall be better able to judge of the prospects of disturbance and of our means of meeting it, after my tour.

I have the honour to be
Sir,
Your most obedient humble servant
Walter J. Sendall
High Commissioner

THE CYPRUS GAZETTE
Friday, 23rd April, 1897

By the HIGH COMMISSIONER
A PROCLAMATION

Walter J. Sendall,
High Commissioner

Whereas a state of war unhappily exists between His Imperial Majesty the Sultan of Turkey and His Majesty the King of the Hellenes;

And whereas it is expedient to make provision for the maintenance of order and tranquillity in the Island of Cyprus during the existence of hostilities between the aforesaid Powers;

Now therefore I, Walter Joseph Sendall, Knight Commander of the Most Distinguished Order of Saint Michael and Saint George, High Commissioner and Commander-in-Chief in and over the Island of Cyprus, do hereby strictly charge and command all persons within the Island of Cyprus to abstain from taking part in any meetings, assemblies or processions to the disturbance of the public peace, and from giving cause or provocation tending to a breach of the public peace by means of any act, writing, word or gesture as they will answer to the contrary at their peril; and I hereby give notice that any assembly, meeting or procession which does not forthwith disperse on being required to do so by any Commissioner or Peace Officer will be dispersed with such force as the occasion may require, and that any person offering such provocation as is herein-before mentioned will be forthwith apprehended and dealt with according to Law.

Given at Nicosia this 23rd day of April, 1897.

GOD save the QUEEN.

By His Excellency's Command,
ARTHUR YOUNG,
Chief Secretary to Government.

IV. Dispatch of W. F. Haynes-Smith, 28 November 1901, and Enclosures (CO 67/128)

A. Letter of W. F. Haynes-Smith, 28 November 1901

The Right Honourable   Government House
Joseph Chamberlain Esquire M.P.   Nicosia
etc.   etc.   etc.   28th November 1901

Sir,

I have the honour to bring under your consideration the nature and the extent of the agitation now being carried on amongst the Greek speaking Cypriots for union with Greece.

2. I have received numerous reports from different officers of the Government on this subject and from these I select the reports of the Chief Commandant of Police and of the Commissioner of Limassol as shortly placing the matter in a clear light. Copies of these reports are annexed. The Chief Commandant stated that he feels it his "duty to represent to the Government lest trouble should arise in the future that the time has arrived for some check to be put upon the disloyal movement spreading among the District population who though content at present may be made the ignorant tools of the demagogues who appear to be desirous of emulating the people of Crete." He alludes to the constant flaunting of the Greek flag which would lead anyone to suppose Cyprus was a Greek Island and which is being increasingly used as the banner of the agitation. Mr. Michell, the Commissioner of Limassol, who has been here since the British Occupation and who views the question quite dispassionately after noticing the effect which events in Crete have had on this agitation points out that Union with Greece is now being held out by the Press and the Town Agitators as a remedy for all the evils attributed to the Government such as excessive taxation the payment of Tribute and other like cries and that it is now linked with baseless attacks on the Government and deliberate misrepresentation of its

acts; and concludes his report by saying that "with a more or less ignorant peasantry the constant repetition of statements based on the grossest misrepresentation cannot fail to have in great measure the effect that it is intended should be produced—and that if the causes which are in operation without check continue to operate the feeling will continue to become intensified."

3. In order to appreciate the motives of the agitation it is fair to look at the matter as it appears to many of those who are leading the movement. The agitation has hitherto been confined to the towns and to the professional classes which are exceptionally large as compared with the population and have little to do. Considerable numbers go to Athens to qualify as advocates and doctors and come back with a superficial education, many of the doctors being mere Apothecaries. They return imbued with the Hellenic propaganda. These men as Cypriotes find they have no Citizenship for they endeavour to repudiate being Ottoman subjects, and they are not allowed to become British Citizens, and they bitterly complain that they have little or no protection in neighbouring countries. They have no flag and there is no outlet for any sentiment of nationality, and no satisfaction for the natural craving to belong to some nation. They belong to a generation which has experienced none of the actual evils of a Turkish Administration, and they are constantly rebelling at the payment of the £60,000 per annum which is annually drawn from the Island to pay a portion of the tribute. They have been bred up in the history of the success of agitation when applied to the Ionian Islands, and they have seen the success of organized agitation and violence in Crete. They have nothing to lose while if they could organize an agitation which would make England willing to give up the administration they would at once gain nationality—and as they believe get rid of the Tribute for they consider that in some way Greece would escape paying it and would never compel the Cypriotes to pay it. How this is to be brought about they do not say—but if their thoughts were expressed I have no doubt that they consider it would be done by violence as in Crete. Some of their Advocates are training themselves to arms and to lead bodies of men; although the violence most often thought of is probably the sniping from behind walls or from places of concealment.

4. The progress of affairs in Crete is a most powerful influence on the Greek speaking Cypriotes, and there are several of the moderate men who watching Crete are beginning to think that union with Greece would be for the material advantage and progress of the Island. As an illustration of this feeling I annex a copy of an article which appears in the moderate paper The Phoni of the 20th of October on the subject of education drawing unfavourable comparisons between the position of Cyprus under the British and the position of Crete under the Government of Prince George and pointing out that while the total taxation in Crete was £80.000 less than in Cyprus £25,000 was allowed there annually for education against the amount allowed in Cyprus which is £5,400. The contribution for the Tribute must always tell in any such comparison, whatever action may be taken.

5. The recent General Election for the Legislative Council has given rise to increased agitation on the subject. I enclose translations of some of the Election papers issued by the successful candidates under the leadership of the Bishop of Kitium. The Bishop some time before the Elections when canvassing for election as Archbishop had an interview with the Greek Consul and then urged that he should be supported on the ground that he was the door through which Cyprus would pass to Greece. I annex a short

account of the interview. The cry of union with Greece has been continued through the Elections. One of the favourite posters was the following:

Long Live Union With Greece

Your greatest enemy is the Government and its friends.

Give this day one good slap both to the Government and its friends.

Vote for those who are fighting the Government and its menials.

I annex copies of some of the other issues which go into particulars and as Mr. Michell points out contain the grossest misrepresentations. The other side amongst the Greek speaking Cypriotes did not dare to resist this cry of Union with Greece. They called themselves the truly National Coalition and urged the electorate that national restoration had been the permanent aim to which they were incessantly looking from their paternal hearths and the school bench. On their glorious Mother Greece would their eyes be fixed and as Members of the Council they would be ready at every proper moment to declare formally the holy and lawful aspirations of the Cypriote people. I annex a translation of some of their Manifestoes.

6. The agitation as previously mentioned has hitherto been confined to Towns and to the professional classes, but the agitation is well organized, has money at its disposal and is engineered from abroad and principally from Greece. The Villagers at present are loyal and contented but the organizers are daily using every means to alter this, and they are past masters in the art of intrigue and in creating seditious discontent. They have captured the Schools, the Schoolmasters and the instruction given in the schools, and they are now actively engaged in endeavouring to corrupt the mukhtars or headmen of the rural towns and villages who are as a rule loyal and true to the Government, and who are most useful to the administration. Professional agitators have arrived from abroad who are introducing a sinister element into the agitation. The Greek speaking Cypriote left to himself when he advocates union with Greece says he desires it and hopes that England will graciously grant it—but does not abuse the British. The professional agitator from abroad has introduced the new element of abuse of the British and harps on the Boer War and the opposition in Malta on the language question and other similar themes. I annex a translation of an article in the Evagoras as a specimen—but abuse of the British is very constantly issued from a section of the press. In the article the writer states that "by means of a dishonest contract torn away from Turkey by a still more dishonest coercion Great Britain occupied Cyprus for the object of guarding the Turkish possessions from any Russian inroad in Asia and has rendered the Cypriot people more ill-fated than they have been under the Franks or the Venetians or the Saracens or the Turks."

7. The two contending parties among the Greek speaking Cypriotes while seeking to out do each other in the fervency with which they each advocate Union with Greece were bitterly divided on the question of the election of Archbishop—the Bishop of Kitium and his party taking their stand on the platform that they would bring it about, or that all their efforts would be directed to this end. The parties are most bitter against each other on the Archbishop's question and I had to take most careful and most stringent measures to preserve the public peace. The elections were carried out without disturbances. The Bishop of Kitium and his party have been entirely successful throughout the Island and the Bishop was elected in two divisions. Showing the spirit and feeling with which the members enter the Council, I annex copies of speeches made by two of the successful candidates at Larnaca in which they declare their resolve to further the "Patri-

otic cause." One of them, Mr. Zanneto, a Greek subject, is the gentleman whose action when temporarily performing the duties of Greek Consul in using the name of the Crown Prince of Greece as the patron of the Pan-Cypriote games was brought under notice in a confidential despatch from Captain Young of the 28th April 1900. He intimated to the people that Mr. Gladstone had given them the Constitution to enable them to bring about the Union with Greece. Mr. Rossos, a French subject, says "forming as the Greek Cypriotes do an inseparable part of that Hellenic body it is not otherwise possible than that we should some day be united with that free country." I also annex a translation of portions of a speech made by another elected member at Morphou. There are two matters alluded to in the election addresses which I may perhaps notice and these are the alleged conspiracy against the Greek language and against the Orthodox religion. The attacks on the first head arise out of the offer of a bonus to the Schoolmasters but they are becoming less. The reference to religion arises from the following circumstances. The party now defeated had, when the Archbishop was alive, asked him to obtain the services of a talented preacher and the Archbishop applied to the Patriarch of Constantinople who sent down a preacher of ability. This preacher attacked the laxity of morals among the people and the low state of education among the Orthodox Clergy and raised a hornet's nest. The preacher in the result was driven out of the country and had to be afforded police protection to escape. He was ill-treated when he landed at the Piraeus. The party now defeated had raised the cry that the Bishop of Kitium and his party were free masons and they on their side retorted that the party now defeated wished "to crown their infernal endeavours by a plot against their religion by the spreading of anti-religious belief through preachers they have invited to Cyprus." This is a matter in which the Government are in no way connected.

8. I bring the present matter thus fully before you because I believe with the Chief Commandant of Police that serious trouble will arise if some prudent measures are not quietly taken which, without inflaming any passions or making martyrs for the cause, will give heart to those who desire to support the British Administration and prevent the agitators ruining the rural population who are as fine a class of peasantry as can be found in any country.

9. The agitation in the towns is led from Limassol and Larnaca where the richest of the Greek speaking Cypriotes reside, and where the principal mercantile business of the Island is transacted. They are exceedingly jealous of Nicosia. The recent elections have been carried, it is alleged, by the money and intimidation of money-lenders, and I think one great reason for their wish for union with Greece is to obtain social position, as well as Greek Nationality. I have for some time thought it would be judicious for the High Commissioner to obtain suitable rooms at each of these towns and meet the people there in social intercourse. The High Commissioner now visits the towns but has to live in a tent in which entertainment is impractical. The objection to obtaining rooms are that it would entail an expenditure of some £500 to £700 and that one might be placing a burden on one's successors for entertaining which they might not like. Still if you should consider that it would be advisable and suitable, accommodations can be provided from the next Public Works vote, steps would be taken to make these towns social centres at certain seasons, and such action might probably heal a good many sore feelings among the wealthy Cypriotes and their families.

10. The main matter, however, is that some arrangement should be made as to Tribute and I earnestly urge that if it is possible to disentangle the question of the Cyprus Tribute from international complications on other matters that an effort might be made to commute the Tribute for the payment of a moderate capital sum in cash to be charged on the Island. It is greatly hoped in the Island that the present necessity at Yildiz might induce the Turkish Authorities to accept a very reasonable sum. This payment of about £60,000 a year is the constant thought of all classes. They speak out on every occasion, they dream of it and I believe never refer to it without a curse in their hearts. As I have said the present generation knows nothing of the inconveniences of Turkish Administration and there is no gratitude in politics. All they look at is that the withdrawal of the portion of the Tribute of £92,000 amounting to about £60,000 a year which is paid by the Island thwarted them at every turn when they want money for public uses; and I believe that the determination is growing to use Cretan methods for deliverance from the burden.

11. In this connection I may refer to the proposed commercial treaty with Turkey which as I have brought under your notice in a numbered despatch will ruin our trade with Turkey because the articles exported from Cyprus to Turkey are similar to those produced on the opposite coasts and the proposed increased Turkish tariff is therefore a protective tariff against the Cyprus goods which will turn the balance entirely against Cyprus. Any alteration of the existing relations with Turkey which are so much to the injury of Cyprus while the Tribute remains as at present will only deepen the resentment against the Tribute.

12. I have already alluded to the desire for some nationality and as this matter is surrounded by so much difficulty I would ask your consideration of the question whether you could favourably place before His Majesty the King the proposal to graciously grant to Cyprus a flag which the Cypriotes might lawfully use. Such a grant would to some extent satisfy the craving for a corporate existence and place the Islanders in this respect on an equally favourable footing with Crete. Samos has its own flag and I understand Crete is allowed its own flag. If Cyprus were granted a flag the use of the Greek flag could be quietly checked without exciting attention of rousing passions. A suitable flag might be devised without offending any sentiment and I think a St. George's Cross, red on a white ground, with the arms of Richard Coeur de Lion in the upper quarter, would be one readily adopted. St. George is one of the heroes of the Greek speaking community. In Famagusta one sees in close proximity churches to St. George of the English, to St. George of the Greeks, and to St. George of the Latin. Such a flag too would not offend the Turkish community.

13. I would also ask that the legal difficulties in the way of raising a military force for service in all parts of the world might be dealt with as soon as can conveniently be done; for the raising of such a force, which might be made an exceedingly fine and useful one, would do much to consolidate the British influence in Cyprus and I believe the adjacent countries.

14. I would further advocate that when a new Archbishop is appointed a concordat should be arranged with the leader of the Cyprus Orthodox Church and thus restore to the Orthodox Church some of the prestige and position which it enjoyed under the Turkish Administration. Such a course would I hope win the great majority of the adherents of the church and would conciliate local public opinion while at the same time such action would not run counter to the Turkish sentiment.

15. The Constitution of the Legislative Council was based on the idea that there would be a proper balance of parties in the Island, because when the Turkish members agreed with the Government the two would form a majority. This safeguard has not worked in practice. The Turks have fallen into the power of the Greek speaking usurers and the Turkish members are of no use whatever to the Government and seem fatally blind to the dangers which threaten to wipe them out. The Turkish members are—a gentleman who was removed from the Headmastership of the Idadi school—a Turk who has been deprived of all his honours and his civil status by the Courts of H.I.M. the Sultan and sentenced to imprisonment for life with confiscation of all his property and the third is a gentleman who has been shot at and wounded for alleged oppression by his debtors and whose brother was murdered for some agrarian dispute. I understand that the line they are taking up is that the Tribute ought to be paid to the Sultan but that it should be wholly paid by the British Government and that no portion should be paid by the Island.

16. The Turkish members have all been supported by the Bishop of Kitium and his party, and the bait which has been held out to them is that the Greek members will help them in a campaign against the Evkaf Delegates to bring the administration of the Evkaf funds under their control if the Turkish members will act with the Greeks in other matters.

17. The Order in Council constituting the Legislative Council in clause XXIV empowers the Council to discuss any question in debate which does not refer to the appropriation of the Revenue or the imposition of a tax or impost. It is quite possible that the Council following the precedents at the Ionian Islands and at Crete may at its meeting formally propose Union with Greece as the expression of the wish of the inhabitants and to satisfy the Turks, also bring forward the proposal that the Evkaf should be placed in the hands of elected administrators. If I were in the Chair as the presiding officer I should rule that any vote or resolution on either of these subjects was not within the competence of the Council as being inconsistent with the Constitution and with the obligation imposed upon His Majesty the King by treaty. The point however is not clear; and as I believe any such action of the Legislative body would be inexpedient and injurious to the Island I would suggest that the Order in Council should be amended by making it clear that such subjects are not within the competence of the Council. This could be done by redrafting the clause and inserting the words "not being inconsistent with any obligation imposed on us by Treaty." Any such alteration would reassure the loyal portion of the community, for the agitators are never weary of telling the people that a large portion of the British people will support the movement for Union with Greece and that official denials are of no weight because a few weeks before the cession of the Ionian Islands the allegation of the intention was officially contradicted in the House of Lords.

18. There is at present no power given to the Chair or presiding officer to maintain his rulings on any point of order whatever. At the last session one of the members who has again been returning to the Council at the head of the poll accused the acting Receiver General of preparing false returns with intent to defraud. The acting Receiver General drew attention to the statements and I required the member to withdraw the statements. He declined to do so, and I then used the only means at my disposal of maintaining order, and that was to adjourn the Council. The feeling of his fellow members was against him on the occasion and at the reassembly of the Council he made a halting apology; but in any case when the feeling was with the offending member he would not

apologize, and a deadlock would be at once created. Of the 9 Greek speaking members, five are advocates and one is a doctor, the Bishop of Kitium holds two seats. If he is made Archbishop and retires two more advocates will probably be elected. These five or seven men as the case may be know that if they appear before a Judicial officer even before so subordinate a one as a village Judge they must behave with decorum and therefore conduct themselves decently. I think the Chief Executive Officer when presiding in the Chair should also have power to preserve decorum by requiring any member not complying with the ruling of the Chair to withdraw and that in case of continued offence the Chair should have power to suspend the member from the sittings of the Council for a limited time. The great object is to avoid "scenes" arising. They will not arise if the Chairman has power to enforce his ruling. They do not arise in the Courts where the advocates know they must behave themselves. The Council will never pass any ruling of order giving the Chair any such power and therefore in the interests of proper administration I suggest that clause XXIII of the Order in Council should also be redrawn and that the latter paragraph of the clause should be as follows "Subject to such Instructions the Council shall conform to such rules and order for the regulation of its proceedings as may be framed by the High Commissioner in Council and may be sanctioned by one of His Majesty's Principal Secretaries of State and such rules and orders when so sanctioned shall have the same effect as if expressed herein and subject to such instructions, rules and orders the Council shall from time to time as occasion may require make further Standing Rules and Orders for the regulation of their proceedings and such Rules and Orders shall take effect when confirmed by the High Commissioner." The reasons why I advocate such a modification are that the possession of such a reasonable and guarded power will prevent the occasion arising for its use and that any open collision in the Legislature on any such question as Union with Greece is highly inexpedient. There is no personal element in the question and since the Elections the newly elected members have called on me to express friendly sentiments towards myself, and a desire to work with me. I quite understand that they wished to ascertain how far the British Government would permit them to go in this matter.

19. (This number was skipped.)

20. The agitation will, of course, be strengthened if the Patriarchs of Constantinople and Jerusalem lend the professional agitators the aid of their influence in their attempt to create an anti-British feeling throughout the Island.

21. I think the whole situation requires care. The rural population are at present with the Administration, and will probably continue so, if the agitation can be judiciously checked, for they are shrewd enough to see that the British Government are as likely to advance their interests as the money lenders and middlemen; but it will be difficult for the rural population long to resist the organized so-called "patriotic" movement if it is unchecked, and they will regard the absence of any action as acquiescence by the Government in the movement. There is a considerable body in the towns who also would support the Government if they receive any encouragement such as the suggested amendment of the Order in Council, which would be an indication to them that the work of the Island was to be quietly carried on. I have fully discussed with my advisers the various aspects of the movement and I now submit to your judgement the suggestions made in this despatch, in the hope that if they are adopted the development of the country may not be arrested by barren or disastrous political disputes and agitations.

I have the honour to be
Sir,
Your most obedient
humble Servant
W. F. Haynes-Smith

B. Newspaper Extract, 11/24 October 1901

Extract from Evagoras of the 24 October 1901.

———

Tyranny with Hypocrisy.

In the process of extending the colonial empire of Great Britain carried on by the English politicians either by the force of arms or by means of gold, foreign and alien peoples are being subjugated by them in the name of civilization and progress of humanity. That hypocritical pretence could have a justification whenever the conquered countries are inhabited by savage or barbarous peoples; but what value can such pretence have when the British guns spread the death amidst civilized people whose only sin has been that they have repelled the English rule and preferred instead their own autonomy and national freedom? What sufficient defence will Great Britain offer to the impartial history for the Anglo-Boeric war which has heaped up on that heroic people fatal misfortunes and has cast on Great Britain excessive sacrifices of blood and money? What other difference can there be between that unequal and unjust war and the abominable Armenian butcheries than that of the number of victims? The Turkish tyranny could justify itself by citing in defence the security of its empire which has been threatened by a heedless patriotism and by foolish and untimely provocations of the rulers by the subjects, but what could England say to justify the bloodshed that reddens, for two years now, the floods of Modder and Tugela and blackens the repute of the British arms?

The Turkish tyranny pursues the extermination of one race because it considers that that race is a danger in its realm and that it threatens, from day to day, to provoke against Turkey an external war which will shake Turkey utterly and will bring on Islamism incalculable misfortunes, whilst England, who runs no danger from the peaceful and pious Boers, has brought upon that unfortunate people all its brutal power for the purpose of seizing the rich mines of their country and completing the conquest of South Africa and, with it, of the whole Dark Continent.

It was in the name of freedom that the Maltese were, on a former occasion, aroused by Great Britain against the French and that the latter were blockaded from the sea by the British fleet and compelled to surrender, and that the people of Malta hailed then the British flag as an angel of freedom and progress. After about a hundred years since, the British rapaciousness and the political hypocrisy of the English politicians, in spite of the progress of civilization, not only have lost nothing of the malevolence and perfidy that has often characterized them, but, alas, have assumed besides a greater rashness and boldness. After a British rule of a hundred years, the Maltese feel to-day all the choking weight of that rule and rise up all of them as one man to protect their language and national existence against those whom they received formerly as liberators and saviours! A cry of patriotic pain has sounded responsively from the breast of the noblest children of Malta whereby the national Maltese denounce to their fellow-citizens and the civilized world the breach of faith and arbitrariness of the English rule.

England has not listened to the solemn request to spare their national language and not to impose new taxes on the poor and rocky island and the Maltese Patriots moaning under the weight of the brutal force and of the inhuman injustice speak as follows to their fellow-citizens.

Fellow-citizens!

"Despotism is victorious for the moment! Our protests have availed of nothing. The supplications to the King have been thrown off. Silly rulers! The Victory you have won is delusive, you have lost the appreciation and won the hatred of the Maltese. Be not deceived! The vengeance of the heart is awful!

We have been stricken, it is true, and the stroke is heavy, but, glory be to God, it is not fatal and never will it be fatal, so long as the people will it.

Fellow-citizens! Be ready to face that struggle! Be ready for sacrifices. Recollect that the surrender of one span of ground is equal to a defeat and, if you give in, all is lost, i.e. the honour, the freedom, the future of our children.

On, then!

We must neglect no lawful means of defence. Whoever is not with us is against us. Whoever is not with us will be treated as an enemy, even if he is a brother.

Brave youth! The fatherland invokes your help. If you abandon her, nothing but disgrace will be left for you; shew that you want to be masters in your own house and that never and in no wise will you renounce your holy rights!"

That clear and sonorous patriotic cry of a people who has been deceived and who, instead of the freedom he expected, runs now the risk of losing both his language and his nationality must move, above all, the patriotic Cypriots who are running the same dangers and have suffered the same disappointment under the English rule.

The Turkish despotism, in spite of its coarseness and arbitrariness, was free of the deceitful hypocrisy and, when it had satisfied its financial wants and the base covetousness of its corrupt Government, it allowed the subject races to enjoy the blessings of their soil and intelligence and never thought of laying snares for their nationality. Strangely enough, the Turkish despotism, in spite of all its savageness and absolution, paid respect to the religion, the language and the nationality and kept subjugated nations stationary, but intact and never thought of exterminating or injuring them by the use of force or through hypocrisy, as the pharisaical and hypocritical tyranny of the English does nowadays.

By means of a dishonest contract torn away from Turkey by still more dishonest moral coercion, Great Britain occupied Cyprus for the object of guarding as she pretended, the Turkish possessions from any Russian in-road in Asia, and thus put herself forward as the guard and champion of Islam against the predominance and extension, to the Islam's detriment in the East, of any Christian power whatever and for such a purpose, she has rendered the Cypriot people more ill-fated than when they have been under the Franks or the Venetians or the Saracens or the Turks.

We say, more ill-fated, because they are taxed more heavily and more unjustly now then they have been under any other foreign rule in the long past and moreover, their language and, with it, their national existence is threatened by those who promise to render Cyprus the PARADISE OF THE EAST. The Turkish tyranny bestowed on the Orthodox Church and on every other Christian community in its realm privileges whereby a state in a state was created and the subdued nations were able to preserve themselves through unhurt, for the most, and intact.

By exercising a hypocritical tyranny the English Occupation in Cyprus has put down the privileges of the Church and of our holy clergy and has even attempted to humiliate and humble the latter in the conscience of the inhabitants and, even now, in collusion with a known antinational faction in the country, has interfered with the purely ecclesiastical question of the Archbishop and prolongs its pernicious suspension, because it loathes the accession to the Archiepiscopal throne of that prelate who will be able to concentrate around the said throne the whole people of the Island and force on the Government justice, good administration and alleviation of taxations.

To that malevolent policy against our church, the English Government add now an undisguised treacherous attack on our national education, not only through hidden operations and advices, but also through an absurd and unjust persistence in entrusting the inspection thereof to an English priest who is entirely unacquainted with the Greek language and is ignorant of the pedagogue science. They have overlooked the solemn protest of the people and have already made his appointment a definite one and have thus shewn that they are firmly determined to prosecute the realization of their scheme in the Island so that, in time, they may distort the national education of the people and tear the latter away from their glorious and holy national traditions and thus render them cosmopolitans without a religious and national conscience.

To that persistence and treacherous attack of the Government the whole people of the Island, united and of one mind, must oppose an indomitable persistence and opposition and they must abstain from no lawful defence for their national existence the means of such defence being manifold and innumerable. To-day by the protests in public meetings tomorrow by the formal language of the elected members of the Legislative Council and, after that, by other more positive and effective means.

It is necessary that the civilized world should learn that the English Government apply in their colonies the jesuitical dogma "the object sanctifies the means" that from none of such means do they abstain in the prosecution of the consolidation of their rule and that they sacrifice for that purpose the national and religious existence of their subjects of a different race.

The imperialistic policy which the Tory Party has declared to be its principle and which the busybody Secretary of State, Mr. J. Chamberlain, has undertaken to force on the Colonies of Great Britain threatens to crush peoples who have rendered the greatest services to humanity and whose destruction will be a great lost to the civilized world.

At a time when nations hitherto unknown and obscure wake up against any attack on their national conscience and put forward claims of national self-existence, it would be a shame and disgrace for the Cypriot people to yield to and tolerate in any way the arbitrary and tyrannical policy of the English Government who aim at the distortion and wiping off of the national education of the Cyprus people.

C. British Commentary

Sir J. Anderson,

This is on the whole a temperate statement of the present condition of the agitation in Cyprus for union with Greece. I think that the time has come to take some steps to check it. The elections have resulted in the triumph of the extreme party, led by the Bishop of Kitium, and the election has been won by false and disloyal representations. Before the new Council has time to make mischief, we should consider what we can do to throw cold water on the agitation. It must also be remembered that the Bishop of Kitium will probably be awarded the Archbishopric by the Patriarch of Constantinople, who is arbitrating on the question. His new position will greatly increase his power. He has given us much trouble in the past and his attitude to the Government in the future will be largely determined by the way we deal with him and his agitation now. I believe that he is a man of considerable common sense, and that he is likely to shape his behaviour according to the course of events. A little tact and firmness now will save rows ahead.

Coming to the recommendations of the H.C. in paragraphs 9 and onward

1. There is a suggestion to try social influence by entertaining at Larnaca and Limassol. The H.C. is apparently willing to bear the cost of entertaining (he is very generous in such matters) but he says that it will cost some £500 to provide suitable rooms. I presume that he means to build. It would be much preferable to hire apartments if such can be found. A moderate provision from the Public Works Vote might well be allowed. I think we might express appreciation of his offer to entertain, and say that if it is absolutely necessary to build for the purposes, the S. of S. is prepared to consider moderate proposals in connection with the allocation of the Public Works Vote, but that it would be preferable if possible to hire suitable rooms and charge the rent to the P. W. Vote, so that if the experiment is unsuccessful, it can be dropped without any considerable expenditure having been incurred.

2. Conversion of the Tribute. The Tribute is, of course, at present allocated to the charges of the guaranteed Loan. There is, therefore, no object in commuting the Tribute except in connection with the conversion of the Loan. The Treas. proposal some years ago was to give the Sultan a lump sum to obtain his consent to the conversion of the Loan, and we should then have reduced the amount of the Tribute payable by Cyprus and allocated the remainder to the service of the Loan. But it was not proposed to reduce the Tribute below some £60,000 or so, which may be taken as the average paid by Cyprus after setting off against their payment the Grant in Aid voted by Parliament. Mr. Chamb. pointed out forcibly in a desp. to Cyprus that the first claim for relief on the conversion of the Loan was that of the British taxpayer. Cyprus would of course benefit by a reduction of the Tribute which would allow them to get on without a Grant in Aid, since they would have the benefit of their own natural increase of revenue and there would be no Treas. control.

Under present circumstances it seems quite impossible to consider the question of the Tribute apart from the Loan, and that cannot be tackled in the present state of the money market and of our own finances.

The question of a fixed Grant in Aid was considered thoroughly the year after Mr. Chamb. came into Office and was dropped. Cyprus has however been treated much more liberally during the last six years, and the Tribute question must sleep at present.

3. The new Commercial Treaty with Turkey. The S. of S. has approved of negotiations being opened for a separate Agreement between Cyprus and Turkey on the basis of the existing tariff. If this can be secured Cyprus will benefit instead of losing over the new Treaty (in which she will not be included) since her goods will enjoy preferential treatment.

4. A flag for Cyprus. We have been immensely hampered by opinions expressed by our L.O. in the early days of the Occupation, who declared that Cyprus ships were Turkish and must carry the Turkish flag. A new letter to the L.O. has now gone, and we hope to get a more reasonable opinion, which will enable us to register Cyprus shipping, and provide a special flag. It would be best that the flag should be some modification of the Union Jack. The flag if granted can be used for purposes of demonstrations, etc. and will it is to be hoped supersede the Greek flag.

5. A Cyprus regiment for general service in the Army. The W.O. approve of this project, and the L.O. allow it, subject to an amendment of the Army Act, which at present limits the proportion of aliens (which Cypriots are) in a British regiment. The amendment was to have been carried out last year but the Army Act had to be passed in a hurry, and the question had to stand over. I think we should now remind the W.O. of the matter, and say that Mr. Chamb. trusts that the amendment will be made in this year's Act. It is important for raising regiments in Protectorates as well as in Cyprus.

6. Concordat with the new Archbishop. We have already told the H.E. that the civil powers to be conferred on the new Archbishop—similar to those conferred in old days by the berat of the sultan—will be settled by an order of the King in Council, when the future occupant of the See is determined and we have received from the H.C. proposals as to the powers required and proper to be accorded. I see no harm in making the grant of these powers conditional on good behaviour on the part of the Archbishop, and the H.C. should tell us what terms he proposes. We have already said that we cannot interfere in questions of the administration of church property, at any rate without the full consent of the Church.

7. Legislative Council. It is evidently undesirable that the council should formally discuss a proposal for Union with Greece, or any similar subject inconsistent with H.M.'s Treaty obligations. I think clause xxiv of the order in Council of the 30th of Nov. 1882 should be modified as suggested by the H.C. This will have a good moral effect generally as showing that the Council may forfeit their constitution if they can't behave themselves, besides being a desirable reform in itself.

As for the standing Orders, we have told the H.C. to rule Members out of order in certain cases, but his inability to enforce his ruling except by adjourning the Council is awkward. The only course seems to be to amend the O. in C. as suggested, giving the H.C. power to frame Rules subject to the sanction of the S. of S., and he can then take power to suspend a member—but perhaps it would be best to give the Council an opportunity of framing a suitable standing Order before proceeding to amend the O. in C. in this respect.

The H.C. makes no recommendation in this desp. with regard to the licence of the Press and the use of the Schools for the purposes of agitation. So far as concerns the Press the view taken here is that it is of no use starting a campaign against the Press unless we can steadily maintain it, and we are liable in this country to get a Parliament which would not tolerate interference with the liberty of the Press, however harmful.

As to Education we have told the H.C. that he might induce the Elected Members to give the Govt. some reasonable supervision over the course of instruction by pointing out that while H.M. Govt. would be reluctant to do anything to check the progress of education in Cyprus yet if they find that the schools are made use of to foster an agitation inconsistent with H.M.'s Treaty obligations, it may become incumbent on them to reconsider the arrangements under which assistance is now given so liberally to Education. (I may however point out that we only give about £5,400 a year for a population of a quarter of a million, and a Cyprus paper which is described as moderate draws very unfavourable comparisons with the state of things in Crete, where it is stated that out of a total revenue of £80,000 less than Cyprus £26,000 is allowed for education.

Encl. 4 gives an interesting account, by whom is not stated, of an interview between the bp. of Kitium and the new Greek Consul. His attitude is a welcome change from that of his predecessor who gave us much trouble and had to be got rid of.

When the attitude to be taken up is settled it will be most convenient to send a draft of the reply which we propose to return for F.O. concurrence, with copy of the despatch. The Treas. should also see the papers with the draft reply.

A. E. Cox 18/1

Mr. Cox,

It is no use trying to kill an agitation of this nature either with tea and cake or with specially devised flags and banners. Even if we could give them Br. citizenship I doubt if it would have effect. Greece is very much nearer and the Cypriots go there to be educated and inherit the Greek language and tradition.

No doubt a Cypriot regiment would be useful to us and might have some influence in damping the agitation—though I have never heard that the large number of Irish who join the Br. Army has had much influence on Irish agitation.

The worst feature in the speeches is the demonstrations of the policy of depriving the suspects of arms. Whether that means anything or not in the quantity of the lawyers and priests who run the agitation, it is difficult to say, and the High Commissioner does not touch upon this point. It is a policy which should be steadily adhered to, and the High Commissioner should be asked whether there has been any special reason furnished by recent events which would account for the prominence of these questions in the various manifestos.

As regards the possible discussion in Council on the subject of union with Greece—no one pays any great attention to discussions in the Cyprus Legislative Council, and the High Commissioner should let them blow off steam and then tell them flatly that H.M.G. hold Cyprus in trust for the Porte, and can only relieve themselves of that obligation by restoring the Island to Turkey. That they are satisfied is not the wish of the inhabitants, and that it is idle for them to ask H.M.G. to hand over to Greece an island which does not belong to us, and that we must refuse even to consider any change to the political status of the Island. He might point out also that we have invested and may invest more of the money of the taxpayers of this country in works of general improvement in Cyprus, and that a continuance of such an agitation is not likely to encourage our efforts in that direction.

Beyond that, I would not go. It is very easy to attach too much importance to the effervescent talk as in election time it is the ebullitions of newspapers which nobody pays any attention to, and prosecution is the only thing which strengthens agitation. If the agitation leads to breach of the peace, let us go for the agitators with a mailed fist or any heavier instrument we can get, but so long as it is froth, we may let it go by. So long as we do not give the Cypriot a bread and butter grievance, it is unlikely that he will do more than applaud these sentiments, and will still be a long way from fighting for them. Initialed 21/1

Mr Ommanney

The press is not nearly so fierce as Dr. Mizzi's organ in Malta and it would be impossible, even were it desirable, to put in force any laws as to seditious writings which may exist.

We are hampered on all sides by the peculiar position of Cyprus but there is not the least chance of our being able to modify or alter the position we have assumed.

I do not suppose the L.O. will give as much help as to the flag on the register of ships and I do not expect that we shall be able to get into the Army bill of this year the clause which the W.O. dropped last year in view of the political questions which would arise. We are, therefore, rather helpless as to the High Comm's suggestions.

I think we shall have to content ourselves with Sir Anderson's suggestion.

H.B.C.
22 Jan

D. Chamberlain's Reply

19 Feb. 1902

Sir,

I have had under my careful consideration your conf. desp. of the 28th of Nov., reporting on the nature and extent of the agitation which is being carried on among the Greek-speaking Cypriots for union with Greece.

2. I have learned with regret from your desp. and its enclosures that this movement is causing considerable embarrassment to administration. Some allowance must however be made for the heat generated by a contest at the polls, and I have no doubt that much of the violent language used is due to the occasion and goes far beyond the sober views of the politicians who employed it.

3. The worst feature of the speeches is the denunciation of the policy of depriving suspects of arms. It is difficult for me to judge of the importance to be attached to this denunciation since you do not touch on the point. The policy hitherto followed must of course be steadily adhered to, but I should be glad if you would inform me whether any events have recently occurred which would account for the prominence of the question in the different manifestoes.

4. The various recommendations which you make in paragraph 9 and the following paragraph of your despatch have had my consideration, and I will now deal with them in the order followed by yourself.

5. I appreciate your liberality in proposing to adopt the plan of entertaining at Larnaca and Limassol, but before expressing a final opinion on the suggestion, I should be glad to be furnished with further information as to the availability of suitable rooms and the charges which would fall on Island funds and also whether the amount you propose to expend in entertaining can be met from your official salary. I am opposed in principle to Governors spending more in entertainment than the amount of their official income.

6. With regard to the Tribute, I must point out that as the Tribute is at present allocated to the payment of interest on the guaranteed Ottoman Loan there can be no question of its function apart from a general arrangement for the conversion of the Loan. Whether the negotiations for the conversion of the Loan will be resumed, and also when, I am not in a position to say, but I adhere to the views contained in my desp. No.67 of the 19th May '99 that if on the conversion of the Loan a reduction of the Tribute is made possible the first claim to relief is that of the British taxpayer who has been called on to make good the annual deficiency in the Cyprus accounts arising from the liberality with which the local expenditure of Cyprus has been allowed to grow as compared with the expenditure in Turkish times. The object of reducing the Tribute would be to make Grants in Aid unnecessary for the future, and further relief reduction for the benefit of the Cypriot taxpayer could only be a very small amount.

7. The question of the effect on Cyprus of the new Commercials Treaty now being negotiated with Turkey is dealt with in separate correspondence. I am now awaiting your views as to the basis of such a separate arrangement between Cyprus and Turkey as you desire to effect.

8. I am consulting the L.O's, of the Crown as to the possibility of a Register for Cyprus shipping and the introduction of a Cyprus flag. I shall inform you hereafter of their opinion.

9. With regard to the proposal for raising a Regiment in Cyprus for general service in the Army I have to inform you that the project is favourably regarded by H.M.'s Government, but cannot be carried out without an amendment of the Army Act, which is now under consideration.

10. I entirely agree with you that the Government should attempt to arrive at a friendly understanding with the new Archbishop. I have already informed you that the civil powers necessary for the execution of the office, such as were formerly conferred by the Berat of the Sultan, will be conferred by O. in C. of H.M. when the proposals for this purpose have been put forward by the Church, discussed by you with the Christian Members of the Council, and sent to me. The settlement of these powers would seem to offer a favourable opportunity of arriving at an arrangement with the Head of the Church, since their nature and extent can within certain limits be made to depend on the assurances which the Archbishop is prepared to give as to his attitude to the Govt.

11. Your proposals as to the Leg. Council do not commend themselves to me. Though I admit that it must be trying to listen to long and irrelevant discussions in the Council to the detriment of public business, and though these discussions may occasionally tend in a direction contrary to H.M's Treaty obligations, I think it is easy to attach too much importance to utterances which can be little known and have little effect outside the Council Chamber, and it must moreover be remembered that such discussions are

useful in providing an outlet for seditious sentiments which are less dangerous as they are openly expressed.

12. I would therefore suggest that if the members of Council wish to discuss the question of Union with Greece, you should after giving them a hearing tell them firmly that H.M.'s Government hold Cyprus in trust for the purposes stated in the Treaty of 1878, and can only relieve themselves of their trust by restoring the Island to Turkey; that H.M.'s Government are satisfied that restoration to Turkey is not the general wish of the inhabitants and must consequently refuse to consider any change in the political status of the Island. It is useless for the Council to ask H.M.'s Government to hand Cyprus over to Greece, since the reversions of the Island belongs to the Sultan and H.M. cannot disregard this Treaty. You might also point out that H.M.'s Government have invested the money of the taxpayers of this country in works of general improvement in Cyprus and may invest more, but that the continuance of such an agitation as the present is not likely to encourage liberality in that direction.

I have, etc.,
J. Chamberlain.

V. Dispatch of W. F. Haynes-Smith, 30 August 1902 (CO 67/132)

A. Letter of W. F. Haynes-Smith, 30 August 1902

The Right Honourable   Government Cottage, Troodos
J. Chamberlain, M.P.   30 August 1902

Sir,

I have honour to report to you that I have waited to reply to your confidential despatch of the 19th of February last on the subject of the agitation which is being carried on among the Greek-speaking Cypriots for union with Greece until I had been able to ascertain what action the Members of the Legislative Council elected on the cry intended to take.

2. They have asked for union with Greece under the form of independent autonomy free from any right of veto of the Crown—and that England should pay the whole of the Tribute, adding their threats that if this is not done the people will refuse to pay taxes—and if this is not sufficient that they will resort to violence. Their threats are I think at present the expression of what the foreign agitators for union with Greece would wish done—and of what they would do if they could. It must be remembered that the movement is engineered from abroad by past masters in the art of intrigue who have established a very complete organization of so called "Patriotic Clubs" throughout the Island and have the command of money. As showing the nature of the organization and the danger to British Officers who in many cases have only native officers around them I annex a copy of a telegram sent to me by Mr. Theodotou and Mr. Chacalli, Members of the Legislative Council. Mr. Theodotou is also an additional Member of the Executive Council. In this telegram they accuse Mr. Percy Ongley, the acting Commissioner at Famagusta, of offering unnameable insults to their religion and calling for exemplary punishment. Within a few hours I received telegrams from all parts of the Island in the same strain. I replied to the Members of the Council in the letter of which a copy is annexed

asking them to give me particulars as to the occurrence of which they complained and although they received the letter nearly a month ago they have not replied. I understand the allegations are perfectly unfounded—and Mr. Ongley proposes to take further action. A clear case can be met; but the acts of an isolated officer may be misrepresented at times by astute and unscrupulous persons if they have a political object to gain. One of the objects of the agitators at present is to discredit the British Administration in Cyprus and to endeavour to show that the administration of Crete under Prince George is much more successful. Crete is an unpleasant neighbour to Cyprus. I annex for convenience of reference an article which appeared recently in "The Times" showing how active political agitation is in Crete and that it is worked as here from Greece and abroad. The writer points out that "fortunately for Crete the Christian peasants who form the bulk of the population are comparatively unaffected by party politics."

3. In reply to the inquiry contained in the third paragraph of your despatch as to whether any events have recently occurred which would account for the prominence in the election campaign of the denunciation of the policy of depriving suspects of arms I think the answer is that those outside the Island who are directing the agitation consider that they can now act more openly and that it may be essential for their purpose that a considerable portion of the population should be armed. They desire to bring about, if they can, a position in Cyprus analogous to that they created in Crete before the intervention of the Powers. The foreign agents of the agitation who have come to Cyprus, as in the case of Dr. Zanettos, openly state that the people will resort to violence—and the local leaders, as in the case of Mr. Theodotou, not to be outdone or to lose influence with the wilder spirits try to outcap the foreigners and each section thus eggs on the other. They realize however that they would have to deal with a very different Government to that of Crete. It is a disadvantage to the administration that foreign subjects should be eligible for seats in the Legislative Council and if any amendment of the Constitution be made it would benefit the island if the Members were required to be either Ottoman or British subjects or native-born Cypriots.

4. The foreign element means to carry out its programme if it can and I do not think it would be of any advantage to try and propitiate it. The case as regards the growing class of the Cypriots who are accumulating money stands, I think, on quite a different footing and here the social question is of much importance. The ladies of the Greek families must feel the social isolation of not generally mixing with the ruling class and one of the uses of Government House is that a tone can be given there to society in a matter of this kind. The visits of the High Commissioner to Larnaca and Limassol, where most of the wealthy Cypriots reside, afford a natural opportunity of meeting them in social intercourse which would promote better mutual acquaintance and remove misapprehensions—social isolation on the other hand leads to many bitter jealousies. The matter could not be forced for if it were thought to have a political object the "Patriots" would make themselves offensive. In reply to your inquiry as to the cost of obtaining suitable rooms I have received estimates showing that one of the buildings not now used, but included in the premises rented from the Military at Limassol, could be altered at a cost of about £300, and accommodation obtained at Larnaca for about £400 making £700. This would perhaps be better than renting rooms. If premises were rented they would cost about £ 75 annually in each place. The entertainment I suggested was only to a moderate extent which could be met from the official salary.

5. As the Cypriots gain in wealth and education there will no doubt be an increasing pressure for posts now held by British Officers—and this is seen in the Legislative Council. One of the causes why the foreign organization and the Elected Members obtain support is that they make themselves the mouthpieces of the native professional men who are in an immense excess of the professional requirements of the Island and for whom there is no employment. I do not well see how this increasing pressure can be avoided—but it certainly would be advisable to turn the current of local feeling into a wholesome channel and instead of making Union with Greece the general cry among the Greeks to turn their aspirations in the direction of developing Cyprus. In this the Moslem and Greek communities can both join.

6. There is a large body of the native Greek community who though they would not dare to incur the odium of being denounced as traitors to the Patriotic cause, would yet be glad to be rid of the agitation and support the British Administration if they received any support from the public acts of the Government. If therefore this move of the foreign agitators in reducing the Education Vote is fully met many would rally to the local administration. While convinced that every overt action should be met with firmness I am seeking to prevent any cause of collision. In each case where the Elected Members bring forward complaints and make specific allegations full inquiry is made. In most cases the allegations are disproved but in every instance where any ground is shown remedial action is taken. I am also endeavouring to remove every just cause of complaint. The most frequent complaints now relate to the Forest Laws or to the collection of taxes. I have in my report on the recent session of the Council stated the outline of the action taken with respect to the forests. I also brought forward a Bill to amend the tithe and tax collection Ordinance 1882 which would have relieved the taxpayer from annoyance and been advantageous to the revenue. I annex a copy of the Bill which would take the issue of process out of the hands of the Medjliss Idare and give it to the Receiver General and would do away with the cumbrous system of numerous installments allowed by the Turkish law by substituting a payment in two installments if desired. On the other hand the whole of the crop of the taxpayer would not be stopped and he would not be driven to the usurer for money as the Bill provides that the collector when taking the tithe may set aside a portion of the produce which at market rates would realize the half of the Verghi and Askerieh taxes then owing. The agriculturists in the villages, to whom the matter has been explained, wish for the Bill and the Elected Members will probably pass some modification of it next session. In other respects the system for the collection of the taxes may with advantage to the revenue be made simpler and less constantly worrying.

7. All the pending questions can, I think, be gradually dealt with and satisfactorily disposed of except that of the elementary education of the Island. However successful the Government may be in securing contentment and the material improvement of the country if the elementary education in the Greek schools be left in the hands of the foreign agitators controlling it from abroad there will be continued and increasing trouble. To deal with other matters and leave this appears as useless as attempting to fill a sieve with water. The action of the agitators in carrying out the first step in their political programme has made some actions necessary and affords the opportunity for placing this matter on a right footing without undue friction. If the proposed draft Order in Council be approved the local bodies would be free to act in all educational matters for the furtherance of Education except that they would have to use the grants in aid to secure the

proper elementary education of the children. I annex a copy of a confidential report of the Inspector of Schools showing that the school organization is being openly used in the Greek schools to further the agitation for Union with Greece and that a system of terrorism has been established over the masters to coerce them into carrying out the programme of the agitators. The so called National Party however are not content with this but desire to get rid of any English Inspectors who, as they consider, act in some way as a restraint on the masters. The present course of education is itself bad and the children are wrongly taught in the ordinary subjects of instructions and especially in arithmetic. It seems positively wrong too for the English Administration to supply funds to be used by the Greek masters to teach the children that among their highest aspirations must be the hope of fighting the Turks who are their fellow subjects and with whom they have to live. Inciting the inhabitants of the Ottoman Empire to take up arms the one against the other is an offence under the Ottoman Code; but the course of instruction in Greek schools paid for by the British administration comes near to this description. It seems too a mistake to permit the public funds granted by the English Administration to be used for the purpose of instructing the youth of the country that they must obstruct and impede the English Administration as "a putrid Government." The agitators may enjoy their own opinions but there does not appear to be any good reason for using the public funds to pay people to inculcate such doctrines.

8. The peasants, both Moslem and Christian, as in Crete, are as yet for the most part unaffected by the political agitation. This state of matters however cannot very long continue. The schoolmaster is subject to annual election and the Hellenic propaganda organization is using this system to stir up trouble and keep villages in constant turmoil. The political schoolmaster when elected is always on the spot and if he is a firebrand fresh from Athens the agitation is kept up. The police reports are constantly showing how often disturbances in a village can be traced to the political schoolmaster who is partly paid by the Government but who advances his interests by obstructing the Government because under the existing system his position depends on his so acting in order to retain the support of the organization.

9. The present system is inflicting grave injury on the Island and the necessity for its alteration lies at the root of any permanent improvement in the country and in fact at any peaceful administration in the future. I trust therefore that the local Government may be empowered to secure for the youth of the island a sound elementary education apart from politics and that this may be carried out either under the authority of the suggested draft Order in Council or in such other way as may appear to you to be best. If such authority be given it would not be necessary to take any action likely to lead to serious friction. If the Order in Council were passed I believe that it would be sufficient for the most part for the Inspectors of schools in a friendly way to warn the teachers to drop politics in the schools and to let them know that the Government were prepared to stand by them and improve their position. The passing of the Order in Council would assure them as to the power and will of the Government to protect them. If the warnings were not attended to flagrant cases could be met by special action, but the Greek Cypriot is very shrewd he will clamour and cry but let him once understand that while there was no compulsion he had yet to conform to the Government requirements and he will govern himself accordingly. The Moslem Board of Education would be quite willing to act in co-operation with the Government if the Order in Council were passed; and although there would be more

difficulty with the Greek Board of Education I believe that if they knew the Government had the power to control that it would be quite possible to induce them to pass reasonable rules from time to time and to obtain a good working compromise. If the Order in Council were passed I should not advise any interference at first at all with the Board. The useful action would be with the Village Committees and the schoolmasters through the English Inspectors. These Village Committees are generally reasonable. The personnel of the Board would be gradually modified. The bulk of the country population would be with the Government and if we secured the position of the teachers we could obtain the services of a body of men who are anxious to improve themselves and who would in time be of valuable service. It is sometimes stated that if any conditions were attached to the grant in aid the money would not be accepted. If so this would be a most excellent result for it would enable the Government with the money thus saved to establish a few model central schools well manned with efficient native teachers fairly paid and working on proper lines. The children are willing pupils and the parents are eager they should be well taught. At present the grant is spread over such a large number of schools that its beneficial effect is to a great extent lost and the programme includes so many subjects that none is properly taught or learnt. The material is good and schools well managed would have effects which would gratify the people.

10. I asked Mr. Collet as knowing the condition of the Country to give me his views on the present position of political matters and he has sent me the memorandum of which I enclose a copy. His suggestion as to the Penal Code being passed by an Order in Council and as to Rules of Order regulating the procedure of the Legislative Council being established by the same means have already been submitted for your consideration but were not approved.

11. The action as to the English Inspectors is a test which has been instituted by the foreign organization to encourage their followers and as an important step in their programme. The Press is full of their intentions and of vilification of the British Administration. Any course of compromise by yielding to it would I think be only taken as so much gained to the movement and as an invitation to the organization to take the next step in their programme for stronger and more adverse action as regards the non payment of taxes.

I have the honour to be,
Sir,
Your most obedient,
Humble Servant,
W. Haynes Smith

B. Report on the Schools, 4 August 1902

A REPORT ON THE HELENIC PROPAGANDA IN ELEMENTARY SCHOOLS
4 August 1902

In response to an enquiry by His Excellency the High Commissioner as to my observation of this Propaganda, I have the honour to report as follows.

Greek Flag.

At nearly every school the Greek flag or its blue and white striped staff is found, either in position outside or standing in a corner of the room, waiting for the next festival or holiday, on which occasions its use is universal.

At a recent athletic display at the Cyprus Gymnasium in Nicosia, (the training school of our elementary masters,) which I was invited to attend, the blue and white was everywhere, the large flag was paraded round the playground, the competitors and masters wore or carried small flags etc., etc.—not a sign of English colours anywhere—and this although the Headmasters and Committee do not belong to the party which claims to be the National Party, and indeed have quarreled with it. The fact that no master is accepted at this school who has not a certificate of qualification from Athens, no doubt tends to influence them in this direction.

The annexed extract, marked "A", from the "Evagoras" newspaper, shows how the flag and the influence on the masters is looked to "to open the eyes of the Greek hearts of the simple villagers."

Pictures.

I find the walls of every Greek-Christian school room, except in some of the remotest villages, adorned with Chromolithographs of the Greek Royal Family, politicians, heroes of the War, a battle piece, and especially an allegorical picture, "The Resurrection of Crete." These have generally been introduced by the master, and are his personal property.

I have found these pictures in poor schools where maps and sacred pictures are wanting, where desks and other requisites are deficient, shewing that in the Master's opinion Hellenic sentiment is the basis of education.

In three or four schools I have seen an old portrait of Her late Majesty, Queen Victoria; and these, I was informed, were given by the Education Department in the early days of the occupation.

Books and Lessons.

On examining the schools I find that the only History that is taught is modern Greek History, and almost the only Geography, certainly the only Geography over which any trouble is taken, is that of Greece. However bad other maps are, there is sure to be a large map of Greece.

The Reading books in use above the lowest classes usually contain, as might be expected from their origin, selections in glorification of the Hellenic people; and, in the fourth class and upwards, modern Greek renderings of the Odyssey and Anabasis are in constant use, one may say to the exclusion of all others. They are most unsuitable books for country children who are quite ignorant of anything beyond their own Island.

Singing.

A song-book is prescribed in the "Programme," out of which it is directed that a certain number of songs shall be taught. It consists to a large extent of matter intended to inflame Greek patriotism, War songs, (against the Turks), Klephtic Outlawry Ballads, or those of a Religio-Patriotic sentiment, of course all referring to Greece. In practice, whenever I ask to hear the children sing, it is a war song, "Forward, follow the drum that leads us against the Turks," or often the Greek Anthem is produced, showing that the character of the selection made by the masters is scarcely suitable for an Island where both nationalities should live in peace under the shadow of the British Flag.

In <u>one</u> school only, under an old master, have I heard a Greek version of "God save the King."

The Authorised Programme.

Unfortunately Books are used and lessons given under the authority of the Programme drawn up a few years ago by the Board of Education, which lends itself admirably to the propagation of Hellenism, and in my opinion, it has been drawn with that obvious intention. In any case it is too complex for village schools, and needs amendment as to the teaching of arithmetic, and by the substitution of the rudiments of Agriculture for other subjects; but this, under present arrangements, would have to be passed through the "Board of Education," which now is even more Hellenistic than formerly. I shall refer to this in another paragraph.

Festivals.

The Three days specially marked by the schools, when the masters lead the children round the village in procession with Greek flags, garlands, etc., are the "Three Bishops," (a school holiday universal in the Orthodox Communion), St. George's Day, (the name-day of "our King"), and the anniversary of Greek Independence; on which days inflammatory speeches are made by the Master, and any leading person, such as the Bishop of Kitium, that they can import for the occasion.

Examinations.

The teachers have been careful not to obtrude their anti-English sentiments on me personally in any offensive way. In fact, the only instance of its introduction directly into the examination was at the Limassol Boys' School, where the headmaster, in asking question on the geography of Greece, made some on the Ionian Islands lead up to a declaration by the pupil that all true Cypriots should ardently strive for the same position.

On another occasion, in conversation away from the school, a master asked me, quite innocently, "Is it true that <u>our</u> King is related to your Queen?"

The English Language.

I may here refer to the English Classes offered to schoolmasters during their holidays with the view that they should be able to teach English in their schools, by gradual introduction, not compulsion, for which they were to receive a small bonus. The first year, 1900, about 40 Greek masters came to the classes, and (I was then taking them myself), seemed to accept the idea with considerable favour. But an attack was organized in the Press; the scheme was represented as an insidious attempt by the Government to destroy the Greek language and religion; the proposed bonus was called a bribe; masters who would accept it were denounced as traitors; and eventually all the masters attending the classes, except two, were induced to sign a declaration that they would never teach English to the children. Each year since then the classes have been denounced beforehand, and in consequence only two came to the class in the vacation of 1901, and five are attending this year.

The annexed extract, marked "B", will illustrate the way the local Press endeavours to discourage the study of English even in Turkish schools; while in extract "C" there is a passing reference, more eloquent, perhaps, than if it were the subject of the article, to a Greek master at Lapithos, who began to teach English in his school, but whom they "dissuaded" by making his name "public" in this paper.

The Teachers.

In spite of much "tall talk" and resolutions calling upon them to exclude the British Inspector from their schools, I have been received with respect and even friendliness wherever I have been; and I do not believe that the majority of the masters are really extreme in their sentiments; but, while Government support is of comparatively little moment to them, they stand in awe of personal attacks in the Papers, and of intrigues that may be organized against them in the Village and District Committees, upon which they depend for their appointments and livelihood.

Nevertheless there are a considerable number who do much mischief in the villages, stirring up disputes and party feeling, and whose position as master is used, not for the benefit of the children, but to command the attention of the villagers.

It is somewhat difficult to disentangle the threads of these disputes; personal feeling, village politics, and the Archbishop question are so intermingled; but I have no doubt that the Hellenic sentiment is the trump card in these encounters; he who shouts loudest for the "Enosis" is the truest patriot and commands the largest following.

Complaints by Commissioners.

The Commissioners see this more closely in their respective Districts than I do, and frequently say to me that "this or that master is nothing but a demagogue, and causes the officials much trouble: I wish you could get him moved."

One instance out of many I have before me under enquiry now. The Commissioner of Paphos on the 26th July last wrote to me enclosing a complaint that the master of Lysso had publicly insulted the Nazir in a café, saying; "You are afraid of this putrid Government; in future the conduct of the Government will make it the duty of conscientious men to refuse to serve under it." The Commissioner says, "I think you will agree with me that the language used by this teacher is most unbecoming, more especially from a person holding a position under Government. I take this opportunity of informing you that this man has during his residence at Lysso caused party spirit to run so high that fears are entertained by the "Police that serious crime may result."

Though there are some schoolmasters who might with advantage be moved, the Government has no power to do so, the appointment resting entirely in the hands of the Village and District Committees, without any confirmation by the Government being necessary: and, even if we know a man to be a drunkard or leading an immoral life, we cannot dismiss him or take away his certificate: and as regards the grant, it would be useless for me to propose to the Board of Education that a grant should be withheld or reduced because the man was a violent politician.

Board of Education.

With the Board of Education as it has been constituted for some time, such a charge would be a recommendation rather than otherwise. A master at Lophos has frequently been reported against by the Inspectors for neglecting his school; and once by me, and various times by the late Inspectors of schools a reduction of his grant has been recommended to the Board; but, because he is a protagonist in his District, his friends on the Board of Education have always refused to reduce it. It was the Board of Education that drew up the Programme of lessons and the Regulations, which, among other things, order the observance of the Greek Independence Day, as already referred do, and the present Board are rather more extreme than their predecessors.

Influence of the Press.

Of the extracts enclosed, "A", "B", and incidentally "C" have been mentioned in illustration of various points.

But extract "C" particularly illustrates the attacks made on teachers by name. In the case in point, three masters came to see me at one of my camping places, and asked questions relative to the Education Law and their work. They appear to have been pleased by a civil answer, and were foolish enough to write to the "Phone" to say so—I need scarcely say, without the least suggestion on my part.

But in this article a vitriolic attack is made on these masters by name for daring to thank a British interloper who has been rejected by the Legislative Council and the People of Cyprus, and all true masters are called upon to show what they think of them.

In the same paper were articles congratulating the people of Varoshia on having got rid from their School Committee a man who was a supporter of the Government, and declaring that if the Government would not give way about the British Inspectors the people must reject the ridiculous assistance now given and work their schools themselves without any Government supervision.

And such articles appear week by week.

Conclusion.

While I find in conversation with the villagers, especially in the remoter districts, that the older peasants, who remember Turkish times, are quite happy and contented with the deliverance afforded by the British Occupation, there is, I believe, no doubt that the Elementary Schools are being used by the Hellenistic party, through the power they obtain over the masters through the Board of Education, the Press, and party organisation, to bring up the younger generations to look for the "Enosis" as a deliverance, not from Turkish but from "English tyranny."

In fact, the money of the British tax-payer, given in grants to the schools, now assist to teach the children that "they must hate the English language and people," and thwart "the English Government" in every possible manner.

But if the masters were brought more under the control of the Government, and were taught to look to it rather than to the party organisers, the majority of them might, I believe, with tact and time, become its useful supporters.

F. D. Newham,
Inspector of Schools.

C. Newspaper Extracts

Extract from The Evagoras 31 July 1902

A PATRIOTIC SCHOOLMASTER

A young man without a schoolmaster's certificate has been appointed schoolmaster of a group of small and remote villages, paid by the villagers. Besides his daily school work he has urged, and by his personal example has persuaded them to repair the ruined church of the village and to apply voluntarily the Public Health Law by keeping clean the court-yards and streets of the village.

He bought cloth and sewed a flag and the villagers seeing the white and blue pieces asked the schoolmaster if they were "children's napkins"? The patriotic master was not discouraged, he sewed during the hours of tuition altogether 5 national flags and one of these floats every Sunday over the Church and the other 4 ornament the school on the festival of the Three Bishops, (a school festival all over Greece), and on the day of Greek Independence (Palingenesis), which the master celebrated with every possible magnificence.

The simple villagers are now filled with enthusiasm at the sight of the national emblem, and worship and are grateful to him who opened the eyes of their Greek hearts.

The name of this obscure but good soldier we pass over for obvious reasons, putting him forward to many certificated Masters as an example to be followed.

THE DESTINY OF THOSE WHO LEARN ENGLISH

His Excellency visited a short time ago the Ottoman School IDADI and urged the pupils to learn English as well as Turkish and Greek, promising that they would be preferred as Zaptiehs.

We are persuaded that those of our Moslem fellow-townsmen who lean towards the Government will have been filled with enthusiasm at the brilliant prospect which is reserved for the Ottoman Youth.

EXTRACT FROM THE ALETHEIA, 19 JULY 1902.

Who would ever have believed that after the unanimous expression of opinion of the people of Cyprus and the scholastic world about the appointment of Mr. Newham as Inspector of Greek Education—who would ever have believed that there would come a day on which there should be found men, and schoolmasters too, to publish letters of thanks to the Inspector "for the amiable and warm zeal with which he listened to the representations of the undersigned upon questions which concerned the Greek-worthy development etc?"

Nevertheless it has been our fate to see this unspeakable thing; and the last number of the Phone published in an out-of-way corner, as if it were ashamed, a famous letter of thanks, signed by three schoolmasters who certainly through this document deserve immortality.

I shall do all that is in my power and possible to satisfy the love of notoriety of the masters of Pitsillia district, and, as formerly we helped a certain schoolmaster of Lapithos, who had taught English in his school, that there should be some mention of his name—previously unknown—so now too we will try that the masters of Alona and Pterykoudhi shall meet with the immortality they desire.

But Messrs. Antoni Kyprianides, Neophytos A. Ierodiakonos, and Christodoulos Y. Kanthos, for these are the gentlemen's names, ought at least to know that there are cases in which notoriety and public discussion give very little honour; and if at all cost they wanted to see their names printed in the Phone, they might have found some other and more simple means than this, and might have had nothing to do with letters of thanks to the Inspector, because the "Hellenistic Development and the fulfillment of our long felt desire," as they write to excuse their shameful deed, are certainly not furthered by such groveling letters of thanks to the English Inspector for "the warm zeal with which he listened" etc. thus giving into Mr. Newham's hands a weapon, not dangerous and indeed ridiculous as those who foolishly gave it to him, but useful to the Inspector who will certainly not omit to profit by it to answer the vote of the people and the Legislative Council when the occasion requires.

So much for these teachers, of whom their brother teachers and the Pancypriot Teaching Union ought to shew what they think, and concerning whom it is not worth while saying more.

But as concerns the Inspector, who is resorting to such means and who extracts from the foolishness or the material necessity of appointed masters letters of thanks and testimonials (bon-services), we assure him that such means tend most certainly to anything else than to better his position. In spite of all the letters of thanks the people of Cyprus and its true schoolmasters will never cease from looking upon him as a simple interloper whom the right of the stronger has put and continues to put over them.

D. Political Matters

In connection with the question as to what would be the best Constitution of Cyprus there must be borne in mind—

(a) that the Christians are born intriguers and that their agitators declare their desire to get rid of British rule;

(b) that they resent the payment of the tribute to Turkey, and oppose anything that will decrease the deficit, even when such opposition is against their own interest;

(c) that from their love of public speaking and their jealousy of each other an inordinate amount of time is wasted by elected Members of the Council in debate, so that measures more or less favourably regarded by the people have to be dropped through sheer exhaustion;

(d) that the canvassing for elections is carried on in an objectionable manner and is attended with bribery and intimidation.

Bearing the foregoing in mind we must come to the conclusion that it is hopeless to induce the Legislative Council to pass any law tending to render political agitation innoxious. The Ottoman law is very defective with regard to the prevention of disturbances, because recourse was not had to the Courts, The Executive always acting as it thought proper.

The Penal Code should be passed by Order in Council and in all matters relating to public disturbance or apprehended public disturbance the law should be assimilated to that of England. The Courts should have the same powers as English Courts have to require sureties to keep the peace or to be of good behaviour.

When prosecutions are dismissed on legal grounds, there should be a power of appeal, if permission is given either by the Court itself, the Supreme Court, or the King's Advocate. It is unlikely that the power of appeal would be used to any great extent; but many cases are out of simple weakness dismissed now by native judges where convictions should ensue. There is no possible appeal against a dismissal, and the native judges have a horror of having their decisions reversed on appeal.

Appeals from Magisterial Courts should be direct to the Supreme Court. Ordinary judges should not, as at present, have the power of reversing the magisterial decision of the President, whose decision once reversed, no matter how wrongly, cannot be restored by the Supreme Court.

The Legislative Council should not have the nominal power of rejecting the estimates. They have no desire for economy, and when they wish to make reductions in votes it is simply with a view to replacing British officials with natives and to further their agitation for rejection of British rule.

The estimates should be framed by the High Commissioner in Council and be in force when approved by the Secretary of State. They should be placed to the Legislative Council at as early a date as possible so as to give them an opportunity of making representations concerning them.

The President of the council must have powers of regulating debate (a) by powers of suspensions, or if necessary of punishment, if his ruling are disregarded, (b) by a power to exercise the closure (a power which should only be exercised when it is obvious the measure in question is going to be thrown out, or when there is no possibility of its being thrown out, such as in the case of the resolution in favour of an agricultural bank, when it took two days to dispose of the unopposed resolution; (c) by restricting the time for which each person may speak without special permission from the chair; (d) by restricting the unlimited right of speaking in Committee, (e) by allowing only two days a week for private motions, with perhaps another ten days for motions on the estimates.

These Rules can only be passed by Order in Council.

In election petitions the procedure is the same as in England and the Court requires the petitioner to find security for £1000 for costs. The amount is too large for Cyprus and prevents petitions being made. The security should be reduced to £200.

I think the voting should be by ballot, with no provision for illiterate voters. The voting boxes should have the candidates names printed in large letters. Specimens of the labels could be circulated in advance and photographs of the candidates might be placed on the boxes. In this way illiterate voters can easily be taught how to recognize the various boxes, but they should not have to record their vote in the presence of a money lender or his agent, as they have to now.

I think the qualification should be same as in elections for Village Commissions. The elector should have at least 50 c.p. Verghi in his own name. Instead of there being for non-Moslems three districts each returning three members there should be nine districts and each returning one member, Nicosia, Famagusta and Limassol would have two electoral districts each, Kyrenia, Larnaca and Papho one.

Although the Estimates should not be under the control of the Legislative Council, no alteration in taxes, or imposition of new burdens should be made without its consent; unless perhaps in matters regarding the water supply and sanitation in the principal towns, where something must be done. But with the alterations I have suggested possibly, the Legislative Council would do what is necessary. Their loquacity is such that they cannot deal with any important measure in less than a month; but with debates brought under control more business could be done.

W. Collet

E. Extract from the Times, 5 August 1902

"The Times," Tuesday, August 5, 1902.

THE SITUATION IN CRETE
(from our special correspondent.)

It is now more than a year since the four protecting Powers, aroused by a series of demonstrations in Crete and a vote of the Assembly at Canea in favour of union with Greece, addressed a somewhat stern admonition to Prince George declaring their firm resolve to maintain the status quo and at the same time requesting the Prince to continue to exercise his mandate, which, under the arrangement of 1898, expired last December. Some four months previously (February 22, 1901), in reply to his urgent advocacy of the union, they had intimated to the Prince that, "while ready to examine with sympathy every proposition made to them with the object of ameliorating the condition of the island"—the promise implied in these words has been somewhat tardy of fulfillment—they could not, in present circumstances, sanction any such modification of the political situation as the Prince had suggested. Since the declaration of June 18, 1901, nothing has occurred to indicate any change in the views of the Powers. Failing the immediate realization of the union, it is hoped at Athens that the Powers will consent to the withdrawal of their troops from Crete and that Greece will be authorized to occupy the island with her armed forces in accordance with the precedent supplied by the Austrian occupation of Bosnia and Herzegovina. The Sultan's *amour propre*, it is urged, might thus be respected and his suzerainty maintained. It will be remembered that a somewhat similar proposition was made by Greece to the Powers shortly after the expedition of Colonel Vassos in the spring of 1897. The idea has hitherto failed to recommend itself to the European Cabinets, which seemed influenced by the consideration that the Sultan, who has not yet recognized Prince George as a civil ruler, would hardly be disposed to welcome him in Crete at the head of a Greek army. Yielding to the representations of the Powers, Prince George, with a sense of duty which deserves all praise, resolved to continue the task he has undertaken with so much success; his mandate was renewed for an indefinite period, and for the past year the history of Crete, from the international point of view, has been almost devoid of incident.

It is otherwise, however, with regard to the domestic affairs of the island. Party spirit runs high, higher perhaps than at any time since the days when, after the signature of the Pact of Halepa, a constitutional *regime* was inaugurated under the mild sway of a ruler who was both a Christian and a Greek. Those were the days when the *Karavanades*, or "well-fed" supporters of the Government, and the *Xypolyti*, or "barefeet," fought out their battles under Photiades Pasha, who ruled in accordance with the time-honoured maxim, *divide et impera*. The methods adopted by Prince George differ widely from those of Photiades; his Royal Highness is strongly disposed to absolutism and discountenances the formation of parties, but years of constitutionalism have left their mark upon the Cretans, who share the passion of the Greeks for political combination and their aptitude for party warfare. The principal figure in the present Cretan Opposition is M. Venezelo. It will be remembered that in March last year M. Venezelo, who was then one of the Prince's councillors, suggested the institution of a temporary principality as a step towards the attainment of the union, that the proposal produced a journalistic tornado at Athens, and that its author was dismissed from office by Prince George. The project might conceivably have obviated diplomatic difficulties, as the Sultan is known to desire a principality in Crete on the model of Bulgaria, but it had the fatal defect of exposing the Prince and the Greek Dynasty to the fury of the Athenian Democracy, which, as the Gospel riots of last November once more showed, is at best a slumbering volcano. Immediate possession of the island is desired at Athens, and any transitory arrangement is regarded with suspicion as tending to encourage the covetousness of certain Powers and to deaden the zeal of the Cretans for annexation. The underlying object of M. Venezelo's proposal was virtually the same as that of the "Bosnia scheme"—the removal of the international troops, which would leave the Cretans practically free to declare the union at their pleasure. The essential difference in the working out of the two plans is that, under the Bosnian scheme, the Greek troops would be in the beatitude of possession when the hour for the union struck, whereas, should M. Venezelo's project be realized, the Cretans, being masters in their own house, would find themselves in a position to bargain for certain financial or administrative privileges—perhaps even the retention of their home-made Constitution. It must be borne in mind that the Cretan Constitution was framed on very conservative lines in view of the evils resulting from unbridled democracy at Athens, and some of the native politicians who drew it up expressed the opinion that it should be retained after the union, or else that the Greek Constitution should be modified.

Since his dismissal in April, 1901, M. Venezelo has become by force of circumstances the centre and rallying point of the malcontent element in Crete. The conflict between him and the High Commissioner, though arising from a divergence of opinion as to the best mode of attaining the union, no longer turns on this question, inasmuch as M. Venezelo has recognized the impracticability of his project and has unreservedly renounced it. It was proposed, in view of foreign misapprehensions, that he should sign a recantation of his heresy, but the document laid before him contained certain phrases of contrition which he refused to endorse. The conflict has, accordingly, proceeded; but its details possess little interest for the outer world. Naturally enough, the Governmental party, in which M. Koundouros, late Councillor for the Interior, and M. Papadiamantopoulos, the Prince's secretary, are the principal figures, has hitherto had the best of it; some prominent partisans of M. Venezelo have been removed from judicial and other appointments, and his sympathizers are no longer regarded as eligible candidates for public posts. In spite of this, or perhaps, because of this, the opposing faction has gained strength, at least among the black-coated politicians of the towns; it displays a growing confidence, and its attitude is somewhat menacing. In all the newly-liberated countries of South-eastern Europe the struggle for places is keen, and every Government gradually becomes unpopular as the number of disappointed candidates increases. M. Koundouros, whose position had enabled him to dispose of a large patronage, found himself face to face with a hostile Chamber last year, but the Prince, who appreciated his services, decided to retain him in office. His resignation has now been accepted, and this timely concession to popular feeling will doubtless mitigate in some degree the growing exasperation of his enemies.

Party rancour has long been endemic in Crete, and there is nothing wonderful in its reappearance now that the first transports of joy over the abolition of Turkish rule have subsided. All controversy on the subject of the union is, of course, absolutely futile, as the settlement of the question rests with the Powers alone. But the charge of treachery to the national cause furnishes a convenient party weapon, and any stick is good enough wherewith to beat a dog. If M. Venezelo's recantation savours of opportunism, it must be understood that, in the circumstances, any programme to which the Prince and the Greek public are opposed is doomed to failure. The Principality has been anathematized; in the union alone, immediate and unconditional, is salvation found. The Venezelists are apparently determined not to allow the dominant party a monopoly of this saving and popular doctrine; in view of the coming elections they mean to "go one more" than their adversaries by clamouring for the union more loudly than they. They will at least enjoy "a position of greater freedom and less responsibility"—to borrow a phrase of Mr. Gladstone's—for the party in power is shackled in some degree by international engagements. In order to meet the threatened danger, M. Koundouros, released from the trammels of office, will be put forward to fight the so-called renegades, ostensibly as the head of an independent party, but in reality supported by the Government. It is to be hoped that this arrangement will have the effect of eliminating from the controversy certain august names, which have hitherto been bandied about in a most unbecoming manner.

The present situation in Crete bears a curious resemblance to that which existed in Eastern Rumelia before the union of that province with Bulgaria. In September, 1885, the "unionist" party were in power at Philippopolis, but their programme remained unrealized till their opponents, whom they denounced as traitors, carried it out by means of a successful conspiracy. A similar *Coup d' Etat* in Crete is, of course impossible, owing to the presence of the international troops, and it is therefore hoped, by the Government party at least, that the four Powers will, at the earliest moment, consent to the substitution of a Greek force for the present army of occupation. When this has been done all will be easy enough, and King George will be speedily invited to land in the island. There is a simplicity in this plan which contrasts with the complicated diplomatic procedure involved in the "Bosnia scheme" or the institution of a transitory principality; no international entanglements are anticipated, the Sultan would not be heard of, and the exodus of the Moslem population, which would probably leave in the wake of the European troops, would not be regarded as a serious drawback, if indeed a drawback at all.

The Moslems insist with great earnestness on the retention of the international troops. The Mahomedan minority, now reduced to a third of its former numbers, is apparently regarded as a negligible quantity, but no description of the allusion to this melancholy remnant of a once dominant race. The Moslems, as a rule, remain congregated in the principal towns; a few families have returned to their homes in the country, but most of the smaller proprietors have sold or abandoned their holdings, while the larger landowners, or "beys," have let their estates to Christian farmers. The positions of the beys will tend to resemble that of the Irish landlords after a further course of remedial legislation in the other "distressful island." They express their gratitude to the High Commissioner for the protection which he has accorded them and admit that their present security belies their former apprehensions; rightly or wrongly, however, they are far from contented, and a certain fellow-feeling in misfortune has led many of them to ally themselves with the Venezelist. Now, as in former times, the Moslems associate themselves with the Christian political groups; fatalistic indifference and a want of initiative prevents them from forming a homogeneous party and playing an energetic part in the Assembly, in which, if duly represented, they would still be proportionally almost as numerous as the Irish party in the House of Commons. The Moslems have, of course, their own special grievances. They complain that the number of Mahemedan officials has been decreased; that portions of the Evkaf, or ecclesiastical domain, have been appropriated by the Christians; that their cemetery at Candia has been desecrated, and that the amnesties granted to Christians condemned by the international Courts have not been extended to Mahomedans. Space forbids me to examine these complaints in detail. The first and the third seem well founded; with regard to the Moslem convicts, it must be pointed out that many of them were sentenced by British Courts at Candia, and that their release would be somewhat premature. The Moslems lament that the foreign Consuls no longer interest themselves on their behalf, but they should remember that fortune helps those who help themselves. A little energy in the assertion of their rights might benefit them more than petitions to the Sultan and the Ambassadors at Rome.

Fortunately for Crete, the Christian peasants, who form the bulk of the population, are comparatively unaffected by party politics. They have little to expect from changes in the Government and they are ready to accept any rulers nominated by the Prince, who is highly popular amongst them. Crime has remarkably decreased in the rural districts, notwithstanding the recent murder of Moslem boatmen in Sphakia, which unfortunately tends to show that the disarmament of the population is incomplete and that the old racial vendetta is not extinct. The magnificent harvest, which has just been reaped, and the excellent condition of the vine and olive crops will tend to promote tranquility among all classes, notwithstanding the feuds of the politicians, and to alleviate in some degree the serious economic situation which the disasters of prolonged insurrections, the exodus of a fifth of the population, and the errors of inexperienced financiers have all contributed to bring about.

Chapter 2
Churchill's Visit and the Aftermath: 1907–1926

The documents in this chapter open with the High Commissioner's account of Mr. Churchill's visit to the island. His letter to the Earl of Elgin, Secretary of State for the Colonies (a position Churchill would later fill) included two important attachments, namely, a copy of the Memorial that the Greek Elected members of the legislative Council presented to him, along with Mr. Churchill's reply. We then jump ahead five years to minutes and other correspondence relating to the riots of 1912. Even though five islanders lost their lives and more than a hundred were injured, the British were not alarmed. "The proceedings and the language are very mild; there is no ground for official repressive measures" (CO 67/166). As we will see, this is in sharp contrast to the official response in 1931 when British property was destroyed. Correspondence from 1914 through 1926 illustrates the continuing press for Enosis and the effects this had on the Turkish community on the island. The last several documents demonstrate the economic underpinnings of the Enosis movement and the resentments generated by the Cyprus Tribute.

I. Dispatch of C. A. King-Harman, 21 October 1907 (CO 67/149)

A. Letter of C. A. King-Harman, 21 October 1907

The Right Honourable   Government House
The Earl of Elgin, K. G.   Nicosia, 21 October 1907
etc., etc., etc.
Secretary of State for the Colonies

My Lord,

Referring to Your Lordship's despatches of the 12th of July and the 30th August, upon the subject of the visit to Cyprus of the Right Honourable Winston S. Churchill M.P., I have the honour to inform Your Lordship that Mr. Churchill arrived in Cyprus on the morning of Wednesday the 9th and departed on the evening of Sunday the 13th.

2. As soon as the news of the approaching visit of Mr. Churchill was made known to the public of Cyprus, the leaders of the Hellenic agitation determined that every effort should be made to impress the Under Secretary of State with the predominance of what is known in Greek circles in the Island as "The National Idea." The columns of the local press teemed with fervid articles calling on the people with one heart and one voice to advocate Union with Greece as the great ideal of the Cypriot nation. Greek flags were manufactured by the thousands; school children were organized and drilled to wave the national standard effectively; addresses were prepared in which Mr. Churchill's visit to Cyprus was likened to the arrival of Mr. Gladstone in the Ionian Islands and in which he was fervently exhorted to follow the example of the late illustrious statesman and to restore Cyprus to her Mother Greece; arrangements were made for the simultaneous despatch of telegrams to Mr. Churchill from all parts of the Island, a telegram being still regarded here as a more important and imperative communication than a letter, and the people were exhorted to assemble in their thousands and to vociferate unceasingly their desire for the Union.

3. On Mr. Churchill's arrival at Famagusta all these arrangements were very effectively carried out and while the wharf and the streets of the town were gay with the colours of Greece, the air was rent with shouts for the Union. The display was at one time in danger of being marred by the Turks of Famagusta who, in their indignation at the Greek demonstration, fell foul of some of the processionists and began what might have developed into a very considerable affray. Fortunately the exertions of the police and the good sense of the Turks themselves combined to maintain the peace and when Mr. Churchill landed on the wharf there was some outward appearance of good order.

4. An address was presented at once by the mayor of the town who, in behalf of the Greeks, gave prominence to their national aspirations. The Turks were also ready with an address of welcome in which they repudiated the pretensions of their Greek compatriots. There was much excitement and shouting, waving of flags and cheering for the Union, in the midst of which Mr. Churchill drove off and joined me at the Famagusta Club where I awaited him.

5. In the afternoon we proceeded by train to Nicosia where a Greek demonstration was organized at the Railway Station. The crowd with their flags were kept outside the station by a strong body of police and admission to the platform was only permitted to the Mayor and members of the Municipality, who presented an address of welcome, and to

the Greek elected members for Nicosia whose spokesman, Mr. Theodotou, addressed Mr. Churchill on the subject of Union with Greece. Mr. Churchill thanked the Mayor for his welcome, declined to discuss politics with Mr. Theodotou and then drove off to Government House with me.

6. By the next day (Thursday) the Greek organizers began to realize that their demonstrations were not entirely to Mr. Churchill's taste and the display of Greek colours visibly deteriorated. Mr. Churchill postponed all political deputations and memorials till Saturday and received only such representative persons as were deputed to approach him on matters connected with the local requirements of the people. He interviewed the heads of the Forest, Public Works, Agricultural and Education Departments and inspected the Central Prison.

7. On Friday I took Mr. Churchill to Kyrenia and there he was requested by the spokesman of the people to give the assistance of the Government for the improvement of their harbour, their water supply and their public buildings. No Greek demonstrations were made and not a single Greek flag was visible; so completely are these docile people at the orders of their political organizers.

8. The next day, Saturday, had been fixed, at Mr. Churchill's request, for the reception of the elected members of the Legislative Council who, as he people's representatives, were deputed to present addresses indicative of the principal requirements of their constituents. It was unfortunate that two of the three Moslem members were absent from the Island on other business at Constantinople, and it devolved therefore on Hami Bey, the member for Larnaca and Famagusta, to present the Turkish views. The Greek members, nine in number, were present in full strength with the Bishop of Kitium as their spokesman.

9. Hami Bey had no memorial to put in. He commenced his speech by apologising for the absence of the Moslems from the railway station on Mr. Churchill's arrival and explained that those who wore the fez could not do so under cover of Greek flags. He complained of the latitude allowed by the Government to the Greek population in the expression of their national sentiments and insisted that the feelings of the Moslems were outraged and insulted by the demonstrations of the nature of that which greeted Mr. Churchill on his arrival in the Island. He deprecated even the idea of the Union of Cyprus to Greece and explained the Moslem view of the Tribute to Turkey; that it was a token of the sovereignty of the Sultan and should continue to be paid by the Island.

10. I should here explain that the deputations were received in the Chamber of the Legislative Council in the presence of the official and elected members, and also of the public, so far as accommodation could be made for them.

11. In reply to Hami Bey, Mr. Churchill assured him that he fully appreciated the motives which had prevented the assembly of the Moslem people at the railway station and that he had not attributed their abstention to any want of respect to himself as a member of His Majesty's Government. He said that he had noticed the display of Greek flags; but had not discerned in that display any attack on the honour or dignity of the Moslems or any discourtesy to the representatives of His Majesty's Government. He regarded the display as an evidence of the anxiety of the Greek population to impress him with the particular views which they held, and, although he could not agree that the methods adopted were the best that could have been found, yet he did not complain of them. Freedom of expression should be allowed within due bounds; but he hoped that the

Greek people would be careful to avoid exuberant manifestations such as might hurt the feelings of others in the Island. He would reserve his observations on the questions of the Union with Greece and the payment of the Tribute until he had heard the address of the Greek elected members.

12. The Bishop of Kitium then presented a memorial from the Greek elected members in behalf of the Greek population of the Island, of which I annex a copy, and addressed Mr. Churchill on the three cardinal points of Union with Greece, the payment on the Tribute and wider political liberties for the representatives of the people. In insisting on the wish of the Greek population for Union with their Mother Country, His Eminence significantly added that such a desirable consummation would doubtless be fulfilled in the plenitude of time and that, in the meanwhile, the people of Cyprus would be content to remain under the British flag.

13. Mr. Churchill's reply to the Bishop of Kitium was carefully reported and I annex a verbatim copy his important speech. The Greeks were greatly pleased at his generous recognition of their national sentiment and I think that they also, as well as the Moslems, were greatly relieved at his pronouncement that Great Britain does not intend to evacuate or abandon the Island.

14. Several other deputations were then received and memorials presented by the representatives of the many different sections into which the Greek and Turkish communities are split up, and also from the Roman Catholics and the Armenians; the two latter being purely complimentary and congratulatory. Further references were made to the leading questions of the day and certain local requirements were brought to the front. Mr. Churchill undertook that his remarks on the Union, the Tribute and Constitutional liberties would be published for general enlightenment and information and he dealt generally with the other matters put before him.

15. On Saturday afternoon, after having dismissed the deputations, Mr. Churchill had a most interesting interview with the Patriarch of Alexandria and the two Exarchs, representatives of the Œcumenical Patriarch of Constantinople and of the Patriarch of Jerusalem. These ecclesiastical dignitaries have now been four months in Cyprus engaged in the discussion of the Archiepiscopal question, and, in reply to Mr. Churchill's sympathetic enquiry, they stated that they trusted to be soon placed in a position to enlighten the Government on the course of their negotiations. They all expressed the most lively satisfaction at the benevolent attitude of both His Majesty's Government and the Island Government towards the attempt in which they were engaged to restore peace and harmony to the Church of Cyprus, and they thanked Mr. Churchill warmly for having accorded them an interview and for the interest he displayed and the anxiety he expressed in regarded to a speedy settlement of the deplorable dispute.

16. Early the following morning (Sunday) Mr. Churchill left Nicosia for Larnaca were he interviewed the leading people of the town. He then embarked on H.M.H. "Venus" and proceeded to Limassol where he landed and was well received by the people. The same evening he left Cyprus for Port Said.

17. In the memorials which have been presented to Mr. Churchill, in the speeches which have been addressed to him and in the conversations which he has held with the leading people of the Island, it has been persistently impressed upon him that there is a wide feeling of discontent and disappointment at what is regarded as the parsimonious policy of the Government in regard to public works, and especially, in regard to the re-

afforestation of the Island. Your Lordship is well aware that under the financial system which obtained in the administration of the Government of Cyprus, prior to the institution, this year, of a fixed grant in aid, the resources of the Island were annually and absolutely depleted in order that as much as possible of the legislative action, wise administration or bountiful harvests, no increase of expenditure for the profit and improvement of the Island accrued thereby. Any augmentation of the revenue was for the advantage of the Imperial Treasury and the sum allowed for the requirements of the Island was most inadequate. Your Lordship's liberal policy has put a term to such a system, and Cyprus, with a fixed grant in aid, should now be at liberty to use her surplus revenue in the development of her great resources.

18. Mr. Churchill, in his examination of the circumstances of the Island, has concluded that there should be no delay in bringing home to the people the realization of the real benefit conferred on Cyprus by the change in the financial policy of His Majesty's Government, and he is strongly of opinion that the surplus revenue which has accumulated as the result of four years of propitious weather and good harvests should be appropriated, as soon as possible, and expended in meeting the many and crying needs of the Island.

19. I need scarcely say that I fully concur in the wisdom of Mr. Churchill's views and I can find no expression in which to explain the satisfaction which would be felt by the people of Cyprus should those views be carried into effect. So little, in comparison with what was expected, has been done since the British occupation, and there is so much that could profitably be carried out. Bewailing spilt milk is an inexpedient occupation; but Mr. Churchill has been able to see for himself and to realize the harm that has been done and the enormous pecuniary loss which has been sustained by the Island by the abandonment of the systematic policy of re-afforestation so wisely advocated by that talented and experienced Forest expert Monsieur Madon in 1881 in his reports which are in Your Lordship's possession.

20. In pursuance of the forward policy adopted by Mr. Churchill, and at his request, I am preparing a scheme of expenditure on Forestry and Public Works which I shall submit to Your Lordship so soon as a correct estimate can be made of the surplus revenue which will have accumulated on the 31st of March next. The amount of that surplus which may safely and properly be appropriated will depend entirely on the prospects of the next harvest and I should hesitate to make a forecast until the winter rains have passed. Should those rains, under the blessings of Providence, be abundant, the surplus will be sufficiently large to enable an appropriation to be made of an amount sufficient to give immense satisfaction to the people of the Island and to cause them to realize at once the great benefit which the fixed grant in aid will confer. As soon as the prospects of the harvest are made evident, I shall address a further dispatch to Your Lordship on this all-important matter.

21. I would add, in conclusion, that the visit of Mr. Churchill to Cyprus has been of the greatest advantage to the Island from every point of view. His pronouncements on the political questions which agitate the people have been most satisfactory in their effect, and although he was not able to satisfy the ardent national aspirations of the Greeks, he has pleased them by his sympathetic recognition of their patriotism and he has given satisfaction to them, as well as to the Turks, by his assurance that His Majesty's Government intended to remain in occupation of the Island. His ready recognition of the eco-

nomic difficulties under which Cyprus is labouring, and of the moral and material advantage to be derived by liberal expenditure on the development of the Island's resources, is not only for the benefit of the people but is extremely encouraging and strengthening to the Island Government; while the opportunity of which he has availed himself of meeting the leading people and of discussing public affairs with them has enabled them to enlighten him considerably on the social as well as the political and economical situations.

I have the honour to be,

My lord,

Your Lordship's most obedient

humble Servant,

King-Harman

B. Letter of Greek Members of Legislative Council

RIGHT HONOURABLE SIR,

By direction and on behalf of the Greek-Cypriot people who compose the four-fifths of the whole population of the Island, we the undersigned Representatives thereof in the Legislative Council, have the honour to express its and our unqualified joy for the visit of Your Honour in our country, and to greet you cordially on this occasion.

The presence of Your Honour amongst us is a strong proof of the lively interest which you and your Government take in order to ascertain closely and more directly, your well known sound judgment, the various aspirations, need and grievances the peoples under the glorious scepter and protection of His Majesty EDWARD VII. Among which, we venture to believe, we hold a prominent position by reason of our descent, history, traditions and language.

The Cypriot people, therefore, quite justly attaches the proper importance to your visit in our country and calls to mind, on this occasion, a pleasant event which has held an immortal position in our national history: We mean the great, for us, national event, the visit to our Sister Ionian Islands of Great Gladstone whose principles you genuinely represent in the present Administration of the affairs of Great Britain. As that great Statesman has been the harbinger of the Union of the Sister Ionian Islands with Mother Greece, so we wish to look at Your Honour, whom we have since long expected as a beloved harbinger, and we do not doubt that from the moment you have landed, you must have certainly understood the strong and earnest desire which burns the breasts of every Cypriot, pushing him, since many centuries, steadily and undeviatingly to the fulfillment of the historical mission.

Long and odious servitude, oppressions and trials have been unable to check the irresistible impulse of this desire, which, gradually increasing, has formed, in stormy ways, the infallible compass of the whole course of the Cypriot people, and has held it always fixed with sacred piety on its great national ideals.

National Aspirations.

Cyprus, Your Honour, as far as the lights of the latest archaeological researches have shown, has been firstly inhabited by Greeks, and successive settlements have renewed the National ties and strengthened National spirit through centuries, which was always preserved strong, and was manifested on every opportunity, in the letters and Arts as in the struggles and martyrdoms for the common Liberty and progress of the Greek race and humanity.

The Cypriot people has solemnly declared its glorious descent and strong National aspirations to the magnanimous English Nation from the first day of the British occupation through the mouth of its highest ecclesiastical chief, and has never ceased declaring publicly on every occasion given, by various Memorials to the Home Government and through its Representatives in the Legislative Council.

In expressing this desire to-day with greatest joy and sacred enthusiasm for the last time, as we venture to hope, we must above all declare that the Cypriot people unhesitatingly believes its realisation as the only basis and inexhaustible source of its true prosperity and as the only final goal of its historical career, from which no interest and no power either moral or material can ever possibly keep it away.

We confidently expect the realisation of this desire as soon as possible from the magnanimous English Nation which, continuing its liberal traditions, as formerly in the Ionian Islands, and adding another immortal page to its glorious history, and attracting the eternal gratitude not only of the people of Cyprus, but of all Hellenism all over the world, will restore this Island to whom it belongs, viz.: to the beloved Mother Greece, in the bosom of which only will it enjoy the blessings of liberty on which every people has imprescriptible rights, and especially a people by reason of descent, language, religion and civilisation, forming as it does an integral part of the immortal Greek race, which has born and promoted civilisation and developed humanity.

On this occasion, we deem it our duty to add that the Hellenic population of the Island follows, with a psychical pain, what takes place in Macedonia and Thrace, where the imprescriptible rights of the Hellenic race are being immolated and where unheard of atrocities are being perpetrated by an intruded people, renewing the savage cruelties of bygone centuries. The Hellenic population of the Island consider it its bounden duty to protest to the Noble Representative of the British Government asserting the inseparable national solidarity of the Hellenic Sections—only politically disunited, but closely united nationally—of the Hellenic Country, and solicits for the Brother victims the high protection of Great Britain.

The recognition and fulfilment of the historical National Rights of the Cyprus Hellenes, the small Mahomedan minority might disapprove, actuated, no doubt, by religious rather than racial feeling: but its numerical existence in the Island is not as strong as to entitle it to dispose of the National fate of this most Hellenic Island, nor can it be alleged that its real activity in civilising and economical progress is possessed of any significance. Trade, Science, Arts, Letters, Industry and every work connected with mental or economical progress, are almost exclusively exercised by the Cyprus Hellenes.

It would be a great injustice to the co-habiting majority and a flagrant denial of the sacred right of Nationalities, were it hampered by a small alien minority from its highest National Rights and the fulfilment of its great mission. The Mahomedan minority will not be prejudiced by following the National fate of the Hellenic Majority but, on the contrary, will in a good many respects be benefited, as the Hellenic race has practically exhibited a remarkable religious tolerance and a tendency to communicate its own blessings to the foreign races, from the remotest years up to to-day, as in Thessaly, Epirus, Crete and elsewhere.

Political Rights.

Moved by the above feelings, the Cyprus people considered very rightly since the very beginning the present political regime as a temporary and transitory one. Viewing it as such, we feel bound, declaring the general wish of the people, to emphasize the fact that the present Constitution granted to Cyprus is very limited and, as such, altogether inadequate both to the spirit of the century and to the character and culture of the Cyprus people who, more than any other, is to-day conscious of the necessity of taking a more effectual part in the management of its own affairs.

We therefore beg to suggest:–

(1) That the Legislative Council may henceforward consist exclusively of Elected Members in proportion to the population of the two predominant races of the Island, the Government being represented by the Members of the Executive Council (*i.e.* Chief Secretary, King's Advocate and Receiver General) who should, however, have no vote.

(2) That the Legislative Council may be accorded full liberty in the management generally of the interests of the Island—the restrictions embodied in the Order in Council of 6th July 1907, Clause 33, being removed—the Crown reserving to itself the power of disallowance.

(3) The aptitude of the Cyprus people and its political maturity point to the need of larger and more effectual co-operation, on its part, in the Executive Authority. The Administrative and Judicial Authority should be entrusted in the hands of the Natives, due allowance being made to the proportion of the population.

Financial Condition of Cyprus.

Your visits to our Island will, certainly, recall to your mind the declarations in regard to the occupation of the Island made by those who administered the affairs of Great Britain in 1878, and will, more especially, remind you of the promise officially given that Cyprus was destined to become, under the British administration, a paradise of the East and a model of administration, as well as of the official and historical proclamation issued in the name of the late Queen Victoria by the first High Commissioner, Sir Garnet J. W. Wolseley, at the time of the occupation of this most famous country, whereby Her Majesty, within the hearing of the whole world, set the seal of her royal approval on the liberal promises of great Britain to Cyprus. Bearing in mind those great promises to the English people by a responsible Government and those royal words promising a marvelous advancement of the Island, and seeing now the actual state of things in the Island, you must have felt your national *amour-propre* wounded and you must have been surprised to see with your own eyes how greatly the state of things in the Island differs from that which was promised.

You have passed, Right Honourable Sir, though that portion of the Island where the most numerous and the most important public works have been executed since the English occupation, and on which the whole of the loan made by the British Exchequer has been spent. It happens that you visit Cyprus at a time when she is in her happiest days owing to abundant harvests though an unbroken series of years and to an enhancement in the prices of all Cyprus products, but it will not, we believe, escape your perspicacity, that this prosperity is but temporary and that, in reality, the Island is an unprosperous state.

It is to be regretted, Right Honourable Sir, that you have not more time at your disposal so as to visit the whole Island and, especially, the most neglected districts, and thus have a fuller picture of our financial condition and perceive from close observation the industry, the intelligence, the merit of the Cypriots, their love for progress and the multitude of their wants, their financial inability to improve their condition and the just vexation aroused by their deplorable financial condition, caused not by the economic conditions of the country itself but by entirely foreign pecuniary obligations—a vexation which, in spite of the gratitude they owe in other respects, leads them to describe the policy of the Government as a totally heartless policy.

It is admitted by all, Right Honourable Sir, that, from a financial point of view, the misfortunes of Cyprus are due to the yearly alienation of a sum of money which, in proportion to her resources and public revenue, is enormous.

His Majesty's successive Governments, the parties in opposition, and the Island's successive Governors—Sir Charles King-Harman occupying a prominent position among the latter—have all confessed that the Island's financial troubles are due to the great annual draining of the public revenue and that, owing to this draining of the public revenue, *all that ought to be done under an English Government has not been done.*

The English Government have, in a manner worthy of the noble traditions of the British nation and in disregard of the integrity and the sovereign rights of Turkey, assumed the initiative in the taking away from the hands of Turkey of the revenue of a most important Turkish province in Europe and in the application of that revenue for the improvement and advancement of that same province. While congratulating the British Government for that, we feel a still greater grief that such a Government and such a nation should, till now, suffer the people of Cyprus, who, by the help of God, have been freed of the Turkish administration for some decades past to be wronged in a manner which is unheard of in the colonial history of Great Britain.

As regards the truly great injustice of imposing an entirely foreign obligation on the people of Cyprus, to which foreign obligation a very great portion of the country's public revenue is annually applied in spite of the just outcry raised by the people from the very first days of the English occupation and in spite of the cogent reasons for which we, on good grounds, consider that Great Britain is herself liable to pay what, on account of the strategical importance then attached to Cyprus, was privately agreed upon with the Sublime Porte, we will, in order not to speak at length herein, request that you will, Right Honourable Sir, have recourse to the copy hereto attached of a memorial of the representatives of the country under date the 12th February, 1903, and more especially to the contents thereof from its fifth to its twenty-eighth paragraphs. We emphatically declare that the squandering away in this manner of the public revenue of the Island was bound to bring about such financial enervation as to place the people of Cyprus at a disadvantage in comparison with other peoples in many most important respects, and to place them at this disadvantage in spite of the fact that they are under British administration, a fact which perplexes both the Government and the people.

The sum £1,781,942 which has, till now, been taken away from the island would have been sufficient to make Cyprus in very truth a paradise of the East as promised by Great Britain. But owing to that action: (1) the grant-in-aid of the people's education is not even the fourth of what it ought to be in comparison to the population, which has manifestly shown hitherto how very eager it is for spiritual and moral development and culture and which, owing to that cruel abandonment, has been compelled to undertake a burden of additional taxation for the sake of education and which, in spite of this extraordinary sacrifice, is unable to make sufficient provision for education because of the fact that it is in want also of school buildings and of school furniture and of school apparatus, whilst, moreover, the school personnel, because of the meagre salaries given, is unable to satisfy the just claims of the country the more so because the best of the teachers give up their profession and follow other safer avocations to earn their livelihood and because even those school-masters who stand by the scholastic profession fail because of want of the necessary means. It is in vain that school groups have been devised whereby many villages maintain schools in common, because the regular attendance of children is rendered difficult by the lack of bridges, and the great distances, especially in winter, and also because of the youth of the pupils. Further, with a view to obtaining higher and more practical education in foreign languages and in business pursuits, a very great number of young men expatriate themselves and seek elsewhere the said higher and more practical education and thus take away with them from this financially exhausted country a great amount of money. (2) Owing to the insufficient provision in the estimates, not even the absolutely necessary public works have been performed, although a period of thirty years has elapsed; moreover, a great part of the public works actually performed— these latter works are the most important ones being the Famagusta Harbour, the Railway and the Irrigation Works—have been made by means of a loan of over three hundred thousand pounds, and the public revenue of the Island has thus been burdened with a yearly charge of £13,000 for interest and sinking fund. With the exception of the Famagusta sea-port town all of the rest of the Island remains without harbours, and, although Cyprus comes third in size among the Islands in the Mediterranean, she is the last of all as regards harbours, notwithstanding that heavy port dues are levied in all natural roadsteads of the Island; a great many torrents in the Island are yet bridgeless and, moreover, many public roads which have been laid out for many years past are still unexecuted and others which have been left incomplete are destroyed, and such of them as have been accomplished are deficiently maintained. Most necessary railway lines whereby flourishing district towns must be connected either with the capital town or other places which are thickly peopled and of a great production and with excellent summer resorts much appreciated by Cypriots and foreigners and especially by Europeans settled in Egypt, have not yet been constructed. In the face of the parsimoniousness of the Government, these progressive people have felt compelled to construct public roads by paying the one-half of the expenditure and to maintain many of those roads for many years out of their own purse, and also to subject themselves to a corvée for roadmaking for the purpose of developing the communication between towns and villages and to grant private properties for that purpose. There are district towns wherein no buildings for the offices of the Commissioners, their Courts and the other branches of the public service have yet been erected. (3) The chief wealth-creating source of the Island, *i.e.*, agriculture, has not been duly protected or sensibly improved, but is still in a primitive state and is, moreover harassed by manifold diseases, by animals and by insects of which the locust has become a permanent financial scourge owing to the extra taxation called the Locust Tax, which the Government has, in a great extent, succeeded to consolidate for the fulfilment of its own obligations, for which the Government ought to spend out of the general revenue. Agriculture is bent down and stifled by the oppressive system of the tithes. (4) Tracts of land which have no trees or have been denuded of their trees have not been re-afforested to the hygienic, climatic and financial detriment of the people. (5) Public health is not duly guarded, sanitary works have not been made, whilst malarious places are to be found not only in the open country but even near the towns. The rural medical service is still very scanty and the villages are in a very unhealthy state, and the loss by contagious diseases of various animals and cattle is great. In the towns, the Municipalities, on account of the heavy taxation levied on townspeople, are yet unable to impose Municipal taxes so that they may be able to make provision for the absolute wants of their communities. (6) No sum of money is provided for archaeological excavations in the Island, although archaeological treasures of great scientific value lie hidden under the soil of Cyprus, nor has it been possible to build an archaeological Museum after such a great period of time. (7) A great many of the villages of the Island are without a mail communication. (8) The living of the native Government officials has become precarious owing to the enhancement in the cost of the necessaries of life and the unusual meagerness of their salaries, and the public service runs the risk of being deprived of its able officials The Police branch, especially, runs the risk of being dissolved to the incalculable detriment of public peace because of the fact that its abler and better elements withdraw from it and idlers and incapable persons are enrolled in their places. (9) No provision proportionate to the resources of the country has been made for the support and encouragement of native industries and for a professional and practical education of the heavily taxed people.

The Cyprus people, Right Honourable Sir, are justified in thinking then that all the above requirements as well as others besides could be satisfied with their own money and it is with good reason that they see, with great pain, this money being taken away from them by force, and themselves in consequent misfortune, but they find a consolation now in the fortunate fact of your presence which enables them to submit an expression of all their feelings and of all their wants and to invoke the kindly attention of His Majesty's Government and the sympathy of the British people for the removal of so great an injustice—an injustice which is perpetrated under British sovereignty and administration.

The fact that Great Britain has now undertaken to disburse in the future more than she has disbursed in the past in meeting the liability under the Convention of 1878 is regarded as the beginning of a rapid and complete deliverance of the country from that burden, and is, therefore, hailed as the dawn of a better future without which any marked progress in the Island is impossible.

We take advantage of this opportunity of tendering our thanks to His Majesty's Government for having entrusted the administration of this Island to the hands of His Excellency Sir Charles King-Harman, who, by his uprightness and sincerity, by his political perspicacity and wisdom, by his deep study of the needs and just complaints of the country, and by his sincere co-operation with the elected representatives of the people, has succeeded in removing, to a very great extent, acute friction between the people and the Government, and has thus deservedly won the appreciation and respect of the Cypriot people.

In conclusion, the Hellenic people of this land of Cyprus, so famed in history, now temporarily entrusted by Divine Providence to the governance of the glorious British sceptre, and under the rule of the most beloved of all powerful sovereigns, ardently yearn for the grant from the great and magnanimous British nation in accordance with the will of God and to the eternal gratitude of the whole Hellenic race—of their most speedy Union with their glorious Mother Greece.

We remain, Right Honorable Sir, your most obedient servants,

The Greek Representatives of Cyprus,

The Bishop of Kition, Kyrillos.
Antonios Theodotou
Theophanes Theodotou
Evangelos Hajioannou
Michael Nikolaides
Loues E. Louizou
Ioannes Kyriakides
Christodoulos Sozos
Spyros Araouzos

C. Reply of Churchill

Mr. Churchill's Reply to the Greek Elected Members.

I find it a great pleasure and a very useful experience in my travels to meet here today so many capable and experienced parliamentary representatives of the people of Cyprus.

I congratulate Cyprus and I congratulate your constituents on the ability with which they find their representatives endowed; and I congratulate you gentlemen, on the eloquence and force with which the Bishop of Kitium has unfolded his case. And this brings me to the consideration of one of the important questions raised in the address, namely, an alteration of the existing Constitution to secure what you describe as a widening of political liberties, but what might also be described as a greater predominance and power for the Greek element in the Constitution of the Island. Because I am quite sure there can be no question of importance affecting the Greek Community, to the discussion of which its representatives are not able to bring a great fund of knowledge, and upon the decision of which they are not able to bring an effective influence.

In reviewing the proceedings of the Legislative Council, it does not appear to me that the wishes of the representatives of the people have suffered from any insufficiency of expression or from any failure to shape or control legislation. I have carefully examined and considered the Constitution of the Government, and I fail to discern at present any way by which the influence and power of the Greek Elected Members could be increased which would not in fact involve a surrender of sovereignty and an inability, not only on the part of the British Government but also in that of the Moslem minority, to exercise any further influence on the course of affairs. It may be that in the course of time such a way may be discovered; and though I do not see it now, I will not fail to think about it.

But when it is suggested that the elected representative element in the Legislative Council should actually have power to initiate expenditure, I am bound to remind you that that power does not belong to private Members of the House of Commons, and that the initiation of expenditure is confined, I believe in all countries possessing parliamentary institutions, to the Executive Government, on which the responsibility also rests.

And when I pass from the question of amending the Constitution to the even larger political question which the Greek Elected Members have brought forward, of the Union of Cyprus with Greece, I must speak at a little greater length.

That is a very grave question, in fact the gravest and most serious question which could possibly be raised by the representatives whom I see before me. It involves not only an absolute change in the Government of the Island, but also the abrogation of the Treaty with Turkey. It involves further the setting aside of the views of nearly one-third of the population, and the creation of what would probably be a permanent and dangerous antagonism between the two sections of the community. Strongly as you, gentlemen, may feel on this question, you will agree with me that it is the gravest which could possibly be raised by the people of the Island.

I think it is only natural that the Cypriot people, who are of Greek descent, should regard their incorporation with what may be called their Mother-country as an ideal to be earnestly, devoutly, and fervently cherished. Such a feeling is an example of the patriotic devotion which so nobly characterises the Greek nation; and while I trust that those who feel so earnestly themselves will not forget that they must show respect for the similar feelings of others, I say that the views which have been put forward are opinions which His Majesty's Government do not refuse to regard with respect. On the other hand the opinion held by the Moslem population of the Island, that the British occupation of Cyprus should not lead to the dismemberment of the Ottoman Empire, and that the mission of Great Britain in the Levant should not be to impair the sovereignty of the Sultan, is one which His Majesty's Government are equally bound to regard with respect.

It has not been represented to His Majesty's Government that the Greek nor yet the Moslem population of Cyprus is actually discontented with the British administration of the Island. Many complaints, some of which are well founded, have been made that the progress of the Island during the British occupation has not been so rapid or so substantial, as had been anticipated. But I do not think that any just-minded man who remembers the past history of Cyprus, and observes the fortunes of other countries in other parts of the world, would commit himself to any absolute condemnation of the existing state of the Government. Nor, be it remarked, even in the memorials presented to me, do I find any facts alleged or any reasons adduced which would lead me to believe that the material welfare of the Island would be appreciably increased were the administration to be transferred to any other Power. His Majesty's Government may therefore be encouraged to hope that the people of Cyprus, while cherishing great national ideals are content, for the present at least, to be governed in accordance with British ideas of justice and freedom.

His Majesty's Government believe that the people of Cyprus appreciate the fact that their condition, social, political and economical, has been considerably improved during the last 30 years; and if complaints exist that the progress of the Island has not been commensurate with the promises made, and the hopes entertained, at the time of the occupation, it will be the duty of the Government by all possible means to remove the grounds which may exist for those complaints.

With reference to the cession of the Ionian Islands to Greece, and the comparison made between those Islands and Cyprus, I must observe that the analogy is by no means complete, if only for this reason—that the Ionian Islands at the time of cession, were in the possession of Great Britain, and accordingly at the disposal of Great Britain—which is of course by no means the case with regard to Cyprus.

In these circumstances, and in view of the considerations which I have put before you, it is the duty of Great Britain to remain in occupation of Cyprus, and I think it is my duty to say to you that His Majesty's Government cannot recognise that the time has come when the Island should be abandoned, or when any change in its political status should be effected.

I have left question of the Tribute to the last, because it is the most practical of the questions on which you have addressed me. It is a matter which has a political as well as a financial aspect. From the political point of view, it is clear that payment could only cease with the abrogation of the treaty by which the occupation of the Island is secured; and His Majesty's Government do not contemplate any abrogation of the treaty.

The financial aspect of the matter has already received the serious consideration of His Majesty's present advisers. By recent arrangements, which fix the amount of the annual grant-in-aid at £50,000 the pressure on the Island Treasury has already been reduced and relieved. I hope that larger funds may be available in the near future for the development of public works in various parts of the Island. But any advantages which may have been conferred on you by these arrangements you owe in the first place to the exertion made on your behalf of His Excellency Sir Charles King-Harman. He is the best friend Cyprus has had for some time; and as I know from my own knowledge, he is neglecting no opportunity of pressing the interests of Cyprus on the Home Government.

Now that I have had the pleasure of seeing your beautiful Island and have had opportunities of making friends, or at any rate of making acquaintance, with so many of its leading persons of influence and authority, I shall join my efforts to his in the attempt to secure more liberal treatment and greater advantages for the Island. It is quite true that the new arrangement of the grant-in-aid is limited to a period of three years. But I daresay that when the time to reconsider it is reached, if the British Government see encouraging results from the new arrangement already achieved, it will certainly not be altered to the disadvantage of the Island.

The financial condition of the island is improving and will continue to improve; and with the increasing prosperity of the people means will be found for repairing past failures and undertaking further improvements. I shall report all that I have seen and all that you have said to me to Lord Elgin when I return to England; and I am sure you will find in him a Minister who is most desirous of using his influence to promote the highest interests and most rapid advancement of the people of Cyprus.

II. Dispatches of H. Goold-Adams and Enclosures, 27 June 1912 (CO 67/166)
A. Letter of H. Goold-Adams, 25 April 1912

The Right Honourable
Lewis Harcourt, M. P.   Government House
etc., etc., etc.
Secretary of State for the Colonies   Nicosia, 25 April, 1912.

Sir,

By last mail I had the honour to report to you, in my dispatch No. 57 of the 18th instant, the resignation of the Greek-Christian members of the Legislative Council, and to forward to you a copy of the communication which they addressed to me on the occasion of their doing so.

Under cover of this confidential communication I desire to lay before you some sidelights bearing upon the present situation.

2. I consider that the present recrudescence, in a somewhat acute form, of the political agitation by the Greek element is mainly to be attributed to the settlement of the controversial archiepiscopal question, the reunion of the two section of the Greeks, and a consequent desire on the part of those persons who gain their livelihood by agitation and unrest to find fresh sources for their energies. The agitator openly urges annexation to Greece, as exemplified in the following resolution adopted at Larnaca:-

"We notify that no oppression, however tyrannical the same may be, can alter our national sentiments or weaken our patriotic aspirations and dissolve our sweet dream, which has always been, continues to be, and will continue to be unalterably, the union with our free Mother Greece."

3. The more astute politicians, consisting of the clerics and the ex-members of Council, pose as the champions of political liberties, and demand redress of what they consider legitimate grievances. In this connexion I attach the translation of a manifesto published last week in the "Phone tes Kyprou," setting fort the reasons which led the members to resign, and signed by all those members.

4. Owing to my action in replying to the memorial addressed to me in November last, I have incurred a considerable amount of public censure from the Greek press and politicians, who accuse me of wantonly insulting their race, and of being opposed to the consummation of their national and legitimate aspirations. The Greek members of the Legislative Council deemed it expedient to refuse an invitation issued to them to attend the High Commissioner's customary official dinner on the evening preceding the opening of the Council, and also to absent themselves from the monthly "At Homes" given by my wife. All these matters have been referred to in laudatory terms by the Greek press, and the members congratulated on their actions. On a tour which I made lately to the Karpass promontory, I deemed it desirable to issue a notice, copy of which I attach, to the effect that I desired all deputations to eliminate from their addresses matters of a political nature, and to avoid the use of political flags and emblems. Immediately on this becoming known in the capital, orders were sent out by the Greek leaders that everywhere were my wishes to be ignored, and Greek flags and banners to be made as conspicuous as possible wherever I went. I accordingly found on my arrival at many villages where I was expected that Greek flags were flying, and addresses prepared dealing only with the question of annexation to Greece. Where, however, I varied my route and visited villages where I was not expected, no signs of the great love for Greece were apparent. In these villages, as well as in those inhabited by Moslems, I discussed with the people in the most friendly manner many matters affecting their material interests, such as the granting by the Forest Department of extended grazing permits for stock, the cutting in the forests of roofing poles and firewood, the cultivation of unplanted forest lands, the question of improvement of roads, postal communications, village courts, fencing of cemeteries, experimental gardens, etc.; thus showing that where the villagers were left alone by the politician, they were quite prepared to bring forward for my consideration many subjects which warranted my attention, and to put aside what is made out by the politicians to be their one and only desire, viz., annexation to Greece.

The most exaggerated and untruthful reports have been spread through the medium of the local press regarding my proceedings whilst on tour, in order to make it appear as if I had gone out of my way to insult and ignore one section of the population at the expense of the other.

5. As above mentioned, I was absent on tour during the period of the Easter adjournment of the Council, and only returned to Nicosia on the 15th instant, the day preceding its reassembling.

Having anticipated some such action on the part of the Greek members as actually took place when they were informed on the resumption of the Council of your reply to their memorial, I directed Captain Orr, the Chief Secretary, to see Mr. Theodotou during my absence, submit to him your despatch, and urge upon him the desirability of carefully weighing the position before taking any hasty action. I am assured by Captain Orr that he had a long and friendly discussion with Mr. Theodotou, and that every endeavour was made by him to induce the Christian members through their leader to see reason. Mr. Theodotou at the end of the interview thanked Captain Orr for the frank way he had spoken, and promised to try to induce his colleagues to take a similar view, but stated that he feared he would be unsuccessful.

6. Within the last few days I have been called upon by the representatives of the Roman Catholic and Maronite Churches, for the purpose of expressing on behalf of the adherents of those Christian Churches their satisfaction with the present administration of the island, and their entire disagreement with the opinions recently expressed, and action taken, by the members of the Legislative Council representing the Christian communities.

7. I submit a confidential report from the Chief Commandant of Police relating to the events in Nicosia on the 16th instant and the two following days, which confirm my telegraphic report to you that all was quiet here. Nothing has since occurred to disturb that quiet, and there are unmistakable symptoms that many of the more respectable among the Greek people already regret the interruption of the friendly relationship between the Government and the people, and are endeavouring to combat the wilder counsels of the agitators. I have every reason to hope that within a very short time things will have returned to normal conditions, namely, a continuance by the politicians of their claims for an extension of executive and legislative powers, with but an apathetic interest taken therein by the people they are supposed to represent.

8. Meanwhile, I understand that a central committee has been formed, consisting of the Archbishop, the Bishops and principal Abbots of the Orthodox Church, and the Christian ex-members of the Legislative Council, to direct a movement in England and on the Continent in favour of granting to the people of Cyprus more extended executive and legislative powers, and, where possible, of furthering the idea of annexation to Greece; also, to direct the course of conduct of the Greek population in the island in such matters as elections, payment of taxes, intercourse with members of the island Government, and resignation of honorary administrative appointments such as membership of the Central and District Mejliss Idares. On Sunday next, 28th instant, mass meetings are to be held in several centres in the island, where prepared resolutions are to be presented for adoption, and for submission to myself when passed. I have no fear that any breach of the peace will take place, all precautions will be taken to keep apart the Moslem and Greek people, and there will be no interference by the Police in any of the meetings provided that the participators do not create a disturbance.

It will most probably be resolved that a deputation representing the Greek section should at once proceed to England to interview you regarding the affairs of Cyprus, but whether this deputation will proceed or not will largely depend upon the amount of financial support forthcoming later on.

9. In conclusion, I desire to say now that should the island not return speedily to its usual tranquil condition, and should I attribute this state of affairs to the continual stirring up of discontent by one or two notorious agitators such as Mr. Katalanos, an Athenian demagogue who has been a resident in the island for the past few years, I shall proceed to have them expelled from Cyprus under Law 8 of 1879, unless, on my referring the question to you, you should consider such a course to be specially undesirable.

I have honour to be,
Sir,
Your most obedient,
Humble Servant
Hamilton Goold-Adams
High Commissioner

B. Letter of H. Goold-Adams, 30 May 1912

The Right Honourable   Government House
Lewis Harcourt, M. P.   Nicosia, 30th May, 1912
etc., etc., etc.
Secretary of State for the Colonies

Sir,

In my telegrams to you of 28th and 29th, I had the honour to inform you that disturbances had occurred between the Greeks and Turks within the past week at Nicosia, Limassol and some outlying villages in the Island. The only really serious trouble occurred at Limassol on the night of the 27th, resulting in three being killed, two from knife stabs and one from a bullet, two dangerously wounded, one of whom from a knife stab and one from a bullet, forty-eight seriously injured by knives and sticks, two slightly wounded by bullets. This particular riot was caused by a brawl in a café between a Greek and Turk, and ended by both sections of the population becoming involved. The matter being reported to me by telegraph, I authorised the Local Commandant of Police to take such steps as he considered necessary to quell the riot, and to call to his aid the local company of the Devonshire Regiment at Polymedia. The Police were eventually ordered to fire on the rioters with the result of injury, as above stated, to four persons and an immediate termination of the disturbance. The troops arrived in time to assist in patrolling the streets but were not otherwise involved. The disturbances at Nicosia and a few villages were of no very serious kind, and resulted in a few persons being more or less injured by sticks and stones.

2. In view of the general strained relationship between the Moslems and Christians throughout the Island, accentuated by the aforesaid rioting, I considered it desirable to ask for some additional military assistance from Egypt, which, as I learned from you last night, has been approved by the War Office. The company of infantry is expected to arrive tomorrow at Famagusta, and will be brought on by rail to Nicosia.

3. It is unnecessary for me to draw your attention to the causes which under normal circumstances give rise, both here and elsewhere, to a certain amount of animosity between the Moslems and Greek Christians. These feelings have been accentuated in Cyprus within the past six months by two causes, viz. the increased agitation which has been organised amongst Greek Christians for annexation of the Island to Greece, the excitable speeches which have been made by the Christian leaders, the writings of the local Greek Press, and the taunts hurled at the Moslems regarding the approaching doom of the Ottoman Empire at the hands of Italy, especially since the occupation of the Turkish Islands in the Aegean Sea. On the other hand, the Moslems have unquestionably been rendered rather despondent by the results of the present Italian war, and many of their fanatical members have become more sensitive to anti-Ottoman displays on the part of the Greek Christians.

4. The principal event which has more or less been the cause of the present rioting was an attack made by some Moslem villagers a few miles from Nicosia upon some fifty students with two masters of the local Greek gymnasium, who unwisely and probably noisily passed through a Turkish village late in the evening after dark. The Moslems turned out and assaulted them; some of the students did not reach their homes in Nicosia until after daylight next morning, their absence being attributed to their being murdered. The following night both sections of the population attempted to come in conflict with one another but were prevented by the Police. The latter however in the course of their task met with some resistance, and both the English Local Commandant and the Moslem Inspector were struck and stoned by the Greek section, the Moslem Inspector at one time being believed to have been shot with a revolver, several of which were discharged by the crowd. The Police fired in the air and eventually restored order. Since then the town has been patrolled by the Police armed, and order has been maintained. I imagine that exaggerated reports of the events at Nicosia were the cause of the rioting at Limassol the next night, and do not believe that there has been any organised attempt on the part of one side or the other to force on trouble. I have kept in close touch with the leaders of both elements, as have the Commissioners in the districts, and I am pleased to be able to report that I believe that they all are conscientiously working with us to maintain law and order.

5. With such inflammable material to handle, it is of course impossible to be certain that matters will quieten down at once, my principal anxiety being the maintenance of peace in the outlying districts. The presence of the Military here, and the enrolment of an additional 120 Police sanctioned by you, will now allow the Country police detachments to be materially strengthened, and this will go a long way to preserve order.

I am taking all necessary precautions to prevent unnecessary gatherings of the people, such as the closing of wine shops at seasonable hours; and am doing all that is possible to prevent any extension of the present trouble. Full enquiries will be instituted into the local causes of the past riots, and the guilty parties will be duly dealt with according to the law in force.

I have the honour to be,

Sir,

Your most obedient,

humble Servant,

Hamilton Goold-Adams

High Commissioner.

C. Letter of H. Goold-Adams, 4 June 1912

The Right Honourable   Government House
Lewis Harcourt, M. P.   Nicosia, 4 June 1912
etc., etc., etc.
Secretary of State for the Colonies

Sir,

With reference to my telegram of 28th May and subsequent dates regarding the disorders which broke out at Limassol on the 27th ultimo, I have the honour to forward to you two brief interim reports by the Commissioner Major Bolton, dated 2nd June.

2. Major Bolton has up to the present been too fully occupied in maintaining quiet, to proceed to the holding of the full inquiry which I have ordered: it is, moreover, desirable from other points of view not to hold the inquiry until the excitement of the people has had a little time to subside.

I therefore propose to withhold until then my comments on the events which have taken place: and will do no more now than to record my conviction that had Captain Gallagher not ordered the police to fire on the rioters, the loss of life would have been very much greater than it has actually been.

I have the honour to be,
Sir,
Your most obedient humble Servant,
Hamilton Goold-Adams
High Commissioner

D. Letters of W. N. Bolton, 2 June 1912

Limassol
Sunday June 2nd 1912

Hon. C. S.

I have the honour to report that the town is quiet and that the ordinary work is being resumed although the Moslems are still showing reluctance to get too far away from their own quarter. I have been trying hard to bring the leaders of both parties together but have so far failed as the Moslems are exceedingly bitter about the desecration of their Mosque but I still hope to be successful in day or so. I am at present holding all the main entrances to the town from the Moslem Quarter by the troops so that there is little likelihood of further trouble in town.

The villages have been exceedingly frightened by absurd rumours of large bands of wandering Turks and many of them have entirely lost their self-control but in the villages and those nearby where Lt. Bellfield and his men have patrolled there is now quiet. The party visited Monagri, Doros, Ayios Georgius, Lania, Silikou, Kontea, Perapedia, Platres, Mandria and Kilani. I am sending them off again on Tuesday to the Moslem and mixed community villages lying in the Evdimou Nahieh.

I regret to report that the feeling is very strong and bitter against the Town Police who fired on the rioters and that the lower classes daily shout insults after them and for this reason the Local Commandant of Police has not at present disarmed them. The truth is that the great majority were Moslems and the people have the idea that they used their rifles against the Greeks picking off more or less harmless spectators. I regret to say that this idea is encouraged by their leaders and I think with a view to cover the fact that in Monday's riot the aggressive party were the Greeks.

I have very carefully examined all the streets in which firing took place and can find very few bullet marks except at 8 ft. and higher from the ground and then only some half dozen which proves to me that the main part of the firing was in the air. I shall be able to let you know later the exact number of rounds fired. It is also a fact that revolvers were fired from various houses and I trust we shall be able to prove this by taking the offenders to Court.

As far as I have been able to ascertain there seems no doubt that the Police behaved exceedingly well and forgot their religion and behaved as policeman should under exceedingly trying conditions.

I have taken every precaution for tomorrow which is another Greek holiday and feel confident we shall have no further trouble, at any rate in Limassol Town.

W. N. Bolton
Commissioner

Limassol
Sunday, 2nd June 1912

Hon. C. S.
I regret I am at present unable to send the lists of injured in Monday's riots as promised. The Police are finding some difficulty in getting an exact return but I hope to do so in a day or so but as far as we know at present besides those already reported there are about 17 Greeks and 48 Turks whose wounds were treated at home. Thus I expect the total will be

5	dead
17	severely wounded—detained in hospital
2	slightly wounded treated by private practitioners
50	dressed at Hospital and sent home
17	Greeks treated at home
48	Turks treated at home.
139	

I hope to be able to start the inquiry on Tuesday or Wednesday but at present I am afraid of hampering the Police.

W. N. Bolton
Commissioner

As regards rifle fire, it is two killed and seven wounded; the remainder are: three killed by knives, and 127 wounded in other ways by knives sticks stones, etc.

E. Letter of H. Goold-Adams, 27 June 1912

The Right Honourable   Government House
Lewis Harcourt, M. P.   27 June 1912
etc., etc., etc.
Secretary of State for the Colonies

Sir,

I am pleased to be able to inform you that peace and order have been restored throughout the Island, and that everywhere the general affairs of the people are being carried on under normal conditions.

2. I have permitted the local company of the Devon Regiment, which was recently called upon at Limassol to assist the Civil power, to proceed, as is usual during the summer months, to Troodos.

3. The Company of the same Regiment which arrived recently from Egypt and which is now stationed at Nicosia, its detention for a few months longer in the Island having been approved by the General Officer Commanding the Troops in Egypt, will also shortly proceed up to Troodos and there join the other.

4. As soon as the decision to move the two companies to the hills became publicly known, I was approached by the representatives of the Moslem communities of both Nicosia and Limassol who asked that these changes should be cancelled on the grounds that they had reason to fear that immediately the British Troops were removed any distance from the two towns named, attacks by the Greek section of the population would be made upon the people of their faith. I have consulted the two experienced Commissioners of the respective districts and they assure me that there is no real reason for the fears expressed by the Moslem community; and I have accordingly made no change in the plans.

5. With reference to the enquiry mentioned by me in paragraph 2 of my despatch of the 4th June, into the circumstances attending the recent rioting and loss of life at Limassol, I have the honour to inform you that I have appointed a mixed Commission for the said purpose, consisting of Major Bolton, the Commissioner of the District, who was not actually present at the time of the riots, as Chairman, and Yorghanjibashizade Mustafa Sami Effendi and Mr. Stavros Stavrinakis as members, both the latter being residents of Nicosia and appointed by me after consultation with the leaders of the two sections of the population. This Commission is now sitting at Limassol.

6. As soon as the proceedings of the Commission are received I will forward them to you together with the reports of the Coroner at the Inquests held upon those who were killed.

7. The prisoners apprehended for participation in the rioting are now being tried by the District Court, at which the Acting King's Advocate is himself conducting the prosecution; and I propose that those who are committed for trial at the Assizes should be tried by a special Assize Court assembled for the purpose early next month, thereby avoiding the delay in their being dealt with which would under ordinary circumstances take place were they to be put back for trial at the usual sitting of that court in September.

I feel that the sooner the whole incident is closed, the sooner confidence in the power of the Government to deal with such cases of rioting will be restored, a matter which at all times is desirable and under present conditions in the Island absolutely essential.

I have the honour to be,
Sir,
Your most obedient humble Servant,
Hamilton Goold-Adams
High Commissioner

III. Dispatch of H. Goold-Adams, 20 November 1914 (CO 67/174)

A. Letter of H. Goold-Adams, 20 November 1914

The Right Honourable   Government House
Lewis Harcourt, M.P.   Nicosia 20 November, 1914.
etc., etc., etc.,
Secretary of State for the Colonies.

Sir,

I have the honour to forward herewith an address presented to me by the signatories, which I was requested to forward to you. I availed myself of the occasion to thank His Beatitude the Archbishop and those who were present for the sympathy expressed in regard to the war being carried on by Great Britain and her allies, and the satisfaction felt by the British people that others who were not of their own flesh and blood such as themselves should unhesitatingly acknowledge that the cause for which Great Britain was fighting was that of justice and liberty.

I have the honour to be,
Sir,
Your most obedient,
humble Servant
Hamilton Goold-Adams
High Commissioner

B. Greek Petition, 8 November 1914

The Right Honourable   Nicosia, 8th November, 1914.
Lewis Harcourt, M.P.,
etc., etc., etc.
Secretary of the State for the Colonies.

Right Honourable Sir,

We, the Archbishop of Cyprus and Greek Members of the Legislative Council, interpreting, as we do, the sentiment of the Church and of the people of Cyprus on the occasion of the official announcement of the annexation of our Fatherland to the British Empire, seize the opportunity in order, in the first place, to confirm the feelings of sympathy and honour with which the Greek people and the Church of the Island view the noble struggle which Great Britain and the Powers allied to Her have, on provocation, undertaken and which is one for the value of civilization, being, emulously fought, under the leadership of Great Britain and Her Allies, by peoples of all the Continents independently of race and creed, and which has for its object the consolidation of peace and progress in the world by the laying down, as the supreme moral principle ruling the international relations, of the principle of respecting the liberty of the peoples, howsoever small may be the position held by them under the sun. In regard to this struggle of Great Britain and Her Allies for principles to which the Greek political spirit is thoroughly adapted, in regard, we say, to this struggle to which, particularly, we Cypriots look with reasonable hopes, Cyprus would feel the highest honour to give herself also, in any way, her contribution in the conviction that by so doing she contributes to a cause which is common to the whole civilized world.

Under the sway of such conceptions and sentiments, we desire, Right Honourable Sir, to become the interpreters of the joy felt by the Church and the people for the final deliverance of our Fatherland from the Turkish sovereignty and to declare that to the change in the political status quo of the Island which has been the outcome of the war circumstances, we look as to a last and provisional station leading to the rapid and definitive national rehabilitation of our Fatherland, that is, to her Union with the free Greek Kingdom to which she belongs of right and which is destined to continue in Cyprus the noble principles of liberty and equality of civic rights.

Whereupon, we remain,
Right Honourable Sir,
With all due honour,

Kyrillos, Archbishop of Cyprus.
P. Constantinides.
Th.Theodotou.
A. Liasides.
J. Economides
J. Kyriakides.
E. H. Hajiioannou.
L. E. Louizou.
N. C. Lanites.
E. Zenon.

C. Letter of H. Goold-Adams, 20 November 1914 [The Muslim document was not included in the file.]

The Right Honourable
Lewis Harcourt, M.P.
etc., etc., etc.,
Secretary of State for the Colonies

Government House
Nicosia 20 November 1914

Sir,

I have the honour to forward herewith a letter, addressed to you by representatives of the Moslem inhabitants of Cyprus, in connection with the future status of the Island.

2. This letter was presented to me by the Chief Cadi, the Mufti, the Hon. Irfan Bey and Shevket Bey at an interview accorded by me for the purpose.

I undertook to forward the letter as requested.

3. I have reason to suppose that copies of this document will be transmitted to various influential personages throughout the Moslem world for the purpose of calling their attention to the desires of the Moslems in Cyprus.

I have the honour to be,
Sir,
Your most obedient,
humble Servant,
Hamilton Goold-Adams
High Commissioner

IV. Dispatch of J. C. D. Fenn, 16 December 1920 (CO 67/199)

A. Letter of J. C. D. Fenn, 16 December 1920

The Right Honourable   Government House Nicosia
Viscount Milner, G.C.B., G.C.M.G   16th December, 1920.
Etc., etc., etc.,
Secretary of the State for the Colonies

My Lord,

With reference to my dispatch No. 386 of the 14th of December, 1920, reporting that nine Greek Christian members had resigned their seats in the Legislative Council as a protest against the announcement made on Your Lordship's behalf by Colonel Amery on the 25th of October to the members of the Greek-Cypriot deputation to the effect that His Majesty's Government could hold out no hope of the union of Cyprus with Greece being sanctioned, I have the honour to inform Your Lordship that bye-elections to fill the vacancies so caused will be held about the 15th of January and that it appears probable that the late members will again be nominated and be returned unopposed. What course of action they will then adopt is not clear at present as further meetings of the political leaders to consider their further action are proposed; it is probable, however, that they will again resign their seats in which event I propose to continue to hold bye-elections until such time as the agitation dies a natural death though the lack of monetary support which the political leaders are finding great difficulty in securing. The period of five years for which the present Council was elected does not expire until October next and I do not consider that any good purpose would be served by dissolving the Council at present.

2. The mass of the Greek-Christian community continue to regard the matter with the utmost apathy and I am glad to be able to report that the mischievous activities of the political leaders have led to no disorder whatever and do not appear to be likely to do so. In any case I anticipate no difficulty in dealing with any situation which may arise.

I have the honour to be,
My Lord,
Your Lordship's most obedient,

humble Servant,
C Fenn
Administering the Government.

B. Letter of J. C. D. Fenn, 14 December 1920

The Right Honourable   Government House
Viscount Milner, G.C.B., G.C.M.G.   Nicosia, 14th December, 1920.
Etc., etc., etc.
Secretary of the State for the Colonies.

My Lord,
    I have the honour to transmit a translation of a letter received from the Archbishop of Cyprus, who, as Your Lordship is aware, has recently returned to Cyprus after his visit to England as head of the Greek-Christian deputation for the union of Cyprus with Greece, protesting against the continuance of martial law and against a warning which I caused to be given to Mr. Nicolaos K. Lanites, a member of the Legislative Council for the Limassol-Paphos Division.

    2. As anticipated in my confidential despatch of the 16th of November, 1920, the announcement made on your Lordship's behalf by Colonel Amery to the Cyprus deputation to the effect that His Majesty's Government had no intention of relinquishing the Island, although received with general acquiescence or apathy by the mass of the Greek-Christian community, has lead to considerable agitation on the part of some of the leading clerics and professional politicians, which is causing uneasiness amongst the Moslem population as evidenced by the enclosed translations of two letters which I have received from the Cadi of Cyprus.

    3. In these circumstances I trust that Your Lordship will approve of the continuance of martial law as desirable with a view to the maintenance of order in the Island. It is only the fear of deportation or prosecution under martial law that prevents political firebrands of the Greek-Christian community from giving vent to utterances which would offend Moslem susceptibilities and would inevitably lead to serious conflict between the Greek-Christian and Moslem populations; especially is this the case during the winter months, when villagers spend most of their time in the cafés where racial brawls are always liable to arise.

    4. Apart from the necessity for the continuance of martial law for the present as a precaution against internal disorder, the Provisional Powers Law, 1919, and the Provisional Powers (Amendment) Law, 1920, of which copies are appended, do not come into force until the declaration of the date of determination of the war. Consequently, in the absence of any legislation analogous to the Defence of the Realm Acts, the immediate result of the withdrawal of martial law at the present time would be the exportation to neighbouring countries of all necessary supplies such as cattle, sheep, pigs, cereals, olive oil, etc., and also the exportation of all transport animals the shortage of which is severely

felt owing to the abnormal exportation during the war of mules and donkeys for military purposes. In addition a number of essential articles such as petroleum, rice and sugar are at present being supplied to the Island under martial law license from the Egyptian authorities and no power would exist to prevent the re-exportation of such articles from Cyprus to other countries.

5. In the ordinary course martial law powers are now only being exercised in respect of the following matters:–
(a) To control the exportation of necessary supplies
(b) To control the exportation of gold and silver coinage
(c) To control emigration and immigration
(d) To legalise the local note currency issue, which amounts at present to £632,169
(e) To provide for the powers of the Public Custodian.

6. With regards to the protest as to the warning given to Mr. Lanites, the facts are as follows. It was brought to my notice that Mr. Lanites had announced his intention of visiting all the villages in the Limassol District with a view to inciting agitation for union with Greece, and that he had commenced his tour with a visit to the village of Ayia Phyla, a suburb of Limassol with a reputation for violent crime where a number of notorious roughs and bad characters reside, and had there delivered an inflammatory anti-British speech likely to excite racial feeling between Greek-Christians and Moslems. In the circumstances I considered it advisable to send the chief Commandant of Police to Limassol to instruct the Provost Marshal to warn Mr. Lanites in the presence of the Chief Commandant of Police that he must be careful in the choice of his language in making speeches to the villagers. I directed him to be informed that if he let himself be carried away to such an extent as to excite racial ill-feeling between the Greek-Christian and Moslem villagers, I should have no hesitation in requiring him under Martial Law to leave the Island as an undesirable alien in the event of his utterances resulting in disturbance. Mr. Lanites is a Cypriot by birth, but acquired Greek nationality some years ago.

7. Mr. Lanites is an advocate practicing in the Limassol Court, and, whilst possibly the only agitator in the Island who has a sincere conviction that union with Greece would be of benefit to the Island, is unfortunately of a most excitable nature and lacking in self-control. Consequently he is very liable, if allowed a free hand, to cause disturbances in Limassol where as Your Lordship is aware very serious racial riots occurred in 1912. The warning given to him appears, however, to have had a most salutary effect throughout the Island and it is significant that the professional orators and leading newspaper editors are careful to announce their determination to continue their struggles for union with Greece by all "lawful means." I anticipate no difficulty in dealing with any situation which may arise.

I have the honour to be, My Lord,
Your Lordship's most obedient,
humble servant,
C. Fenn
Administering the Government.

V. Dispatch of Malcolm Stevenson, 13 April 1921 (CO 67/202)

A. Letter of Malcolm Stevenson, 13 April 1921

The Right Honourable   Government House
Winston S. Churchill, P.C., M.P.,   Nicosia, 13th April, 1921.
etc., etc., etc.
Secretary of State for the Colonies.

Sir,

With reference to my telegram of the 9th of April, informing you that there had been disturbances at Nicosia on the 6th and 7th of April on the anniversary of Greek Independence Day, I have the honour to submit the following report regarding the occurrences on those days.

2. It has been the custom each year on the occasion of this anniversary for the Greek Church to hold a Te Deum Service and for the other ceremonies to take place; but this year very elaborate programmes were drawn up for celebrations in the principal towns on an unprecedentedly large scale. These programmes which were not divulged till the 1st and 2nd of April, when they appeared in the newspapers, included, in addition to the customary religious services and other celebrations, organised processions through the streets with Greek flags and bands, the singing of the National (i.e. the Greek) Anthem, torchlight processions, the salutation of the Greek flag by the firing of mortars. Soldiers who had served in the Greek Army were ordered by the organising Committees to attend the processions in their military uniforms and it was stated that the bands would play national warlike airs (ἐθνικὰ θούρια). I attach translated copies of the programmes prepared for Nicosia and Limassol.

3. The publication of these programmes gave very great offence to the Turkish population, which is always liable to become excited by Greek demonstrations and the parading of Greek flags. On the present occasion the Turks appear to have been more than usually incensed by the proposed action of the Greeks, in view of the military situation in Asia Minor, and also because the persons responsible for the programme had taken the opportunity to include among the ceremonies the usual resolutions for the union of Cyprus with Greece and had given directions that such resolutions should be passed in all Greek Churches in the Island on the 7th of April. Both the Greeks and the Turks are naturally very excitable and are possessed of little self-control at any time, and apart from the impropriety of permitting such public celebrations by British Subjects in a British Colony, I was not prepared to allow any such organised processions in the public streets as I was fully convinced that, if carried out, they would lead to serious trouble. I accordingly had instructions given to the Commissioners of Nicosia, Limassol, Famagusta and Larnaca to inform the Committees responsible for the drawing up of the programmes that, while it was not desired to interfere in any way with any Church services or festivities in private places, it was not possible, in the interests of the public peace and security, to permit any organised processions in the streets or public places. The Commissioners acted accordingly and there was no untoward incident in any of the outstations.

4. In Nicosia, however, this was unfortunately not the case. Here the persons responsible for the programme were the Archbishop, Messrs. Theodotou and Severes, Members of the Legislative Council, and Messrs. Economides and Liassides (Mayor of

Nicosia), ex-Members of Council. The latter four gentlemen were sent for by Major Bayly, the Commissioner, who informed them of my decision, and Mr. Televantou, Chief Inspector of Police, who is a Greek, communicated the decision personally to the Archbishop at his place. This occurred on the 4th of April.

5. On the morning of the 6th of April, in spite of the order regarding processions in the streets, a very large procession of the students of the Gymnasium carrying about 300 Greek flags was formed near the Gymnasium, and proceeded to march through the streets of the town towards the Stadium, singing and shouting. They were soon joined by other disorderly elements, but the procession was turned back by the Police. The authorities of the Gymnasium took immediate steps to disclaim responsibility for the incident and promised to deal with the ringleaders among the students. The same morning a circular was issued from the Archbishopric to the Greek Community laying down a programme for the following day which, notwithstanding the order communicated to the Archbishop and the other Members of the Committee regarding processions, including a procession through the streets to be headed by a band playing the Reveille. I had no doubt that this was a deliberate attempt to defy the Government and I at once directed the Commissioner and Provost-Marshal to send for His Beatitude, to point out that he had already been informed that such processions could not be allowed and to require his explanation. On appearing before the Commissioner the Archbishop attempted to shuffle and stated that he did not know that a procession of this nature would be considered a procession within the meaning of the prohibition order. The Commissioner directed him to take immediate steps to cancel this part of the programme which he promised to do and in fact did cancel it the same afternoon. The Archbishop subsequently addressed a letter to me protesting against the Commissioner and Provost-Marshal for having summoned him to explain his action. I attach a copy of His Beatitude's letter and of two letters in reply which I caused to be sent to him.

6. During the whole of the 6th there was very considerable uneasiness manifested by the Turks and a large crowd of them, numbering several hundreds, gathered together near the Police Station in anticipation of any disturbance. Through the indefatigable efforts of Irfan Bay, Member of the Executive and Legislative Councils, they were however kept in check, though with difficulty.

7. On the afternoon of the same day an incident occurred which might have had very serious consequences. Three Greeks were observed by the Police driving near the Archbishop's Palace in a carriage which contained a small harmonium, to the accompaniment of which they were singing "patriotic" songs. All three of them were drunk and they carried with them a large picture, of which I enclose a photographic reproduction, representing a Greek in the hands of three Turks. This picture, which was surmounted by a Greek flag, is, I am informed, a well known one, representing a Greek hero who fought in the Revolution of 1821, but was eventually captured and roasted alive by the Turks. It appears to have been the intention of these persons, who were forming a procession at the time, to drive round the streets and inflame the minds of the Greek population. Fortunately they were discovered by the Chief Commandant of Police who promptly stopped the procession and arrested the three men. They were all bad characters with many previous convictions (including convictions for homicide and creating disturbances) and on their production before the Provost-Marshal's Court, which was effected at once, were sentenced to terms of imprisonment varying from six to nine months. After this incident I

gave instructions for the closing of all liquor shops which were kept shut for the remainder of the 6th and on the 7th of April.

8. On the morning of the 7th of April, a Te Deum Service was held in the Phaneromeni Church at which Mr. Theodotou made a speech protesting against the prohibition of processions. After the service in the Church a very large procession was formed, whether spontaneously or otherwise is not clear, which proceeded through the streets carrying Greek flags. The procession does not appear to have contained any one of note, being composed mainly of persons of the lowest class. It eventually came into collision with the Police who attempted to get it to disperse. The Police were stoned but managed to hold their ground, and eventually part of the crowd moved off elsewhere to form a large and unruly mob outside and in the neighbourhood of the old Post Office buildings. Here they refused to disperse and continued to stone the Police and the Commissioner and the Magistrates who had been called out. The situation eventually became so serious that the Commissioner, after the refusal of the mob to disperse, gave the order for the Police firing party, which had been brought up, to get ready. At this stage, the Abbot of Kykko, who was present and who alone among the crowd seems to have realized the seriousness of the position, rushed forward and begged for permission to address the crowd. This was granted and, after about five minutes, his speech had the desired effect and the crowd dispersed. After this, order was gradually restored and since then no further untoward incidents have occurred. Several arrests have been made and the persons charged are being dealt with. There were no fatalities among either the crowd or the Police Force, but Captain Bradburn, Local Commandant of Police, sustained serious injuries from stones and other missiles and had to be removed to hospital subsequently. One zaptieh received injuries which necessitated his removal to hospital, and there was a number of minor injuries sustained by officers, other ranks and horses.

9. So far no evidence which would enable successful action to be taken against the wirepullers in this matter has been secured. There is no doubt, however, that the persons primarily responsible for the whole occurrences were the Archbishop, Mr. Theodotou and Mr. Catalanos. Mr. Theodotou, since his return to Cyprus in November last from London, where he was engaged for two years in agitation for the union of Cyprus with Greece, has been persistent in his efforts to bring about a boycott of the Government by the Members of the Legislative Council, and has been consistently occupied in holding secret meetings with the political agitators, presumably with the object of devising further measures for promoting the campaign for Union. His principal aim in life now appears to be to prevent, at any cost, the agitation for Union from subsiding. He has latterly been joined by an Australian journalist named Lloyd, who is an advanced panhellenist, and is at present living with the Archbishop. While both of them have been active behind the scenes they have been careful to cover their traces so far. Mr. Catalanos is a Greek subject who came to Cyprus in 1893 as Professor of Mathematics at the Greek Gymnasium, Nicosia. He is a bitter Anglophobe who like Mr. Theodotou manages, after long experience, to keep within the law. Since his arrival in Cyprus he has twelve sentences recorded against him in Criminal Courts, the last one being for shooting and wounding in 1910, for which offence he was sentenced to six months' imprisonment. A number of years ago he was in the habit of delivering inflammatory speeches against the Moslems. The Archbishop, who is a weak man physically and mentally, is merely a pup-

pet in the hands of Mr.Theodotou who makes him, and indeed the other agitators, do what he wants.

10. As indicated in my telegram of the 9th of April I applied to the General Officer Commanding the Troops in Egypt to strengthen the garrison in Cyprus by the addition of two platoons of British troops and these are expected to arrive on the 14th. I have also informed him that it will be necessary for some time to come to maintain the garrison in Cyprus at a strength of at least one full Company. At present the garrison consists of a weak half Company only. I feel sure that the moral effect of the few additional troops which are being sent will be sufficient to prevent any disturbance at Greek Easter. As you are aware the Police Force in Cyprus is composed of both Turks and Greeks, and although the discipline of the Force is very good there is always the risk that they may take sides in any racial disturbance which may occur.

11. I attach, for your information, copies of two reports which have been furnished by the Chief Commandant of Police regarding the disturbances in Nicosia. I also forward a copy of a Bill to regulate Public Processions in Cyprus, which I propose, subject to your approval, to introduce to the Legislative Council. There is at present no law governing the regulation of such processions and I think it most desirable that this deficiency should be remedied. I enclosed, in this connection, a copy of a memorial which I have received from the Moslem Members of the Legislative Council relative to the recent disturbances. I also enclose for your information an Extract form a personal letter addressed to the Chief Secretary by Irfan Bey regarding the disturbances.

I have the honour to be,
Sir,
Your most obedient,
humble Servant,
Malcolm Stevenson
High Commissioner.

B. Memorial from Moslem Members of Legislative Council, 11 April 1921

To
His Excellency   Nicosia, 11th April, 1921.
The High Commissioner,
etc., etc., etc.,

May it please Your Excellency,

We the Moslem Members of the Legislative Council beg leave to lay the following before Your Excellency.

As your Excellency is well aware the agitation carried on by the Greek-Christian politicians for the union of Cyprus with Greece was, for a long time, of spontaneous nature, but since two years they have assumed the character of an organized propaganda, such as the sending of deputations to England and demonstrations in Cyprus.

These demonstrations appear to have taken the form of organized processions which are provoking the indignation of the Moslem Community.

The Moslems of Cyprus are law-abiding, and respect the authority, but these recent organized agitations are becoming very trying to their temper, and if continued, we venture to submit, the time may come when it will be a question if their patience and law-abiding dispositions will stand the strain, and in spite of every endeavour it may not be possible for their leaders to keep them under control.

We, therefore, earnestly pray, in the interests of peace and order, that steps may be taken, in time, to put an end to these vexatious organized public agitations which, we fear, may lead to very serious and deplorable consequences.

We are, Sir,
Your Excellency's obedient servants,
(Signed) M. IRFAN.
(Signed) M. HAMI.
(Signed) A. SAID.

C. Extract from Letter of M. Irfan, 11 April 1921

Hon. C. D. Fenn, Esq.   Nicosia, 11th April, 1921.

Dear Chief Secretary,

With reference to the letter sent in by the Members of the Legislative Council this morning on the subject of the agitation of the Greek politicians for union with Greece, I thought it my personal duty to inform you of my feeling and experience on the whole situation, as we avoided in our official letter to deal with the question in detail.

As we stated in the letter, the agitation has of late been so much aggravated that nobody can foresee the degree of disaster to which it will lead if allowed to go too far.

The hatred that the Greek politicians are trying to imbibe into the heads of schoolboys and riff-raffs of the Greeks, against the Turks, are simply boundless. Besides the lectures delivered and the speeches made in private, you see pictures of a very inciting nature exposed here and there such as the one the Police fortunately captured the other day, and prevented its being taken round, in a carriage, through the streets of Nicosia, by a drunken lot playing harmonium and singing songs. If those people were allowed to come to a main Turkish quarter I fear the consequences would have been very grave indeed.

Sometimes several of the Greek politicians try to assure us that they bear no ill-feeling against Turks, but putting this assurance and their actions and attitude together, one cannot help becoming very suspicious of their intentions.

Then, on the other hand, one hears of a lot of inciting accounts such as a Greek telling some Turk that "when Greeks come to Cyprus we will revenge the year 21 when our Bishops and laymen were massacred by the Turks, etc.", and this sort of feeling is strengthened in recent years by the erection of a monument in the Archbishop's palace, in the image of the late Archbishop Kypriano, the martyr as they call it, of whom so much fuss is made every year since.

In view of all these organized propagandas, the arrangements made this year for the celebration of the anniversary of the independence of Greece, had certainly made the Moslems of Nicosia suspicious and all sorts of ideas were brewing up in their minds; and on the 6th and 7th April you could see some several hundreds of them coming together to be on the look-out, just outside the Police Station, but happily the effective measures taken by the Police prevented the Greeks coming into contact with them by preventing processions through the Turkish quarters, and the Turks were advised by me to keep away from the Greek quarters, for a few days, and not to give the slightest cause to anything, and I am glad they have listened.

Sincerely yours,
(Signed) M. Irfan.

VI. Dispatch of Malcolm Stevenson, 15 May 1925

A. Letter of Malcolm Stevenson, 5 May 1925

The Right Honourable   Government House
L. C. M. S. Amery, P.C., M.P.,   Nicosia. 5th May, 1925.
Secretary of State for the Colonies

Sir,

With reference to your despatch No.78 of the 30th of March, 1925, and to previous correspondence relative to the elevation of Cyprus to the status of a Colony, I have the honour to transmit a translation of a memorial from the Archbishop of Cyprus protesting against the retention of Cyprus as part of His Majesty's dominions and reiterating the alleged aspirations of the Greek-Christian population for Union with Greece.

2. I would explain that the Archbishop attended in person at a ceremony in the Konak Square at Nicosia on the 1st of May when the Letters Patent constituting the officer of Governor and Commander-in-Chief of Cyprus were publicly read and proclaimed in accordance with your instructions. On taking his departure at the close of the ceremony which, I may say, was conducted with due pomp and ceremony His Beatitude, with that lack of good manners which is habitual among the small coterie of Cypriot agitators, handed to the Commissioner of Nicosia, who had just finished the public reading of the Letters Patent, an envelope which on subsequent examination was found to contain the memorial under reference.

3. The protest made by the Archbishop is purely formal. It is in no way expressive of popular sentiment, but was, I understand, considered necessary by the extreme section of which, through weakness of character, His Beatitude has been forced to become the unwilling mouthpiece. Omission to protest at this juncture would, it was considered, have been interpreted as a tactic renunciation of the creed of "Enosis."

4. I would suggest that I should cause a reply to be sent to the Archbishop to the effect that you have received his memorial and desire that he should be informed that he must clearly understand that, as has already been pointed out to him on more than one occasion, the question of Union of Cyprus with Greece has been finally closed and cannot be reopened. I would propose, subject to your concurrence, that a copy of the Archbishop's memorial and the reply sent to him should then be published in the official gazette for general information.

I have the honour to be,
Sir,

Your most obedient,
humble Servant.
Malcolm Stevenson
Governor.

B. Memorial from Archbishop, 1 May 1925

Translation

The Right Honourable   Nicosia,
The Secretary of State for the Colonies,   1st May, 1925
London.

Right Honourable Sir,

On the occasion of to-day's official pronouncement of the declaration of the Island of Cyprus as a Colony, We, the Archbishop of Cyprus, President of the Holy Synod of the Autocephalous Church of Cyprus and National Leader of the Hellenic population of Cyprus, express, in the name of the clergy and people, their very deep grief, and lay an emphatic protest against the renewed ignoring by this political action of the indefeasible historic national rights of the Hellenic people of the Island to their national restoration, which it was expecting soon to receive from the Liberal English Nation; and we declare that the burning and unalterable desire of the Hellenic people of the Island was, is and will always be its union with its mother Hellas.

We remain,
With deepest respect and honour,
Kyrillos,
Archbishop of Cyprus.

VII. Dispatch from the Treasury, 19 November 1926 (CO 67/219/13)

A. Letter from A. Barstow, 19 November 1926

The Under Secretary of State,   Treasury Chambers
Colonial Office.   19th , November 1926.

Sir,

I have laid before the Lords Commissioners of His Majesty's Treasury your letter of the 17th July (X3884/26) and the accompanying copy of a dispatch from the Governor of Cyprus forwarding copies of two resolutions concerning the share of Cyprus in the Turkish Debt charge.

In reply I am to say that My Lords agree with the view of Mr. Secretary Amery that the matter cannot have been properly explained to the Cyprus legislature and that it is desirable to send a despatch for their information and to disclose such facts as can properly be made public at the present time.

I am accordingly to transmit (a) a memorandum giving a brief historical résumé of the facts relating to the Cyprus 'Tribute' and (b) a confidential note on the investment of the surplus of the Tribute. In view of the absolute necessity for complete secrecy with regard to the arrangements referred to in the latter note I am to request that its contents may not be disclosed or allowed to become public property.

My Lords note Mr. Amery's suggestion that the interest on the invested surplus should be applied in reduction of the contribution by Cyprus. However much they may sympathize with the desire of the Islanders to be relieved of the charge, they feel no doubt that the present is not a time when the heavily-burdened British taxpayer can be asked to re-open the question, particularly as such action would inevitably increase the difficulty of terminating the default of Egypt. It may be sufficient to point out that taking £42,800 per annum as in effect the sole contribution made by Cyprus towards debt and defence charges, that sum represents only (s.d.) 2/6 per head of population, whereas the corresponding payment by the British taxpayer, say £480,000,000 per annum represents £11 a head.

I am, Sir,
Your obedient Servant,
A. Barstow

B. The "Cyprus Tribute"

THE "CYPRUS TRIBUTE"

1. Under Article 3 of the Convention with Turkey in 1878, Great Britain undertook, in return for the right to administer Cyprus, to pay to the Porte the then excess of the Island's revenue over expenditure on the average of the five preceding years. The land revenues were reserved to Turkey. The Article reads as follows:–

> "III. That England will pay to the Porte whatever is the present excess of revenue over expenditure in the island; this excess to be calculated upon and determined by the average of the last five years, stated to be 22,936 purses, to be duly verified hereafter, and to the exclusion of the produce of State and Crown lands let or sold during that period."

This payment was ultimately (in 1882) fixed at £87,800 per annum.

By a Supplementary Convention in 1879 the right of the Porte to the land revenues was commuted for an additional annual payment of £5,000.

The total annual payment then became £92,800.

By the Order in Council dated 30th November 1882 relating to the Constitution of Cyprus a sum equal to the annual amount payable to Turkey was charged permanently on the consolidated revenues of Cyprus. The relevant provisions are:–

> "XXVII. The several sums required for the undermentioned services shall be permanently charged on the Consolidated Revenue of the Island, and shall be payable to Her Majesty, Her heirs and successors, every year until it shall be otherwise ordered by Her Majesty, Her heirs or successors, with the advice of Her or Their Privy Council:–
>
> £92,686 being a sum equal to the sums payable under the Annex dated the
> 1st of July 1878 to the Convention of Defensive Alliance between Great

Britain and Turkey, signed on the 4th of June 1878 and under an agreement respecting Cyprus lands signed by the Representatives of Great Britain and Turkey on the 3rd of February 1879 . . . "

2. Under these arrangements Cyprus was liable to Great Britain for £92,800 a year and Great Britain was liable to the Ottoman Empire for the same sum. In practice, however, the liability of Cyprus to Great Britain was reduced by Grants-in-Aid from the Imperial Exchequer: originally these varied from year to year, the amounts being determined by the Annual deficits of the Cyprus Budget, but since 1907 the Grant-in-Aid has been fixed at £50,000 reducing the net payment by Cyprus to His Majesty's Government to £42,800.

3. In point of fact the Porte has never actually received any portion of the Cyprus tribute, for it refused to realise the sums which were placed at its disposal in the years immediately following the Convention of 1878, pending negotiations as to the amount due and other questions. Up to 1885 the tribute account remained in suspense. Meanwhile the Ottoman Empire in 1875–6 defaulted on both Interest and Sinking Fund of the 4% Loan of 1855, the interest (but not Sinking Fund) on which was jointly and severally guaranteed by the British and French Governments.

The amount of this loan outstanding in 1876 was £3,815,200 and the annual interest amounts to £153,752. This Loan of 1855 was secured upon the whole revenues of the Ottoman Empire and specially on (1) the balance of Egyptian tribute available—viz: £72,000—and (2) the Customs of Syria and Smyrna. Thus when the Ottoman Empire defaulted, and only £72,000 was available from the Egyptian Tribute, an annual deficit of £81,752 for Interest and £50,000 for Sinking Fund was caused. The Law officers of the Crown advised His Majesty's Government that the "Cyprus Tribute" formed part of the revenues of the Ottoman Empire and could be withheld from the Porte and used towards the service of the 1855 Loan so long as the Porte continued to default. Accordingly the £92,800 (gross) received annually from Cyprus has been applied to make up the deficit of £81,752 on the Interest of the 1855 Loan, the annual surplus of some £11,000 being invested and accumulated.

4. Thus the pre-war position was that

(a) Cyprus owed His Majesty's Government £92,800 under the order in Council of 1882 relating to the Constitution of Cyprus, this liability being in practice reduced to £42,800 by the Grant-in-Aid.

(b) His Majesty's Government owed £92,800 to the Ottoman Empire under the Convention of 1878 and in fact applied this sum towards meeting a liability on which the Ottoman Empire had defaulted.

On 5th November, 1914, Great Britain being at war with the Ottoman Empire annexed Cyprus and the British liability to pay £92,800 a year to the Ottoman Empire ceased.

The payment by Cyprus, however, of an equivalent sum to the British Crown under Article XXVII of the Constitution was in no way abrogated by the war with Turkey or by the annexation of the Island: and this payment accordingly continued and was applied, as previously, to the service of the Guaranteed Loan of 1855.

5. The annexation of the Island was recognised by Turkey (with retrospective effect) in Article 20 of the Treaty of Lausanne. That Treaty provided, in accordance with what is now a generally accepted principle of international law, that the territories detached from Turkey should assume liability for a share of the Turkish pre-war public debt. Cyprus was not required to assume such a liability, as the payment of £92,800 for the Service of

the Guaranteed Loan of 1855 was treated as her contribution to the Ottoman public debt. Had it not been for this payment, Cyprus would undoubtedly have been required to take over a share of the Ottoman Debt in the same basis as the other territories detached from Turkey as the result of the war, and on that basis her contribution would have been substantially more than the gross amount of the Tribute.

6. The position of Cyprus as regards the Treaty settlement was closely analogous to that of Egypt. Egypt became a British Protectorate on 5th November 1914 (and an independent State in 1922) and by Article 17 of the Treaty of Lausanne Turkey renounced all rights over Egypt as from the 5th November 1914. The Treaty of Lausanne was not signed by Egypt, but the Treaty made it clear that it was the intention of the Signatory powers that the former Egyptian Tribute should continue to be paid as Egypt's share in the Ottoman Public Debt. This is the result of Article 18 which reads as follows:–

"Turkey is released from all undertakings and obligations in regard to the Ottoman loans guaranteed on the Egyptian tribute, that is to say, the loans of 1855, 1891 and 1894. The annual payments made by Egypt for the service of these loans now forming part of the service of the Egyptian Public Debt, Egypt is freed from all other obligations relating to the Ottoman Public Debt."

This arrangement that Egypt should continue to meet the service of the loans secured on the "Egyptian Tribute" and should be accordingly exempted from the share of Ottoman Public Debt which would otherwise have been assigned to her, was in accordance with the proposals unanimously adopted by the Paris Commission which met in 1913 to consider the distribution of the Ottoman Debt, but was unable to finish its work before the European war.

7. The position of Cyprus is so closely analogous to that of Egypt that it might have been expected that a similar clause would have been added freeing Cyprus from all other obligations relating to the Ottoman Debt, provided that she continued the annual payment of £92,800. On April 24, 1923, Hassan Bey, the Turkish financial expert at Lausanne proposed that there should be added to (what is now) Article 20 the words "Turkey is freed from all obligations in regard to the Ottoman Loans secured on the revenues of Cyprus." (Receuil des Actes de la Conference de Lausanne—2eme Serie—Vol. 1 page 177). This proposal had already appeared in the Turkish counter-proposals made between the two stages of the Conference in March 1923. The Foreign Office consulted the Colonial Office on 25th March, pointing out that the proposal was probably due to a mistaken belief that the loan of 1855 was specially secured in law upon the Cyprus revenues, but suggested that if the Turkish proposal were to be accepted the clause should run as follows:–

"In view of the fact that the obligation of Cyprus to make annual payments heretofore made by her for the service of the Ottoman loans of 1855, now constitutes a part of the Public Debt of Cyprus, Cyprus shall not be called upon to undertake any further liability in respect of the Ottoman Public Debt, notwithstanding the provisions for the distribution of this debt contained in Part II of the present Treaty."

The Colonial Office, however, thought that as the liability of Cyprus was a domestic matter between His Majesty's Government and the Island, it should be left to be decided by his Majesty's Government and it did not require to be dealt with in an international instrument (Colonial Office letter 14443/1923 of 24th March 1923). As a result of the Colonial Office communication the British Delegation explained to Hassan Bey that the loan of 1855 was already covered in Article 18 and the Turks agreed to drop the proposed addition to Article 20.

If the clause proposed by the Foreign Office had in fact been included in the Treaty, it would have had the advantage of making clear that the payments by Cyprus represent her share of the Ottoman debt.

C. Cyprus Tribute Account

Cyprus Tribute Account

There is at present in the Account Turkish Guaranteed Loan to the face value of £642,400. Since the default of Egypt in 1924 on her contribution to the service of the 1855 Guaranteed Loan, any cash in the Account, and some British War Loan previously held by the Account, has been utilised towards payment of interest on the 1855 Loan as it fell due. Normally, some £41,000 would be paid over half-yearly from the Cyprus Tribute Account in respect of this Loan, but owing to the default of Egypt, the following sums have in fact been paid from the Account (in addition to further sums from the Consolidated Fund):

In July 1924	£46,048
In January 1925	£72,669
In July 1925	£56,678
In December 1925	£56,678
In July 1926	£56,320

that is a total of £288,393 in all, or some £83,000 more than would normally have been paid.

There appears to be some prospect that Egypt will before long resume payment on the 1855 Loan, including arrears now due, and His Majesty's Government are taking every opportunity to press upon the Egyptian Government the desirability of terminating the default. If and when this is done, the amounts taken from the Cyprus Tribute Account in excess of the amounts which would normally have been paid will be restored to it, and it will continue to grow by the accumulation of the annual £10,800 as in the past. It is understood however that the Egyptian Government will insist, as a condition of terminating their default, that some scheme of amortisation of the loan should be arranged to which Egypt and Cyprus would contribute in the same proportions as they do for interest at present. Such an arrangement would be to the interests of the island, as it would eventually enable the payment of the Cyprus Tribute (and of the Imperial grant-in-aid) to be terminated: but it is clearly essential if such a scheme is to be elaborated (i) that there should be no undertaking to amortise any part of the loan unless Egypt agrees to amortise her due proportion and (ii) that the proposal should be kept absolutely secret, in order that the market may not put up the price of the Bonds, which at present carry no rights of redemption. The fact that His majesty's Government has reinvested the surplus Cyprus Tribute and at present holds some £642,000 of the Loan should help to persuade the Egyptian Government to buy up a similar amount: and thereafter an annual sinking fund of substantial amount can be provided by (a) the surplus Cyprus Tribute plus an equivalent extra payment by Egypt and (b) the interest on the Bonds already purchased for the Sinking

Fund. Clearly, however, it will be many years before the loan can be totally redeemed, and in the meantime the net payment made by Cyprus cannot be reconsidered.

Chapter 3
British Debate and Rising Demand for Enosis: 1929–1931

This chapter begins with minutes by Colonial Office personnel who are trying to determine how to respond to the latest Memorial from the Archbishop praying for Enosis. The Enosis campaign of 1929 was different because the Archbishop targeted so many "high personages" that the Colonial Office was at a loss as to how the response should be coordinated. We also get a sense of the antagonism lurking under the surface of interactions between the Foreign Office and the Colonial Office (CO 67/228/1). Two of the minutes in CO 67/228/5 provide a list of the individuals in the Colonial Office whose opinions were solicited on the various documents. The dates next to their names indicated when each of them had signed off on the various pieces of correspondence. There is also some correspondence that indicates the impact and role of the press in Athens vis-à-vis the Enosis movement. The 1929 Memorial in CO 67/227/6 is the annotated version that Governor Storrs sent to London. Further minutes and correspondence record the uncoordinated and awkward response to the Greek Cypriot Delegation in London. Finally, on October 25, 1929, the Secretary of State met with the deputation and the next day entered a minute in the Colonial Office records saying that he had decided that a detailed reply to the Memorial was justified. The original Memorial along with the reply from the Secretary of State was published in the form of a "White Paper" in December, 1929. Governor Storrs evidently greatly resented the burden such a detailed reply placed on him. Rather than the very formal customary ending to his letters, as in "I have the Honour etc," Storrs had some unusual ways of expressing himself. On September 11, 1929 (see below, III.A.) he ended his letter to the secretary of State by referring to the deputation of Greek Cypriots in London with sarcasm and complaint:

> I have submitted, for obvious reasons, that they should be answered as soon as conveniently possible. Heaven knows I grudge no man his jaunt to London nor his quail and peche Melba at the Mayfair Hotel, where I understand they will be modestly established. But I do faintly resent the futile and unnecessary researches and verifications imposed upon my unhappy Departments and not least, upon
>
> Yours very sincerely,
> Ronald Storrs

The persistence of the Enosis agitation in 1930, even after the "White Paper" had been published and following the visit to the Island of Dr. Sheils, the Under-Secretary of State for the Colonies, led to frustration and amazement in Downing Street. Mr. Dawe called the Memorial a "piece of impudence" and judged that it "illustrates the complete childishness of the Cypriot Politician."(CO 67/227/7) These documents set the scene for the British formal and informal reaction to the riots of 1931.

As the documents make clear, just prior to the island-wide riots of 1931, British officials were at pains to claim that Enosis had no popular support. As the officer administrating the government in Cyprus in February 1929 put it: "the agitation . . . has been due solely to the Greek Orthodox Church in alliance with a small clique in the principal towns . . . The Greek population is wholly indifferent."

I.   Dispatch from R. Nicholson, 6 February 1929 (CO 67/228/5)

     A. Letter of R. Nicholson, 6 February 1929

     B. Commentary

II.   The Greek Press and Athletes, April–May 1929 (CO 67/228/1)

III.   Memorial, 20 July 1929 (CO 67/227/6)

     A. Letter of R. Storrs, 11 September 1929

     B. Letter of R. Storrs, 18 September 1929

     C. Letter of Armenian Prelature, 12 September 1929

     D. Letter of the Maronites, 10 September 1929

     E. Letter of the Moslems, 10 September 1929

     F. British Commentary, Sept-Nov, 1929

IV.   Reactions to Memorial, November 1929–February 1930 (CO 67/227/7)

     A. Extract from the Near East and Cyprus, 21 Nov 1929

     B. Letter from R. Storrs, 20 November 1929

C. Dispatch from Secretary of State, 28 Nov 1929
D. Letter of J. Shuckburgh to Storrs, 5 Dec 1929
E. Letter to S. Wilson, 14 Jan 1930
F. Letter from Passfield, 6 Feb 1930

I. Dispatch from R. Nicholson, 6 February 1929 (CO 67/228/5)

A. Letter of R. Nicholson

The right Honourable
L. C. M. S. Amery, P.C., M.P.
Secretary of State for the Colonies.
Sir,

Government House
Nicosia, 6th February, 1929

    I have the honour to transmit to you, for your information, the accompanying copy of a letter which I have received from the Archbishop of Cyprus enclosing printed copies, in English and in Greek, of a Memorial which His Beatitude states that he has already forwarded direct to the English Houses of Parliament, requesting that the Island may be ceded to Greece.

    2. It is not necessary that I should deal with the various statements contained in the Memorial. It attempts to raise anew a question which His Majesty's Government has repeatedly and definitely declared to be closed.

    There is however one point to which I would draw attention.

    It will be observed that His Beatitude, speaking as Supreme Prelate and Ethnarch, and also in accordance with a resolution of the Holy Synod and with the advice and consent of the Greek Members of the Legislative Council and of the Mayors of the Island, refers throughout the Memorial to the demand for union with Greece as proceeding from and representing the desires of the Greek population of the colony, and to the public meetings, memorials, resolutions and missions to England by which, he states, they have not ceased to demonstrate their wishes.

    3. I can only repeat in this connection what I have already said in my confidential despatches marginally noted. There is no demand on the part of the Greek community for union with Greece.

    The agitation carried on with that object has been due solely to the Greek Orthodox Church in alliance with the small clique of politicians in the principal towns who work together because they believe it to be for their ultimate aggrandizement.

    The public meetings, memorials, resolutions and the mass of the Greek population is wholly indifferent to them.

    4. I enclose also a translation of an article published in the Greek newspaper "Nea Phoni tes Kyprou" of the 2nd of February in which it is stated that copies of the Memorial in question have been sent to His Royal Highness the Prince of Wales, the Archbishop of Canterbury, the Prime Minister and others.

I have the honour to be,

Sir,

Your most obedient,

humble Servant,

R. Nicholson

Officer Administering the Government.

B. Commentary

Downing Street
28 February, 1929.

To: A. J. Sylvester, esq.

I have your letter of the 18th February, in which you ask for my advice as to the reply to be sent to the enclosed communication which Mr. Lloyd George has received from the Archbishop of Cyprus.

I think the best thing I can do to enable you to deal with the matter is to send you the enclosed copies of (1) the letter sent by Philip Kerr at Mr. Lloyd George's direction to the Cyprus Mission in November, 1919. This is no doubt the letter referred to in the communication: and (2) a Confidential despatch just received from the Acting Governor of Cyprus forwarding officially a copy of the Archbishop's memorial to the two Houses of Parliament.

You will see that it is quite untrue to say that Mr. Lloyd George, in his letter of November, 1919, recognised any "right" such as the senders of the communication allege. You will also see from the Acting Governor's despatch that the Archbishop and his supporters have really no claim to speak in the name of "the Hellenic people of Cyprus." The demand for union with Greece is the cry of only a small clique gathered around the Archbishop. There is of course no question of handing Cyprus <u>back</u> to Greece, since the Island has never been under the political sovereignty of that country.

Copies of the memorial are being broadcast to various eminent personages in this country. The question of the reply which Mr. Lloyd George should send to the copy which has reached him is of course one of policy, which he alone can decide. Since, however, you ask for my advice, I think it would be to the advantage of Cyprus if a thoroughly discouraging reply were sent. A real effort is now being made to develop Cyprus and improve its administration. A good deal of British capital is finding its way to the Island, and it is hoped that in the near future more and more will be attracted by the undoubted possibilities which the country offers. It is clear, however, that it will be difficult to realise this object if the impression gets abroad that there is any possibility of Cyprus being handed over to Greece. It is [inadvisable that] Government would take such a step. A number of petitions similar to the enclosed and emanating from the same source have been received during the last decade at the C.O., and each Govt. for the time being in office has returned the same negative answer. I may add that in Greece itself no support has been forthcoming from the Greek Government for the movement led by the Archbishop. M. Venizelos indeed only recently declared that there is no Cyprus question outstanding between Greece and Great Britain.

I hope the above will give you what you want, and if you would like it amplified in any particular, you have only to let me know.

Lieutenant Colonel
Sir Ralph Verney, C.I.E., C.V.C.

Downing Street,
21st March, 1929.

Dear Sir Ralph Verney,

This refers to our conversation about the petition (which I return herewith) addressed to the Speaker by the Archbishop of the Greek Orthodox Church in Cyprus praying for the union of the Island with Greece.

In view of our discussion I think that the only answer which could be sent by the Speaker would be a bare acknowledgment; and the higher authorities here have now authorised me to suggest that this should be done.

If you would like the exact words of the acknowledgment, I suggest the following might meet the case:

"I beg to acknowledge the receipt of your letter dated the 26th
January, 1929, in which you transmitted a petition praying for the
union of Cyprus with Greece".

It is advisable not to use any words which would suggest that we accept the contention that this petition is put forward by "the Greek people of Cyprus" as the Archbishop would have us believe.

If you could kindly let me have a copy of the reply, we would then let the Governor know what has been done.

Yours sincerely,
A. J. Dawe.

II. The Greek Press and Athletes, April–May 1929 (CO 67/228/1) [The Archbishop's Memorial referred to in this section is not in the file.]

The right Honourable   Athens
Sir Austen Chamberlain, K.G., M.P.   April 8th 1929.
&c., &c., &c.

Sir,

I have the honour to inform you that the news of the recent dissolution of the Cypriot Legislative Council has provoked adverse comment in the Athens press of all shades of political opinion.

2. Generally speaking, the view is expressed in the papers that the dissolution is an illiberal measure unworthy of the traditions of Great Britain.

3. A summary of the more important articles is enclosed herewith.

4. A copy of this despatch is being forwarded to His Majesty's Representative at Cyprus.

I have etc.,
Percy Loraine

SUMMARY OF TRANSLATION.

"Proia" says that it is astonishing that England should be endeavouring in Cyprus to sully a splendid liberal tradition, a tradition which has lasted for centuries. The Acting Governor of the Greek island has insisted upon a Greek member of the Executive Council resigning, because he is in favour of the union of his country with Greece, and has prorogued the business of the Chamber indefinitely, because the Cypriot deputies will not approve the granting to civil servants of the pensions out of proportion to the revenues of the island. But the English must be convinced that nothing can kill the national spirit of a Greek people, and that Cyprus will continue to demand union with Greece as long as Cypriots exist.

"Hemerisios Typos" says that Acting Governor of Cyprus has forgotten the liberal traditions of his country.

"Hestia" says that the dissolution of the Cypriot Chamber has been carried out in a manner unprecedented in the history of Parliaments—if the Legislative Council can rightly be called a Parliament. The pensions paid by the Cypriot people to British functionaries absorb, according to "Hestia," nearly ten per cent of the whole budget. A certain policeman received a pension far larger than that of Marshal Foch and as his four hundred and fifty pounds sterling was not enough for the Governor of a province he was given the post of Farm Inspector with three hundred pounds sterling so that, for his twelve years' service, he received seven hundred and fifty pounds. The Cypriot people cannot put up with the accumulation of pressure and wrongheadedness on the part of the Government. Greeks and Turks are united, fortunately, in defence of the slender purse of their country, and are resolved, if necessary, to refuse to pay the taxes. We do not know what measure of "honesty" Sir Austen Chamberlain will attribute to the Law, but it is certain that the words with which the British Acting Governor dissolved the Chamber have reechoed painfully in every Greek heart.

In a second article, "Proia" says: "Cyprus had a chance not only of being liberated from the Turkish yoke by England—to be transformed forty years later into a British Colony—but also of being administered by the worst British Colonial functionaries. And the Acting Governor, on the pretext that he was interrupted by a deputy, has dissolved the Cypriot Chamber in order 'to teach the deputies how to behave.' The true reason of the dissolution was that the Cypriot Chamber refused to pass a measure providing fresh increases of the pensions of the Government employees. This action on the part of England is very regrettable, and pushes the unfortunate islanders to despair. The situation also profoundly afflicts Greek public opinion, which is forced to draw a contrast with the liberal action of England in 1864."

"Politeia" says "Because the Cypriot deputies, or rather legislative Councillors, ten Greeks and two Mussulmans, rejected the bill concerning pensions, Mr. Nicholson, the Colonial Chief Secretary, replacing the absent Governor, dissolved the Chamber. Wonderful liberty! Why did the Deputies reject the bill? Because the pensions paid to British officials absorb already one-tenth of the Budget of the island."

The Right Honourable   Athens,
Arthur Henderson, M.P.   August 31st 1929.
etc., etc., etc.

Sir,

From time to time I have had the honour to address despatches to you reporting articles in the Greek press on the subjects of the British occupation of Cyprus. Such articles, which are a perennial feature in the press, notably in "Hestia," whose editor is a Cypriot, have been much stimulated of late by the advent of the labour Government to power, and they are now pitched on a much more confident note.

2. A further stimulus to Greek hopes has been given by the announcement of the proposed terms of settlement with Egypt. Egypt is not more Egyptian than Cyprus is Greek, so runs the argument, and it is not possible that His Majesty's Government should be less generous to the one than to the other.

3. The recent trouble in Palestine, however, coupled with the intended reduction of British forces in Egypt, have erected a certain uneasiness lest British naval and military authorities should now deem it necessary to make Cyprus a new place d'armes in the Near East, and thus a fresh argument should be forged against eventual union with Greece. It appears that a certain Colonel Gunliffe-Owen has written to the "Times" in some such sense, and quite undue authority has been attributed to his letter. A rumour reached me yesterday in fact, that His Majesty's Government had decided to transfer the whole base at Malta to Cyprus.

4. Although nothing so far as I am aware, has ever been stated officially on the subject, responsible organs in the press have more than once made plain that Greek public opinion would gladly guarantee His Majesty's Government any military, naval or air facilities which they might require in Cyprus, in return for the cession of the island to Greece. An English informant, who was recently dining with Monsieur Michalacopoulos when the question happened to crop up, has told me that His Excellency said once that of course Greece would be only too pleased to afford any such facilities.

5. I have naturally refrained from engaging in any discussion of the subject.

I have honour to be,
with the highest respect
Sir,
Your most obedient,
humble Servant,
Oliver Harvey

Local commandant of Police   5 May, 1929
Nicosia,

Sir,

     In continuation of our report dated 5.5.29, regarding the athletes of Greece and Egypt, we have the honour to report that some of them arrived here today at 12 noon.

     2. Soon after their arrival here they proceeded to the "Commercial Club" where the Mayor of Nicosia delivered a speech briefly as follows:–

> "Greek brothers, on behalf of the Greek people of the Capital of this enslaved Island I salute you. You have come from our free mother in order to celebrate with us, the slaves, the sports which our grandfathers have established. Our nation has a long history and the whole civilized nations respect it.

Hurrah the free brothers, Hurrah the Union with Greece."
Then the Leader of the Greek and Egyptian athletes named Delas said as follows:–

"Cypriot Greeks, as a representative of the Greek and Egyptian athletes I thank very much the Mayor of the Capital of Cyprus for the gentle reception which he organized for us and I assure him that this reception will be kept in our heart.

Gentlemen, believe me that we recognise your national feelings as ours and we keep them in the depth of our heart. Let us fraternally celebrate the Pan-Cypriot sports as the sports are the only means by which a struggle is successful. Cheers for athletism."

Then they proceeded to "Cleopatra Hotel" headed by the Municipal Band.

3. At 3.30 p.m. they proceeded to the Stadium "Pancypria." The athletes held a procession in the Stadium. Mr. G. Poullias thanked the athletes of Greece and Egypt.

4. Mr. Th. Ioannides advocate of Nicosia, read a decree of the Committee "Pancypria" by which the valuable services of Mr. Th. Theodotou were mentioned. He said that Mr. Th. Theodotou was an elected Member of the Legislative Council and Executive Council for 35 years, he is the founder and president of the "Pancypria" for 25 years, he was sent to Italy by the British Government on 1901 in order to study the Cooperative Associations, and he went to England three times as a member of the mission for the political affairs of Cyprus. Mr. Poullias decorated Mr. Theodotou and proclaimed him as honorary president of the "Pancypria."

Then Mr. Th. Theodotou addressed the people briefly as follows:–

"I am about to terminate the last years of my life but I shall sacrifice the rest of my life for our enslaved country by every struggle and even by blood. Greek brothers, we are ruled by a tyrannic Government and this is the English Government. They are endeavouring by every fraudulent trick to reduce the Greek feelings but they will never succeed in this. Let them put heavy taxes on us, let them rule us like the uncivilized nations, they shall never succeed to reduce our national feelings, on the contrary our feelings are strengthened and we become more courageous. If they leave us ragged we shall call for Greece, if they turn us into Lords we shall again call for Greece and only Greece. The Prisons are strengthening us, the deportations are beautifying us and the hanging is sanctifying us. This is witnessed by the 300 martyrs who were killed by the barbarous nation, also the hanging of Archbishop Kyprianos and Patriarch Grigoris and so many others whose blood painted the waters of the Bosphoros. By our strong will and sacrifice we shall succeed our liberty and will fly to the bosom of our mother Greece and under the blue-white flag we shall go forward together with our brothers of Dodecanisos and Vorioipirotes (Northern Epirus) we shall march to the town

of our dreams (Constantinople). We shall wake up the dou-
ble-headed Eagle who is sleeping in the Churches, we shall
give him power to fly under the arches of St. Sophia. Hurrah the Union with Greece, Down with Tyranny."
There were about 2000 people present. The Greek national anthem was played by
the municipal Band at the end of the sports and the athletes left for Limassol at 7 p.m.

We have etc.,
Nicola, Corporal
Kleanthi, L/Corporal

III. Memorial, 20 July 1929 (CO 67/227/6)

MEMORIAL
Dealing with the chief grievances
of the people of Cyprus addressed to his
Lordship the Secretary of the State for the
Colonies by the Greek elected members
of the Legislative Council.

1929

The right Honourable
The Lord Passfield, P.C.
Secretary of State
Downing Street
London.

Your Lordship,

1. We the respectfully undersigned Greek members of the Legislative Council of
Cyprus, representing about the 5/6 of its population, have the honour to submit for your
Lordship's kind consideration and earnest solicitude the following:
[British comment:

Last Census figures
    Greek 244,887)
   Moslem 61,338) = $\underline{244,887}$ = $\underline{4}$ approximately.
   Others   4,480)   65,818   1
Accordingly the Greek population is 4/5 of the total.]

2. The victory of Labour party at the last general election in England and its consequent accession to power has been a source of particular gratification to the Greek people of Cyprus. The more so as having been exceptionally oppressed and greatly wronged
by the Conservative party—the governing body of yesterday—they reasonably hope for a
more humane treatment from a Government coming from a party, which was formed by
the rousing of consciences against a bourgeois dictatorship, and in consequence better in
a position to appreciate the righteous struggles of a people—such as the people of Cy-

prus—fighting against foreign oppression. The recent declarations of policy made by the Labour party during the last general election campaign and the ideology both of the present Government and its eminent Leader so officially proclaimed by him at the Socialist Meeting of Berne in 1919, afford the Cyprus people a cause for rejoining in the Labour Victory.

We, therefore, in their name and on their behalf request to be allowed to submit to the Labour Government and to its Leader on the occasion of their victory and their assumption of authority, the expression of the most cordial congratulations of this people.

3. A foremost and basic complaint of the Greek people of Cyprus is that, contrary to their expressed unanimous will and against all justice, they are being kept separated from their Mother country Greece, with whom sacred and unbreakable ties of blood, religion, language, traditions and national conscience link them together.

Cyprus was without the knowledge of its people subjected to British administration in virtue of the Treaty of 1878, which has been very rightly declared by great British statesmen and famous English papers, to be a shame for British policy. This treaty has confirmed an unconscientious and unprincipled act of purchase—sale of a people, by agreement between England and Turkey, without the knowledge of the Cyprus people themselves who were thus made like livestock the subject-matter of a shameful dealing. This in accordance with the aforesaid Treaty, Cyprus has been administered by Great Britain and badly administered too and despite its persistent claims for national restoration it was kept by England and was made a British Colony in 1914, under the lively and strong protest of the Island which in written form was handed by the Archbishop and Ethnarch to the Governor on the occasion of the annexation official ceremony.

And all this on the morrow of the great war, during which the peoples in general and individuals in particular voluntarily shed their blood, having given faith to the sincerity of such Liberal promises as were held out and widely proclaimed by Great Britain and the Allies regarding the Liberty and self-determination of small nations. But as a result of all this sacrifice the world has seen again the 'right of might' only prevail.

The bitter disappointment felt by the Greek people of Cyprus on the frustration of their hopes for a national settlement, far from disheartening them in pursuing their national aspirations has certainly caused in their minds a diminution of the prestige enjoyed by Great Britain, as a country proud of the strict adhesion to her promises, and a country where justice both internally and internationally reigns as law supreme.

[British comment:

1920 Deputation informed by the Under Secretary of the State at interview on the 26th October, 1920, that no change in the status of Cyprus was contemplated and that he could hold out no hope of reconsideration of this question in the near future. (Secretary of State's decision published in 1920 Gazette, p.535.)

To sundry Resolutions sent by the Members of the Legislative Council and the Archbishop protesting against the Secretary of State's decision, and asking for the taking of a plebiscite, the Secretary of State replied that His Majesty's Government could hold out no hope of Union being sanctioned and disallowing plebiscite proposal. (S. of S. despatches of 3/5/21 and 18/4/22.)

Archbishop's Memorial of 1922. Informed that no good purpose served by submission of further Memorials in view of the fact that His Majesty's Government could hold out no hope of Union with Greece. (S. of S. despatch of 18/4/22.)

Archbishop's Memorial of 1925. Informed that he must clearly understand that as already pointed out to him the Union question was finally closed and cannot be re-opened. The Secretary of State's reply was published in the Gazette. (Gov. despatch 148 of 5/5/25; S. of S. despatch 118 of 21/5/25.)

Memorial by Greek-Christian Members of the Legislative Council of the 17th November, 1925, for Union with Greece or failing that for self-government. Informed that Union question definitely closed and cannot be re-opened, and reminding them of their Oath of Allegiance to His Majesty.

As to self-government they were told that Cyprus had not yet attained such a degree of political development as to justify grant of increased constitutional powers. (Gov. despatch Conf. of 16/12/25; S. of S. despatch Conf. of 21/1/26.)

Archbishop's letter re alleged aspirations of Cyprus people for Union—The Secretary of State stated that the Archbishop's animadversions re "enslaved people" with "national aspirations" were most unseemly and deprecated such disloyal expression coming from an Archbishop in a British Colony. (Gov. despatch 213 of 2/7/25 S. of S. despatch Conf. of 21/7/25.)

Memorials 1928. In letter to the Governor dated 4th June, 1928, submitting congratulations on His Majesty's Birthday the Archbishop at the request of the Greek members of the Legislative Council and Mayors submitted a prayer that Cyprus be restored to "Mother" Greece. In transmitting to the Secretary of State the Governor offered no observations as views of His Majesty's Government had already been publicly stated and the Secretary of State was well aware of them. (Gov. despatch 206 of 6/6/28.)

Further Memorial from Mayors, Greek Members and Synod on the occasion of the "Jubilee" reiterating demand for Union. Transmitted by Governor's Confidential despatch of 5/6/28 suggesting "nothing to add to last communication." The Secretary of State approved of this reply.

Memorial 1929. Letter from the Archbishop transmitting copies of Memorials for Union addressed to Houses of Parliament, Members of the Royal Family, etc., etc. Copies sent to the Secretary of State by O.A.G's despatch Confidential of 6/2/29 pointing out that no demand from general community, agitation solely Church movement in alliance with a small clique of politicians, mass of population indifferent, etc.

NOTES.   (a) Venizelos' declaration at Rome that no Cyprus question exists between Greece and His Britannic Majesty's Government and his observations this summer to Mr. Artemis, local advocate, (by him reported to me) that "Enosis" representations were inopportune, and that Cypriots should cooperate with the Cyprus Government.

(b) Apart from vociferous Cypriots in Athens there is said to be very little demand for Union from Greece.

(c) "Union" would mean increased taxation (and, as in Crete, expenditure thereof in Greece), military service, inrush of Greek officials.

(d) With regard to the reference to the "agreement" between England and Turkey whereby Cyprus came under British administration it is pertinent to remark that without this "agreement" Cyprus would have remained under the Turks and by now would have been under ?

4. Great Britain in denying to satisfy the just national claims of this Island put forward only by way of excuse and certainly not as a serious reason, her obligation to protect a small Turkish Minority which, it was alleged, would be wronged by the change of the political status of Cyprus.

[British comment:

The Turkish minority is one of many considerations.]

It is, though, evident that in thus excusing herself Great Britain on the one hand disregards the principals of the law of nations and introduces a fallacious theory, (which, were it to be adopted would have to reverse many post-war international conventions) and on the other hand on the pretense of doing justice to a small minority, exercises great injustice and oppression on the large majority. England moreover in handing over Cyprus to Greece would have every opportunity and all means of protecting the rights of the minority by "convention," the observance of which would be amply guaranteed by her own power, though the great rights and the protection already enjoyed by the minorities in Greece would afford sufficient assurance.

5. Having denied justice to this Island as to its claim for a national settlement Great Britain has not acted in a fairer way in her treatment of Cyprus in other respects. The same unjust and imperialistic policy of administration as was first established continues till this day and in worse form.

[British comment:

Denial of justice is a gross exaggeration and perversion of facts. The liberty of speech and action enjoyed by Cypriots is the cause of comment from most visitors, including Greeks, and is frequently cited in the Athenian Press.]

A clear manifestation of such an autocratic administration and its chief cause and reason at the same time, is the so-called constitution of the Colony, which was granted to her by the Letters Patent of the 1/5/1925 and the Instructions attached thereto and by the Legislative Council Order of the 6th February, 1925. This constitution is exactly the same as, and in those respects where it differs of a still more restricted application than the pseudo-constitution which was granted to the Island, very soon after the British occupation (vide Order in Council 14th Sept., 1878 and Feb., 1882).

According to the existing constitution there is no Legislating Assembly, but merely a Legislative Council. Its powers are very limited and where they are a little extended are so much restricted as to annihilate the voice of the whole people of the Island in general and of the large majority in particular. That is to say:

a) The Legislative Council can introduce no vote, resolution or law for the appropriation of part of the public revenues or purpose a bill imposing a tax without having previously obtained permission from the Governor.

[British comment:

This is governed by the Letters Patent and Royal Instructions thereunder which in turn are presumably modelled on similar documents in force in most Crown Colonies.]

b) It has no control over the whole of the sums to be appropriated during the voting of the Budget, a great portion of them being beyond its control by virtue of existing Imperial Orders in Council and laws.

[British comment:

Usual Crown Colony procedure providing necessary safeguards for provision of essential services which cannot safely be left to the vagaries of an unbalanced electorate.]

c) It enjoys no substantive participation in the preparation of the Budget, nor is it entitled to exercise any control over the estimates of expenditure.

[British comment:

No Legislature participates in the preparation of the Budget. It has however full opportunity of criticism and power of amendment and modification, and exercises it amply.

In general its obtaining rights and privileges are further curtailed by the power reserved to the Governor or the King in the exercise of the prerogative of disallowance and they are completely annihilated by the King's right to legislate for the Colony by Order in Council not only where the circumstances are such as to call for such extraordinary measures but also in respect of current routine in the service.

[British comment:

Recognised Crown Colony procedure.

The prerogative is exercised in exceptional circumstances only although constitutionally it may be exercised without any limitation.]

We cite the following most recent examples of this latter party:

a) The Budget of 1927 rejected by the vote of the elected members of the Legislative Council was nevertheless put into force in its entirety by an order in Council from the King.

[British comment:

There is no suggestion how the machinery of Government was to function if supply was withheld. "The most drastic form of obstruction to which Elected Members can resort is the complete refusal of supply." (S. of S. despatch No.47 of 24/2/27.) There was and is no alternative but to invoke Royal prerogative and the Members of the Legislative Council were clearly warned of this and graver possibilities in my Speech to them of the 26th December, 1926, attached.]

b) Connected with the Budget and for the purposes of covering a deficiency provided therein a new levy to the sum of £40,000 was also imposed in the same year without the advice and consent of the Legislative Council.

[British comment:

This refers to the introduction of the Cyprus (Customs, Excise & Revenue) Order in Council, 1927, imposing additional taxation on luxury articles, and articles other than necessaries of life. Additional duties estimated to bring in £39,400, which formed part of the above rejected Supply Bill. (O.A.G's despatch No.401 of 29/11/26.)]

c) The Penal Law published in the Government Gazette as a draft bill in order to be later introduced into the Legislative Council as expressly stated in the preamble to the said bill, was imposed as law from London by Royal Order, without its being laid before the Legislative Council and the advice of its members thereon being obtained.

[British comment:

The new Code lay published as a Bill for over 10 months. At the request of Members of the Legislative Council a Committee of 5 of its Members was appointed to consider draft and suggest amendments. After a lapse of over 8 months it had not functioned in any way. During all this time no constructive amendments had been suggested from any local source. Reform of Cyprus Criminal Code urgently required. Judiciary for years had pointed this out in open Court. Old Code inadequate and in consequence both moral and social conditions of Colony prejudicially affected. (O.A.G's Conf. despatch of 19/12/28.) District Commissioners and Police all subscribe to the beneficial effect the Code has had. Figures show that the number of cases of serious crime for the first six months of 1929 as compared with the same period in 1928 are 1069: 798. Decrease 278 or 25 %.]

d) During the last session of the Legislative Council a Pensions bill, as proposed by the Government was rejected. The same measure has just been sanctioned from England as law, by means of a Royal Order in Council.

[British comment:

This measure was thrown out by the "elected" majority of the Legislative Council on the first reading without any consideration of the Bill on its merits. (O.A.G's despatches Conf. of 15th March and 20th March, 1929.)]

6. But if by all these it is shown that the present constitution of the Island in nothing else than a mockery for the people of Cyprus as a whole, for the Greek people of Cyprus forming the 5/6 of the population, it constitutes a daring and unconcealed provocation, as, owing to the composition of the Legislative Council with 9 appointed officials, 3 Moslem and 12 Greek elected members under the chairmanship of the English Governor, the stifling of the voice of the 5/6 of the population is nearly secured, the majority in the country being thus turned into a minority, a form of tyranny is thereby established over the heads of the majority of the inhabitants of the Island.

[British comment:

The fact remains that there is an unofficial majority, which places Cyprus in a more favourable position than many Crown Colonies. When the Moslems and Greeks combine Government is in a minority of 6. Numbers of cases are on record where measures have been thrown out by the unofficial majority, nor is there any justification for the assumption that the Turkish Members of the Legislative Council have a perverted or inferior sense of the interests of Cyprus, which indeed they view with more objectivity and much less bias than their elected colleagues.]

The administration of the country is substantially in the hand of the English Governor and the English officials as his Executive Councillors. The Governor being in fact responsible and answerable to the Home Government in London only, has no responsibility towards the tax-paying people of Cyprus.

[British comment:

The administration of the Government must lie in the hands of the British Governor and his senior British officials, for with notable exceptions the Cypriot for a variety of reasons cannot yet be relied on to be fair, unbiased, or in cases honest. Regrettable but indisputable instances are available where they have been granted unchecked or unsupervised power, e.g. Municipalities, Boards of Education, Hospitals, etc., and the standard of personal, commercial and general morality is lamentably low.]

That is to say:

a) The Executive Council consisting of not more that four persons appointed from among the high English Officials is, like a Cabinet, only an Advisory body, the Governor not being bound by their advice.
[*British comment:*

True: but if the Governor acts in opposition to the advice of his Executive Council he has to report the grounds for so doing to the Secretary of State, whilst members may require their opinions to be recorded on the Minutes (Royal Instructions of 10th March, 1925.)]

b) The Governor is not bound to nominate members of the Executive Council from among the native elements.
[*British comment:*

He is not: but in practice always does so.]

c) The additional three members who are in fact called to attend its meetings are not always and necessarily taken from among the elected members of the Legislative Council.
[*British comment:*

Under the Royal Instructions they are not required to be, but for the last few years at any rate two out of the three have been Members of the Legislative Council. There are many objections, though some advantages, to the same unofficial persons serving on both the Executive Council and the Legislative Council. Furthermore, local representation is wider if they do not.]

If should thus be observed that under (c), the most liberal of the above cited instances, the constitution of the Executive Council, gives to the 5/8 of the opinion therein to the foreign Government and reserves to the tax-paying inhabitants of the country the 3/8 only. Furthermore to the Greek element which forms the 5/6 of the population a 2/8 portion is granted. But it also should be pointed out that there always exists the possibility of either the one or both the native elements being absolutely excluded from the said Council or of their being unevenly and disproportionately represented therein, in as much as it is not at all binding for the Governor to make his nomination and selection of the additional members according to their actual numbers in the Island. In addition, the fact that the Governor is not bound to invite always the additional members to attend the meetings of the Council and to participate in its deliberations, should not be lost sight of.
[*British comment:*

It is not necessarily intended that the Executive Council is selected on a "party" basis.]

[*7. Missing.]*

8. Consequently the present constitution of the Executive Council allows of many serious transgressions either on the part of the all-powerful Governor alone or of the other official members, whereby foreing interest may be favoured or promoted to the grave prejudice of important interests of the country or of private individuals. Unfortunately the policy of the Government, during these last years, tends to give its wholehearted and unqualified support to British capital alone, thus endeavouring to facilitate its introduction and domination in the country to the detrimental prejudice of local capital and of the existing enterprises.

Examples do not lack to testify to this conduct of the local Government. On the one hand exemption from import duty allowed to English Companies in order to import foreign materials and goods abounding locally and on the other denial to grant similar privileges to Cypriot enterprises to import raw material not abounding in the country; facilities on the part of the Government to English Companies and imposition of difficulties in the way of Cypriot or Graeco-Cypriot capital during these last years; these are sufficient evidence to support the statements made above.

[British comment:

Cyprus is a British Colony, and an integral part of the British Empire, and it is therefore natural that British capital should be encouraged. But foreign, including "Graeco-Cypriot" capital, is welcomed (cf. American mines) when forthcoming for purposes other than of usury.

It is unfortunate that the Memorialists do not furnish the examples at which they hint. One case in mind no doubt is that of the Cyprus Silk Filature which Government is endeavouring to keep going for the benefit of silk growers throughout the Colony and part of its population employed by the Filature. The closing down of this enterprise would deprive many inhabitants of a living and be a serious set back to an important and potentially more important local industry, but would be a matter of indifference and even satisfaction to local usurers.

They make no reference to the concession granted to the Cyprus Tannery, a purely Cypriot concern, regarding free importation of hides and tanning material.

The concession granted to the Filature does not affect Revenue: that to the Cyprus Tannery reduces import duty revenue by several thousands of pounds.

The above are the only two instances which can be traced.

It has to be remembered too that without "foreign" i.e. British capital the Agricultural Bank could not have been established and the financing of Cooperative Credit Societies made possible. It was made clear in the deliberations of the Agricultural Bank Loan Committee, 1927, that local capital could not be looked for for this purpose.

Mr. Pilavachi, a Cypriot capitalist from Egypt who visited the Colony in 1928 in order to found a much needed and loudly demanded Cyprus Hotel Company, left in despair, having failed to collect from the whole Island more than £2,000 in conditional promises. I alluded to the local investment problem in the last section of paragraph XXIV of my Speech (attached) of April 17th, 1928, and later in paragraph 9 (attached) of my Confidential despatch of the 5th June of the same year.]

9. We wish to lay special stress on the constitutional monstrosity created in Cyprus by the establishment of an Executive Council, holding the place of Government yet complete in itself and entirely independent of the representation of the people in the Legislative Council.

This forms the main cause of continuous troubles, for on the introduction by the Government of any measures into the Legislative Council for its sanction in case of measures not approved by the Greek elected Members, either of the following things will occur, namely: The Government will either succeed in getting them past by the assistance of the votes of the Turkish elected Members, being added to the official votes, much to the displeasure and annoyance of the 5/6 of the population, or else the proposed measures will be rejected by the united votes of the elected Members, who having no voice in the

formation of the Government and consequently not being connected with it by political programme or otherwise, will, as it is very natural, disagree with the Government in many cases and throw out its Bills. And though the Government has at its disposal the Royal Orders in Council in order to meet with any resulting difficulties, yet, it should be remembered, this policy is certainly not conductive to smooth relations between Government and people, and badly serves the regular function of the Government machine.
[British comment:

I cannot follow the basis of argument. The Executive Council in Cyprus is constituted in the main similarly to that of other Colonies.]

10. Under such conditions of Government for the last fifty years it is but a natural consequence that this place reached its present deplorable state. Agriculture, its principle source of wealth, is found in a primitive condition compared to other countries. There are no harbours, though we have been governed for the last fifty years by the first naval nation of the world. Local means of communication are in such a ruinous state that an estimate of £360,000 was made for their repair and restoration. And so long as the annual budget could not be charged with such an exorbitant burden, it became necessary to apply for the sanctioning of a big loan. Elementary education is but recently assisted by half measures, and secondary education is left entirely to itself and to the care of the Communities. The forests, or what still remains of this beauty and wealth of the Island in ancient times, are half destroyed, and very little has been done for reafforestation, while the Government has completed the destructive work of fires by cutting down large wooded areas for the needs of war.
[British comment:

The "deplorable state" is refuted by figures of increasing imports and exports. The spending power of the population is increasing day by day as the import figures show, as also the decreasing figures of "forced sales."

Agriculture is admittedly backward, but the responsibility lies partly with the farmers who, despite all the efforts of Government and the Agricultural Department, are conservative to a degree and will not change their archaic and uneconomical methods. In spite of all these difficulties however agriculture is going ahead apace. All over the Island are Government agriculture, experimental and demonstrational plots, gardens, vineyards, fruit groves, etc. Within the last 10 years the increase in orange gardens, potato fields, vineyards, etc., has been very large, and in tobacco and many other items phenomenal. With the advent, last year, of a capable, experienced and energetic Director of Agriculture with a constructive and progressive policy, all that is wanted is active cooperation on the part of the Cypriot for agriculture to boom. See also the Director of Agriculture's Report for 1928, transmitted with Governor's despatch No.280 of 21st August, 1929.

Harbours. "No harbours." Famagusta, although small and circumscribed, is a good harbour of its kind and enjoys a good reputation. In 1926 Mr. Haji Pavlou in the Legislative Council stated "For the present we might take pride in Famagusta Harbour . . . sufficient for the present requirements of trade." Mr. Kakoyannis objected strongly to raising of a loan for Harbour Works. Seven elected Members (including 5 of the present signatories) voted against the Resolution for provision of funds for harbours. The open roadsteads of Larnaca and Limassol compare most favourably with similar parts in the Mediterranean, and Government is continually improving the facilities.

Communications. In 1878 there was but one road (Nicosia-Larnaca). Now there are about 900 miles of main and secondary roads under the control of the Public Works Department. This is apart from village roads, including which Cyprus has more miles of road than England and Wales in proportion to population and than Scotland in proportion to area. The present condition of many of the Cyprus roads is due to lack of funds and false economy in the past accentuated by the fact, common to many parts of the world, that roads are now called upon to carry very much heavier, and a different type of traffic, than that for which they were originally intended.

A valuable and progressive road scheme at an estimated cost of £300,000 is now under way.

Education. Grant to Elementary Education in 1913–14, £6,200.

Grant to Elementary Education in 1929, £59,000 and will I hope be substantially increased for 1930.

Forests. The guilt for the destruction of the Forests cannot be laid entirely at the door of Government. The depletion was a "fait accompli" when Great Britain assumed occupation. Remedial measures were put in hand forthwith, Laws were passed in 1879 and 1881 the main purpose of which was to protect the forests from the ruinous practices of the people.

Large sums of money have been spent on re-afforestation, but illicit cutting of timber, indiscriminate grazing of goats, and other prejudicial actions on the part of the people themselves have proved serious obstacles. During the last 10 years no less a sum than £78,000 has been provided for planting and re-afforestation. Prevention of fires and measures thereto bulk large on the work of the Forest Department which in this work has to contend against the dryness of the climate, and the lawlessness of certain elements of the population.

The timber sold for war purposes was but a very slight proportion of the forest resources and exceptionally good prices were obtained.

The Forest Enquiry Report of 1927 and the visit of Professor Troup this autumn will determine future policy.]

11. And all these at a time when the burden of taxation has long since reached the highest possible limit of endurance of the Cypriot tax-payer. The total amount of taxation paid by him yearly is £750,000 approximately and his yearly gross production, mostly agricultural is computed according to official statistical elements at 3½ million pounds, i.e. the proportion of taxation to the gross production is between 20 to 25% which represents, if it does not exceed, the amount of capitalization.

[British comment:

This figure of "taxation paid by the Cypriot" viz. £750,000 is the total Revenue of the Colony which is of course not all raised by taxation; neither is all the Revenue contributed by Cypriots. It is estimated that the rate of taxation per head of population in Cyprus is £2.1.0. So far as can be ascertained, in Greece it is £4.0.0. This year's "Whitakers" gives:–Australia £9.1.6. Canada £6.19.4. France £8.5.10. Germany £5.6.5. Italy £3.8.9. New Zealand £14.0.9. South Africa £11.17.2. United Kingdom £15.2.8.

In the opinion of the Comptroller of Customs and Excise the production figure of 3½ millions is greatly underestimated. He estimates it now at 5 millions.]

12. But why is this? Because a Government foreign to the country, a Government composed of officers in the public service—another form of constitutional monstrosity—a Government, the actions of which lie beyond the effective control of the representatives of the people, in as much as by Royal Orders in Council, a facile source of legislation, it can easily fill up any gap and get over the refusal of the elected Members to pass a legislative measure even the most injurious—such a Government will always prove to be, in its disposal of the revenues of the Island, unscrupulously and unreasonably lavish and also devoid of any correct scientific criterion of public finance.
[British comment:
See comments on paragraph 6 of memorial.]

13. Thus in a country where no charge for war debts and the maintenance of an army and navy exists; in a country without any important and serious public works to maintain and with no considerable support for education and agriculture, the total amount of expenditure in the Budget of 1929 has, save the contribution to the Public Ottoman Debt, reached the amazing figure of £735,000. Out of this sum, sufficient, according to certain authoritative statements by non official English residents in the Island for the administration of a country with an area thrice or four times larger than Cyprus and with a population thrice or four times greater than the population of this Island, an amount of 0,57 is appropriated for expenditure in respect of purely administrative matters and a 0,27 portion only is assigned for the welfare of the country. The remainder being spent for the various other departmental services and the maintenance of the property of the state.
[British comment:
The Treasurer reports that he cannot understand how the Memorialists arrive at their figure of £735,000. He computes that of the estimated expenditure of £720,171 for the current year, the amount set aside under the Appropriation Law, 1929, and other statutory authority for cost of administration (Personal Emoluments) represents roughly 42.5% of the total expenditure. (N.B. Even taking into account the heavy expenditure on the Land Registry Department which has a counterpart in very few Colonies, this figure of 42.5% compares most favourably with Personal Emoluments expenditure in five Colonies selected at random. The Treasurer estimates that of the 42.5% allocated to Personal Emoluments the share drawn by British officials is about 18%.

".27 portion assigned to welfare of the country." It is indeed difficult to follow the argument here. Expenditure on personal emoluments of doctors, judges, police, and all other public officers are not unconnected with the general welfare of the country.

There are but half-a-dozen "non-official English residents": not one is in a position to speak with authority or experience of other Colonies.]
Owing to the fact that the Government of Cyprus is composed of English officials from among those employed in the local public service, the waste of the Island revenues becomes altogether unreasonable, developing into a serious financial question, in respect of the very high figure, charged for public salaries due to a supernumerary personnel and to exorbitant emoluments.
[British comment:

"Exorbitant emoluments, supernumerary personnel."

The Memorialists would be absolutely unable to prove justification for use of these adjectives, as both are demonstrably incorrect.]

The fact that there is supernumerary personnel in the service, is admitted even by the public officers themselves, can also be demonstrated by the number of the Government employees in 1913 by comparison to that in 1920 and 1929.

[British comment:

There has most certainly been an increase of personal, but this is a natural corollary to the increase of the activities of Government in order to bring about and keep pace with the progress of the Colony. Many of the Laws which the Memorialists have helped to pass in recent years have of necessity entailed an increase of staff for consequent administration.

"Supernumerary personnel admitted by the public officers themselves." A wild and unsupported statement.]

Thus we have 925 permanent officers in 1913, about 1000 in 1920 and 1220 in 1929, i.e. their number was increased by 30% without an analogous increase of the work in the various departments.

[British comment:

"Without an analogous increase of work." It is most unfortunate in their own interests that the Memorialists make statements of this nature which they cannot prove.]

In order that the high increase of salaries should be well and clearly understood it is sufficient to note that while the number of men in the service increased from 1913 to 1929 by 30%, the amount appropriated for personal emoluments was increased by 200%. It should be further noted that the amount in the Budget of 1929 to be appropriated for personal emoluments covers the 0,477 of the total of the general expenditure therein, the share of Cyprus to the Public Ottoman Debt excepted. This is no doubt due to the fact that the Government, during the period between 1920 and 1921, when the cost of living reached its highest pitch, consolidated the war allowances into fixed salaries without making any provisions for analogous reduction consequent upon the falling of the cost of living.

[British comment:

The Treasurer disputes the statement that Personal Emoluments have increased by 200% during the period stated. He makes the increase 173%.]

In 1920, as far as we know, in England after a determination of the cost of living for the year 1920, at 230, taking as basis 100 for 1914, the Government regulated the increase in respect of the salaries of public Officers as follows: For the first £91.5.0 of the salary an increase of 130% was allowed for any salary exceeding that sum but being under £200.0.0 an increase of 65% was given and for any sum over and above £200.0.0 an increase of 45%. And it was decided also that for any future alternate increase and decrease in the cost of living by 5 units, an alternate increases and decreases by 1/26 should be effected.

[British comment:

The cost of living in England and Cyprus can hardly be said to bear comparison, conditions and circumstances being wholly different.]

In Cyprus the same principle in respect of the increase of salaries was approximately followed. According to certain official data published in the Blue book we have been able to come to the conclusion that the cost of living in Cyprus was raised from 100 in 1913-1914 to 230 in 1920-1921, the latter being the year of the consolidation of the salaries as explained above. It has fallen to-day to 130. Thus in Cyprus as in England approximately the same principle in respect of the increase of salaries prevailed, no provisions whatsoever having been made for proportionate reduction of the allowed increase consequent upon the falling in respect of the cost of living. Owing to this latter omission and the continuous changes both in respect of the classification and the scale of the salaries in the service, it so happened that not only the above referred to salaries (small salaries exempted) were not reduced but in some cases further increases over and above the increased salaries of 1920-1921, were made. The following off hand instances may be taken to illustrate how the salaries would stand had the principle applied in England been made applicable to Cyprus as well.

[British comment:

The Memorial gives the present index figure of cost of living at 130 as compared with 100 in 1913-14 and 230 in 1920-21, but it furnishes no figures in support of the statement.

Unfortunately, we have no exact figures, but from a calculation made with the help of Blue Books, and based on <u>essential commodities only</u> the drop in 1928 as compared with 1920 is 30-35%.

The consensus of opinion amongst officials who have long residence in the Colony is that, taking everything into consideration, the general cost of living now differs but slightly from that in 1920. It is indisputable, too, that it is rising.]

	Salary 1913/4.	Salary 1920/1.	Salary 1928/9.
Colonial Secretary	£800 (100)	£1200 (150)	£1400 (175)
The maximum increase should have reached			£1253
It ought to have been reduced to			£965
He draws to-day			£1400
1st Assistant	£400 (100)	£600 (150)	£675 (187.5)
The maximum increase should have reached			£673
He ought to be drawing to-day			£453
He takes in fact			£675
The Treasurer	£400 (100)	£900 (150)	£1000 (166)
He should have taken as maximum			£963
He should be drawing to-day			£680
But he draws in fact			£1000
A 1st class clerk	£200 (100)	£360 (180)	£325 (162.5)
He ought to be taken as maximum			£383
He ought to be drawing to-day			£243
But he actually takes			£325
A 2nd class clerk	£120 (100)	£185 (154)	£200 (168)
He ought to have taken as maximum			£257
He ought to be drawing to-day			£152
But he actually takes			£200

[British comment:

Salaries in 1913–14 were scandalously low in Cyprus, and even had there been no increase in general cost of living, increases would have been necessary. The 1920 increase was from all accounts wholly inadequate and it is stated on good authority that in 1920 most Government officials found themselves in debt.

The salary of the Treasurer in 1913–14 was £600—not £400. A typographical error.]

14. A further important reason, one of detail but essential, of the heavy salaries paid by Cyprus is the continuous appointment to high-salaried post of officers coming from England—who are in most cases supernumerary in their department, and sometimes prove to be completely inefficient and unsuitable for the post which they are appointed to fill—despite the fact that there are local persons adequately equipped and trained to occupy these posts. Any off hand investigation into the various departments can at once establish that the main service is carried out by the native officers. That most of the English Officials are supernumerary can be proved by the fact that many of them taking advantage of the provisions of the Colonial Regulations, they travel on leave to England without the regular functioning of the machine of the Government being in the least upset or interfered with. How much does the maintenance of such sumptuous personnel cost for the Budget of Cyprus, is evidenced by the official statistics namely: British Officers take to-day £48320.

The English officers who form the Government in order to justify their luxurious salaries did not hesitate to suggest that the salaries of the native officers should be also increased disproportionately to the scale of salaries in force before the war, the financial endurance of the country and the cost of living.

[British comment:

It is necessary to appoint British officials, as save in a few exceptional instances there are no Cypriots "adequately equipped and trained" to occupy the posts.

If there are inefficient British officials it is because the inadequate salaries do not attracted the proper stamp and partly because some have been left in Cyprus too long. Colonies offering better conditions will naturally get the best men.

"Main service is carried out by the native officers." A ludicrous and libellous statement, read with mixed feelings by those British officers who sacrifice health, recreation, domestic life, etc., in an endeavour to carry out the "main service" and train Cypriots in the hope that they may gradually prove themselves capable of administration with less British control and supervision.

When A British official goes on leave, the machinery he has installed goes on working smoothly because in the majority of cases a brother British official undertakes to do his work temporarily in addition to his own.

The Treasurer calculates that British officials take £55,795 not £48,320 as stated.

At the end of 1927 there were on record here 18 cases of British officials in which the Secretary of State had either negatived reductions or requested that salaries be increased. There have been others since, whilst recently occurred that of Engineers, wherein Cyprus had to institute an increase to come into line with "market rates."]

15. Incidentally and with reference to the question relating to the present position of the public officers in the Island, the fact that the local Government favours the Moslem and the other less significant minorities in the country in order that it should enjoy the support of their representatives in the Council, should also be noted. This unjustifiable favouritism and partiality on the part of the Government has been the chief cause of the above referred to alliance and co-operation by means of which the Government has, even since the occupation, been imposing its will on the country against the expressed opinion and desire of the large majority of the Greek population. The following table conclusively proves the partial policy of the local Government:

STATISTICAL TABLE OF 1927 (a)

		Proportion in respect of the total of officers	In proportion to the population it should have been	Salaries in £	Proportion in respect of the total of salaries	Average per head
Greeks	1101	0.56	0.80	123,820	0.481	112. 9. 0
Turks	699	0.36	0.17	70,680	0.275	101. 2. 3
English	76	0.04	0.03	48,320	0.190	635. 0. 0
Catholics	56	0.03	0.03	10,792	0.042	192. 0. 0
Armenians	21	0.01	0.03	3,180	0.012	159. 0. 0

a) NOTE.–In accordance with an official answer to a question by the Hon. Hadji-Eftychios HadjiProcopi M.L.C. for the Orini division. And it should further be noted that the sum of £256,792, the total amount of the salaries, does not agree with the sum as mentioned in the estimates for 1927-1928 published in the Blue Book of the year according to which the total is much higher in 1927. (The total of the personal emoluments together with the amount of pensions (£38,090) being £312,910, in 1928 the total of the personal emoluments together with the amount of pensions (£42,100) being £326,425).
[British comment:

The insinuation of favouritism and partiality is unfounded. Selection for various posts is made on the merits of the individuals. As stated, the figures were supplied officially in reply to a question in the Legislative Council. A copy of the question and full reply furnished is enclosed. See also O.A.G's despatch to the Secretary of State No. 369 of the 5th October, 1928.

The conclusion to be drawn from this representation is that, given power to do so, the Greek element would fill appointments with Greek-Cypriots irrespective of capabilities, etc.]

16. In addition to this partiality on the part of the Government it should also be noted that in pursuance on the same as above stated policy, it pays by way of compensation, since the time of the abolition of the tithe, and out of the public revenues a sum of £5,959, to the Evcaf, a Moslem institution, and to other Moslem private owners of tithe. This is done arbitrarily, against the existing laws and without a shadow of legal obligation for the Government, it being purely an act of grace as was admitted in Council by the Hon. the Attorney General himself.

[British comment:

This matter was raised in the Legislative Council on the 8ᵗʰ of December, 1927, when in reply to questions by Messrs. Stavrinakis and Kakoyannis an undertaking was given that the Attorney-General should furnish a Memorandum on the history of Evkaf and Moslem Private Owners' Tithe Compensation. The Greek-speaking electives had requested that their writing should be submitted to the Secretary of State after they had considered the Attorney-General's statement. Further copies were laid on the table at the Legislative Council meeting of the 23ʳᵈ December, 1928, but up to the date of submission of the present Memorial (which makes no allusion to the Memorandum) no representations have been received.

As however the Officer Administering the Government gave an undertaking that their views in writing (together with the Speeches of the meeting) would be forwarded to the Secretary of State, I attach herewith copies of the Attorney-General's Memorandum and the relevant minutes of the Legislative Council.

I agree that the compensation is without legal obligation and purely an act of grace for which however the Cyprus Government is bound by the promise of my predecessor. I have reasons to believe that, if the Private Tithes Compensation could be settled (presumably by commutation), the objection to the continuation of Evkaf compensation might be withdrawn but, as above stated, I still await any concrete suggestions from the members of the Legislative Council for dealing with the problem they have raised.

The Memorial surprisingly omits reference to the standard and, in my opinion, justified grievance of the payment of the Sheri Courts out of General Revenue, of which I hope before long to submit suggestions for a solution.]

17. If for the facts explained above the local Government is to a great extent to blame for the suggestion in each case made by it to the Colonial Office, the Central Government in England is wholly responsible for the grave injustice done to this country from 1878 till 1928 by means of yearly financial extortion on the ground of payment of the so called Tribute to Turkey or, as it was later called share of Cyprus of the Turkish debt charge. By virtue of the Treaty of 1878 and especially of the Appendices attached thereto, England undertook to pay to Turkey a sum of £92800 which was calculated to be the excess of revenues over the expenditure in the Island. But contrary to the clear provision of the Convention that England should pay this sum to Turkey, Cyprus was made to provide its payment unjustly out of its own privation; nor can this injustice be excused on the ground that the principal signatory to the terms of the Convention helped Cyprus to make it payments by means of the so-called grant-in-aid, which were yearly voted by the Imperial Parliament. During the whole of the 50 years that elapsed since the British occupation a sum of £2640000, apart from the aforesaid grants-in-aid went out of Cyprus and has served to secure the payment of interest to the bondholders of the Ottoman Loan of the Crimean war, which had though been denounced by Turkey since 1881.

[British comment:

According to a calculation made by the Treasurer: -

PERIOD – JULY 1878 – DECEMBER 1928

Share of Cyprus of the Turkish Debt charge	*£4,675,332*
Less Grant-in aid………………………	*1,989,885*
	£2,685,447]

18. From the sum thus yearly paid a sum of about £11,000 remained as a surplus after the payment of the interest on the above referred to bonds which has been invested, ever since, with the Bank of England and forms a separate fund.

A capital of £475,000 has accumulated until 1914, which though morally at least belonging to the financially oppressed and exhausted people of Cyprus is nevertheless retained by wealthy and prosperous England.

[British comment:

There is no record available locally to enable these figures to be checked.]

19. If, the act of England in thus retaining the said sum is from a moral point of view blameable, her conduct in charging Cyprus with the same sum in a new form and name i.e. "share of Cyprus of the Turkish debt charge" is undoubtedly far more reprehensible; the reason being that if, until 1914, in forcing Cyprus to make payment of this sum, England put forward the obligations arising from the Treaty of 1878, after the abolition and avoidance of that Treaty, by the annexation of Cyprus on the 5th of November 1914, no such justification could any more be pleaded. Because: a) in the Treaty of Lausanne, which settled all question with Turkey after the war, no reference whatsoever is made to Cyprus, as being in any way liable for a share in the payment of the Turkish Public Debt. b) The loan of 1855 did not form part of the Turkish Public Debt since 1881, nor does it appear in the table attached to the said Treaty and c) no legal relation exists between this loan and the revenues of Cyprus—the surplus of the Tribute of Egypt and the revenues of the ports of Smyrna and Syria being answerable for its payment.—It therefore becomes manifest how arbitrary was the act of the British Government in depriving Cyprus for 14 further years of these important sums, in order to relieve herself and France from the onus of providing as guarantors the amount of the interests payable to the bondholders of the Turkish loan of 1855. The sums so unjustly paid by Cyprus amount to £588,000.

[British comment:

See Governor's despatch No. 349 of the 19th October, 1927.]

20. At long last Great Britain having felt the injustice of such payments tried to make amends by raising the annual grants in aid to £92,000 on condition however that the sum of £10000 be annually paid by the Island towards the Empire defence. But the charge for this same sum of £92,000 continues formally to be made on the estimates, for unknown future purposes, though outbalanced by an equal grant-in-aid. Yet the Island until 1922 are still fully felt in their different manifestations.

21. We have so far tried to explain in broad lines the anomalous and unfortunate state of the Island and its disastrous effects, due to the basic cause which is that this place is governed against its will by foreign rule, arbitrary and autocratic in its essence.

In laying these facts before your Lordship, we have the honour to request your Lordship's kind consideration and earnest attention to the matter, trusting that the Government, adorned by your Lordship and other eminent Leaders of the Labour party, will grant as the only real remedy and solution, which is Union with our Mother country Greece.

We have to declare to your Lordship, to the British people, and to the whole world that the Greek people of Cyprus, being fully aware and conscious of their national rights, and desirous of the real and true advancement of their interests in general, will never cease to demand and claim from the ruling Power their national settlement, as an act of justice and a beneficial solution of their problems

The Greek people of Cyprus, far from being inspired by any anti-British feeling and truly caring for the Imperial British interests, trust that Great Britain can in her power, grant the just claims of the people of Cyprus and at the same time safeguard her own interests by special Conventions. They further hope and are fully confident that the new Government, under the enlightened leadership of that great herald of the liberties of nations at the Socialist Meeting of Berne, will, during its life do justice to them, thus honouring the ideology of its party in particular, and England in general.

22. In regard to the other questions explained in this present Memorandum, if the British Government is of opinion that nowise injures primely itself and its reputation and secondly the Cyprus people can and may leave the same political state. But, if it cares to preserve the prestige of the British name, it must and it is an imperative duty with it to:
[British comment:
In other words apparently "If Union with Greece" is not approved.]

A) Grant to this Island a constitution by which:
   a) The representatives of the people in the Council will be vested with full and unlimited legislative power regarding all local matters; but making the necessary exemptions and reservations for matters affecting the general interest of the British Empire.
      The Members of the Council to be only elective the two elements, forming the population, to be represented therein in proportion to their numbers.
   b) In the Executive Council the majority will be given to persons elected by the Legislative Council from among its own Members or from outside persons, only three British born officials participating in the Executive i.e. the Colonial Secretary, the Attorney General, and the Treasurer of the Island.
   c) The Governor will have only the right of disallowance in the ratification of laws.
   d) The decision of the Executive will bind the Governor.
   e) The king in Council will not enact laws for the Island except in extraordinary cases provided for in the constitution.
B) Have British born officials removed from Cyprus and leave only three the aforementioned i. e. the Colonial Secretary, the Attorney General, and the Treasurer.
C) Have the rights of the minorities protected by a special clause in the constitution and also their appointment in the public service in proportion to their numbers.
D) Discontinued the following payments:

a) Compensation to the Evcaf and to individual owners of Tithe now paid as an act of grace.

b) The taxes of conquest paid to the Evcaf.

[British comment:

"Taxes of Conquest." This reference is not understood.]

E) Return the following sums and place them at the disposal of the Cyprus Government:

    a) The surplus of the Tribute as stated in paragraph 18 of the Memorandum amounting to £475000 and

    b) The sums unjustly and illegally collected as stated in paragraph 19 of this Memorandum amounting to £588000. These two sums coming up to £1,063,000 would be sufficient if applied to the Island to supply its great and vital needs, and form the basis of its future prosperity.

23. We have, Your Lordship, endeavoured to describe in outline the miserable state of the Island in every respect, after 50 years of British administration, and to point out the chief causes of such a state, interpreting thus the aspirations and conceptions of the people we represent. But in order that the Honourable Ministry of State for the Colonies may be able to form a clear and responsible opinion thereon, from first hand information, it is most desirable and necessary that a special Royal Commission of Inquiry should be sent to Cyprus empowered to inquire into the matter and with full liberty of action both in respect of the questions to be investigated and of their mode of action all of which should be carried out independently of the opinion of the local Government and in an absolutely unbiased and free way. We ask for the envoy of such a Commission on behalf and in the name of the people whom we represent, and we feel certain that this Commission, on visiting the Island, will draw appaling inferences of the 50 years British rule, which must form a quite unique instance of British maladministration. In returning to England the Commission will be able to make to the Ministry such suggestions and recommendations as would enlighten it to do the best for the prosperity of the Island.

Nicosia the 20 July 1929.

We have the honour to be

Sir,

Your Lordships most Obedient Humble Servants

	[British comment:
Bishop of Kitium Nicodemos	*A Churchman of questionable moral character*
S. G. Stavrinakis	*An Advocate*
G. Hadjipaulou	*Advocate (reputed to be mentally deranged)*
K. P. Rossides	*Advocate and Journalist*
P. Cacoyiannis	*Advocate*
M. H. Michaelides	*Merchant and Moneylender*
Hj Eftychios Hj Procopi	*Farmer of the villager type—practically illiterate*
Ph. Joannides	*Advocate (Brother of Hadjipavlou)*
L. Z. Pierides	*Merchant. Ex-clerk in Government Service (Grade III). Pension £57.4s. p.a.*

D. Severis   *Advocate, Merchant and Moneylender*
N. Nicolaides   *Advocate and Moneylender*
G. Emphiedjis   *Advocate and Moneylender]*

A. Letter of R. Storrs, 11 September 1929

The Right Honourable   Government House
Lord Passfield, P.C.,   Troodos, 11th September, 1929
Secretary of State for the Colonies.

My Lord,

I have the honour to confirm my Confidential telegram of yesterday's date reading as follows:–

"My despatch 16th July Confidential two persons named left for England to-day via Athens and Venice. Expected to arrive London about 22nd September. Memorial handed to me by delegation prior to leaving follows with despatch by tomorrow's mail."

and to inform you that a Delegation consisting of the Honourable S. G. Stavrinakis, M.L.C., and the Bishop of Kitium, M.L.C., waited upon me on the 6th instant with a Memorial which they requested me to transmit to Your Lordship and in support of which they are proceeding to London on the 10th instant. As it was not addressed to me I accepted the Memorial without further comment than that some of the questions raised had been previously answered by the Secretary of State and that others had for some time past engaged my attention, and undertook that it should reach its destination.

In accordance therefore with this undertaking and the provisions of Colonial Regulation 203 I forward herewith in duplicate the original Memorial in Greek, signed copies of a translated version, together with printed copies of the translation, all of which were received by me from the persons named.

2. The idea of presenting a Memorial by Delegation or otherwise appears to have originated after the incidents in the Legislative Council recorded in Mr. Nicholson's despatches quoted in the margin, but from the beginning it received no popular support and up till to-day has aroused so little interest that outside the larger cities it is hardly known. General conditions indeed recall with curious exactitude those described in the second paragraph of my predecessor's Confidential despatch of the 15th of April, 1920. Shortly after my return to the Colony in July the project was dropped owing to differences of opinion as to its expediency among the Greek-speaking Elected Members of the Council, some of whom opposed it as a manoeuvre of the Orthodox Church to make use of the "National" question in order to settle in its own interests that of the Church property in Cyprus. Colour is lent to this theory by the records of a subsequent secret meeting when, on a second impasse being reached, the Archbishop appeared with a written undertaking that the Ecclesiastical question should form no part of the purposes of the mission. Upon this undertaking, together with His Beatitude's promise to finance the proceeding from Church revenues, the opposition of the dissentients was tardily and, I am informed, unwillingly withdrawn. A recent incident which divided and shook the credit of the Greek-

speaking Electives and almost wrecked the Delegation was the passing of a list of recommendations for transfer of teachers, submitted by some of them in their capacity of Members of the Board of Education. As a result I received lively protests from their own colleagues, scores of petitions from the teachers, threatened, for political reasons wholly unconnected with Education, with transportation to distant corners of the Island: and the matter was taken up by the Press urging me to exercise the discretion vested in me under Law 32 of 1923. So great was the scandal caused by these revelations that, after careful consideration, I felt myself compelled to resort to this extreme measure, in respect of which I attach the relevant notice published in yesterday's Gazette. So uncertain, at all events up to the last week, was the departure of the Delegation that the loyal minorities, Turks, Armenians and Maronites, usually prompt and even beforehand with counter memorials for the preservation of what is to them a matter of life and death, forbore on this occasion, until the Members should have actually sailed, to draw up their representations, which will consequently have to be transmitted by a subsequent mail.

3. The circumstances which have combined to encourage the Greek-speaking Members of the Legislative Council to take these steps are as follows:–

(a) The unsatisfactory impression made by them upon the moneyed interests which control the electorate, by their conduct in walking out of the Chamber last December over the Estimates discussion and yet lacking the necessary self-sacrifice to resign and forfeit their annual emoluments.

(b) The general belief that, consequent upon such incidents and the general obstructiveness recently displayed, a new constitution is on the point of promulgation by His Majesty's Government: and the desire to "get in first" with an anticipatory complaint.

(c) The discontent of the lawyer-politician-usurer class at the constantly increasing success of the Cooperative Credit movement, which is freeing the peasant and small holder from the clutches not only of the usurer but also of the Law, and consequently decreasing operations and profits under these categories.

(d) The salutary effect of the introduction of the Penal Code, which has decreased crime both serious and petty, and with it the opportunities of the Bar.

(e) (As stated in the Memorial) the recent change of Government in England.

(f) Recent events in Egypt, which have been interpreted in sections of the extremist Greek Press as an encouragement against "Imperialism."

4. I am informed that the Orthodox Prelacy, whose intervention in politics, traditional throughout the Balkans and Near East, is in Cyprus a legacy of the days of Moslem domination, has been moved in the person of its Archbishop or "Ethnarch" to take advantage of the above circumstances because of the increasingly violent and, I would add, deserved general criticism of their neglect of their spiritual and educational duties; and it is unhappily characteristic of this traditional attitude that, for the provision of this purely secular enterprise, some hundreds of pounds should be perverted from Church revenues and the offerings of poor villagers (over £3,000 have been thus exacted in the past three years in order to purchase aeroplanes for Greece) to preserve the good will of politicians who are not prepared to make any sacrifice themselves but hope to regain, at the expense of others, their lost prestige in time for the forthcoming Elections of 1930.

5. The sum of £645 (popularly estimated at £600) for current expenses of the Delegation has been provided in its entirety by the church, whilst special additional contributions of £150 each are being made by the Archbishopric and the See of Kitium to-

wards the travelling expenses of the Bishop. (Mr. Stavrinakis is travelling at his own expense). Part of the total amount provided is intended for Press and personal propaganda, as Members of the Legislative Council have proclaimed throughout the Island, presumably on the local analogy, that a good cash balance is a useful agent in dealing not only with the Press but with prominent politicians of all parties. For this and other reasons I need hardly suggest to Your Lordship that the less publicity, even of an adverse character, received by the Delegation the better.

6. Of the two Members that compose the Delegation Mr. Stavrinakis enjoys the reputation of an honest and reasonable man. He is by nature inclined to moderation, nor have I found him anti-governmental in tendency but on the contrary anxious to do his best for his country as a member of the Executive and Legislative Councils. His chief defect is a weakness of character which prevents him under extreme pressure from maintaining and acting up to his personal convictions and better judgment. He is incidentally the most confirmed economic pessimist I have ever met and no statistics, official or unofficial, no evidences of prosperity however obvious are sufficient to lighten the gloom of his outlook. He rendered valuable service on the Executive Council, his expulsion from which last spring logically perhaps, but in my opinion unnecessarily and impolitically recommended, accounts for his present appearance in the unhappy and unfortunate part of the "Broken Roader." The Bishop of Kitium is a clever, determined and extremely ambitious man. He aspires to the succession of the Archiepiscopal Throne of Cyprus on the demise of his kinsman the present Archbishop, and it is his hope and intention to assist his candidature by the publicity shed on him by this mission. He is a master of intrigue and behind most of the anti-British agitation. His natural disposition is by no means priestly and he announced some days before his original nomination as Archiepiscopal Locum Tenens that if not appointed he would abandon his frock and make his career in Paris. His moral character in private life is such as I think it only fair should be intimated to the Dignitaries of the Anglican Church, who might otherwise be disposed to receive the representative of an ancient and honourable diocese. The Secretary of the Delegation, Mr. Zenon Rossides, is an agreeable but decadent young lawyer with an exceptionally good command of English. His services were somewhat reluctantly, and only at the last moment, accepted; largely, it is said, to conciliate his uncle, Mr. L. Z. Pierides, M.L.C., and his father-in-law, Mr. M. H. Michaelides, M.L.C., by whom he is being jointly financed.

7. The extent and degree of serious popular inclination or mandate for the Delegation are pleasantly, if cynically, illustrated by the enclosed cartoon published in "Yelio" (Helios), the local Punch, on the eve of their reception by me.

8. The Memorial which, as translated and printed, is badly expressed, abounding in typographical errors and containing many inaccuracies and misleading statements, necessitates extensive research and verification to meet the various issues raised and therefore prevents my submitting more than the above general observations upon the cause, purposes and circumstances of the Delegation; my detailed considered commentary upon the various points of the Memorial must be reserved for the next mail.

I would suggest that, as early as possible after the receipt of this further despatch and assuming that Your Lordship accepts in general my observations on the Memorial, the memorialists should be informed, with regard to paragraph 21 of their representations, as they were by the Under Secretary of State on the 26th of October, 1920, and on subsequent occasions, that His Majesty's Government can hold out no hope that union with Greece will be sanctioned, and have nothing to add to previous declarations on the subject: that with regard to paragraph 22, sections A B C and E cannot be considered and that, as they are aware, section D is already occupying the attention of the Cyprus Government. As for paragraph 23 my opinion is that, unless Your Lordship should, for reasons unknown to myself, think otherwise, the appointment of a "Special Royal Commission" is, in the circumstances, unjustifiable, would serve no useful purpose and, however limited in scope, could hardly fail to raise false hopes and unprofitable issues.

9. I would venture meanwhile, in general reference to the constitutional, political and administrative situation, to refer Your Lordship to the minute and thorough summary contained in Mr. Nicholson's Confidential despatch of the 30th of January last, as well as to Chapter V, "The Cyprus Parallel," in "The Seventh Dominion," by the Right Honourable J. C. Wedgwood, and, in dealing with the sweeping criticism of British rule in Cyprus, to the comparison "1878–1928" forwarded in my Confidential despatch of the 5th of June, 1928.

I have the honour to be,
My Lord,
Your Lordship's most obedient,
Humble Servant,
Ronald Storrs
Governor.

Extract from d.o. letter from Sir Ronald Storrs to Sir J. Shuckburgh.

Government House, Cyprus.
11th September, 1929.

By next week I hope to have despatched to you ample material for dealing with the latest Memorial and Delegation. The document is no less absurd than pathetic and in a way makes me blush as a result of 50 years British Administration: for the great mass of the people are indeed deserving of sympathy and encouragement though not the Delegation nor those they really represent. If you knew as much about the Bishop as I do, you would appreciate even more my suggestion that Lambeth and Fulham should receive fair warning.

I have submitted, for obvious reasons, that they should be answered as soon as conveniently possible. Heaven knows I grudge no man his jaunt to London nor his quail and peche Melba at the Mayfair Hotel, where I understand they will be modestly established. But I do faintly resent the futile and unnecessary researches and verifications imposed upon my unhappy Departments and not least, upon

Yours very sincerely,
Ronald Storrs.

B. Letter of R. Storrs, 18 September 1929

The Right Honourable
Lord Passfield, P.C.,
Secretary of State for the Colonies.

Government House
Troodos, 18TH September.1929

My Lord,

In continuation of my Confidential despatch of the 11th of September, I have the honour to forward for Your Lordship's information annotated copies of the Memorial transmitted in original last week. The commentary is inserted, for speed and ease of reference, inter-paginally, and in order that Your Lordship should have before you the amplest possible material for consideration, I have been at pains, even at the risk of repeating the known or the obvious, to err if anything on the side of excess rather than deficiency of facts, figures and observations submitted.

2. I have no changes to suggest in the recommendations contained in paragraph 8 of my above quoted despatch nor indeed anything to add thereto beyond the attached relevant extracts from the Police reports of Nicosia and Larnaca on the departure of the Delegation together with an article from the local press indicative of public opinion even in the larger cities.

I have the honour to be,
My Lord,
Your Lordship's most obedient,
humble Servant,
Ronald Storrs (signed)
Governor

C. Letter of Armenian Prelature, 12 September 1929

ARMENIAN PRELATURE OF CYPRUS

His Excellency
Sir Ronald Storrs, K.C.M.G., C.B.E.
Governor and Commander-in-Chief
Of the Colony of Cyprus.

Nicosia, 12th September, 1929
P.O. Box No. 287

Your Excellency,

I have the honour to refer to the Hon. Colonial Secretary's letter to me No. 951/28 of the 1st August, 1928, whereby I was informed that the Union of Cyprus with Greece is not contemplated by His Majesty's Government.

I would not have troubled Your Excellency again but for the present new movement by the Greek inhabitants of the Colony who are sending a deputation to England to put forward various claims amongst which stands foremost the claim for Union with Greece or alternatively, Autonomy.

The object of my present memorial is to strongly protest on behalf of the Armenian Community of Cyprus against any of the above requests being granted.

Knowing well the mentality and disposition of the Cypriot Greeks towards the minorities resident in the Colony, my community are perfectly convinced that life under Greek rule or even under an autonomous Cypriot Government under the sovereignty of His Majesty, would be absolutely intolerable and are therefore, very anxious and apprehensive.

Consequently, I would request Your Excellency to be kind as to communicate to His Majesty's Government the present protest and the earnest request that the Status Quo may be maintained because we are quite satisfied with the present administration and any change would be unwelcome.

I have etc.
B. Saradjian,
Archbishop of the Armenian
Church of Cyprus.

D. Letter of the Maronites, 10 September 1929

The Right Honourable
The Secretary of State for the Colonies
London.

Cyprus
10th September, 1929

Right Honourable Sir,

We, the respectfully undersigned, representing the Latin and Maronite communities in Cyprus have the honour to respectfully submit, for consideration, our protest against the memorial of the Greek members of the Legislative Council, a text of which has been published in the local Greek papers, containing the Greek National aspirations and demanding Union of Cyprus with Greece.

2. We understand that a deputation has already left Cyprus for London in order to pursue their memorial and make special efforts with a view of obtaining Autonomy pending the Union of Cyprus with Greece. We, as representatives of our respective communities, beg to lay before Your Lordship our most emphatic protest both against Union and Autonomy and to express our entire satisfaction with the present rule which we now thoroughly enjoy.

3. We most respectfully beg to lay before Your Lordship our earnest desire that the present administration may continue, as, if any wider powers in any form are granted to the Greek element, it would certainly be disastrous for the whole Colony and undoubtedly the minorities will suffer terribly in the hands of the Greek inhabitants of Cyprus.

4. We shall be most grateful, Your Lordship, if this our memorial is taken into serious consideration when the demands of the Greek deputation and the memorial of the Greek representatives are being considered.

We have the honour to be,
Right Honourable Sir,
Your most humble and obedient Servants.
The Vicar General of the Maronites
of Cyprus

E. Letter of the Moslems, 10 September 1929

The Right Honourable
The Secretary of State
for the Colonies,
Downing Street,
London

Nicosia, Cyprus
10th September, 1929

Right Honourable Sir,

We have the honour to submit, on behalf of the Mohammedan Community of this Colony, the most emphatic protest against the alleged grievances and so called claims which are formulated in the printed Memorial dated the 20th July, 1929, and addressed to Your Lordship by the non-Mohammedan Honourable Elected Members of the Legislative Council, and which culminate in their stereotyped political leitmotif or programme of agitation, i.e. Union of Cyprus with Greece and, in the meantime, Autonomy.

2. A Deputation, consisting of the Hon. the Most Reverend the Metropolitan N. Mylonas and the Hon. S. G. Stavrinakis, is we understand on its way to England with the view of pressing by all possible means the pretensions of the Memorialists.

3. The intestine personal altercations to which has given rise the discussion of the Memorial and which have transpired in the local Greek papers, should illustrate the level of the signatories' ideology (sic), their reciprocal mistrust and their utter lack of conviction in the cause which they have made up their mind for obvious reasons to espouse.

4. The indignation and disquiet aroused amongst the Mohammedan population and the other non-Greek Christian elements in the Island on similar outburst of chauvinism and crusades of misrepresentations in recent years, have been voiced in our Memorials of the 10th December, 1925, and the 3rd June, 1928, to the Right Honourable the Secretary of State for the Colonies, to which we beg leave to solicit attention.

5. We have on no occasion demurred from cooperating with our Hon. Non-Mohammedan Colleagues in matters connected with the general prosperity of the Country, provided such were free from unwarranted political intrigues and petty individual interests and systematic antagonism to his Britannic Majesty's Government, in which the greatest waste of vitality is unfortunately indulged by the oligarchy of Greek agitators.

6. Incapable of mental and moral height and breadth such as should place them—in the spirit of the Annexation which regards all Cypriots alike without distinction of creed or religion as BRITISH SUBJECTS, and in the true interests of the Island—above racial bias and prejudice, jealousy and intolerance of the other Communities' opinions and susceptibilities, and prompt to magnify and to distort with characteristic shrewdness the most futile impediment to the realisation of their one-sided pursuits, our Hon. Non-Mohammedan Colleagues cannot help seeing Cyprus affairs except through the lens of their inveterate arbitrary and selfish idiosyncrasy.

7. Were they ever allowed the upperhand, they should not hesitate to inaugurate and enforce in this Colony an era of castes and favouritism—with Greeks as the privileged class and all others as pariahs—and to revive persecution, serfdom and servitude which the British Nation has made it a national pride to eradicate throughout the British Empire.

8. In its unfaltering loyalty and devotion to the British Rule since the British Occupation of the Island, the Mohammedan Community ventures through its Representatives to appeal once more for protection and relief to the Right Honourable the Secretary of State for the Colonies as to "the pilot who weathered the storm" in the past.

Your Lordship may rest assured that our earnest appeal is anxiously and most cordially shared by all the non-Greek elements of the Colony.

We have the honour to be,
Right Honourable Sir,
Your most obedient,
Humble servants,
(signatures)
Mohammedan Members of the
Legislative Council of Cyprus.

F. British Commentary, September–November 1929

Sir John Shuckburgh,

The Delegation should reach this country early next week; and you may care to glance though this before they arrive.

No action on our part appears to be called for for the moment. The Governor is sending a further despatch dealing with the substance of the Petition and we must await it. You will observe that the Governor suggests that we should convey to the "Dignitaries of the Anglican Church" a warning as to the moral character of the Bishop of Kitium in private life. I do not very much like this idea and would suggest that at any rate it should be kept in abeyance for the time being.

I doubt whether we need take this deputation too seriously. There have been two such deputations since the end of the War and many petitions. I may call attention to the action taken on a similar petition which was received in 1924 when the present Prime Minister was formerly in office. The usual negative reply was sent with Mr. Ramsey MacDonald's concurrence. Please see 10845/24, Cyprus and Lord Arnold's Minute thereon, 21998/24, Cyprus, at green flags below.

? Wait.

A. J. Dawe
21.9

Sir S. Wilson.

I think that the Secretary of State ought to see this file again at the present stage. The position is that the Delegation has now arrived in England. We have not heard from them yet, but we may do so at any moment and we shall then have to decide what our attitude towards them is to be.

Meanwhile, we must await a further promised despatch from Cyprus before we are in a position to deal with their memorial in detail.

Presumably the S. of S. will think it desirable to see the Delegation at some stage or other. I suggest that he need be in no hurry to make their acquaintance. If they approach the Office they might be seen in the first instance by Mr. Dawe and myself. We could then hear what they have to say and report to the S. of S. who could then in due course give them an appointment if that course is thought desirable.

Meanwhile there is one paramount point of policy upon which we must be clear. The substance of the Greek demand is Union with Greece. The other points raised in the memorial are of minor importance and may be ignored for the moment. I presume that the present Cabinet, like its predecessors (including Mr. MacDonald's earlier Cabinet of 1924) will stand firm on this point and will not be prepared to consider the question of transferring the Island. If so, there will be very little to say to the Delegation. It will really amount almost to the single word "NO": but the point is obviously one upon which we must have clear instructions.

(I am not sending down the voluminous previous papers but these can of course be produced if required).

Initialed 25/9/29

The Secretary of State held the discussion referred to above on the 7th October. Mr. Lunn, Sir Samuel Wilson, Mr. Cowell and I were present.

Lord Passfield intimated that it would not be possible for him to receive the Deputation during the next few days, since he was at present occupied with the Conference on the Operation of Dominion Legislation. He is, however, prepared to see them a little later on. He expressed the wish that in the meantime Sir John Shuckburgh should give them a preliminary interview, and directed that a reply should be returned to (31) accordingly.

Lord Passfield stated that he thought it would be preferable for Sir John Shuckburgh not to make any pronouncement on the questions of policy raised in the Memorial from the Greek Cypriots which the Deputation have come to support. He considered that the preliminary interview should be directed rather to ascertaining what the mind of the Deputation is upon the various matters at issue. Lord Passfield also intimated that he did not consider that it would be necessary for him to refer to the Cabinet before disposing of the Memorial.

I should add that Mr. Howard Smith of the Foreign Office rang me up the other day to enquire what the position was with regard to this Deputation. He stated that the Italian Ambassador had expressed some anxiety with regard to the possible repercussions in the Dodecanese of the reception accorded to the delegates in this country. I promised that I would keep him informed of developments.

A. J. Dawe
8.10

Mr. Cowell,

I annex a note of Sir John Shuckburgh's interview with the Cyprus Deputation on the 11th of October. The Deputation handed in this further letter at the interview, but it does not, I think, bring out any new points.

The next step will, I presume, be for the Secretary of State to receive the Deputation and give them an answer. The question of what the answer should be raises matters

123

of policy which are rather outside my sphere, but I take it, that it can only be a negative one, as on previous occasions.

? The papers should now be submitted to the Secretary of State for directions as to the date for which the interview is to be fixed.

A. J. Dawe 14.10.29.

I assume that it is not desired to give serious consideration to this demand on the application of a deputation which, however it may describe itself, is in reality self-appointed. Before any question of union with Greece could be even discussed it would be necessary not only to attempt to ascertain the real wishes of the people at large, and to estimate the difficulties arising from the attitude of the minority communities, but also to obtain the views of the Foreign Office and the Defence Departments.

The interleaved copy of the memorial (enclos. in 25) summarizes the previous history of the matter and expounds the Governor's views on the statements in the memorial and on the importance to be attached to the deputation.

H. R. Cowell 16/10/29

Sir S. Wilson,

The Secretary of State is to see the Cyprus Delegation Friday morning at 10 a.m. He may like to see these new papers in the meantime.

I am not sure what line Lord Passfield proposes to take with the Delegation. Presumably so far as concerns their principal demand, viz., Union with Greece, his answer will be plain no. Similarly, with regard to their alternative demand, viz., that they should be given "Dominion Status," no reply other than a simple refusal seems practicable.

There remains the question of constitutional reform, which the Delegation may possibly press. As you know, proposals have already been submitted to the S. of S. by the Cyprus Government for constitutional changes in the Island. These proposals, however, are in a direction contrary to what the Delegation are likely to ask for. They contemplate a restriction, not an extension, of self-government in Cyprus. Whether these proposals will, or ought to be, carried any further is a question on which a decision is still awaited. Whatever the decision may be, it seems quite clear that the time is not ripe for a movement in the opposite direction, viz., towards an extension of self-government. I can only suggest that if the S. of S. is pressed on this point, he should say that he is not in a position to make any statement on the subject.

Clearly it would be undesirable, without further consideration and consultation with the Governor, to say anything to the Delegation that they might interpret as a promise of constitutional concessions. To do so would place the Governor in a very embarrassing position, and would in effect negative his own proposals without more ado.

On general grounds, it is, I submit, important that if any concessions are to be made to the Cypriots (and my own view, as I have said above, is that the time is not ripe for them) they should not be made to appear as an outcome of the present Delegation. We do not want to create an impression among the Cypriots that they can squeeze anything they like out of us by sending a delegation to London. Moreover, the right of the present delegation to speak in the name of Cyprus is at any rate open to dispute. The Governor's latest despatch would seem to indicate that they are not taken very seriously in Cyprus itself. In any case, they cannot claim to represent more than the Greek section of the population; there are others (Mohammedans, etc.) who hold diametrically opposite views and have in fact submitted counter petitions to the Secretary of State.

 Mr. Dawe and I will be present at the conference on Friday as instructed by the S. of S. I do not know whether there are any points that you would like to discuss with us before the meeting takes place.

Initialed

23/10/29

P.S. Since writing the above, I have seen Mr. Gerahty, Attorney-General, Cyprus, now on leave pending transfer to Trinidad. He confirms the view that the Delegates are not regarded very seriously in Cyprus itself, and that it would be a mistake to let them go back with the impression that they had wrung concessions of any kind out of us by their visit to London.

Mr. Cowell,

 I now submit the draft of a reply to the Memorial from the Greek Elected Members and to the counter Memorials in (26). I regret that I have not been able to prepare it earlier, but the reply to the Greek Elected Members has entailed a certain amount of consideration and research.

 In the past it has been the custom to reply to these Memorials simply to the effect that we have "nothing to add to previous replies" etc. This Memorial is more elaborate than those of recent years, and it may do some good on this occasion to try the effect of a reasoned statement of the British case. The politicians will no doubt criticise whatever we say. But I am not sure that a considered reply may not have some good effect on the general public and the younger generation of educated Cypriots. In any case we can hardly pass over without comment the many misleading implications contained in the Memorial. The draft reply is therefore rather long, and, as you will see, written entirely with a view to publication.

 The weakest portion of the proposed reply is that dealing with the "Tribute." You will remember that the Elected Members requested that the surplus of the Tribute accumulated up to the date of the Annexation and all the money paid subsequent to that date should be refunded to the Island. With this request I think we must have a certain amount of sympathy. The rights and wrongs of the matter are discussed in my minute of the 19th March, 1927, at (1) in 22246/27 Cyprus, and also in the Memorandum for the Cabinet contained in that paper. When in 1927 His Majesty's Government agreed to increase the grant-in-aid to the same amount as the "Tribute," it was made a condition of the settlement that the question of the Tribute must be regarded as closed for the future. I therefore do not think that we have a good enough case to go to the Treasury again on the matter. In the draft I have therefore put the best complexion I can on the case.

A. J. Dawe 16.11.29

I think that Mr. Dawe has prepared an admirable reply to the memorial. That document is, in great part, of so vague and general a character that it does not lend itself to detailed reply. In particular, the changes of inefficiency and neglect of the interests of Cyprus made against European officials in general are entirely unsupported by evidence; and they are perhaps better ignored.

On the question of procedure, I think that there can be no question that the full reply to the memorial should be sent through the Governor, and that the members of the deputation are not entitled to be made the channel of communication of the S. of S's views.

H. Cowell 18/11

In the past, so far as my knowledge goes, these Deputations from Cyprus have always been disposed of by the Parliamentary Under Secretary of State. The Deputation on this occasion has been received by the Secretary of State himself, and that seems to me to be as far as they should be allowed to go.

In any case the Secretary of State has now given them a reply with regard to their main demand for union with Greece, which has now been confirmed by Mr. Lunn's answer to a recent question in the House; and there seems therefore to be no point in their re-opening the matter with the Prime Minister at this stage. The draft of a considered reply to all the subsidiary points in the Memorial has now been prepared, and, subject to approval, will presumably be despatched at an early date.

If the Deputation were to be received by the Prime Minister, it would look as if His Majesty's Government attached a real importance to their mission and would give an occasion for undesirable publicity in Cyprus and possibly in this country.

? the Private Secretary should return the letter (keeping copy) to the Prime Minister's Private Secretary saying that this Deputation has come to this country to support a Memorial to the Secretary of State from the Greek Elected Members of the Cyprus Legislative Council, the main demand of which is for union of the Island with Greece: that the Secretary of State received them some weeks ago and informed them that there was no hope of His Majesty's Government being able to accede to this request, and that this reply has since been confirmed in an answer to a question in the House of Commons: that we feel it would be very undesirable for the Deputation to be given an opportunity at this stage of re-opening the matter with the Prime Minister: that if they were given such an interview it would give the impression that His Majesty's Government attach undue importance to the mission, and might give rise to embarrassing misconceptions in Cyprus. Suggest therefore that the reply might be that the Prime Minister understands that the Deputation have already been given an opportunity of laying their representations before the Secretary of State for the Colonies, and fears that in all the circumstances no useful purpose would be served by the grant of an interview for the further discussion of these matters with himself. Ask for a copy of the reply as sent to be forwarded to us, in order that we may keep the Governor acquainted with what has passed.

A. J. Dawe 20.11

IV. Reactions to Memorial, November 1929–February 1930 (CO 67/227/7)

A. Extract from "The Near East and India" of 21 November, 1929

<u>The Problem of Cyprus</u>

Elsewhere in this issue we publish a Memorandum forwarded by the Cyprus Delegation, which has come to London to lay before His Majesty's Government the claims of the Greek-speaking population of the Island. This Memorandum is not the document that has been presented to the Secretary of State for the Colonies, but reproduces in abbreviated form the Memorial that was drawn up by the Greek-speaking members of the Legislative Council for submission to the Government by the Delegation. In the interval that has elapsed since the preparation of the Memorial and the compilation of the Memorandum the Cyprus Delegation has been received by the Secretary of State for the Colonies, and has been told that the British Government can hold out no hope of meeting its request for the union of Cyprus with Greece. It may be inferred, therefore, that the Memorandum lays much less stress than the original Memorial on the subject of Union. Very wisely the Delegation, which, when it left Cyprus, was concerned mainly if not solely, with the case of union, has realised that the rejection of its claim by Mr. Ramsay MacDonald's Government in language as emphatic as that used by any of its predecessors, renders the possibility of union with Greece out of the question in the near future. In order, therefore, not to return empty-handed to the Island, it has supplemented the demand for union by the more reasonable request that present conditions in Cyprus should form the subject of an inquiry by a Commission. In support of this request the Memorandum refers to a number of factors that render the situation, in the opinion of the Greek-speaking population, "far from satisfactory." The proposals regarding constitutional changes and administrative reforms now being considered by His Majesty's Government and an answer given to a question in the House of Commons last week stated that no final decision had at that time been taken on the subject. The purpose of the Memorandum now issued is to direct "sympathetic attention" to the case of Cyprus and to insure that as wide a body as possible of public opinion in Great Britain is acquainted with conditions on the Island.

No one with first-hand knowledge of Cypriot affairs can contend that British administration has done all that it might have been expected to do for Cyprus. At the same time it has to be recognised that the obstacles in the way of the Island's progress have not been due solely to the shortcomings of successive Governments. Cyprus is a poor country, and much of the inaction of which Administrations in the past can be accused has been imposed upon them by the need of rigid economy. The history of the Tribute carries with it, if not its own condemnation, at least a strong argument for a more generous attitude towards the Island in the first instance. On the other hand the Cypriots themselves have a large measure of responsibility for their own lack of progress. Not only have the innate conservatism and the inertia of the inhabitants prevented them from making the most of their opportunities, but they have also imposed upon the Government the necessity of a cautious policy. In this way the Island has condemned itself to a vicious circle. The people have become too prone to look to Government for help instead of helping themselves, and the Government has been deterred from launching ambitious schemes by the backwardness of the people and their hesitation to abandon primitive ideas and methods. Until recently the Greeks in Greece itself, however ready to form political organisations and to discuss politics among themselves, have shown individualistic tendency in matters of commerce and industry. The same lack of co-operation for economic ends has manifested itself among Greek-speaking Cypriots. Since the war, when Great Britain has come to appreciate the fact that more might have been done for Cyprus, the situation has been complicated by the insistence of the leaders of the Greek-speaking community that the demand for union with Greece should override all other considerations. It is not correct to say that Cyprus has stood still under British administration; progress there has been in many directions, and of recent years much leeway has been made up; but it goes without saying that with closer co-operation between the people of the Island and the Government the rate of advance might have been greatly accelerated.

A new era will have been inaugurated in the history of Cyprus, if, as a result of the visit of the Delegation now in London, the Greek-speaking population accepts, albeit with disappointment, the decision of the British Government that no hope can be held out for the cause of union with Greece, and set to work loyally with the Administration in the interests of the Island as a whole. The constitutional change for which the Memorial asks bespeaks more responsibility for the Greek-speaking community and a more direct share in the administration. It will be evident to every man of intelligence that there can be little inducement to any British Government to meet such a demand, unless it can be assured that effect will be given to the new regime by the Cypriots themselves in complete loyalty and sincerity. Rightly or wrongly, the British Government has decided, in its capacity of trustee of Imperial interests, that Cyprus cannot at this time be ceded to Greece. Can the same Government reasonably be asked to run the risk, by handing over control of the Island's legislature to the Greek-speaking community, of having the whole administrative machinery brought to a standstill because the demand for union with Greece which has been refused is still to be pressed in season and out of season? All uncertainty on this point could be removed, if the Greek-speaking Cypriots pledged themselves to abandon the union-movement for a period of, say, twenty years, during which a whole-hearted attempt to promote the material development of the Island on agreed lines would be made in co-operation with the authorities. Never in the history of Cyprus has a more favourable opportunity presented itself for a straightforward effort on the part of elements hitherto mainly at variance to understand one another and to work together in the real interests of the Island. There is a general desire to remove from Cyprus the reproach of having been the Cinderella of the Empire; no Government in Great Britain is likely to lend a more sympathetic ear than the present one to the requests of Greek-speaking Cypriots, and in the present Governor the latter have an administrator of broad views, of ready sympathy, with a shrewd and practical mind. The attitude of the Delegation in London gives rise to the supposition that the other leaders of the union-movement also realise that they have done their duty to their compatriots by pressing home their request as long as there was the least hope of success, and that now statesmanship and common sense alike require that personal considerations should be subordinated to the interests of the Island. Every point that the Memorandum makes calls for specific action on the part of the Cyprus of the British Government; it is against the dictates of reason that concession should be granted to people who may be liable to stultify them by an attitude of non-co-operation. When once this danger has been eliminated by a self-denying ordinance of the Greek-speaking community, the case for a the Greek-speaking community, the case for a constitutional change and administrative reforms in Cyprus becomes overwhelming.

B. Letter from R. Storrs, 20 November 1929

Government House
20th. November, 1929

My dear Schuckburgh,

I find myself somewhat perplexed with regard to the exact position of the Memorial, or Memorials, submitted by the Cyprus Delegation. The only information as yet to hand from the Secretary of state is his telegram of October 25th. All that we have heard this end is that, during or after a visit to Paris in which Venizelos refused, almost ostentatiously, to receive the Delegates (though in Cyprus opinion is unanimous that he really did receive them) they took the decision to substitute a second Memorial confined to Enosis for the first embracing Autonomy and other matters originally submitted through and by me. But I find this account difficult to reconcile with your above telegram for presumably, once you had disposed of the revised version (superseding and thus withdrawing that authorised by the M.L.C's) it would seem that the subsidiary issues raised in the first would no longer require handling. Yet it is clear from the S of S's cable, as well as the Reuter Communiqués (of which I sent Dawe specimens last week) together with the articles in the Athenian Press communicated from our Legation on November the 6th, to say nothing of statements such as the enclosed issued by the Archbishop, that something in the nature of a further reply is genuinely expected by the Delegation, if not by the Island. I would therefore venture to suggest that if it is deemed necessary to deal at all with the withdrawn Memorial, no sort of undertaking should be given for the sending of any Commission or Mission which could be in any way connected with the Delegation. I would, as you know, welcome, and have indeed urged a visit from the Under-Secretary whenever it should suit him best, but would, I must say, from all points of view infinitely prefer and earnestly recommend that he should come, so to speak, proprio motu, rather than as if impelled by external forces.

The Education, Estimates and subsequent Sessions are, at best, not going to be easy during the next few months. They will be rendered infinitely more difficult if any demonstrable and, I may add, wholly unexpected countenance be lent to the representatives of the policy of sterile non cooperation and obstruction, characteristic of the Greek-speaking Electives in and out of Council during the last few years.

Believe me,
Yours sincerely,
Ronald Storrs

C. Dispatch from the Secretary of State, 28 November 1929

Despatch from the Secretary of State for the Colonies to the Governor of Cyprus

Downing Street,
28th November, 1929.

Sir,

I have before me the Memorial signed on the 20th of July last by the Greek Elected Members of Legislative Council of Cyprus in which they formulated certain requests for change in the political status and administrative system of the Island. This Memorial has now received my attentive examination; and I have had the opportunity of listening to the arguments urged in its support by the Bishop of Kitium, Mr. Stavrinakis and Mr. Rossides during their recent visit to London. My reply to these representations is contained in the following paragraphs and I should be obliged if you would communicate this despatch to the Greek Elected Members and then publish it.

2. The first request contained in the Memorial is a renewal of the demand that Cyprus should be ceded to Greece. My answer on this point can only be the same as that which successive Secretaries of State have in the past returned to similar demands, namely, that His Majesty's Government are unable to accede to it. This subject, in their view, is definitely closed and cannot profitably be further discussed.

3. In paragraph 22 of the Memorial the Greek Elected Members put forward certain requests for consideration in the event of the rejection of their major demand for union with Greece. The first of these contained in sub-paragraph A is the submission that the Island should be granted a form of responsible Government. This is a request which has been given very careful consideration. The conclusion at which I have arrived, not without regret, is that the time has not yet come when it would be to the general advantage of the people of Cyprus to make a trial of a constitutional experiment in this direction. Those institutions already established in the Island which are subject in varying degrees to popular control cannot be said to have attained that reasonable measure of efficiency which could be looked for before any extension of the principle is approved. The requests contained in sub-paragraphs B and C do not, in these circumstances appear to arise. In sub-paragraph D it is represented that the payment to the Evcaf and to individual tithe owners should be discontinued. I can only say in regard to this that the matter is, as the Elected Members are aware, already occupying the attention of the Cyprus Government.

4. I will now refer to the so-called "Tribute." The points made by the Greek Elected members with regard to this subject are contained in paragraphs 17–20 and in sub-paragraph E of paragraph 22 of the Memorial. Up to the annexation in 1914, the payment of the Tribute was made in virtue of the Convention with Turkey of 1878. His Majesty's Government are unable to share the view advanced by the Memorialists that the payment of this sum from Cyprus revenues was contrary to the provisions of the Convention. It is true that Clause III of the Annex to the Convention stipulated that England should pay the money to Turkey. But it is clear from that document and from the terms of the Allied negotiations that the intention was that England should pay the money from the revenues of Cyprus, or in other words, that it should come from the same source as in the past. The effect of the arrangement was that Cyprus became liable to Great Britain for £92,800 a year, and Great Britain became liable to the Ottoman Empire for the same annual sum. When the Ottoman Empire defaulted on the 1855 loan, the interest on which had been guaranteed by the British and French Governments, Her Majesty's then Government was advised that the "Cyprus Tribute" formed part of the revenues of the Ottoman Empire and could be withheld from the Porte and used for the service of the

Loan so long as the default lasted. The whole of the money was, therefore, and always has been, devoted to the liquidation of a liability on which the Ottoman Empire defaulted. The Greek Elected Members state that no legal relation exists between the 1855 Loan and the revenue of Cyprus. The 1855 Loan, however, was secured upon the whole revenue of the Ottoman Empire as well as specifically on the balance of the Egyptian Tribute and the Customs' revenues of Syria and Smyrna. In these circumstances the British Government clearly had ample justification in diverting to the service of the Loan the payment for which they were liable to the Ottoman Empire under the Cyprus Convention. It has never been their contention that the 1855 loan had any specific connection with Cyprus.

It is hardly necessary for me to point out that the liability of Cyprus to Great Britain for the annual payment of £92,800 was in practice greatly reduced by Grants-in-Aid from the Imperial Exchequer. After a period of fluctuation the Grant was definitely fixed at £50,000 a year in 1907, and remained at that figure until 1927. During that period Cyprus had, therefore, to find only £42,800 a year. On a purely material evaluation this sum cannot be considered an excessive price to pay for the practical benefits which accrued from the establishment of a British administration.

On the Annexation in 1914, the 1878 Convention was abrogated: and I agree with the Greek Elected Members that the payment of the Tribute then ceased to find any sanction in that instrument. The payment was, however, continued as the share of Cyprus in the general Public Debt of the Ottoman Empire. It is contended that in accordance with the generally accepted principle of international law Cyprus, as a Succession State of the Ottoman Empire, could properly be charged with this liability. It is true that, as the Greek Elected Members state, no reference to the liability of Cyprus in respect of the Ottoman Public Debt is made in the Treaty of Lausanne, although under Article 20 of that Treaty Turkey recognised the annexation of the Island by Great Britain. The reason why the liability of Cyprus was not mentioned in the Treaty was that the Island was already paying the sum of £92,800 a year which had been appropriated for the service of the 1855 Loan. The matter was carefully considered at the time, and it was decided that this payment should be treated as the contribution of Cyprus to the Ottoman Public Debt, and that the matter did not, therefore, require to be dealt with in an International Instrument. Had it not been for this payment, Cyprus would no doubt have been required to take over a share of the Ottoman Public Debt on the same basis as the other territories detached from Turkey as a result of the War, and on that basis her contribution would have been substantially more than the gross amount of the Tribute.

In 1927 His Majesty's Government, with the desire of accelerating the progress of the Island, decided to increase the grant-in-aid to the same amount as the Cyprus contribution to the Ottoman Public Debt charge, namely, £92,800 a year. The only condition attached to this increased grant was that Cyprus should contribute £10,000 a year towards the cost of Imperial defence. The grant on this condition was accepted by the Legislative Council. In the reply to the offer of His Majesty's Government dated the 5th of September, 1927, and signed by the Elected Members, which was handed to you on your return from your visit to Rhodes in that month, they stated: "The happy answer of the Imperial Government has fulfilled all Cypriot aspirations concerning this burden." His Majesty's Government, therefore, regard the settlement of 1927 as having finally closed the question of the Tribute; and it is one which they are not prepared further to pursue. They feel that after studying the facts set out above, all reasonable opinion in Cyprus will agree that Cyprus has been treated not ungenerously in the matter.

5. In paragraph 23 of the Memorial, it is suggested that a Royal Commission should be appointed to inquire into the condition of affairs in Cyprus. This proposal has received my consideration, but after careful reflection, I have formed the view that the appointment of such a body would, at the present juncture, be of no real benefit to Cyprus. An inquiry of the character proposed would raise unprofitable issues, and could only distract attention from those more practical matters on which the progress of the Colony depends. There is much to be said for the view that what Cyprus needs at present are fewer occasions for political discussion and more occasions for constructive work.

6. Before concluding this despatch, I desire to make the following observations with respect to certain of the statements contained in the Memorial. His Majesty's Government do not wish to make any immoderate claims for the achievements of British rule in Cyprus. They are conscious that the material progress of the Island has not been so rapid as they would have hoped. This is in large measure attributable to certain special causes. The first of these is the anomalous and uncertain position of the Island up to the Annexation in 1914. Cyprus was until that date a territory leased by Great Britain from the Ottoman Empire. Owing to this ambiguous situation, the Island was unable to attract the capital necessary for its development, and no Government loan for that purpose was raised in the open market. After the Annexation, the War and the subsequent economic depression further retarded development.

7. A further cause is to be found in the peculiar nature of the Cyprus Constitution. Responsible observers have contended that had Cyprus possessed an officially-controlled Legislature its progress would have been more rapid. There is much weight in this contention. The divorce of power from executive responsibility is rarely conducive to efficient administration, however much unofficial control over the Legislature may be valued from other standpoints. Had the Executive Government had full control it could, for example, have paid salaries which would have attracted highly qualified experts to the service of its technical departments. The Greek Elected Members have argued that salaries paid to the British officials in the Island have been too high. In doing so they are, to my mind, failing to take a long view of their own material interests. Until recent years the salaries paid have in my opinion been too low. Had they been nearer to the market rate for the best ability, the progress of the Island would have been accelerated and the extra outlay would have been more than repaid in the added wealth derived from the development of the Island's undoubted resources. I think it is desirable that the Greek Elected Members should realise that on this subject they have adopted a policy of false economy, which is responsible to no small extent for the lack of progress of which they now complain.

8. In spite of these admitted obstacles to the advancement of the country, I am unable to admit that the picture drawn in the Memorial of the British achievement in Cyprus is a fair one. No person who is correctly informed as to the condition of the Island in 1878 could refuse to recognise the very great advance which it has made in only fifty years of British rule. In 1878 the population was only 180,000. At the time of the British occupation the only road in the Island was a track of some 26 miles between Nicosia and Larnaca. Under the rule of the Ottoman Empire there were no hospitals; and the protection of public health was a matter which received no attention from Government. The encouragement of agriculture and the preservation of the forests were equally neglected. No

effort was made to develop the Island's mineral resources. Taxation was abusive, and rates of interest were usurious. The administration of justice was defective, and access to the Courts was difficult.

9. The Island to-day shows considerable improvement upon this state of affairs. The population has nearly doubled. There are, apart from village roads, a thousand miles of roads which can be traversed by motor. The revenue has increased from £176,000 to nearly three-quarters of a million, and the whole of this money is devoted to the public service which was not the case under the rule of the Ottoman Empire. A railway has been built and harbours have been considerably improved. Regular post, telegraph, and mail services have been instituted. The development and protection of the forests has been taken in hand on scientific lines. The growing revenue from royalties attests the attention which is being paid to the Island's mineral resources. The spread of education, which has been largely assisted by Government grants, is illustrated by the fact that there are now over 46,000 children attending the schools, whereas in 1881 there were fewer than 7,000. Increasing regard has been paid to the important subjects of agriculture and irrigation. The co-operative system has received every encouragement from Government, while credit has been made available to the farmers upon reasonable terms.

10. It is, however, broadly true to say that until recent years the main work of the Government has been not so much to develop the country by direct administrative action to create conditions favourable to the natural growth of prosperity. For fifty years Cyprus has enjoyed the benefits of law and order and the equitable and honest administration of justice. There has been no public disorder within, and there has been immunity from attack from without. During the War while neighbouring countries were the scene of military operations, Cyprus remained secure and peaceful. In the economic dislocation which followed the War, the Island preserved the advantage of a sound currency financial system. The inhabitants of the Island have enjoyed a wide liberty of speech and action which compares favourably with that permitted in adjacent territories. They have escaped the obligation of compulsory military service; the more prosperous classes have not been called on to bear the heavy direct taxation which has been a feature of other fiscal systems. These conditions have not only allowed energy and enterprise to reap their due rewards, but have also a moral value which cannot be computed in merely material terms.

11. I have not written this despatch in any narrow spirit. In many ways I welcome the high standard of achievement which the Greek Elected Members set in their criticism of the British administration. These conceptions are in some sense a tribute to the change in outlook which has resulted from half a century of British rule. The anxiety of the Greek Elected Members for improvement in the conditions of the Island has my entire sympathy. I am confident that in the next few years considerable improvement in the equipment of the country and in the development of its resources is possible. Government can do much to assist the people of the Island to take advantage of their opportunities, and I trust that this frank interchange of views may do something to foster the spirit of co-operation and mutual understanding which is a desirable condition to the attainment of this common goal. If this spirit is forthcoming, it will meet with a generous response.

I have, etc.,
Passfield.

D. Letter of J. Shuckburgh to Storrs, 5 December 1929

5 December, 1929,
Downing St.

My Dear Storrs,

Many thanks for your letter of 20th November about the Greek Memorial Delegation etc. I hope that our telegram of the 27th and the various despatches of the 28th will have resolved the perplexities that you mention. The Deputation handed to me the purely "Enosistic" Memorial at the preliminary interview which I gave them at the request of the Secretary of State; but neither at that interview nor at their subsequent interview with the Secretary of State himself did they confine their representations entirely to the question of union with Greece. They made it clear that, if it was not possible for their main aspiration to be fulfilled at present, there were other grievances which they wanted remedied. They referred at some length to the request for responsible government, to the Tribute question, and the various other points raised in the original Memorial. As that Memorial was signed by all the Greek Elected Members, we regarded it as putting forward the real issues which we had to face. We looked upon the Deputation as a body chosen by the Greek Elected Members to support in person the requests put forward in the Memorial, and we accordingly considered their representations to be really subsidiary to the document in chief.

It was for this reason that the considered reply was communicated through you to the Elected Members instead of to the Deputation. You will, I fell sure, agree that this was the correct procedure.

The Deputation, although they made one or two spasmodic attempts at propaganda, including the circularising of members of the House of Commons, seem to have evoked no public interest here at all. The Archbishop of Canterbury, I believe, saw the Bishop of Kitium; but their interview received little or no publicity. I am not aware that anything of any importance passed between them. The Deputation asked the Prime Minister to see them, but he declined. I trust that for a time at least there may now be a close season for memorials and delegations.

Yours Sincerely,
J. Shuckburgh

E. Letter to S. Wilson, 14 January 1930

Sir S. Wilson,

This White Paper is now ready for presentation.

There is one point on which I should like your instructions. Please see the second footnote (which I have bracketed in red) on p. 3 of the proof. The genesis of this note is as follows. It occurred to the Department, when the publication of a White Paper was decided upon, that it might be useful to include in it, side by side with the Greek Memorial, certain counter-memorials, opposing the Greek demands, which we have received from other Communities in Cyprus (Muhammadans, Latins, Armenians, etc.). The Governor, whom we consulted by telegram, did not favour the proposal, which he thought would arouse ill-feeling; but he suggested that a note might properly be incorporated in the White Paper, merely stating that counter-memorials had been received. Hence the footnote, which is based closely on the wording of the Governor's telegram.

I feel some doubt about this. First there is the question of Parliamentary procedure. It is, I believe, a more or less established principle that if a document is quoted or referred to in a Parliamentary Paper, the Government may be called upon to produce it. Hence the footnote may lead to a demand (which we may find it difficult to resist) for publication of the actual text of the memorials. That is just what the Governor has advised us is against the public interest.

From the wider point of view, I think that our refutation of the Greek case can well stand on its own merits, and that there is no need to call in the dissident minorities to our assistance.

On the whole I would omit the footnote.

Initialed 14/1/30

F. Letter from Passfield, 6 February 1930

Downing St.
6 February, 1930

Sir,

I have etc. to refer to my despatch No. 45 of the 6th February transmitting copies of the Paper (Cmd. 3477) presented to Parliament containing the recent Memorial from the Greek Elected Members of the Cyprus Legislative Council, together with my reply thereto.

2. In connection with the telegraphic correspondence noted in the margin, I have to inform you that it was decided that it would be undesirable to include in the paper a statement that memorials of protest against the Greek Memorial had been addressed to me on behalf of the religious denominations in the Island other than the Greek Christians. It is a general principle of procedure that if a document is quoted or referred to in a Parliamentary Paper, the Government may be called upon to produce it to Parliament. Having regard to the terms of Mr. Henniker-Heaton's telegram, it seemed wiser in these circumstances to omit all mention of the counter-memorials.

I have etc,
Passfield

Chapter 4
The Riots of 1931 and the British Response: 1931–1935

The first document in Chapter four is the report on the riots of 1931. This is a thorough and factual account of events, though the more thoughtful and analytical assessment of the political situation in CO 67/247/10 provides a better account of how and, more especially why, the disturbances took the particular form that they did, namely, an attack on the Governor's residence. The exchange in CO 67/244/7 regarding Professor Toynbee's analysis of British policy on Cyprus is quite revealing. Later instructions from Downing Street to Sir Charles Woolley, forbidding him to censor Enosist telegrams will seem quite hypocritical in hindsight (CO 67/319). British Legislation finally defined Enosis as sedition, though, as we will see in chapter five, circumstances in World War II prevented them from consistency in application. CO 67/244/9 lays out the role of Enosists in Athens and suggests the thoroughness of British intelligence, whereas CO 67/254/6 demonstrates how little control over events their intelligence afforded them. It is surprising to learn that terrorism and violence were being openly advocated as early as 1934, and that the British were aware of it.

I. Storrs' Report on the "Disturbances in Cyprus in October, 1931," 11 February 1932 (CO 67/243/1,2)

The following report is published as Cmnd. 4045, *Disturbances in Cyprus in October, 1931.* (London: His Majesty's Stationery Office, 1932).

Despatch from the Governor of Cyprus to the Secretary of State for the Colonies.

(Received 20th February, 1932.)

Government House, Nicosia.
11th February, 1932.

Sir,

1 have the honour to submit the following report on the disturbances which occurred in Cyprus in October last.

2. The immediate occasion of the outbreak was the resignation of the Bishop of Kitium and other Greek-Orthodox members from the Legislative Council of the Colony. The Bishop resigned on the 17th October. One other member, Mr. N. K. Lanitis, resigned on the 19th October. The resignations of the Nicosia members, or their intentions to resign, were announced or known to the populace at Nicosia in the evening of the 21st October, just before the first and capital act of violence, the assault on Government House, was perpetrated. Copies of the letters of resignation, which are significant of the state of mind of the writers at the time, have been forwarded to you.

3. The secret deliberations of the Orthodox elected members of the Council which led to their resignation opened on the 12th September, 1931. After several postponements, due to the absence of certain members in Europe, they had been summoned by the Bishop of Kitium to meet that day at Saitta, a summer resort near Troodos partly owned by the see of Kitium, to decide what attitude they should adopt and what course of action they should follow in consequence of a statement made in Parliament by the Chancellor of the Exchequer on the 8th July to the effect that the accumulated surplus from the payments made from Cyprus revenue as tribute to Turkey under the Convention of 1878 had been disposed of for the sinking fund of the Turkish loan guaranteed by Great Britain in 1855. It was assumed, correctly, that they would also discuss and attempt to define their attitude towards the Imperial Order in Council introducing a new Customs tariff which had been published in the Colony three days previously.

4. The treatment of Cyprus by His Majesty's Government in regard to the tribute has been one of the two main planks in the platform of local agitation for union with Greece. Much has been made in political speeches of the cry that Cyprus was bought from Turkey in 1878, and has since been cynically exploited by Great Britain for financial gain. In pursuance of the campaign of anti-British propaganda, acceptance by Cyprus of the settlement of the tribute question in 1927 has never been admitted by the politicians: and any public mention of the tribute based on the 1927 settlement afforded opportunities for indignant expostulation which the Orthodox leaders were quick to seize.

5. As regards the Imperial Order in Council amending the customs tariff, a deficit was envisaged in the Colony's budget of some £60,000, and of this not more than £40,000 could be met immediately by reduction of expenditure. Owing to the general fall in commodity prices the tariff stood in need of readjustment and revision to safeguard the revenue, and additional revenue of £20,000 was required to avoid encroachment on the Colony's small reserve of £90,000. The elected members of the Council had refused, however, to agree to any legislative measure involving fresh taxation. Taking their stand on the second plank of the platform for union, namely, that Cyprus was misgoverned, the Orthodox members had chosen logically to obstruct good government by refusing, as on so many former occasions, to co-operate with the administration in remedial measures, and once again in the history of their obstruction in the vital sphere of finance the neces-

sary legislation had been passed by Royal Order. A memorandum explaining the contents of the Order and setting out, in terms conciliatory to the Legislature, the reasons for recourse to legislation by Order in Council was published simultaneously. The necessity for the new tariff was recognized among leading merchants. But for the campaign of misrepresentation that was launched against it, it would doubtless have remained a public matter of ordinary indifference to the community generally.

6. There is no reason to deny sincerity to the Orthodox members in their reaction to the Chancellor of the Exchequer's statement, and no suggestion need be made that they were not genuinely reluctant to accept responsibility for additional taxes in the trade depression or, when the responsibility had been accepted by the Government for them, genuinely conscious of lost prestige. Consideration of their attitude to individual questions borders indeed upon irrelevance, and is totally misleading, unless the extreme degree in which they were bound by the theory that in politics unique value belonged to the cause of union with Greece is first appreciated.

7. No announcement was issued after the Saitta meeting, but it was generally known, and mentioned in the Press, that the members had formally resolved to address a manifesto to the people calling upon them to refuse to pay taxes and to boycott British goods by way of protest. The resolution was, it was stated, subject to the approval of the National Organization, and, until this had been obtained, no action was to be taken. Meanwhile, certain of the Orthodox members proceeded to include in their public speeches some indirect but non-actionable exhortation or reference to refusal to pay taxes.

8. The National Organization was a body, first formed in 1922 under the title of the National Assembly, which claimed as members "all adult male Cypriot-Greeks and all Cypriot-Greeks living abroad" with the object of employing "all powers and means" to achieve union with Greece. The President of the Assembly of the Organization and of the Executive Committee was the Archbishop of Cyprus, and the Bishops presided over the District Committees. The Organization, which was supported by subscriptions and by the Church, maintained a representative in London for propaganda, and employed a secretary in Cyprus who had recently established a number of "National Youth" clubs in the villages to extend the movement. The Orthodox members of the Legislative Council were ex officio members of the Assembly of the Organization, which contrived to exercise strict control over their functions in the Legislature. They were answerable both in theory and practice to the National body, rather than to their constituents, for all political opinions and activities. Reference, therefore, to the Organization of the Saitta resolution accorded with precedent.

9. The Orthodox members and the members of the National Organization eventually met to discuss the Saitta resolution at the Archbishopric in Nicosia on the 3rd October, soon after the return of the Government from Troodos. Dissension at once ensued principally, it appears, because the Orthodox members were unwilling to resign their seats in the Legislative Council, and they were pressed to do so. I enclose a copy of a *communiqué* issued after the meeting announcing an adjournment of the discussion, which had dissolved in uproar. Meetings were held again on the 10th and 11th, and on the 17th October, but no decision resulted. Apart from the question of resignation from the Legislative Council no agreement had been possible on the terms of the draft manifesto, which were reluctantly but progressively modified to meet the general opinion, openly acknowledged by the Press, that an appeal to the people to resist the payment of taxes

was doomed to failure. The inability of the national leaders to come to conclusions, the futility of their suggested boycott of British goods, and the fact that they had already paid their own taxes for the year exposed them to ridicule. They were allowed no dignified way of retreat to a rational standpoint. Foreseeing retreat and refusing to be involved in any weakness, the extremist section of the National Organization resigned in the course of the meetings.

10. It will be convenient at this point briefly to review the capacity of the National movement to support the prosecution by its leaders of desperate counsels. The policy of memorials for union, delegations to England, local demonstrations with flags and processions, anti-British invective from the Press and platforms, and non-co-operation and obstruction in the Legislative Council had come to nothing; and among the extremists in the movement the cry had gone up that they must look in future to deeds rather than (Enclosure 1.) words to achieve their object. The new policy of action had, however, no apparent programme and the cry for deeds seemed only to connote a change of words. Invective against British rule became more bitter and more direct in the political speeches, and vague incitement to unspecified deeds was more frequently included, with occasional references to the revolutionary example of other dependent countries. Many of these speeches were delivered in villages whither the leaders had carried the campaign with determination, not only for electioneering purposes, but in order to prepare an atmosphere contradictory to the criticism that adherence to their cause was restricted to town-bred advocates, priests, and schoolmasters. In 1930 (a year of elections) reports of 555 political speeches delivered in villages were received from the police, and 246 in 1931 before the 17th October. Numerous speeches also were made in village churches, and there were others of which, for various reasons, no record was obtained. Among the peasantry the campaign of misrepresentation and abuse of Government had been favoured by the deterioration of economic conditions and by rustic ignorance. Dislocation of markets in the trade depression might have shaken the apathy of the villagers towards agitation, but their confidence in the established order was deep-rooted; they would take no initiative in opposing the Government, and, if any consequence was to follow from the flow of rhetoric, would look for it to the towns whence the lead should come.

11. In the towns the movement had in the process of time continued to make headway. Fresh generations of youth sedulously indoctrinated with disloyalty had been launched by the secondary schools (in Cyprus non-governmental) on all the professions; and, outside the Government service and the realm of Government influence and activity, every branch of public life in the Orthodox community was in some way allied to the cause of union. Athletic and social clubs in particular were identified with the movement. The boy scout organization, apart from three loyal troops, those of the commercial and English schools and that organized by my aide-de-camp, was subjected to it. Ceremonies of a quasi-martial nature staged by an "ex-service" association of a few Cypriots who had fought in the Greek wars excited fervour not only among the students but the people generally, to whom the realities of any kind of military service were quite unknown. In connexion with demonstrations for union the consistently correct attitude of the Greek Government had in previous months been gravely compromised by the acting Greek Consul, a young man of Cypriot antecedents who had taken it upon himself to accept public homage in his official capacity from the disloyal elements. His indiscretions were flagrantly

exploited and an impression created that with sufficient clamour diplomatic intervention might be invoked in the cause of union.

12. Undesirable as these manifestations of disaffection were they differed only in scale and intensity from those which had been tolerated in Cyprus for over fifty years. Personal memories of such manifestations in past decades vary considerably and official records incline to reticence on this subject. They were not in themselves illegal nor, in the light of experience, a likely prelude to illegality in any serious form. A strong counteracting tendency existed in the tacit but increasingly widespread recognition among educated Cypriots of the generous benefits attaching to the status of Cyprus as a British colony. Appreciation of the many-sided development of the island's resources in recent years was by no means confined to the mercantile community. Apart from Orthodox politics, sympathetic relations and additional points of contact with the Government were increasingly perceptible. The very vehemence of the anti-government propaganda was an unpremeditated tribute to this growth of understanding. Moreover the habit of respect for law and order was firmly rooted in the inhabitants of the country and enabled the hostile movement to be conducted—securely, as it seemed—like a game of make-believe. The danger lay with the irresponsible elements in the town populations which, in the intensity of feeling that had been engendered, might fail to respect the rules of the game.

13. During my absence on leave in the summer minor disturbances had occurred at Nicosia and Larnaca in consequence of the opposition of the national party to the spread of communism. The communist party had openly attacked the national movement and succeeded in gaining many adherents. The national leaders thereupon decided to suppress all communist meetings, and they had secretly persuaded large bodies of the riff-raff in the towns to attack the communists. The disturbances were well handled by the police and kept in check, and the leaders on both sides were severely warned. But sufficient assaults had been perpetrated and injuries sustained to frighten the communists. As your predecessor was informed at the time, the successful employment of mob violence by the national party was a disquieting factor in the general situation.

14. When the Orthodox members met on the 17th October, the Bishop of Kitium had read out to them and sought their approval of a manifesto he had drafted, of which I here enclose a translation. To this the members agreed generally but stipulated that the draft should be considered at a further meeting in a week's time. The next day they learnt with astonishment that a manifesto in precisely the same terms had been published by the Bishop independently under the previous day's date and had been widely circulated together with a letter tendering his resignation from the Legislative Council. Eight of the members thereupon abandoned all their previously professed intentions and concentrated upon denunciation of the Bishop's treachery. I enclose a translation of a public announcement of their attitude which they (Enclosure 2., Enclosure 3.) issued immediately. A supplementary attack on the Bishop appeared in a voluminous broadsheet entitled "Above all sincerity" under the signature of George Hajipavlou, one of their number. The problem of the joint manifesto passed into oblivion and the ground of the political crisis shifted.

15. I shall now allude to the measures of precaution that were taken by Government after the nature of the deliberations at Saitta had been reported. Intelligence of the subsequent meetings was immediately communicated to me, and my principal advisers remained on duty in Nicosia in readiness for developments throughout the week-end holidays in which meetings were held. The Treasurer was instructed to expedite the col-

lection of all outstanding taxes, and the police were warned to be prepared to assist collectors in the event of an emergency. Arrangements were made for the issue of warrants for seizure of property on a large scale should that become necessary, and special directions were imparted to the tax collectors. Through the Commissioners the collaboration of the mukhtars was enlisted in advance. It was arranged to proceed against all well-to-do taxpayers in the first instance. I had decided that if the Orthodox members were actually to issue any form of manifesto of the kind they threatened, I should immediately dissolve the Legislative Council. At the same time I was anxious to assist them, if possible, to withdraw from the compromising position in which they had placed themselves. I, therefore, caused two invitations to be addressed to them invoking their cooperation with the Government in the study respectively of the Estimates for 1932, then in course of preparation, and of certain measures that were contemplated in assistance of agriculture. Neither invitation was accepted.

16. From the 18th October the situation centred in the Bishop of Kitium. His advocacy of illegal measures was hailed with ratification by the extremist elements. His manifesto and resignation were followed the same day by a speech at Larnaca in which he was reported to have used the following words: "For the benefit of this country we must not obey their laws. Do not be afraid because England has a fleet. We must all try for union and if necessary let our blood flow." I was subsequently advised that it was doubtful whether this speech would support a prosecution for sedition under the criminal code, but the Bishop, as I was informed at the time, hourly awaited apprehension by the police. Arrest, martyrdom, and widespread demonstrations at the scene of his trial or for his release from prison were it appears to be the phases of his scheme. As it was, no consequences ensued of any sort. I made my preparations for a flying visit to England on urgent business somewhat eased in mind by the turn political events had taken. I was due to sail on the 22nd October.

17. On the 20th October the Bishop arrived in Limassol. He had come, it seems, at the request of Mr. N. K. Lanitis, who announced that the Bishop would explain his reasons for resigning from the Council. Church bells were rung to summon the people, and a cortege headed by a slowly moving motor car draped with a large Greek flag went out between 4 and 5 p.m. to meet him. He was thus escorted to the Stadium, where a crowd of about 3,000 people, including schoolboys, had assembled. I enclose a translation of the speech he made. After a few more speeches the crowd moved off singing and cheering to a club in the town where, from a balcony, the Bishop again addressed them briefly in inflammatory terms. He was followed by Lanitis and Zenon Rossides, recently the representative in London of the National Organization, who reminded the people that the struggle should now be pursued not with words but deeds. At 7 p.m. the crowd quietly dispersed, and there were no signs whatever of impending trouble. On the 21st the Bishop attended a church ceremony in a neighbouring village and again urged his audience to disobey the laws.

18. The Bishop's words appeared to have fallen on deaf ears in Limassol, and his call to revolt was destined to be answered by those who had not heard them. In the afternoon of the 21st Mr. N. K. Lanitis telegraphed the following exaggerated account of the meeting in the Stadium the day before to Nicosia: "An unprecedented huge meeting of the town and suburbs. Bishop of Kitium spoke to the crowd which filled the Stadium. Mayor addressed the Bishop, a demonstration followed without precedent and under

leadership of Bishop of Kitium, mayor, and ourselves followed by many thousands of people from town and villages, students and ex-service men. The crowd assembled below the club where the Bishop of Kitium, Lanitis, and Rossides spoke. Never before has there been a more panegyric approval by town and district." The effects of this telegram were instantaneous.

19. In Nicosia the campaign against the Bishop's independent action had failed to carry conviction, and it was generally felt that the Bishop's policy had been forced on him by the procrastination and half-hearted counsels of his colleagues. The younger men of extreme persuasions saw their opportunity to discredit and perhaps displace the leaders. Provocative discussion, fed by the fabrication of tendencious rumour, allied with secret scheming, pervaded the clubs and political meetings before the outbreak. The first blow had fallen on the Orthodox members when, on the night of the 18th October, a printed announcement of the formation of a new and radical National Organization for Union was widely published. I enclose a copy of the announcement. The programme was vague and many of the signatories, who came from all over the island and from many trades and professions, were little known. (Enclosure 4., Enclosure 5.) The announcement was generally interpreted as a threat to the unresigning Orthodox members to tender their resignations, and was supposed to have been inspired either by the Bishop of Kitium or the Bishop of Kyrenia, Loizides' confederate. The young leaders of the new Union were, however, more self-sufficient than was supposed at the time, and their aims were not confined to the immediate crisis. They were out to precipitate the crisis and also to exploit it. They had acquired the allegiance of a political journalist of extreme opinions and quiet resolution, and with his assistance proposed to launch a subversive newspaper on the country in support of their programme.

20. The sequence of events on the 21st October in Nicosia after the telegram from Lanitis had been delivered was as follows. Manuscript copies of the telegram were made and posted in the club. The news spread. At 5.30 p.m. it was generally known that the Orthodox members of the Legislative Council in Nicosia had decided to resign. Members of the new National Union collected at the Commercial Club and sent emissaries to cause the church bells to be rung to summon the people. Others went round the town telling the shopkeepers to shut their shops and assemble at the Club. Speeches began and the crowd swelled from 300 to about 3,000 persons who swarmed inside and around the Club's extensive premises. The resigning members arrived and spoke in turn. The keynote of the speeches was that all differences of opinion and party must be set aside. The members had lost ground to recover and rose to the occasion. Hajipavlou raised one discordant note of criticism of the Bishop and was shouted down. Both he and Theodotou referred to my impending departure for England the next day, and the cry arose "To Government House. To Government House." Dionysios Kykkotis, chief priest of the most important church in Nicosia, then stepped forward and "declared revolution." A Greek flag was handed to him and he swore the people to defend it. One more speech was made, the speaker kissed the flag and the cry "To Government House" was renewed with frenzy. The leaders seized the flag, and about 6.45 p.m. began to lead the crowd in procession through the town. It is about a mile and a half from the Club to Government House. A straggling advance guard, which greatly increased en route, impeded the main body. The main procession moved in dense formation and very slowly. There was not much noise apart from occasional outbursts of cheering, mostly from spectators. Passing the Gov-

ernment timber yard, at about one-third of the distance to Government House, the crowd helped themselves to sticks of various sizes, and they tore up the wooden tree-guards along the roadside. At this point some of the crowd or stragglers diverged from the main road and moved in a parallel procession of almost equal density through the suburban village of Ayii Omoloyitades. A spectator from a house on the main road recalls that there passed for ten minutes a broken stream of men and students and for ten further minutes a thickly massed column. Ten minutes later the final stragglers were clear. Sticks, bicycles, lanterns, electric torches, and huge banners are remembered and, among the stragglers, priests holding their skirts up as they hurried forward. The advance portions of the crowd began to reach the first gate of Government House about 7.45, and the main body after 8 p.m.

21. Police headquarters had learnt immediately and were kept continuously informed by telephone of these occurrences. Eight mounted police and a baton party of twelve foot police had been despatched before 7 p.m. with instructions to prevent the crowd from entering Government House grounds. A patrol of five foot police was sent to watch and report by telephone the movements and action of the crowd on its way to Government House. Five mounted police were in line across the first gate of Government House drive and eight foot police with batons in the road in front of them. Here the advance parties of the crowd stopped and thickened gradually from the rear. The police who tried to push the crowd back were assailed with sticks and stones and eventually the horses stampeded and the crowd poured into the drive. I had learnt before 7.30 p.m. that a crowd was on its way to Government House and some ten minutes later the acting Colonial Secretary and the Commissioner arrived and reported to me. I arranged that the Commissioner should go down to the first gate and consent to speak to three representatives. When he and the acting Colonial Secretary went to the gate the main procession had not arrived and eventually, when the police broke, they were driven back at the head of the crowd to the top of the drive some 30 yards from the house. Here for about 20 minutes the crowd waited for the main procession and the Commissioner spoke to some of them. They were mostly students with a few irresponsible spectators. The police reformed and kept the people from pressing forward into the large circular terrace in front of the house. The crowd thickened suddenly and was pressed from behind. It surged forward right across the terrace up to the front door of the house. The Commissioner, acting Colonial Secretary, and the Inspector and police that had not been dispersed in the crowd took up their position at the porch facing the people. Theodotou, Hajipavlou, Pheidias Kyriakides of Limassol, the priest Kykkotis and a few others who appeared to have been leading the main procession struggled through the mass, which now enveloped the whole terrace and surrounding garden, to the porch. With them was a man carrying a trumpet and a large Greek standard. A noisy demonstration ensued with cheering and clapping and continuous shouts of "Enosis" (union). At this stage I informed the Commissioner that if the crowd withdrew to a respectful distance I would see one or two of their leaders. He and the leaders from the step of the porch attempted to tell the crowd to withdraw, but without avail. Their words were drowned in cheering and only those nearest the porch could have heard them at all. In the uproar Theodotou was heard to exclaim "The Governor justly (δικαίως) refuses to see us." A few stones were thrown and some windows broken and, as I learnt afterwards, a Greek flag was hoisted on the roof of the house. It became increasingly clear that words would not move the crowd to go and that its enthusiasm and determination would not easily be exhausted. About an hour after their arrival,

i.e., about 9.30 p.m., the leaders, realizing that they had no control, and fearing the consequences, sent messages of apology to me and decamped. It seems that quite a number of the crowd followed them and thereafter the crowd tended steadily to diminish though the movement was difficult to follow and there was much coming and going, and shifting of position. Along the road between Government House and the town parties came and went. Large groups of people stood about and jeered and threw stones at any police that passed.

22. About 9 p.m., police headquarters had learnt by telephone that stone throwing was going on and that windows had been broken, and the Local Commandant, with the Chief Commandant's concurrence, despatched the armed party of 40 men that had been held in reserve at the barracks under the senior police inspector. The inspector by a devious route avoided the crowd and brought his men into Government House from the rear without opposition. He reported to the Commissioner at the porch. The Commissioner and leaders were then attempting to parley with the crowd. Not long afterwards violent stone throwing began and the Commissioner and police were driven from the porch into the house. Further police reinforcements and a copy of the Riot Act were sent for. The bombardment of stones increased and soon all the windows in the front of the house had been smashed, a number of police were injured, many of the electric lights were broken, and the telephone room, near the porch, had been wrecked and rendered untenable. The police reinforcements of an inspector and 22 men arrived in four cars in front of the house. They were heavily stoned and entered the house, as best they could, through the broken windows; at about 10.15 p.m. Before this the Commissioner had ordered the police to make a baton charge. Only the small original police party of twelve had batons and there was a long delay in collecting them. Eventually the party attempted to debouch from the front of the house, but they were quickly driven in by the fusillade of stones. Many of the stones or rocks thrown that night were larger than coconuts and some, propelled with slings, arrived with sufficient force to shatter the masonry of the porch and to break in the front door. The door was propped up with heavy furniture but was again smashed in by timber used as a battering ram. The senior police inspector had asked for permission to fire, but the Commissioner refused because the crowd appeared to him to be composed largely of young students and because he considered that further effort should be made to disperse the rioters with unarmed police. The chief difficulty was that the now greatly diminished crowd was disposed in groups on and around the terrace and many had withdrawn into the shadow of the trees facing the house, across the terrace, whence they directed the cannonade of stones with increasing volume and accuracy. To the occupants of the house the only clearly visible target was the parties of youths in front. The roughs behind made occasional sallies to support them in destructive acts.

23. Soon after the arrival of the 22 police reinforcements the acting Colonial Secretary's car just in front of the porch was seen to be on fire. It had been wrecked and overturned earlier in the evening. A little later the crowd set fire to three of the four cars in which police reinforcements had arrived in front of the house. The crowd then threw burning sticks and blazing material through the windows of the house. Where possible police were posted under cover along the front of the house inside the windows, but the torrent of stones and havoc wrought made it difficult to maintain an effective guard. When he was satisfied that definite attempts to set the house on fire had been made the Commissioner decided that rifle fire must be employed, but first ordered the baton party again to charge, this time from the west side of the house. The charge was launched under

a hail of stones and failed to reach any of the groups of the crowd. The Commissioner had previously succeeded in reaching some of the students in front of the house. They were too excited to take any notice of what he said. Having ordered the firing party to get ready he again went out to satisfy himself that no other method but rifle fire would stop the riot. He then led the firing party round by the back of the house to the east side. Here further attempts at incendiarism were seen. The Commissioner read the Riot Act, the sense of which was also shouted in Greek by a policeman. The bugle sounded and further warning was shouted. About 100 of the crowd were visible and these at first withdrew but came back quickly shouting insults at the police. The bugle sounded again and the order to fire was given. The party, composed of twelve men, was told to fire one round per man and to aim at the legs of the crowd. The volley was fired, followed by a few scattered shots. The crowd dispersed and was pursued by the police, who were ordered to clear the grounds by charging. Two wounded rioters were left on the ground; seven in all were wounded, of whom one died later. Almost simultaneously the flames from the curtains at the west corner of the frontage of the house spread to the roof and took hold of the whole building, which five minutes later was completely burnt out. The police reported that the grounds were clear. It was then just after 11 p.m. Medical assistance was sent for the wounded and with a guard of two policemen I left in a motor car for Secretary's Lodge with the acting Colonial Secretary. We passed small groups of spectators along the roadside. In the town demonstrations continued until 1 a.m.

24. On arrival at Secretary's Lodge I sent immediately for the troops from Troodos and decided that further military reinforcements would be required. The permanent garrison consisted of three officers and a hundred and twenty-three men. Allowing for guards, transport, and men in hospital, less than a hundred would be available for parade. The police were trained and employed almost exclusively in the prevention and detection of crime and were in no sense of the term a military force. The siege of Government House had shown that they could not be expected to cope with serious disorder adequately except by rifle fire. The outrage at Nicosia appeared to have been partly prompted by a sense of rivalry with Limassol. Further rivalry and disturbance were sure to arise and should be dealt with firmly at the outset before more damage could be done without, if possible, recourse to firing. The political agitators had roused the mob but could not, even if they wished, control it. In Nicosia, it seemed, the mob had taken charge. If similar situations were to arise in the other towns and spread to villages, or if there was to be any concerted outbreak, widespread anarchy was likely to follow. The swiftest precautions were necessary to ensure that any such consequence could be forestalled. I therefore telegraphed to the General Officer Commanding British Troops in Egypt for additional troops to be sent by air as soon as possible and to the Commander-in-Chief of the Mediterranean Fleet for an aircraft carrier or cruiser. I cabled an account of the situation to your predecessor and cancelled the leave granted to me. I also caused all Commissioners to be advised by wire to take precautions in their districts and to report the situation by wire twice daily until further notice. They were informed that grave disturbances had occurred at Nicosia.

25. During the night the Chief Commandant of Police ordered the various posts around the town envisaged in the Internal Security Scheme to be manned. An office for the Officer commanding the troops was prepared at the depot (police headquarters) and the acting Colonial Secretary arranged for certain members of his staff to be there in rota-

tion on continuous duty. He himself remained with me at Secretary's Lodge, which was soon connected to the depot with a direct, and additional, telephone line. The Telegraph Company was asked to submit all private cables for abroad to the Secretariat for censorship and all inland telegrams were to be censored by the Commissioners. The necessary warrants were duly issued. The Commissioner issued large printed notices, stocks of which were kept available at all district headquarters, warning the public to remain within doors from sunset to sunrise, prohibiting assemblies of more than five persons, the carrying of firearms, and provocative conduct. These were posted in the town by daylight on the 22nd.

26. These warning notices were part of the Colony's emergency scheme for disturbances. Though it was not often possible to enforce them completely they were found useful as a preliminary measure both in Nicosia and other districts. It was clear, however, that further powers than those for "apprehended rioting" would be necessary. Tense excitement was reported from Famagusta and disturbance was expected both there and at Larnaca before the end of the day. The situation in Nicosia was extremely uncertain. I conceived that strong confident government should succeed the régime of apprehension as soon as possible and that extraordinary powers of wide and, if necessary, permanent character, should be immediately acquired. Other considerations apart, the prestige of the Government demanded that martial law should at all cost be avoided. I, therefore, sought and in the short interval of three hours obtained by telegraph your predecessor's approval to introduce the Defence (Certain British Possessions) Order in Council, 1928.

27. The Officer commanding the troops with one platoon had arrived from Troodos at 7.30 a.m. and reinforced the police piquets. Three more platoons arrived at 10.30, bringing the military strength at Nicosia to 3 officers and 91 other ranks. Excited gatherings inside the walled town were reported, schools were shut, and normal business suspended, but the exits from the town were now under control and all important Government property was protected. Before noon the Officer commanding the troops decided to send two platoons via Larnaca to Famagusta to clear up the situation there.

28. At Larnaca the Commissioner had mustered the police in the barracks and sent for the political leaders to warn them of their responsibilities. He informed them that the police had orders to shoot if any burning or looting occurred. A mass meeting had been arranged for the afternoon and, as he had not sufficient force with which to prevent it, the Commissioner decided to allow it on the understanding that the organizers and speakers would be held responsible. The meeting took the form of a heated protest, led by the mayor, against the action of the Government in shooting unarmed people in Nicosia. The meeting broke up just as the two platoons arrived on their way to Famagusta: the officer-in charge detained one platoon to assist in the preservation of order and there was no disturbance.

29. At Famagusta an ugly crowd had gathered and persistent rumours reached the acting Commissioner that Government property was to be attacked. The leaders were sent for and warned. They promised to use their influence to prevent rioting, but said they could not guarantee to keep the mob in check. One of them stated his policy would be to urge the people to passive resistance and to diminish the Government revenue by ceasing to smoke tobacco and refrain from using imported goods. Urging an excited mob to passive resistance to Government and to refrain from smoking was, of course, tantamount to provocation; and this absurd contradictory assurance was typical of the irresponsibility and dangerous equivocation of even the more serious-minded of the leaders throughout the disturbances. The need for sacrifice and bloodshed was freely mentioned in their

speeches and, at Famagusta on this occasion, the "meanness of the English in fighting unarmed people." From noon onwards an attack was expected. All British women and children were evacuated on board an Imperial steamship in the harbour and, thanks to the example and energy of the General Manager, Railway, a volunteer force of 20 British officials and others was organized and armed in support of the police. The platoon of military arrived at 5 p.m. and a protected area was established and certain key positions guarded. Notices were issued closing all licensed premises.

30. The Commissioner, Limassol, had telegraphed in the morning that all was quiet and that he did not anticipate trouble. His view was shared by the local Commandant of Police. The police were kept in barracks in readiness for an emergency and reserves were called for from the district. Quiet continued until 6.30 p.m. when two motor lorries arrived with a few soldiers from Nicosia to procure provisions. The market was opened, but while supplies were being brought out to the lorry from the market a crowd collected. The crowd soon showed signs of resentment at the market being opened for British soldiers, and eventually they rushed at the lorry and threw the sacks of supplies to the ground. Soon afterwards the church bells began ringing and the people were urged to assemble at the Bishopric. A police officer and a zaptieh were present there when the Bishop addressed the crowd from a balcony. They made no notes at the time but reported immediately that he had spoken as follows: "Since the Nicosia people refused to supply rations to the troops it is a shame for the Limassol people to give them. We must prevent by every means the taking out of rations from Limassol. Please allow us five minutes time to consider what action should be taken." A patrol of police was soon afterwards sent to the Army supply depot whither the crowd was reported to be proceeding.

31. At 8.15 p.m. the Commissioner telegraphed the situation as follows: "Town quiet but excitement prevails. Bishop still here and if more propaganda is made we shall probably have trouble. The mob has just prevented lorries loading food for troops. When warships arrive consider it advisable to send one here." Having despatched his telegram the Commissioner proceeded by bicycle to his house a mile and a half distant. About half way he overtook a crowd heading in the same direction and getting thicker as he progressed towards its front. The people were shouting "Union" and were carrying sticks. Some of them manifested hostility to him, and his bicycle, from which he had dismounted, was struck. He arrived at his house simultaneously with the head of the crowd and entered his house through the back yard. The crowd entered the yard also and began stoning the house and smashing the windows and wooden shutters. They set fire to a pile of prunings and cut the electric wires. A car arrived with tins of petrol and the crowd set fire to the back door of the house. Inside the house the Commissioner, alone with his wife, twelve-year-old daughter and two servants, was powerless. He had attempted to go out to speak to the crowd but was driven in by a hail of stones. One of the servants whom he sent to warn the police was turned back by the crowd but eventually succeeded in getting through. Seeing that the house was well alight, the Commissioner and his family made their escape from the front door. They were led by two well-disposed persons down to the sea and rowed to the Customs shed where they landed and went to the police station. When the police arrived at the scene of the fire they were too late to extinguish it and the bulk of the crowd had departed leaving a residue of spectators. The police had had no warning of any intention to burn the Commissioner's house, their attention had been diverted to the Army supply depot and their movements were handicapped by lack

of motor transport. One private car which they used stuck in a bank of sand at the side of the road and had to be abandoned. It was burnt by the crowd.

32. I received the Commissioner's telegram reporting that his house had been burnt and that the police were unable to cope with the situation at 10.45 p.m.; and the Officer commanding the troops agreed to send him the platoon from Larnaca, which since the dispersal of the meeting at 6 p.m. had been quiet. Had there been any warning of serious disturbance from Limassol military assistance might have been sent much earlier, but the lorry incident was quite unexpected and it is not unreasonably contended that but for that incident the further outbreak might not have occurred. The platoon reached Limassol at 3 a.m. the next morning. From Paphos excitement and demonstrations had been reported, and the telegraph wire had been cut. It had not been possible to send reinforcements, but as will be seen later the situation was still in course of development. At Nicosia the church bells had been rung in the afternoon and the crowd had collected and refused to move. Six thousand people were said to be massed in Lydra Street, heading towards the New Entrance, where they opened a bombardment of stone-throwing and threatened to rush the piquet. The New Entrance is on the direct approach to the town from the Government offices and Secretary's Lodge. A barricade of barbed wire "knife rests" was erected, the piquet withdrawn and a Lewis gun posted. Warnings were shouted that anyone approaching the barricade and attempting to move it would be fired at. Great credit is due to the troops and police for the skill and patience exercised on this and similar occasions under great provocation. Before midnight the crowd had dispersed.

33. In the course of the 22nd I attempted, but failed, to establish direct wireless communication with the fleet through the Khedivial steamer at Famagusta. At length I learnt that two cruisers and two destroyers were on their way to Cyprus and I requested, and it was agreed, that the two cruisers should proceed respectively to Limassol and Larnaca and the destroyers to Paphos and Famagusta. The fortunate decision of the Commander-in-Chief to send four vessels when one only had been asked for enabled the troops to take the initiative in suppressing the insurrection much earlier than would otherwise have been possible and it ensured in the meanwhile the prevention of further extensive destruction of property in the towns. The ships were due to arrive next morning and the Officer commanding the troops informed his headquarters in Egypt that in the circumstances he would not require the reinforcements, additional to those arriving by air, that had been offered. The reinforcement by air (one company) was due at 11 a.m. on the 23rd. They arrived punctually in troop carriers at the emergency landing ground 5 miles west of Nicosia where preparations had been made for their reception.

34. On the arrival of H.M.S. *London* at Larnaca the Commissioner, in accordance with my directions, proceeded on board and described the situation generally to the Rear-Admiral Commanding. It was arranged that the Admiral should motor under escort to Nicosia for a consultation with me at mid-day. He was asked and consented to land immediately 200 men at Limassol, 100 at Larnaca, and as many as possible up to 50 at both Famagusta and Paphos. At my conference with the Admiral the respective rôles of the navy, military and police were decided on. The closest co-operation with Commissioners was to be maintained and daily conferences held by them with police and naval or army officers in charge in all districts. The Admiral made it clear that only to meet a grave emergency would he send naval parties inland. In the event of necessity for armed intervention by His Majesty's Forces, the senior naval officer on the spot was to take com-

mand at the ports, elsewhere the responsibility for command was in such circumstances to rest with the Officer commanding the troops. Thereafter I communicated with the Admiral at pre-arranged hours twice daily by telephone. The arrangements for cooperation and command were successfully maintained throughout.

35. At Famagusta and Paphos the situation was complicated by the incursion of villagers into the towns. Agitators were busy in the district urging them to come in. At Paphos the Commissioner was the only British official, and he and his wife the only British residents. The force of police was limited to 38, and on the morning of the 23rd he wired for military support. Throughout the 22nd mass demonstrations had continued, and the leading citizens, when warned of their responsibilities had confessed that the situation was beyond their control. The populace awaited in tense excitement the promised arrival of the Bishop of Kitium. The Commissioner placed a small guard on his house, and with the bulk of the police awaited developments at the police barracks. At 10 p.m. the crowd dispersed and the Commissioner learnt that a deputation was proceeding to Limassol to urge the Bishop to come to Paphos on the 24th to address a meeting to which all villagers were to be summoned. On the 23rd at 10 a.m. two officers and a naval party landed from the destroyer and went straight to the police barracks. The Commissioner's wife was received on board. Demonstrations had recommenced early in the morning, the telegraph wires were again cut, and attempts were made to block the road to the harbour. A platoon of the Royal Welch Fusiliers that had been relieved by the Navy at Limassol arrived at 6 p.m. They turned back a procession which was moving in the direction of the Commissioner's house intent on destruction. The officer commanding the platoon was anxious to take immediate steps to break up the disturbance, but the Commissioner had decided that he would withhold the initiative until the day following, when the deputation of ringleaders would return, perhaps with the Bishop, from Limassol. Meanwhile the situation was closely watched, and guards were posted on Government property. The Commissioner prudently matured his plans.

36. At Nicosia one of the wounded rioters had died in hospital in the night. When this was known bell-ringing started, a crowd assembled at the Archbishopric, and a deputation proceeded to the Commissioner to obtain permission for a funeral procession. After consideration I allowed this to be granted on the strict understanding that a prescribed route approved by the military would be followed. The funeral was at 3 o'clock and a crowd, estimated at 8,000 persons, proceeded from the church in the town to the cemetery outside. Boy scouts, ex-service men, representatives of all the political clubs carrying banners and Greek flags attended, and speeches were made urging the people to continue the struggle. In the church a collection had been made for a fund with which to support the police, who were to be persuaded to desert the Government. A number of hooligans attacked the house of a police officer just outside the town on the prescribed route, and a party of the troops, who had been withdrawn to special dispositions at a discreet distance, was sent to drive them off. At the same moment the procession arrived from the cemetery on its way back to the town. With admirable coolness the troops succeeded in dispersing the hooligans and holding up the procession under a hail of stones. Later the crowd again stoned the piquet at the New Entrance, and it was some hours before they could be persuaded to disperse. The Commissioner, assisted by the mayor, warned them of the consequences if they did not do so, but, as on all such occasions in the towns at that time, the

excitement, pressure of people, and confusion were such that the threat of force had little effect.

37. A disturbance which started at 5 p.m. that day at Larnaca was very successfully handled by the police and navy. A crowd gathered, summoned by bell-ringing, and was seen to be moving towards the Commissioner's house, which lies a mile away from the centre of the town. The local Commandant of Police ordered his twelve troopers to ride through the rear of the crowd and disperse them, using their whips if necessary. The Commissioner and local Commandant followed with an armed party of 14 police in two motor-cars. The troopers, six of whom were injured in doing so, drove the crowd on to the sides of the road, and the cars rushed through heavily assailed with stones. The windscreens of the cars were smashed and personal injuries sustained. The armed party took up a position blocking the way to the Commissioner's house, and the Commissioner went forward and shouted to the crowd, which had re-formed and was advancing, that unless they dispersed fire would be opened. The crowd wavered and it was seen that a naval platoon, which had been warned by the Commissioner to watch developments, was coming up from behind, using their entrenching tool handles as batons with excellent effect. Soon the crowd broke and fled in various directions. From one party that was pursued two revolver shots were fired. The naval officer ordered a volley of six rounds to be fired in reply. No casualties resulted. Two much smaller crowds, one composed of villagers, were broken up by the police in the town later that evening. No demonstrations were reported from Larnaca afterwards.

38. In the course of the day the Commissioner of Paphos had telegraphed that it was essential that the Bishop of Kitium should be prevented from going to Paphos, and the Commissioner of Limassol had been told by wire to prevent him. Meanwhile a large crowd supplemented by villagers was on guard outside the Bishop's house as his arrest was anticipated. To consider the situation I summoned a conference at which among others were present: the acting Colonial Secretary, Officer commanding the troops, Chief Commandant of Police, and Commissioner, Nicosia. All were agreed that the Bishop should be arrested that night, and that if possible the most prominent ringleaders in Nicosia should be arrested simultaneously. However important it might be to suppress the Bishop, the situation, it was strongly held, centred in Nicosia, and until order and obedience had been restored in the capital it would not be possible to deal effectively with disturbances elsewhere.

39. The Officer commanding the troops and Chief Commandant of Police undertook to effect the arrests that night. I proposed that the arrested leaders should be deported under the powers I had by then acquired under the Defence Order in Council and regulations, and that they should be removed forthwith to the warships until arrangements could be made to deport them finally. I was advised that this proposal was preferable to any alternative both from the legal aspect and that of public security. No adequate alternative, indeed, was seen. There could be no serious question of the criminal guilt of the responsible ringleaders. The removal of their influence and reassertion of the Government's authority by force of examples were an urgent necessity. Their detention within reach of the populace would be likely to provoke the crowds to further excesses in the hope of securing their liberation. I viewed with apprehension the prospect of an assault on the prisons such as was actually threatened in Nicosia. The avoidance of situations which would lead to bloodshed was my constant duty. In my belief and that of all compe-

tent observers at the time it was mainly due to the power of deportation that I was able to take the initiative decisively at this critical stage.

40. It was thereupon decided to arrest and deport the following Nicosia ringleaders:–

> George Hajipavlou.
> Dionysios Kykkotis.
> Tieofanis Tsangarides.
> Theofanis Theodotou.
> Theodoros Kolokassides.

41. By 5 a.m. on the 24th the six prisoners were on board warships. In Nicosia private cars from the Volunteer Force with soldiers and police had collected the prisoners, within half an hour, just outside the town on the road to Larnaca whither they were conveyed under escort by lorry. No resistance was met with except from Hajipavlou who locked his front door, attempted to escape, and when apprehended refused to move. The Volunteer Force was also employed that night in distributing to all district headquarters supplies of the Defence Order in Council and large printed posters containing translations of the Defence, Regulations.

42. The arrest of the Bishop at Limassol was successfully effected. A small crowd on guard at his house was found asleep and no resistance was offered. A rocket let off as an alarm from the roof of the house appeared to be unanswered. Half an hour later the church bells rang and a crowd collected and approached the building, while police and sailors were still inside searching the villagers for dangerous weapons and taking their names. The police officer sent for reinforcements and brought out eleven police to stop the crowd. His party was stoned and driven back to a position guarded by a naval party facing the house. The crowd increased and began to force in the door of the house and the police opened fire. Twenty one rounds were fired, six casualties inflicted, and the crowd dispersed; one of the wounded subsequently died. No further rioting occurred in Limassol.

43. Early on the 24th it was reported that a number of cars and lorries were leaving Nicosia for the villages to bring in villagers and firearms. Precautions were taken by additional piqueting, and a deputation from Morphou which arrived at the entrance to the town by motor car was stopped, severely warned and sent back to Morphou. I arranged for the troop-carriers to fly round the island demonstrating above the chief towns, and following a route above those villages from which excited meetings had been reported. The news of the arrests did not become general in Nicosia until about midday when a crowd gathered at the Archbishopric and a meeting was held there to discuss what measures should be taken to force the Government to liberate the ringleaders. At this meeting a reconciliation, engineered by Emilianides, was concluded between the communist leaders and the church. Vatiliotis, the Moscow-trained communist, kissed the hand of the Archbishop and promised him the support of his party in the immediate struggle against the Government.

44. Shortly afterwards the Archbishop sent his chaplain to seek an interview with me. I caused him to be informed that I was willing to see him but that his route to and from Secretary's Lodge would be prescribed by the Officer commanding the troops. Both the Officer commanding the troops and the acting Colonial Secretary were present at the interview. I enclose a translation [Enclosure 6] of the communication which the Archbishop read to me. I then requested him to withdraw in order that I might frame my reply. On his return I told him forcibly that I had no intention of liberating any of the

ringleaders, that the Government and not he was responsible for law and order, and that the armed forces would not hesitate to take extreme measures to repress any further disturbance. His proper sphere of responsibility, I said, was to urge his flock to obey the civil power and to warn them, as I had warned him, of the consequences of disobedience. The chaplain took notes of what I said and I dismissed them.

45. In the evening the crowd again stoned the piquet at the New Entrance and refused to move. Assaults on the electric light plant and law courts within the walls and on the Government offices and central prison outside had all been threatened; and the Officer commanding the troops decided rightly that the crowd must be dispersed. One round was fired by the piquet and one man wounded by it; the crowd dispersed immediately. The wounded man died the next day. All British women and children living outside the guarded zone were concentrated that night in an hotel within it. The police reported that the height of feeling in the town endangered the lives of British officials. Inside the walls in the Greek quarters the police had no control. Cyclist-patrolling out of range of the crowd was all that was possible.

46. At Paphos on the 24th demonstrations outside the police barracks again started early in the day. The telegraph wires were still being cut, and the navy had erected a wireless installation within the barracks. The deputation that had gone to Limassol to persuade the Bishop of Kitium to come to Paphos returned without him at 11 a.m. Among them was Galatopoulos, ex-member of the Legislative Council, who on the way back, as was learnt later, had incited the inhabitants of Pissouri, an intervening village, to destroy some valuable Government property in the neighbourhood. The return of the deputation was a signal for the crowd to assemble in force and they massed outside the barracks. The Commissioner, who had been awaiting this opportunity, emerged from the police barracks and proceeded towards the crowd followed by a naval and military party, with fixed bayonets, which extended in line on either side of him. He spoke to the crowd and briefly explained the regime which had been introduced under the Defense Order in Council. Police came forward and unfolded like aprons in front of them and exposed to view the large posters of translated regulations under the Order. The Commissioner then called on the crowd to disperse and the line of soldiers and sailors advanced upon them. The crowd melted, the notices were posted and all clubs and cafés were closed. Patrols of police were sent out to all adjacent villages to warn them of the consequences of their expected incursion into the town. In the town curfew was rigidly enforced. Thereafter the Commissioner rigorously suppressed irregular bell ringing and the flying of flags. Any symptoms of disturbance were immediately and firmly dealt with, and the police were soon able to turn their attention to outlying villages.

47. The situation at Kyrenia in both town and district had so far been quiet. Savvas Loizides and two other agitators were known to have gone on the 20th to Dikomo, a village in the southern foothills of the Kyrenia range, to consult the Bishop who was touring his diocese and thereafter Loizides was heard of, now in Kyrenia now in Nicosia. The police expected trouble but none resulted. On the 23rd the Commissioner had suggested that as there were 54 Europeans in the town naval or military protection should be sent there. He added that he did not contemplate any disturbance, and that there was no hint of rioting; and he was informed on the 24th that assistance could be sent only if he reported a serious emergency. Kyrenia is only 16 miles by road from Nicosia. He was advised to organize the male British residents and visitors as a defence corps. The same evening in-

telligence was received that the Bishop of Kyrenia intended to visit Nicosia the next day and the Commissioner confirmed by wire that this was so. It was most undesirable that the Bishop should be allowed to fulfill his intention at that moment, and it was decided to refuse him admission to Nicosia. The Commissioner was advised by wire of this decision.

48. The Bishop arrived at the outskirts of Nicosia at 7 a.m., was stopped by a piquet, and, after a scene of violent protest, obeyed the order to return to Kyrenia. He proceeded straight to the church where a service was concluding. He was seen to be pale with anger and suppressed emotion, and when the service ended he addressed the congregation on what had happened. "I went to Nicosia," he said, "and was stopped by bayonets." He raised his voice to a shout and words and phrases followed in a tumult. "This is a Greek place and must be given to Greece. Englishmen are tyrants and malefactors" are reported phrases and, finally, "I shall hoist the Greek flag where it should be." He led the people—about 300 followed him—straight to the Government offices and, at his direction, the Union Jack was hauled down and torn in pieces. The Bishop's personal servant hoisted the Greek flag in its place. Warned of the event the Commissioner came running to the scene, mounted the stairs to the balcony and called on the crowd to disperse immediately. "Speak to us in Greek," the Bishop shouted, and, after further warnings, led the procession back to the town. The Greek flag was hauled down and a new Union Jack was at once hoisted.

49. The Commissioner summoned and warned the leading inhabitants. They would be responsible, he said, for any failure to exert their influence in preventing further disturbance. The telegraph wires had been cut and he sent a report of the situation to Nicosia by motor-car. At 12.30 p.m. two sections of soldiers arrived under the command of a sergeant and were used for patrolling and piquets in the town in support of the police. It was not possible to guard the entrances to the town completely and throughout the day the crowd at the Bishopric greatly increased. Villagers from neighbouring and even distant villages continued to come in. Some came in buses which stopped well outside the town, allowing the villagers to cross the fields straight to the Bishopric. By 8 p.m. one thousand people were assembled there, most of them armed with heavy sticks and pieces of iron. About 9.30 p.m. it was reported from Karmi, a hill village five miles distant, that most of the inhabitants were on their way to the town. A party of troops and police, sent to prevent them, found that they had already reached the Bishopric where speeches and shouting recommenced. Soon a yelling mob advanced on the armed party. The police inspector stepped forward and ordered the people to drop their sticks and return to their villages. The armed party advanced with fixed bayonets and were heavily stoned and forced to retreat. Stones continued to be hurled and both the inspector and army sergeant were hit. After a further warning the armed party fired twelve rounds. The crowd recoiled and then came on again. A second volley was fired whereupon the crowd retired to the Bishopric. Three rioters were found to have been wounded and were instantly removed to the hospital. One of the wounded died.

50. On receiving the Commissioner's situation report in the morning I had asked the Admiral whether he could send one of the seaplanes attached to the cruisers or, now that an additional cruiser had arrived, release the destroyer from Famagusta to reinforce Kyrenia until sufficient troops could be sent there to quell the disturbance and arrest the Bishop. Naval support was not, however, practicable owing to distance. The officer commanding the troops had arranged to send a platoon there after dark, when the

Bishop's arrest could best be effected, but could not spare more than the two sections until then. He was still engaged in clearing up the situation in Nicosia, his first and most important objective, where desperate elements of the crowd were still active and were reported to be arming themselves with miscellaneous weapons. He succeeded in dispersing the crowd that day without firing, by raiding the town in a lorry protected with wire netting. The communist, Vatiliotis, was caught in this way in the act of addressing the people and was brought back in the lorry under arrest.

51. Reports were now coming in of numerous demonstrations and of acts of sabotage and defiance of law in the villages. At the usual conference on the 25th with my advisers, the Officer commanding the troops was asked whether further military reinforcements from Egypt would not be necessary. He replied that he would not require them but that he would ask for a section of armoured cars to expedite suppression of disorder in the villages. He agreed also, in view of the continued cutting of telegraph wires, to ask for wireless installations for all district headquarters. The Royal Air Force had established wireless at the depot in Nicosia, and, so long as the Navy remained, wireless communication was assured with all the port towns except Kyrenia. I had, however, to look father ahead to the time when the warships would be withdrawn.

52. The Commissioner, Kyrenia, had been warned that the Bishop would be arrested that night and that reinforcements would be sent. When, therefore, the platoon arrived there, after 1 a.m. on the 26th, they were immediately escorted to the Bishopric and they surrounded and entered the building. Fifty men armed with sticks were found inside but offered no resistance. The Bishop attempted to shake off his escort but was overpowered, placed in a lorry and brought straight to the central prison at Nicosia. In view of the serious developments at Kyrenia the arrest of Savvas Loizides had also been ordered. He was found to have escaped to Nicosia, where he was apprehended later. I decided that he, the Bishop of Kyrenia, Vatiliotis, the communist, and his colleague Costas Skeleas should all be deported with the other ringleaders. Skeleas was seized later in the day at Limassol, where he had arrived from Nicosia with pamphlets announcing the communist party's decision to join the nationalists.

53. At Famagusta (Varosha) the crowd was still out of hand and many villagers were congregated in the town. There had been a mass meeting of about 8,000 people on the 24th, at which the leaders, in response to further warning, made some attempt to discourage violence, but continued to equivocate. The mayor's speech was thus reported: "We have called you here to demand our rights and in order to approve the measures taken by our representatives. My position does not allow me to go farther." The Archimandrite followed, telling the crowd that freedom could not be realized without sacrifice and bloodshed, but adding that freedom should be fought for lawfully. Others continued in the same strain, and called on the people to disperse quietly. Considerable resentment was manifested against the leaders. The police clerk who reported the speeches records that he heard much "grievance" expressed that rioting was not allowed by the English soldiers. "While the British soldiers and zaptiehs are killing our brethren and innocent school boys who are unarmed in other towns, must we leave them here untouched?" they asked. "How can we go back to our village after we have kissed our wives and children and bade them good-bye?" exclaimed some villagers from Paralimni.

54. On the 25th, the cruiser *Colombo* arrived and landed 30 marines. The substantive Commissioner returned from leave in England and took over. It was decided to retain

the women and children on board a steamer in the harbour in view of persistent rumours of mob action, though already there were signs of a return to normality in the town. The decision was justified soon after 5 p.m. when, urged by certain communists, the mob forced the proprietors of licensed premises to reopen. This was followed by a concerted attack on the Varosha police station, a building in the town isolated from the local police headquarters and little used during the disturbances. Windows and doors were smashed and police property and records thrown into the street or destroyed. The captain of the *Colombo* with two officers, two ratings, and a part of police, proceeded to the police station and established a guard there. Returning through the town they were insulted and stoned by the crowd. Adzes, bottles, and earthenware pots were also thrown at them, some being dropped on their heads from balconies. An officer with seven marines and a few police was sent to bring in the guard from the wrecked police station. Threatened by the crowd on two flanks and assailed with various missiles, including iron shovels, the party opened fire. One rioter was killed and two wounded. Minor injuries were sustained by the marines, and the officer's steel helmet was heavily indented. The activities of the crowd continued until midnight. The collection of large stores of missiles was reported, and, in order apparently to created a diversion, which would weaken the armed forces in the town, a wooden bathing hut belonging to the English community some little way outside was set on fire. Additional forces were landed from H.M.S. *Colombo*, and additional guards posted. There was no further rioting in the town after that night.

55. On the arrival of the *Colombo*, the Rear-Admiral agreed to relieve the army platoon at Famagusta. He also relieved the platoon at Paphos. This enabled the Officer commanding the troops to concentrate his force at Nicosia and strike out quickly into the districts wherever required. Reports of disturbance in villages were disquieting and demanded prompt measures of suppression. In Nicosia district telegraph and telephone wires had been cut, the railway line had been interfered with, and, in two villages, payment of taxes had been refused. Many rebellious demonstrations had been reported. The platoon from Paphos left in lorries in the evening of the 25th, spent the night on Troodos and proceeded early on the 26th to Nicosia, deviating from the direct route in order to visit certain villages in which disturbances had occurred. A flight of day bombers, which had been sent from Headquarters, Middle East, Royal Air Force, accompanied the troops and demonstrated without bombs above the villages. At the village of Zodia a crowd of some 300 people attempted to stop the lorries and stoned the soldiers. They paid no attention to warnings that were shouted by the police and, taking cover behind a wall at the side of the road, continued to throw stones. The officer in command ordered fire to be opened and dispersed them. One man was killed, another wounded. A ricochet bullet wounded a girl inside a house. In Akacha, another village in the Nicosia district, a ration lorry was held up by a crowd that morning and the warrant officer in charge, who had an escort of two men only, was forced to open fire. Two men were wounded, one of whom died later. In a village in the Paphos district, the police opened fire in defence of a police station, and one man was slightly wounded. No other casualties were inflicted by rifle fire in the villages during the disturbances.

56. Another platoon from Nicosia perambulated a sector of the Nicosia district during the 26th, certain arrests were made and general warnings given. Small army patrols with British officials as guides and interpreters were also sent by motor car to culpable villages in remote areas, and this system proved most effective. I enclose, for the purpose

of illustration, a report [Enclosure 7] by the Chief Veterinary Officer of action taken in this way at Kambos, a village in the Paphos Forest (Nicosia district), where since the 22nd disorder had prevailed, telephone wires had been cut, and Mr. G. W. Chapman, Assistant Conservator of Forests, had been held up by the villagers on his way to Nicosia and forced to return to his station in the forest. When opposition was met with, the patrols dispersed the people and imposed obedience with the threat of force, supported where necessary by the butts of rifles. By the 27th, the Defence Regulations had been posted throughout Nicosia district and thereafter there was no more rioting either in the capital or the villages. The sight of military patrols, the scope of the Defence restrictions, the knowledge that ringleaders had been arrested, and the increasing consciousness that crime would be punished and damage paid for by those responsible sobered the turbulent and encouraged the law-abiding to exert their influence even in the town.

57. Order had by the 27th been restored in all the towns in the island, but in other districts, which had not had the advantage of the military patrols, disturbance and sabotage continued in villages. In the Paphos district the Navy co-operated with the police in village patrols. Apart from two attempts to burn police stations, which were successfully resisted, the disturbances there were not serious. In the Larnaca district the damage done was confined to destruction of telegraph lines, the cutting and blocking of a road and illicit collection of fuel. In Kyrenia district telegraph wires were cut, one police station was broken into and one salt store looted. In Limassol and Famagusta districts more serious conditions prevailed.

58. On the 25th, in the Limassol villages there were, apart from demonstrations, two thefts from police stations, and in three villages the police were forcibly disarmed. The destruction of valuable Government property at Pissouri on the road to Paphos, to which I alluded in Paragraph 46 above, occurred the day before. A tax collector was robbed and many villagers collected salt from the Limassol lake. The majority of villages were reported to be opposing the police, and a small police patrol sent out to deal with the robbery of the tax collector (at Apeshia) was met and threatened by a crowd and failed to enter the village. The District police were ordered to return to Limassol, and a strong police patrol left there in a lorry at midnight, with orders to use sufficient force to restore order and effect arrests in offending villages. The patrol made a lengthy and successful tour next day. One further rifle was stolen and, on the 27th, a small detachment of police was ambushed and forcibly disarmed on its way to Limassol. Salt continued to be stolen, villagers coming from far and near with donkeys, and even motor lorries, to collect it from the lake. On the 27th an army platoon visited Limassol in troop carriers and penetrated into the district in support of the police. On the 28th all the stolen rifles were returned. On the same day the inhabitants of Mandria repaired, on my orders under the Defence Order in Council, a bridge on the main road from Troodos to Limassol which they had destroyed. On the 29th the Principal Forest Officer, with a party of soldiers and police, dealt summarily with the responsibility of certain villages in the hills for offences against the Forest Laws: extensive destruction of the forests by fire had been threatened. Investigations and arrests proceeded, and in the course of the first week of November the District police were all returned to their normal stations.

59. On the 26th in the Famagusta district two forest plantations and some forest buildings were set on fire, four police stations were broken into and wrecked and one customs building was looted and destroyed by fire. On the 27th one police station was burnt

and another broken into, three forest buildings were destroyed by fire and three salt stores looted. Two further forest stations were burnt on the 28th and 29th respectively. On the 28th an army platoon arrived at Famagusta by air from Nicosia and patrolled certain villages in the immediate neighbourhood which were considered responsible for the continuous damage to the telegraph and telephone lines and the railway track. The platoon returned the same day to Nicosia. A police patrol was sent on the 29th to the Karpass peninsular whence the most serious damage had been reported. On the 30th, K. P. Rossides, a former member of the Legislative Council, who was known to be touring the district and alleged to be inciting the people to acts of destruction, was ordered under the Defence Regulations to quit the district and to reside in Nicosia, where his activities could best be controlled. The same precaution was subsequently taken in respect of other political leaders who were suspected of continued agitation against the Government. A small detachment of troops under the command of a sergeant was sent to reinforce the police in the Karpass on the 31st. By the 2nd November order was restored throughout the Karpass, many arrests had been made and the villagers in that area had begun to rebuild the Government property which a week before they had destroyed. To enable the police to expedite their investigations the Captain of the *Colombo* relieved them of all duties connected with the enforcement of curfew in Varosha.

60. There were in all some 200 villages in which excitement prevailed and demonstrations were made, but without breach of the law. Less than 70 villages were guilty of destruction of property. Many outrages were the work of small gangs of malefactors or individuals, but no satisfactory distinction can be drawn between communal and individual responsibility for incitement. There are 598 Greek-Orthodox villages and mixed Orthodox and Turkish villages in the island. Three hundred and eighty-nine of these took no part at all in the disturbances.

61. The nature of the occurrences in disturbed villages is, as will be appreciated, difficult to define. The news that the towns had defied authority appears to have been brought to many villages by special emissaries from the towns who assured the villagers that the Government was overthrown and the millennium approaching. Meetings were held at which the shout was raised, "There is no Government—this is the end of the English period—this is the day of revolution and hurrah for union." Drunkards and bad characters generally made the most of the occasion. Law-abiding villagers who continued to pay their taxes were derided. Police and tax collectors were avoided or ignored. If they obtruded themselves and persisted in unpopular duties they were told that they were no longer required. No tax collectors and only a few police were assaulted in the villages. Thus situated, some of the police went out discreetly on patrol until conditions should improve, and others displayed very considerable courage and resource remaining at their posts to reason with the people and resisting, sometimes single-handed, illegal acts and acts of violence on the part of the crowd. Many mukhtars and elders announced their resignation. Some resigned under pressure and others, to avoid calumny, said they had done so when they had not and bided their time. Those resignations which were actually received by the Commissioners were not accepted and were soon withdrawn. A few mukhtars confidently supported the police. The notion that the Government had been overthrown was, it appears, very superficial, and amid the turmoil an acknowledgment of authority persisted by sheer momentum. At Apeshia, where the tax collector had been robbed of his collections, only their recent payments were taken by the people. The bal-

ance in the tax collector's satchel was handed for safe custody to the treasurer of the church. In the Famagusta district, it is told, one villager who had stolen salt complained to the police that some of the salt he had taken from the looted salt store had been stolen from him by a fellow villager. One troublesome village in the Paphos district was effectively threatened that, if it did not behave, the detachment of police there would be removed to another village. In the Famagusta and Limassol districts, villagers with disputed grazing and other rights in the state forests seized the opportunity to attack the property of the Forest Department. A large number of offending villages were situated on the borders of the forests. The most general offence was the theft of salt. The opportunity to profit materially from the relaxation of normal control was readily appreciated.

62. The speed with which order could be restored in the districts was only conditioned by the availability of visiting patrols and the time required for reaching distant villages. The process was complete in the first week of November. The return to normal life in the disturbed villages was, moreover, absolute. Agitators and malefactors were freely blamed and the investigations of the police welcomed and openly assisted by well-disposed villagers. At Lythrodonda, a village responsible in October for a hostile demonstration, it was possible on the 9th November to allow unrestricted attendance at the annual fair. As many as 5,000 villagers were present and no manifestation of unrest or disorder supervened. In the towns, however, subterraneous agitation continued and no sign of public regret or repentance was forthcoming. A section of the populace was still open to persuasion that the insurrectionary movement might, after all, prove successful, and might yet be reinforced with outside assistance in the form of arms or diplomatic intervention. Every nerve of government has been strained to dispel these illusions and to teach obedience. I can here record good progress, though completion of the task is not even now in sight.

63. On the 30th October I had been able to publish widely throughout the Colony your predecessor's telegram of the 28th. The unqualified approval there expressed of my action in arresting the ringleaders and the statement that sedition and disorder would not be tolerated by His Majesty's Government were of vital assistance. On the 3rd November six of the deported ringleaders sailed for England and Gibraltar, and the remaining four followed them on the 6th. The fact of the ringleaders' departure and that they were deported for life was announced through the local Press. This helped to clear the air of the rumours which were fabricated that the extraordinary powers and measures taken by Government would soon be cancelled. These rumours still persist, but their power of conviction continues to diminish. On the 3rd November a notice was published announcing that the cost of reparation of Government property destroyed would fall on Greek-Orthodox communities in relation to responsibility, and that a law to give effect to this decision would be promulgated shortly. Notice of the issue of Letters Patent abolishing the Legislative Council was published on the 16th November, and on the 1st December three new laws passed by me under the new Letters Patent were promulgated. Respectively they prohibited the unauthorized flying or exhibition of flags, restricted the ringing of church and other bells to prevent recurrence of their abuse as tocsins, and vested in me, as Governor, the power of appointment of village authorities. The Reparation Impost Law, implementing the decision that destroyed property should be replaced and repaired at the cost of the responsible towns and villages, was passed on the 21st December. The imposts amounted in all to £34,315 and over 80 per cent. of the total has since been paid.

More than 2,000 persons have now been convicted by the assize and magisterial courts for specific offences connected with the disturbances and have received adequate sentences.

64. Meanwhile the garrison of His Majesty's forces in the Colony was progressively reduced. On the 5th November an additional company of infantry arrived from Egypt and relieved the naval landing parties at Famagusta, Larnaca, Limassol, and Paphos. His Majesty's ships sailed the next day for Malta. The section of armoured cars that had been asked for also arrived. They toured the island and then, being unnecessary for practical purposes, were returned to Egypt by the first available opportunities for steamship transport. One infantry company was stationed at headquarters in Nicosia, the second company was divided equally between Famagusta and Larnaca, and the third was stationed at Limassol with two sections at Paphos. At the end of November the detachment at Paphos was withdrawn and those at Famagusta and Larnaca each reduced by half. One of the two reinforcing companies then returned to Egypt. On the 31st December the second reinforcing company also returned to Egypt, the original garrison company having in the meanwhile been brought up to full strength (4 officers and 175 men). The curfew restrictions, the enforcement of which had been undertaken by the military, acting in support of the police, were removed in all towns in which they had been imposed on Christmas eve. The restrictions had been rigid: no lights or noise of any kind had been permitted during curfew hours.

65. The goodwill of the large Moslem population and the other minorities towards the Government never wavered throughout the disturbances, though they suffered the hardships of the curfew orders and other restrictions in common with their fellow townsmen. Their loyalty was fully shared by their Greek-Orthodox compatriots, who formed the majority of the civil service and the police. A greatly increased burden of work and responsibility was cast upon almost all branches of the administration: it was borne cheerfully. The police responded to every call made upon them without hesitation.

66. In the opening paragraphs of this despatch I have described at length the circumstances existing in the Colony which rendered possible the outbreak in October. The facts and considerations there set out have for the most part long been known to His Majesty's Government. They are all directly related to the seditious agitation which has been tolerated in Cyprus for over fifty years. There is no evidence to show that the outbreak was premeditated or prearranged. Any such theory would be sufficiently contradicted by the haphazard nature of the deplorable events, which, in preceding paragraphs, I have placed on record. The nature of the events disposes also of any suggestion that the upheaval represented a widespread desire on the part of the Greek-Orthodox inhabitants for the transfer of Cyprus to Greece. The ground for disturbance was prepared by the leaders of the union movement in the hope that the occurrence of generalized demonstrations would advance the cause of union by means of publicity. Demonstrations occurred, but rapidly degenerated into orgies of criminal violence on the part of mobs and malefactors over which the union movement had no control. The destructive crowds were largely composed of roughs and students. The majority of respectable citizens either kept out of the way or, in order to avoid the stigma of disloyalty, cheered for union. It is indeed in this stigma of disloyalty that the strength of the union movement chiefly resides. Until the shadow of union is finally removed from the political horizon, the leading inhabitants are not likely to come forward in large numbers to support the Government and co-operate openly in the progress of their country under British rule.

67. In conclusion, I desire to reiterate and place on record in this despatch my deep appreciation of the services rendered by the contingents of His Majesty's naval, military, and air forces which co-operated in the restoration of order in Cyprus. The unfailing readiness of the officers respectively in command to understand the peculiar problems of the administration and the needs of the moment rendered their assistance a source of strength which could not be measured by platoons and companies. For the support and sympathetic guidance of your predecessor, yourself and your department throughout a most anxious and difficult period I am profoundly grateful.

I have, &c.,
RONALD STORRS,
Governor.

Enclosure 1.

(*Translation.*)

NATIONAL ORGANIZATION OF CYPRUS.

Communique.

Last Saturday, 3rd October 1931, the National Organization held a lengthy meeting. After a short introduction by His Beatitude, as President, regarding the matter to be discussed, the members of the Legislative Council explained their views in connexion with the disposal of the surplus balances of the Colony and the enforcement of the Customs duties by Order in Council and as to the measures to be adopted in order to face the state of affairs thus created.

After a long discussion, decision on these matters was postponed for the next day, but on account of the absence of many members it was considered advisable for the National Organization to hold another meeting next Saturday, 10th October, 1931.

FROM THE OFFICE OF THE NATIONAL ORGANIZATION.

Enclosure 2.

(*Translation.*)
GREEK BRETHREN,

* * *

Fifty-three years of English occupation have persuaded all and have proved most clearly:-

    (a) that enslaved peoples do not get liberated by means of prayers and solicitations and appeals to the tyrants' sentiments;

    (b) that the reply to the latter is contempt for the beseeching humble slaves, and arrogance;

(c) that our only salvation from all points of view is our national liberation and that the foreigners are here in order to serve their general and special interests with a certain result, our moral and material misery.

Looking therefore steadily at the bright star of new Bethlehem and our national salvation we have one and only one way to walk, the way which is narrow and full of sorrows but leads to salvation. We should hoist under the light of the day the flag of union and in the kiln of our continuous endeavours standing close together round it, reconciled and setting aside our differences we should with sacrifice and every means pursue our national liberation by getting united with mother Greece. In the name of God, the Protector of justice, morality, and liberty, of these benefits in life which are insulted by the foreign tyrant, in the name of the eternal ideal for a united Greek Fatherland, let us be obedient to the voice-law, voice-order which comes down from the Mount Sinai of the National Legislations.

Let us be disciplined trusting in the triumph of justice over might. What even if the foreign tyrants rely upon colossal columns of beastly force and power? Against force let us set up the justice of our cause which is sure to be triumphant at last, especially so when it is inspired with all the force of the soul. Against beastly force let us oppose the unconquerable arms of the soul which are inspired and fortified by the steady strength of unenslaved faiths knowing and capable of being always victorious and of moving even the motionless steep mountains of impossibilities.

Let us show obedience to this voice, which is the voice of the Fatherland, a voice ascending from the graves of those who for seven centuries had sown their bones in the bosom of the land of Cyprus without the realization of their aspirations and dreams for a national salvation having sweetened the miserable days of their life of many woes. Citizens in thought of a free Greek land we betray those while being obedient to the laws and orders of the foreign ruler to whom and to whose illegal laws we owe no obedience. Let us oppose his unjust and arbitrary wishes and let us strain every nerve in order that he should clear out from our country for the sake of his own purification, this abomination which is called English occupation and Administration of Cyprus.

I have said that this way is narrow and full of sorrows and leads through sacrifices to the salvation of liberation. Children of that race which set up the triumphs of the heroism of the holocausts of Messolonghi and Arcadi, let us not interrupt our way, the way which leads to the steep tops of the success of victory.

Let us on then and let the youth lead the way. Let them show that they are not young in body only but that they have also a young soul rushing towards the difficult aims and the difficult struggles for a free country, for a happy morrow which belongs more to them than to us. Let us on for God who has not created his peoples and his creatures to be the slaves of others is with us.

NICODEMOS, Bishop of Kitium.

17th October, 1931.

Enclosure 3.

(Translation.)

COMMUNIQUE BY THE BODY OF THE GREEK MEMBERS OF THE COUNCIL.

The body of the Greek Members of the Legislative Council surprised at the one-sided and secret resignation of the Bishop of Kitium met in the afternoon of Monday last in the great refectory of the Archbishop's residence and resolved upon abstaining for the present from duly characterizing the strange attitude of the Bishop of Kitium who has secretly retracted at the last moment, torpedoed the unity of the body of the Greek members and annihilated by his one-sided action and the manner in which he carried it out, the significance and the weight of a collective resignation with a Pancyprian and well-defined programme, and especially by means of a document much more radical and revolutionary than his own and bearing the signature not only of the whole body of the Greek members but also that of the Ethnarch.

We further decided, in the face of the treacherous activities of certain infernal circles who have, unfortunately, led astray a few Cypriots of good faith, to remain upon the asphyxiating battlements on which we have been ordered to stand as martyrs by the people if not for anything else at least for preventing the repetition of the tragic story of the time of "The Seven," a story that soiled the history of our Island and delivered the liberties of the people chained by our own hands to the foreign ruler.

We further decided, *inter alia*, to remain on the battlements owing to the lack of a collective, harmonious, and responsible struggle, as those who have already resigned (except Mr. Pheidias I. Kyriakides) had not declared that in case of re-election they would not attend the meetings of the Council or that they would resign again, and because we have recently marked out a specially radical and revolutionary policy aiming principally at the attainment of Union, which we will pursue with all powers and sacrifices when the Council will shortly be supplemented.

> The Members of the Council.
> ST. STAVRINAKIS, Member for Nicosia.
> TH. THEODOTOU, Member for Dagh.
> G. HAJIPAVLOU, Member for Morphou-Lefka.
> M. SHACALLIS, Member for Famagusta.
> D. SEVERIS, Member for Kyrenia.
> K. P. ROSSIDES, Member for Karpass.
> CHR. GALATOPOULOS, Member for Paphos.
> CHAR. NICOLAIDES, Member for Khrysokhou-Kelokethara.

Enclosure 4.

RÉSUMÉ OF A SPEECH DELIVERED BY THE BISHOP OF KITIUM, NICODEMOS MYLONAS, ON 20TH OCTOBER, 1931, AT THE SPORTS GROUND AND AT "ENOSIS" CLUB, LIMASSOL (AS REPORTED BY THE LOCAL COMMANDANT OF POLICE).

GREEK BRETHREN,

I thank the deputy Mayor, the President of the Labourers' Confederation, and the people of Limassol who received me on my arrival. In the name of God and people I declare the union with mother Greece and the disobedience and insubordination towards the illegal laws of the immoral, vile and reproachful régime which is called "English régime" and which rules Cyprus without any human right, without our consent, the consent of a people which is more dignified and capable than they are. Yes, England is a great nation, but they must know that they will fall because they ill-treat the other peoples, they do not know how to rule them and they consider them as brutes.

The time that some people in the world had other peoples under them as slaves has passed. The Roman Empire which used to rule and torture the poor has fallen, and there is no doubt that English reign will also fall one day because it is dishonest and immoral. I was blamed that I am inconsistent and insincere but it is not the time now to apologize. I shall, however, apologize before my twelve comrades and before the whole people of Cyprus when we shall be united with Greece. I do not want to appear as a vanguard, but the vanguard will be the one who will act in actions. I declare the disobedience and insubordination to the illegal laws of this immoral, vile, and shameful régime; I invite every Greek Cypriot to the highway of sacrifice. The time has come to show to the foreign rulers that we are a people with national sentiments and educated and that we must live free under the Hellenic flag. Down with the vile and reproachful régime! Long live Union.

Enclosure 5.

(Translation.)

THE CYPRUS NATIONAL RADICALIST UNION.

TO THE PEOPLE OF CYPRUS,

A common impatience of the slavery of our Island, a common yearning for freedom and a common readiness for work have brought us to-day from the four corners of the Island to Nicosia to form the "Cyprus National Radicalist Union."

What we aim at, how and where we shall march, is stated below in the principles of the "Cyprus National Radicalist Union" which constitute its programme, of which principles we shall henceforth be the plain soldiers and faithful keepers.

Principles Constituting the Programme of the Cyprus National
Radicalist Union.

The members of the Cyprus National Radicalist Union—Greek inhabitants of the Island of Cyprus—being profoundly conscious of their obligations to themselves as human beings on the one hand and on the other of their great Greek fatherland and the immortal Greek civilization (decide as follows):–

(1) They lay down as their aim the fanatical pursuit of the union of Cyprus with the Greek political whole.

(2) They firmly believe that the annexation of Cyprus to the free Greek political whole not only satisfies an inalienable human right but is the only means of

creating (suitable) conditions for the real spiritual and material progress of the inhabitants of the Island.

(3) They proclaim without fear before God and man that their moral world as human beings and as Greeks is in no way consistent with any state of bondage or dependence, however much it might be relaxed at any time.

(4) To show their indignation at the slavery of their Island and manifest their intractable bent for freedom, they oppose absolutely any co-operation with the foreign Government in its legislative, executive, or administrative jurisdiction—both under the present form of government and under any other which might be given to Cyprus in the future.

(5) They shall regard as an enemy of their country any Greek inhabitant of the Island whose conduct is opposed to or in any way slackens the national struggle, which has one aim—union and nothing but union.

(6) They shall work untiringly for the sound and national education of the people—they shall endeavour to make as close as possible the ties with their free fatherland—they shall support with fanaticism everything Greek and shall avoid doing anything inconsistent with Greek dignity.

(7) They shall support to the best of their ability the products of the land, the industries and the handicrafts of Cyprus.

(8) They shall be closely bound to one another in their national activity and they shall give one another all possible moral and social support.

(9) They shall observe strictly the principles of the Cyprus National Radicalist Union—they shall be inspired with these only, looking solely to the idea and not at all to persons in the carrying out of their national struggle.

(10) They shall work with perseverance for the propagation of the Cyprus National Radicalist Union and they shall follow faithfully its programme and decisions.

Greek Cypriots.

Those of you who embrace the above principles of the Cyprus National Radicalist Union, and desire the speedy and sure fulfillment of its stated aim, come to its bosom.

The Cyprus National Radicalist Union will have as its official organ for regular communication with the public the newspaper *Irreconcilable*, which will begin to be published as from next Saturday, the 24th October.

Nicosia, 18th October, 1931.

> ANDREAS CH. GAVRIELIDES, Advocate, Varosha.
> ANTONIS CH. OEKONOMOU, Journalist, Larnaca.
> ANTONIS E. GEORGIADES, Doctor, Yialousa.
> ARGYROS DROUSHIOTIS, Headmaster of the Gymnasium, Limassol.
> GEORGHIOS PHASOULIOTIS, Journalist, Limassol.
> EVAGORAS G. PAPANICOLAOU, Advocate, Nicosia.
> THEOKLITOS SOPHOCLEOUS, Headmaster of the Gymnasium, Kyrenia.
> THEOPHANIS TSANGARIDES, Merchant, Nicosia.
> IOANNIS PIGASIOU, Doctor, Nicosia.

K. ZACHARIDES, School-usher, Nicosia.
COSTAS PIKIS, Merchant, Nicosia.
LEFKIOS EVGEN. ZENON, Advocate, Limassol.
XENOPHON COUMPARIDES, Professor, Evrychou.
PETROS ADAMIDES, Merchant, Varosha.
PIPIS CONSTANTINIDES, Dentist, Nicosia.
POLYKARPOS S. IOANNIDES, Clerk, Kyrenia.
SAVVAS LOIZIDES, Advocate, Kyrenia.
STELLIOS KLYTIDES, Advocate, Nicosia.
CHRISTOS TRACHONIDES, Grocer, Nicosia.
PHOTIOS GEORGIADES, Advocate, Paphos.
ALEXANDROS DIMITRIOU, Merchant, Varosha.

Enclosure 6.

(*Translation.*)

YOUR EXCELLENCY,

In my capacity as Ethnarch of Cyprus and on the insistence of the people who have of their own accord assembled outside the Archbishopric I came here in order to bring to Your Excellency's knowledge that on account of the arrest of certain citizens of Cyprus the situation created is such as to be pregnant of imminent dangers in general.

I have felt it my duty to inform Your Excellency of the situation and to recommend, for averting any untoward events, that all those arrested should be released. This measure will ward off any danger.

I divest myself, Your Excellency, of any responsibility in case you will not be willing to enforce this measure, so imperatively called for in the present circumstances and highly beneficial for the interests of the Government and the country.

This is what I had to state, Your Excellency, with the certainty that His Majesty's Government will not delay any longer the fulfillment of the sacred and just national aspirations of Cyprus which is unanimously demanded by the entire Greek population of the Island.

I have, &c.,
CYRIL,
Archbishop of Cyprus.

Archbishopric,
24th October, 1931.

To His Excellency
The Governor of Cyprus.

Enclosure 7.

REPORT ON ACTION TAKEN AT KAMBOS, 26TH OCTOBER, 1931.

OFFICER COMMANDING TROOPS,

* * *

Two sections of the Royal Welch Fusiliers accompanied the volunteers to Kambos—there were no incidents *en route*. On arrival all villagers (men) were assembled at the main coffee house, where Mr. Chapman addressed them in the terms of the proclamation, and informed them that they must return the stolen telephone instruments, yield their arms, help to repair the telephone line, and refrain from hostile demonstration or other action against the interests of the Government.

After some parleying the telephone instrument was produced and troops searched the houses for arms, recovering six shot guns and one barrel of a broken gun.

I then informed the assembled villagers of the true state of affairs in Nicosia and elsewhere, the action already taken by Government in dealing with the ringleaders and the serious consequences which would follow any attempt on their part to fail to comply with the Defence Regulations—the latter being explained in detail. Those present expressed their willingness to comply with the regulations and not to create any breach of peace, it being understood by them that any punishment for such offences would be general. It was further explained to the people that the telephone line must be repaired by this evening, and that thereafter any interruption of the telephone service would produce punitive expeditions by air and other means.

A Greek flag found in the coffee-shop was seized and, together with the arms mentioned above, taken to Nicosia and lodged at Police Depot.

Mr. Chapman, Mr. Dommen, and the police corporal left for Stavros, retaining their rifles, and the other volunteers returned to Nicosia with the two sections of the Royal Welch Fusiliers, arriving at 4.15 p.m.

ROBERT J. ROE.

4.40 p.m., 26th October, 1931.

Extract from a telegram from the Secretary of State for the Colonies to the Governor of Cyprus. (Sent 8.45 p.m., 9th March, 1932).

Immediate. No. 28.

My telegram 8th March, No. 26. As every Member of Parliament has received copy of Coundouriotis' circular I think it is right you should have immediately by telegraph a summary of allegations in enclosure "Information regarding recent uprising of the Cypriots and its suppression."

Following is summary main allegations:—

Ten Cypriots killed, about hundred wounded; two Archbishops, one priest, two late members Legislative Council, four other citizens banished for life, their property seized and relatives forbidden to send money for their subsistence. Number of other political leaders deported to villages far from their homes.

Large number of men and women maltreated and homes destroyed; thousands of arrests made, mostly on absurd or even imaginary grounds. e.g., arrest of all inhabitants of Limassol owning Underwood typewriters.

Following are cited as well-authenticated facts giving concrete idea of methods employed in suppressing revolt:

21st October. After burning of Government House when bulk of crowd had dispersed police wounded stragglers, eight by gunshots, fifteen by bayonet thrusts, three of whom died next day.

23rd October. Kyriakos Mathaios, of Limassol, bayoneted by British soldier while entering Nicosia, died same night in hospital; at celebration of Mass at Varosha police attacked congregation, killed two men, Christou and Papaiossif, wounded eight others, of whom one, Phylis, died two days later.

24th October. On occasion arrest Metropolitan of Kition, British troops fired on crowd "by way of intimidation" wounded eight persons, of whom two, Dimitriou and Constantinidis, subsequently died: same night fifty sailors entered residence of Archbishop of Kyrenia and demanded delivery Archbishopric flag; on receiving no answer they struck him in the face.

25th October. British officer with sixty soldiers entered village Akaki and ordered George Ioannou take down Greek flag flying from church; on his refusal officer ordered soldier to fire killing Ioannou.

26th October. Same officer and detachment proceeded Kato Zodia: in panic following arrival two women, Helen Polycarpos and Maria Zodiatis (latter pregnant), wounded; Zodiatis died soon after; hundred sailors commanded by Army captain and Unwin proceeded to Arsos, ordered priest sign bond £60 for fellow villagers for sticks gathered without permit; on his refusal they dragged him half naked to village square and maltreated him in presence assembled parishioners; eight villagers then caned till blood ran; detachment then departed after forcibly taking £134 from inhabitants.

27th October. Sixty British soldiers under Police Sergeant Pinkerton entered Pissouri, assembled men of village, tied them up, flogged them, to make them denounce the person who had set fire to neighbouring customs station. Christodoulou, youth of twelve, tortured by twisting rope into flesh of head in order to force father to give desired information. Detailed report of this filed at office of Archbishop of Limassol; also report of rape two women, Marie Prokopi and another of tender age, name not stated: same detachment proceeded Trimiklini, broke into church and destroyed Bishop's chair and carried off sacred vessels, etc.

28th October. Detachment thirty sailors sent Mandria to force villagers repair burnt bridge, dragged from bed old man named Saloumis where lying with high fever, loaded him with heavy beam and order him carry it to bridge. On the way as old man slow, stumbling, one of force bayoneted him in back; victim died few minutes later.

29th October. Detachment British troops led by Armenian police officer proceeded Angastina, assembled villagers and selected four younger men beat them with butts of rifles until dropped unconscious. Summary ends.

On 12th November I gave official casualty figures in Parliament as Cypriots six killed thirty wounded (one wounded died later). Police casualties thirty-nine. Are these figures correct?

Am publishing your despatch of 11th February but please telegraph any further information which will enable me to reply to charges summarized in this telegram.

II. Dispatch of R. Storrs, 25 November 1931 (CO 67/237/11)

A. Letter of R. Storrs, 25 November 1931

The Right Honorable Sir Philip Cunliffe-Lister,
Secretary of State for the Colonies.

Government House
Nicosia
25th November, 1931

Sir,

I have the honour to forward for your information a memorandum on the subject of the legal aspect of the demand for Union with Greece prepared, at my request, by the Attorney General. This document exposes concisely the roots of the difficulty experienced in framing prosecutions or obtaining convictions in respect of activities of an apparently seditious nature such as were responsible for the recent disturbances in Cyprus. I shall doubtless have occasion to revert to this question in later correspondence.

I have the honour to be,
Sir,
Your most obedient,
humble Servant,
Ronald Storrs
Governor.

B. Memorandum on the Legal Aspects of "Enosis," 25 November 1931

Governor's Despatch 25/11/31
Memorandum

ON THE LEGAL ASPECTS OF "ENOSIS"

On several occasions prior to the recent disturbances this Department has had occasion to consider whether or not certain activities in connection with Enosis (union) brought the persons responsible within the ambit of the Criminal Law and if so whether, in the circumstances, proceedings should be instituted.

2. Such activities usually took the form of speeches, processions and meetings generally accompanied by the carrying or flying of the Greek flag and a general shout or cheer for union, and in some instances by the singing of the Greek national anthem.

3. So far as it is possible to generalise, I think it may fairly be said that the speeches consisted of,

    (a) a mere or less justifiable criticism of the Government, its constitution, policy and activities,

    (b) a complaint of high taxation,

    (c) some half truths,

> (d) some fantastic statements, (e.g. that England was 100 million pounds in debt which she was seeking to obtain from her Colonies, especially Cyprus. That the Government encouraged the Communists because they were against "union"),
>
> (e) an invitation to the audience to embrace the idea of union, to work for it, and to try and persuade others to do the same.

I think it may fairly be added that the majority of speeches of which I have seen reports did not contain any instigation to overthrow or drive out the existing Government by force.

4. In the consideration of the questions set out in paragraph 1 we were faced with the following difficulties:–

> (a) There had for many years been a policy of laissez-faire.
>
> (b) Isolated cases could not well be dealt with without raising the whole question (I expressly called attention to this in a minute paper on the subject of the registration of clubs).
>
> (c) The evidence with which we were furnished was often unsatisfactory, particularly reports or speeches where there was the twofold difficulty of reporting and translating.
>
> (d) The requirements of clause 205 of the Cyprus Courts of Justice Order, 1927, as interpreted by the Courts, as to corroboration were frequently lacking.
>
> (e) The results obtained in somewhat similar cases (e.g. the Kyrenia procession case and communist prosecution) made us doubtful of the view the Courts might take.

5. Whether or not the inculcation of the idea of union, without the counselling of any other criminal act, is itself a criminal act (e.g. treasonable felony or sedition) must, I think, be academic having regard to the fact that a deputation asking for union has been received by the Secretary of State and a petition to the like effect has been received by the Governor from the Archbishop and forwarded to the Secretary of State . . .

C. Letter from H. Henniker-Heaton, 26 November 1931

The Office of the Attorney General
Cyprus, 26th November, 1931.

My Dear Bushe,

We have received a cable from the Secretary of State asking for a weekly report of the cases tried in connection with the disturbances. This gives the impression that it may be thought at home that nothing has been done. You will have gathered from my letter of last week that this is not so. The police have done their best but it is always difficult to get evidence here at any time owing largely to the fear of reprisals, which fear is accentuated at times like the present.

I think the disposal of the small offences has had a good effect, particularly upon the villagers. They are very simple and got an idea into their heads doubtless in some cases from agitators that there was no longer a Government so they seized the opportunity to do a little damage. They have now realised their mistake. The fines in some cases appear small, but their value of money is different to ours, and they do not like paying.

As to the major cases, I have just seen a copy of a despatch sent home yesterday in which it is said I advised that there was no chance of a conviction for the burning of the Government House and the Commissioner's House, this is a little misleading. I did so advise on the original police reports but further enquiries have now been made and further evidence obtained, but it is in my opinion far from satisfactory. At best for Government House, there is one man for setting fire to it, and to a car; one man for setting fire to a car, four men for throwing stones; sixteen for being present but no evidence that they took any part; sixteen more for being present, the only corroboration of their being present, being statements obtained from them by the police which I doubt if the Court will admit and there are six persons the only evidence against whom is that they have been wounded by rifle fire. None of these persons are in any sense leaders, some of them are known bad lots.

The Pissouri case which I mentioned to you last week should be committed today and I have arranged with the Chief Justice for a special assize next week when I hope it may be taken. I propose to prosecute myself.

As to the "leaders" at present under arrest, the police reports so far have not been satisfactory from the point of view of prosecutions, and they are trying to get further evidence.

I do not think there is anything wrong with the Criminal Law. I have always had doubts if the mere promulgation of the idea of Enosis (union) is seditious, but from a practical point of view we could hardly prosecute for it as successive Governments have more or less sympathetically received petitions asking for it. The difficulty is to get reliable evidence of acts and words to bring the persons concerned within the Law.

Yours sincerely,
H. H.

D. British Commentary

1. Persons who made an attack on, and burned down Government House for the purpose of depriving the King of his sovereignty over Cyprus, or, in other words, of procuring Union with Greece, are, in my opinion, guilty of high treason.

2. Persons who publish such matters as are contained in enclosures 1 & 2 are in my opinion, guilty (a) if the publication is written, of treason felony, and (b) if it is verbal, of sedition.

Whether the advocacy, written or verbal, of union with Greece is by itself treason felony or sedition is a difficult question, though I am inclined to think that it is. We need not, however, go deeply into this point, since I gather from Mr. Trusted's remarks that Governors and Secretaries of State have dallied with persons who advocated such policy.

I have been driven to the conclusion that the real truth lies in paragraph 4(a) of Mr. Trusted's memorandum, and that sedition has been allowed for years to raise its head unchecked. I attach a further letter which I received today. I suppose it is a good and useful thing that all the dupes should now be prosecuted, but I still regret that they have not got the Bishops and other ringleaders, so that justice should appear to be impartial and no respecter of persons.

H B 8/12/31

III. The Toynbee Affair; the Greek Press, April-July 1932 (CO 67/244/7)

A. The Toynbee Article, 23 April 1932, *The New Statesman and Nation,* April 23, 1932.

CYPRUS

CYPRUS needs ventilation; and it has never been properly ventilated since its present connection with this country was started by the British occupation of this ex-Ottoman island in 1878. Every time that the Cypriot Greeks have stated their case to the British Government in a pacific and constitutional manner and have been given the invariable "No" for an answer, British public opinion has been too deeply preoccupied with more important and interesting questions to pay attention. It is, of course, one of the glaring evils of our over-rushed modern world that it should be so much more difficult to gain a fair hearing by orderly than by obstreperous behaviour. The barbarous truth is that, for anybody who really wishes to get anything done, there is almost a premium nowadays on sensationalism which usually means violence; and the recent history of Cyprus is a case in point. The disturbances in Cyprus last October gave Cyprus "news value" for a few weeks in the press of the United Kingdom; and in due course the disturbances have elicited a White Paper ("Disturbances in Cyprus in October, 1931" Cmd. 4045 [1932]) which may be "news" now for a few days.

The situation here revealed is one that is common enough in the world at large, but uncommon (if we have been justified of our pride) in the British Empire. A great Power finds itself in possession of a small territory in which the politically conscious and active element among the majority of the local population does not wish to live under this foreign Power's rule, but desires political union with another country of its own nationality. (In the case of Cyprus, where four-fifths of the local population are Greeks, this other country with which union is sought is Greece.) The great Power simply says: "What I have I hold, and that is that. The Cyprus Question is closed"—or, rather, "no Cyprus Question exists." The Cypriot Greek nationalists remain unreconciled and recalcitrant; H.M.G. professes grief at their "disloyalty" and "ingratitude." At length certain local events—a controversy over the control of education and a controversy over the balancing of the Budget—bring the hostility towards British rule to a head, and there are disturbances. H.M.G. suppresses the disturbances and gives a crack of the whip. Six leaders of the Cypriot Greek national movement are deported, at least nominally, for life; the Cyprus Legislative Council is abolished; a Reparation Impost Law imposes collective responsibility on towns and villages for damage done during the disturbances to Government property to the tune of £34,000; other laws prohibit the unauthorised flying or exhibition of flags and restrict the ringing of church and other bells; and the appointment of Cypriot village authorities is vested in the British Governor (White Paper, p. 30). On the ruling Power's part, to sit tight and to go on saying "No" remains the Alpha and Omega of policy. As the Governor himself sums it up, "until the shadow of union [with Greece] is finally removed from the political horizon, the leading inhabitants are not likely to come forward in large numbers to support the Government and co-operate openly in the progress of their country under British rule." But how "remove the shadow"? By saying "No" again, on the Bellman's principle in *The Hunting of the Snark*: "What I tell you three times is true"? The remedy is not convincing, for already we have repeated the magic formula time and again, and the Greek national movement in Cyprus has thriven on it. Is this policy of negation, which failed to avert the disturbances, likely to prevent their recurrence?

The answer to this question depends, of course, on what the real strength of the Cypriot Greek national movement is. It appears, according to the White Paper, to have started among "town-bred advocates, priests and schoolmasters"; to have "continued, in the process of time, to make headway in the towns"; and latterly to have gained a footing in the villages. "Fresh generations of youths sedulously indoctrinated with disloyalty had been launched by the secondary schools (in Cyprus non-governmental) on all the professions; and, outside the Government service and the realm of Government influence and activity, every branch of public life in the Orthodox community was in some way allied to the cause of union". As for the countryside, "there are 598 Greek Orthodox villages and mixed Orthodox and Turkish villages in the island. Three hundred and eighty-nine of these took no part at all in the disturbances . . . There were in all some 200 villages in which excitement prevailed and demonstrations were made, but without breach of the law. Less than 70 villages were guilty of destruction of property." Apart from statistics, the strength and extent of Cypriot Greek nationalism can be gauged from the fact that on the eve of the disturbances the existing National Organisation was "gingered up" by the formation of a new and radical National Organisation for Union, and that, after the outbreak, there was a public reconciliation, in the name of national unity, between the Archbishop of Cyprus and the leader of the local Communists. All this is in the normal course of modern nationalist movements all over the world.

So, too, unfortunately, is the stifling political atmosphere which the conflict between Cypriot Greek nationalism and British imperialism has exhaled. "In 1930 (a year of elections) reports of 555 political speeches delivered in villages were received from the police, and 246 in 1931 before the 17th October." And we hear of a "Defence (Certain British Possessions) Order in Council, 1928," and an "Internal Security Scheme." This is an unpleasant whiff of the nineteenth-century Hapsburg "police-state" with an alien officialdom living in a potential state of siege. There is a Hapsburg touch, too, about the Governor's official language. The word "Greeks" burns in his mouth, and in the earlier paragraphs of his despatch he sedulously writes "Orthodox" instead (as who should say: "Here are some common-or-garden British subjects who just happen to be domiciled in Cyprus and to be members of the Orthodox Church"). But as the narrative proceeds a more natural language asserts itself, e.g., "One round was fired by the piquet and one man wounded by it. The wounded man died next day. All *British* women and children living outside the guarded zone were concentrated that night in an hotel within it. The police reported that the height of feeling in the town endangered the lives of *British* officials. Inside the walls in the *Greek* quarters the police had no control." (Italics mine.)

What of the future? The outcome of the disturbances of last October shows that the Cypriot Greeks are not yet in a mood to fight for their independence *à outrance*, as the Moreot Greeks fought in 1821–29 and the Irish in 1916–21. This is shown by the slightness of the casualties (six Cypriot civilians killed and 30 wounded, of whom one died later, and 38 casualties among the police), and also by the fact that in an island of some 350,000 inhabitants, of whom four-fifths are Greeks and one-fifth Turks, the British military garrison, which numbered three officers and 123 men at the outbreak of the insurrection, had been reduced again to four officers and 175 men by the end of the year.

There is evidently no truth in the (inevitable) allegation that the suppression of the insurrection was accompanied by atrocities. It looks as though Cyprus were one of the few patches of the British Empire which we are capable of holding for an indefinite time by force, if we choose. But do we choose, when we give our minds to it? The reality of the Cypriot Greeks desire for union with Greece is surely evident. The protection of the local Turkish minority has ceased to be a formidable problem now that Greece and Turkey themselves have buried the hatchet. The French Government have a lien over the disposal of Cyprus by treaty, but there is no evidence that the French would object to a transfer of the island from the British Empire to Greece. As for our own British title deeds, they do not bear inspection. We extorted the military occupation and civil administration of Cyprus in 1878 from the then sovereign, the Sultan of Turkey, at the point of an ultimatum, under threat of throwing the Sultan forthwith to the Russian wolves, who were at that moment baying at the gates of Constantinople; and our occupation was conditional upon our defending the integrity of Turkey-in-Asia by force of arms! That title, surely, is void; and on every ground of common sense and decency we ought to make up our minds to clear out at no distant date.

The choice lies between staying in Cyprus and losing face or leaving Cyprus and adding to the honours which we won for the British Empire when we left Wei-hai-wei in 1930 and the Ionian Islands in 1864. We do not regret that Corfu and Ithaca are under the Greek instead of the British flag to-day. This Ionian precedent for British policy towards Cyprus is singularly apposite.

Arnold J. Toynbee

B. Letters about the Toynbee Article, April-May 1932

British Legation,
Athens,   April 30, 1932

My dear Sargent,
The efforts of the Grand Cyprus Committee are bearing fruit. Professor Arnold Toynbee's Cyprus propaganda in the Statesman and Nation of April 23rd and the Bishop of Kitium's propaganda in the precincts of the House of Commons are calculated to encourage agitation if not violent disorders in Cyprus and to undermine the Governor's position.

Yours ever,
Patrick Ramsay

May, 1932

Mr. Parkinson,
I had not heard before of Professor Toynbee's article in "The New Statesman and Nation" for the 23rd April, but I have obtained a copy which I annex.

From our point of view it would scarcely be possible to write a more mischievous article. He himself sums up his conclusions in the statements that our title to Cyprus is void, and that on every ground of common sense and decency we ought to make up our minds to clear out at no distant date.

I think that we should, if necessary, invoke the assistance of the Foreign Office to prevent the Professor from repeating his exploit in "The Journal of the Institute of International Affairs." It might be useful if I now wrote to Professor Toynbee asking when he will be able to send us the revise of his article.

Since I wrote this I have since gathered from you that steps have already been taken to prevent the publication in question.

CRD 11/5

Downing Street,   19th May, 1932.

My dear Van,

You will remember our correspondence ending with your letter of the 7th April about Professor Toynbee's article on Cyprus for the "Survey of International Affairs."

We had heard nothing more, until Bevir who was up at Oxford picked up some interesting, not to say entertaining, information about what was happening. I enclose a note which he has given me on the subject.

You already know about the article in the "New Statesman and Nation" of the 23rd April, as Ramsay has drawn attention to it in his letter to Sargent of the 30th April.

Yours ever,
S. H. Wilson.

Downing Street,
19th May, 1932.

My dear Storrs,

This is just to let you know that we have reason to think that, owing to objection in the Council of the Institute of International Affairs, the article by Professor Toynbee on Cyprus, about which you and we have had correspondence with him, may not be published at all!

Meanwhile, Professor Toynbee has written an article for the "New Statesman and Nation," which appeared in the issue of 23rd April. I refrain from comment on the article. We know that the Minister at Athens has had it; so doubtless you have seen it too.

Yours sincerely,
A. C. C. Parkinson.

I met Sir Arnold Wilson on Sunday last, in Oxford, and on his hearing that I was in the Colonial Office he at once said that he had been fighting our battles for us, or words to that effect. I asked him what he meant, and he told me that, as a member of the

Council of the Institute of National Affairs, Toynbee's article on Cyprus had come before him for inclusion in the Institute's Journal. He said that he had told the Council that he regarded the article as tendentious and unsound, that Toynbee was wooly headed, and a few years before had been violently pro-Turk, and was quite likely to turn violently anti-Greek; and that it might do the Council no good to have his paper published in their Journal. Moreover, he did not think it a suitable place for attacks on British government, and that if they insisted on publishing it, he would resign and circularise all the members of the Institute saying why he had resigned. He said that he told the Council that that would lose them a great deal of money through resignations, as the article was such as to alienate most sensible people. He was told that the Council must publish what they considered to be true and ought not to be moved by financial considerations. He retorted that if they did not get the money from subscribers they would have to get it in the City, and they would then have to sing the tune that the City called.

The net result was that the article was not published.

But the Council seem to have satisfied their annoyance by refusing to publish an article of Sir Arnold Wilson's. I might add, though it is not wholly relevant, that that Sir Arnold Wilson at once had it published in another magazine, with a note that it had been refused publication in the Journal of the Institute of International Affairs, and headed by a quotation of Roosevelt's to the effect that we should beware of softness of the head and hardness of the heart.

It may be this action which has precipitated Professor Toynbee into print in the "New Statesman."

I did not tell Sir A. Wilson that we had considered trying to get the article stopped: but I think I did say that I knew of its existence and that it had been sent to us for comments.

A. Bevir
13. 5. 32

C. The Toynbee Article in the *Survey of International Affairs*

Toynbee, Arnold J., *Survey of International Affairs 1931* (Oxford University Press and London: Humphrey Milford 1932). Part III. Europe, B. South-eastern Europe, Section (iii): "Cyprus, the British Empire and Greece," pp. 354–394. This article was published by Oxford University Press for the Royal Institute of International Affairs, London, to whom we owe our gratitude for the permission to reproduce it here.

Cyprus, the British Empire and Greece
by Arnold J. Toynbee

In the year 1931 the island of Cyprus, which in political status was at that time a British colony, became the scene of political disturbances which drew attention to the changes that had taken place in the status of the island during the preceding half-century.

These disturbances broke out among the Greek inhabitants, who constituted approximately four-fifths of a total population which at that time stood at a figure of rather more than 350,000 souls. Greek had been the predominant language in Cyprus since the latter part of the second millennium B.C., when it had been introduced by an influx of Greek immigrants from the Aegean; and from that time onwards Cyprus had shared the general fortunes of the Greek-speaking world. In the 'classical' age of Ancient Greek history, Cyprus, like other parts of the Greek world, was parcelled out among a number of sovereign independent city-states.[1] Like other Greek lands, Cyprus eventually became a province of the Roman Empire; and in the Middle Ages, like other Greek lands again, Cyprus was successively seized by the Crusaders, acquired from the Crusaders by the Venetians, and conquered from the Venetians by the Ottoman Turks. The Ottoman conquest of Cyprus took place in A.D. 1570; and the Turkish garrison which was introduced into the island then and thereafter accounted for almost the whole of the non-Greek fifth of the population as it stood in the year 1931, when the population of Cyprus was approximately four-fifths Greek and one-fifth Turkish, the other elements represented being almost negligible.

The Ottoman phase in the history of Cyprus immediately preceded the British phase; and this social heritage of membership in the Ottoman Empire was shared by the people of Cyprus not only with inhabitants of other Greek lands but with a much wider circle of peoples and countries ranging from Serbia to the Yaman and from Algeria to 'Irāq. In this connexion it may be noted that, by the year 1931, the long-drawn-out process of the break-up of the Ottoman Empire had reached its conclusion, and that the ex-Ottoman territories and peoples had all passed out of the hands of the Ottoman Pādishāh, the Sultan-Caliph,[2] into one or other of two alternative régimes. The majority had reorganized themselves into sovereign independent national states on the Western pattern; a minority had passed from the dominion of the 'Osmānlīs into the dominion of other alien Powers. The independent successor states of the Ottoman Empire included the 'Balkan States', namely Greece, Albania, Bulgaria, Jugoslavia, Rumania; the Turkish Republic; and two fully independent Arab states, namely the Najd-Hijāz and the Yaman. In 1931, the catalogue of fully independent Arab states of Ottoman antecedents seemed likely to be enlarged, in the near future, by the addition of 'Irāq and Egypt, and, at some later date, by the further addition of the Lebanon and Syria. There remained a small minority of ex-Ottoman territories under French Italian and British rule for which, in 1931, the national independence attained by the Ottoman successor states was not in prospect. These territories included Algeria, which was a French possession, and Tunisia, which was a French protectorate; Libya and the Dodecanese, which were Italian possessions; Palestine, which was a British mandated territory, and Cyprus, which was a British possession. In studying the 'post-war' histories of any of these countries in their international bearings, their exceptional situation has to be borne in mind. They were patches of territory which had exchanged Ottoman rule for Frankish rule in the midst of far larger and more important territories which had exchanged Ottoman rule for national independence. It is only in the light of this fact that their 'post-war' histories can be understood.

It may be convenient to recall, briefly, the stages by which the transfer of Cyprus from Ottoman to British rule had been accomplished.

The first stage was the signature at Constantinople, on the 4th June, 1878, of a 'Conven-

---

[1] The city-state was not, of course, an exclusively Greek institution. The Ancient Greek city-states had their Syrian contemporaries and their Sumerian predecessors. The Greek city-states in Cyprus, like the Greek and Syrian city-states on the Asiatic mainland, alternated between independence and subjection to the suzerainty of neighbouring Oriental empires.

[2] The Sultanate-Caliphate itself had ceased to exist. The Sultanate had been abolished by Ghazi Mustafā Kemāl and his companions in 1922, the Caliphate in 1924 (see the *Survey for 1925*, vol.i, Part I, section (iii)).

tion of Defensive Alliance between Great Britain and Turkey with respect to the Asiatic Provinces of Turkey' (commonly called the Cyprus Convention) in the following terms:

> Article I. If Batum, Ardahan, Qars or any of them shall be retained by Russia, and if any attempt shall be made at any future time by Russia to take possession of further territories of H.I.M. the Sultan in Asia as fixed by the Definitive Treaty of Peace, England engages to join H.I.M. the Sultan in defending them by force of arms.
>
> In return, H.I.M. the Sultan promises to England to introduce necessary reforms, to be agreed upon later between the two Powers, into the Government and for the protection of the Christian and other subjects of the Porte in those territories. And in order to enable England to make necessary provision for executing her engagements, H.I.M. the Sultan further consents to assign the Island of Cyprus to be occupied and administered by England.[3]

This instrument was signed during the interval between the signature, on the 3rd March, 1878, the Russo-Turkish Peace Treaty of San Stefano and the opening, on the 13th June, 1878, of the Berlin Conference in which the Concert of Europe, on British initiative, revised the Russian peace-terms in Turkey's favour and replaced the Treaty of San Stefano by the Treaty of Berlin. During this interval between war and peace, the Cyprus Convention was imposed by the British Government upon the Ottoman Government through a secret telegraphic ultimatum, in which the Sultan was given forty-eight hours to make up his mind. The text of this telegram, which Lord Salisbury dispatched to the British Ambassador at Constantinople, Mr. Layard, on the 23rd May, 1878, ran as follows:[4]

> Propose most secretly to Sultan following defensive alliance, to secure his territory for the future in Asia:
>
> [A recital of the terms thereafter embodied in the Cyprus Convention, as cited above, and in the Annex of the 1st July, 1878, mentioned below, here follows.]
>
> Press an immediate acceptance of these terms with all energy in your power. Point out that this arrangement makes safe Asiatic Turkey, the field from which the Sultan's army is supplied with men, and that it must be accepted at once if Sultan wishes to retain the goodwill of England. The present opportunity, if neglected, will never recur. We are on the point of an arrangement by which Russian army will be withdrawn from Constantinople, and the autonomous Bulgarian Principality will either be limited to north of the Balkans or got rid of altogether. If the Sultan does not consent to the above arrangement, these negotiations will be broken off at once, and the capture of Constantinople, and the partition of the Empire, will be the immediate result. Nothing has saved the Sultan from this extremity, for which not only Russia, but other Powers, wished, except the friendship of England; but England will desist from all further efforts unless Sultan agrees to allow her to protect his Asiatic Empire by an alliance on these terms. Make Sultan understand that you must have written engagement as above not later than Sunday evening, and that the most absolute secrecy must be observed.

This ultimatum was duly accepted by the Ottoman Government on the 25th May, 1878; the Cyprus Convention, in the terms quoted above, was signed on the 4th June; and an annex to it was signed on the 1st July. In this annex the two most important terms were the following:[5]

> That England shall pay to the Porte whatever is the present excess of revenue over expenditure in the Island, the excess to be calculated upon and determined by the average of the last five years.

---

[3] The text is taken from the Foreign Office *Handbook on Cyprus* (London, 1920, H.M. Stationery Office), p. 67.

[4] The text was made public for the first time in a posthumously published collection of papers by Sir James Headlam-Morley, late Historical Adviser to the Foreign Office: *Studies in Diplomatic History* (London, 1930, Methuen), chap. vii; 'The Acquisition of Cyprus in 1878.'

[5] The full text will be found in the Foreign Office *Handbook on Cyprus*, pp. 67–8.

> That if Russia restores to Turkey Qars and the other conquests made by her in Armenia during the last war, the island of Cyprus will be evacuated by England and the Convention of the 4th June, 1878, will be at an end.

On the 7th July, 1878, just a week before the Berlin Congress completed its work by the signature of the Berlin Treaty on the 13th July, Lord Salisbury communicated the text of the Cyprus Convention to the French Government.

'The disclosure created in France alarm and resentment, and also a feeling that Great Britain had not acted straightforwardly.'[6] On the following day, 'the 8th July, a British squadron, under the command of Lord John Hay, appeared before Larnaca; and on the 11th July the administration of the island was formally taken over from the Turkish authority.'[7]

The new regime which was thus inaugurated in Cyprus was avowedly provisional and contingent; yet on this precarious basis it lasted *de facto* more than forty-six years, from the British occupation on the 8th July, 1878, down to the outbreak of war between the Ottoman and British Empires on the 5th November, 1914. Thereat, the Cyprus Convention lapsed according to a doctrine of international law which rules that bilateral agreements are extinguished by an outbreak of war between the two parties; and in Cyprus, as in Egypt, the British Government found themselves in an anomalous position. They were in friendly occupation of territory which, juridically, was under the sovereignty of an enemy state; and they were in political control of a population who, juridically, were enemy subjects. In both instances, the British Government cut the Gordian knot. They severed the political connexion of both Cyprus and Egypt with the Ottoman Empire by unilateral action. But, whereas they were content to declare a British protectorate over Egypt on the 18th December, 1914, they annexed Cyprus to the dominions of His Britannic Majesty by an Order in Council of the 5th November, 1914;[8] and thereafter the respective British policies towards Egypt and towards Cyprus continued to diverge.[9] The British protectorate over Egypt was renounced by the British Government in a unilateral declaration of the 28th February, 1922;[10] and from that date onwards the British Government made repeated attempts—recorded in previous volumes of this *Survey*[11]—to replace the unilateral declaration of 1922 by a freely negotiated and comprehensive An-

---

[6] *The Cambridge History of British Foreign Policy, 1783–1919* (Cambridge, 1923, University Press), vol. iii, p. 136.

[7] Headlam-Morley, *op. cit.*, p. 202.

[8] Text in the Foreign Office *Handbook on Cyprus*, pp. 68–9.

[9] An apologist for this differentiation in British policy towards Egypt and towards Cyprus might plead that the two cases were not altogether parallel, in spite of the fact that both countries were ex-Ottoman territories which had come under British occupation at approximately the same time (Cyprus in 1878, Egypt in 1882). Whereas Cyprus had been under the direct administration of the Porte until the moment of the British occupation, Egypt had already been autonomous under the viceroyalty of Mehmed 'Ali and his descendants *de jure* since 1841 and *de facto* since Mehmed 'Ali's appointment to the Pashalyq in 1805 or indeed since the previous local domination of the Mamluks, whose power in Egypt had survived the Ottoman conquest, and had revived as the Ottoman Power had decayed. On the other hand, a cynic, seeking to explain the aforementioned differentiation in British policy since 1914, would be inclined to attach less importance to the differences between the local historical antecedents and more importance to the fact that the 280,000 Greek Cypriots were manifestly more amenable, in the last resort, than the twelve or fifteen million Egyptians to coercion by British *force majeure*—and particularly to coercion by British sea-power.

[10] See the *History of the Peace Conference of Paris,* vol. vi, pp. 203–4.

[11] See the *Survey for 1925,* vol. i. Part III, section (i); the *Survey for 1928*, Part III B, section (i); the *Survey for 1930*, Part III, section (ii).

glo-Egyptian treaty: attempts which resulted in a gradual approximation of the British and Egyptian points of view, though complete agreement had not yet been attained at the time of writing. Meanwhile, British policy towards Cyprus was more variable. There was a moment when the British Government were willing to relinquish possession of Cyprus completely; but this was followed by a long period during which the authorities in White-hall declined to consider this eventuality altogether.

The British Government's offer to relinquish possession of Cyprus completely was conveyed in a telegram dated the 16th October, 1915 from the British Secretary of State for Foreign Affairs, Sir Edward Grey (afterwards Lord Grey of Fallodon), to the British Minister at Athens, Sir Francis Elliot. This telegram concluded as follows:[12]

> Now that Serbia has been attacked by Bulgaria, if Greece is willing to come to her aid His Majesty's Government is ready to cede to Greece the island of Cyprus.
>
> If Greece joins the Allies for all purposes, she will naturally participate in the advantages secured at the end of the war, but the offer of Cyprus is made by His Majesty's Government independently of this consideration, and on the sole condition that Greece gives Serbia her immediate and complete support with her army.
>
> Time is pressing and you will ask M. Zaimis to give you his reply without delay.

The situation at the moment was that the German General Mackensen, after having broken through the Russian front in Galicia and compelled the Russian armies to make their great retreat, was leading a combined German and Austrian army against Serbia in order to complete the discomfiture of the Entente in the land-war in the east. Simultaneously, Bulgaria had entered the War on the side of the Central Powers. This raised the question of a treaty, concluded after the Balkan Wars between Serbia and Greece, in which the contracting parties had undertaken to come to one another's military assistance in certain contingencies. In October 1915, Serbia and her allies were representing to Greece that her treaty obligations were now engaged, while King Constantine's Government at Athens were contending that the contingencies contemplated in the treaty were not those which had actually arisen. Sir Edward Grey's offer of Cyprus was made in the hope of inducing the Greek Government to interpret the Graeco-Serbian Treaty in accordance with the Entente Powers' desire. King Constantine's Government, however, were unwilling to fulfil the condition attached to the British Government's offer by entering the War forthwith on the side of the Entente; and accordingly the British offer of Cyprus to Greece lapsed, although, at a later stage of the War, Greece did intervene on the side of the Entente under Monsieur Venizelos's leadership.

Meanwhile, Cyprus remained in British hands; and the unilateral Cyprus (Annexation) Order in Council of the 5th November, 1914, was eventually confirmed by the coming into force on the 6th August, 1924, of the Peace Treaty of Lausanne, in which the sovereignty over Cyprus was formally transferred to Great Britain by the previous sovereign, Turkey. [13] Thereafter Cyprus was given the official status of a British Colony in Royal Letters Patent, dated the 10th March, 1925, which were read and proclaimed at Nicosia on the 1st May of that year. Therewith, Cyprus became in law an integral part of the British Empire.

---

[12] This quotation is taken from S. P. O. Cosmetatos, *The Tragedy of Greece,* English translation (London, 1928, Kegan Paul), pp. 70–1, where the full text will be found.

[13] Peace Treaty of Lausanne, Art. 20: 'Turkey hereby recognizes the annexation of Cyprus proclaimed by the British Government on the 5th November, 1914.'

The island, however, was not, even now, at the British Government's entire disposal, the British diplomacy had given a new lien over Cyprus to France before it had succeeded in getting rid of the old lien held by Turkey. After the lapse of Sir Edward Grey's offer of Cyprus to Greece in the autumn of 1915, Great Britain had given France a veto over the disposal of Cyprus in the secret Anglo-French agreement for the partition of Ottoman territories in the Middle East (the so-called 'Sykes-Picot Agreement') which was concluded in the early summer of 1916. The 'Sykes-Picot Agreement' was never officially confirmed in public; but the majority of its provisions were eventually reproduced in public instruments forming part of the peace settlement; and the provision concerning Cyprus only reappeared as Article 4 of a 'Franco-British Convention of the 23rd December, 1920, on certain points connected with the Mandates for Syria and the Lebanon, Palestine and Mesopotamia,'[14] to the following effect:

> In virtue of the geographic and strategic position of the island of Cyprus, off the Gulf of Alexandretta, the British Government agrees not to open any negotiations for the cession or alienation of the said island of Cyprus without the previous consent of the French Government.

The series of diplomatic transactions, just recorded, determined the juridical status of Cyprus as it stood at the time when the disturbances broke out among the Greek inhabitants of the island in the autumn of 1931. Juridically Cyprus was then a British possession which the British Government could administer as they chose, but could not alienate without the consent of a particular foreign Power—the Power in question being neither Turkey nor Greece but France. Yet the inhabitants of Cyprus had become British subjects in law without ceasing, in speech and sentiment, to be Greeks and Turks; and these Greek and Turkish Cypriots' respective political hopes and fears proved to be psychological factors of international importance. The Greek majority in the population of Cyprus wanted, and the Turkish minority did not want, to secede from the British Empire and to become united with the *ci-devant* Kingdom and subsequent Republic of Greece.

These conflicting Greek and Turkish desires had been present in Cypriot minds, as distant aspirations or anxieties, from an early date in the history of the British occupation. There had been a decided expectation that the British régime, which in the terms of the Cyprus Convention was avowedly contingent and transitory, would actually be a transitional stage in the transfer of Cyprus from Turkey to Greece—a transfer which seemed probable in the light of the general tendency of Ottoman affairs. In general, the old Ottoman Empire was breaking up into national successor states. During the century which ended in the final Ottoman catastrophe of 1911–24, province after province had passed to these ever-growing successor states from the ever-dwindling Empire; and most of these ex-Ottoman provinces had gravitated—in accordance with the recognized modern Western political principles of national self-determination and majority rule—to the respective successor states with which the majority of the local population was nationally affiliated. On these precedents Cyprus, no less than Crete, seemed ultimately destined to become part of Greece; and on the first day of the British occupation in 1878, when Sir Garnet Wolseley arrived at the capital of the island, Nicosia, in command of the British occupying force, the Greek deputation which received him there, with the Archbishop at its head, declared in its address to him that the Cypriots welcomed the British occupation as

---

[14] The text was published as a British Parliamentary Paper *Cmd.* 1195 of 1921.

a stage towards the union of Cyprus with Greece.[15] So long, however, as this prospect remained remote it did not arouse either the Greek or the Turkish Cypriots to violent feelings or violent action. In Bosnia-Herzegovina, another Ottoman province of mixed Christian and Muslim population which had been occupied by Austria-Hungary—as an offset to Russian gains at Turkey's expense—in the same year in which Cyprus had been occupied on the same grounds by Great Britain, such feelings were aroused, and this with wide international repercussions, when the Occupying Power annexed the occupied territory, by a unilateral act, upon the outbreak of the Turkish Revolution in 1908. On that occasion, the Power in occupation of Cyprus had studiously refrained from following the Austrian example; and when the British Government did proclaim the annexation of Cyprus unilaterally, some six years later, upon the outbreak of war between the British Empire and Turkey, this act did not arouse violent excitement in Cyprus itself. In 1915, again, the offer of Cyprus to Greece produced no profound psychological effect. The violent feelings, which finally found vent in the violent action of October 1931, first began to show themselves in Cyprus during the six years beginning with the Peace Conference of Paris and ending with the proclamation of the 1st May, 1925. During these years it was becoming increasingly apparent that the British Government now intended the incorporation of Cyprus in the British Empire to be permanent; and accordingly, in Greek Cypriot minds, the British Empire now took the place of the Ottoman Empire as the obstacle to the union of Cyprus with the Greek national state.

This local conflict between British policy and Greek nationalism, which thus declared itself in the 'post-war' period, has to be viewed in the light of certain 'post-war' circumstances. There was the general circumstance, mentioned above, that by this time a great majority of ex-Ottoman countries and peoples had already attained, or were patently on the eve of attaining, their local national independence. There was also the particular circumstance that by this time every one of the conditions on which Great Britain had originally occupied Cyprus, under the Cyprus Convention, had fallen through. Instead of defending Turkey-in-Asia by force of arms against further Russian aggression, Great Britain had herself invaded Turkey-in-Asia, in alliance with Russia, in the General War of 1914–18; and in 1916 she had actually signed a secret treaty with Russia and France for the partition of Turkey-in-Asia between the three Powers. Instead of securing the protection and good government of the Asiatic Christian subjects of the Porte, Great Britain had found herself impotent, notwithstanding her occupation of Cyprus, to prevent the annihilation of these Christian communities by a process of massacre and eviction which went on intermittently from 1896 to 1922. As for the undertaking, enshrined in the annex to the Cyprus Convention, that Cyprus would be evacuated by England and that the Cyprus Convention would be at an end if Russia restored to Turkey the three Caucasian districts of Qars, Ardahan, and Batum which had been conquered in the War of 1877–8, it is to be noted that the whole of this territory had been restored to Turkey temporarily in the abortive Russo-Turkish peace treaty which had been signed on the 3rd March, 1918, at Brest-Litovsk, and that thereafter the whole of it except the actual port of Batum had again been restored to Turkey—and this time definitively—in the Russo-Turkish treaty signed at Moscow on the 16th March, 1921, and in the treaty between Turkey of the one part and the Soviet Governments of Georgia, Erivan, and Azerbaijan of the other, which

---

[15] Article on 'the Meaning of Enosis,' by a special correspondent at Nicosia, published in *The Times*, 9th December, 1931.

was signed at Qars on the 13th October, 1921.[16] Thus, at an early stage in the 'post-war' period, the conditions on which Great Britain had originally occupied Cyprus had become entirely obsolete. Juridically, as between Great Britain and Turkey, this was without import, since the Cyprus Convention itself had lapsed upon the outbreak of war between Great Britain and Turkey on the 5th November, 1914, and the subsequent annexation of occupied enemy territory by the victorious belligerent was in accord with the traditions of international law and custom. Morally, as between Great Britain and the Greek inhabitants of Cyprus, the lapse of all the conditions on which Great Britain had originally occupied Cyprus was a point in the new 'post-war' situation which impressed itself on British consciences in so far as the Cyprus question secured attention, at all, from British minds outside 'official circles.' In the 'post-war' years, a Cypriot Greek national movement in favour of secession from the British Empire and union with Greece declared itself with increasing energy. The leaders of this movement claimed to represent the opinions and sentiments and aspirations of those four-fifths of the population of Cyprus who were Orthodox Christians in religion and Greeks in nationality; and an active and prominent part was taken by the hierarchy of the Autocephalous Orthodox Church of the island, who, in a community bred in the Ottoman social tradition, were the recognized leaders of their flock in temporal affairs as well as in spiritual. The British Government at Westminster, on the other hand, took the view that the people of Cyprus—Greeks and Turks alike—were unripe for self-government;[17] and the British authorities in Cyprus held that the Cypriot Greek national movement, while general and genuine among the urban minority of the Cypriot Greek population, was neither spontaneous nor deep-rooted among the peasantry. The history of this national movement was sketched as follows, in retrospect, on the morrow of the outbreak of October 1931, by the British Governor of Cyprus at the time, Sir Ronald Storrs:

> In the towns the movement had in the process of time continued to make headway. Fresh generations of youth sedulously indoctrinated with disloyalty had been launched by the secondary schools (in Cyprus non-governmental) on all the professions; and, outside the Government service and the realm of Government influence and activity, every branch of public life in the Orthodox community was in some way allied to the cause of union. Athletic and social clubs in particular were identified with the movement . . .[18]

During the two years immediately preceding the outbreak,

> many . . . speeches were delivered in villages whither the leaders had carried the campaign with determination, not only for electioneering purposes, but in order to prepare an atmosphere contradictory to the criticism that adherence to their cause was restricted to town-bred advocates, priests, and schoolmasters. In 1930 (a year of elections) reports of 555 political speeches delivered in villages were received from the police, and 246 in 1931 before the 17th October. Numerous speeches also were made in village churches, and there were others of which, for various reasons, no record was obtained. Among the peasantry the campaign of misrepresentation and abuse of Government had been favoured by the deterioration of economic conditions and by rustic ignorance. Disloca-

---

[16] For these two treaties, see the *Survey for 1920–3*, pp. 370–2.

[17] It may be noted that the same British Government, during the same period, took the opposite view about the people of 'Irāq—another ex-Ottoman territory under British tutelage in which the majority of the population was still in the feudal or even in the tribal state of society. For the history of the British policy in 'Irāq, see the *History of the Peace Conference of Paris*, vol. vi, Part III C; the *Survey for 1925*, vol. i, Part III, section (x); the *Survey for 1928*, Part III B, section (x); the *Survey for 1930*, Part III, section (vi).

[18] Dispatch, dated the 11th February, 1932, from the Governor of Cyprus to the Secretary of State for the Colonies, printed in the British Parliamentary Paper, *Cmd.* 4045 of 1932. (The passage here quoted will be found on p. 5.)

tion of markets in the trade depression might have shaken the apathy of the villagers towards agitation, but their confidence in the established order was deep-rooted; they would take no initiative in opposing the Government, and, if any consequence was to follow from the flow of rhetoric, would look for it to the towns whence the lead should come.[19]

Notwithstanding the (perhaps inevitably) hostile language in which this British official account of the Greek Cypriot national movement is couched, it is evident that the British authorities in Cyprus did not subscribe to the view, which was sometimes expressed in less responsible British quarters, that the Cypriot Greek nationalists were merely a handful of unrepresentative and self-interested agitators.[20] The British authorities did, however, hold the opinion that, at the time of the outbreak of October 1931, when the priests, the advocates, the school-teachers, and the urban population in the larger towns were, with few exceptions, in favour of union with Greece, and when the control of the Cypriot Greek press was in the Unionists' hands, there was still a majority, including the merchants, the farmers, and the peasants in general, who were either politically apathetic or else were in favour of British rule.[21]

The strength of any political movement in any country at any given moment is notoriously hard to measure, since it is a psychological entity which cannot accurately be

---

[19] *Op.cit., pag. cit.*

[20] A succinct statement of this point of view will be found in an article on 'the Meaning of Enosis,' from a special correspondent at Nicosia, published in *The Times*, 9th December, 1931.

[21] The political state of mind of the Cypriot Greek peasantry might perhaps be gauged to some extent by the reception given to a memorial, asking for the union of Cyprus with Greece, which the Greek Orthodox Archbishop of Cyprus caused to be circulated, in 1930, to nearly every village in the island where there was a Greek population. The Archbishop requested that the memorial should be signed by the village commission and the Church authorities in every village and quarter. The village commission was a body which, until the constitutional and administrative changes consequent upon the disturbances of 1931, had been appointed biennially, in each village, by the District Councils elected by the people and by the elected members of the Legislative Council, to manage the village areas inhabited by Turks or Greeks as the case might be. The District Councils appointed two out of the five members of each village commission, and members of Council three. These village commissions, like all elected bodies, were obviously subject to pressure from their electors, and, in the case of Greek villages, it is evident that the electors of the commissions (i.e. the Greek members of District Councils and of the Cyprus Legislative Council) would be largely Unionists, so that the Greek members of village commissions would feel an inducement to accede to the Archbishop's request for signatures in favour of the union of Cyprus with Greece. The results of the circulation of the memorial were actually as follows. The memorial was circulated to 496 villages or quarters out of the 598 Greek and mixed Graeco-Turkish villages and quarters in the island. In 52 of these villages, some members of the village commission refused to sign, and in 66 the whole commission refused signature. A number of cases were also reported in which the village authorities refused at first and signed under pressure afterwards. The Cyprus Government appear to have abstained, in pursuance of a settled policy, from any intervention, direct or indirect, in connexion with the memorial, and the local authorities appear to have been aware that they had nothing to hope or fear from the Government or its officers in the matter. On these grounds, the refusals of the signatures to the Archbishop's memorial were regarded, in British 'official circles' in Cyprus, as indications that, in 1930, the hold obtained by the Cypriot Greek nationalist movement in the country-side was still far from being complete. In the event, a number of those who refused their signatures duly lost their positions. On the 29th November, 1930, a meeting was held at the Archbishopric in Nicosia of the representatives of the 'National Organization' of Cyprus and the Greek elected members of the Legislative Council. It was then decided that all the Greek members of the District Councils should be instructed not to appoint as village authorities any Mukhtars or Azas who had refused to sign the memorial. In one district, Limassol, the District Council refused to pay any attention to the instructions received; in others it happened that the influence of the Mukhtar was too strong locally for him to be set aside. None the less, large numbers of the Mukhtars and Azas who had refused their signatures were not renominated.

gauged by external marks and which is always subject to violent and rapid fluctuations. In regard to the Cypriot Greek nationalist movement, it can only be said that, on the showing of the British authorities in Cyprus, it was following the normal course of modern nationalist movements everywhere, which had almost always originated among small nuclei of 'intellectuals,' spread from them to the professional classes at large, then captured the whole urban population, and finally penetrated into the country-side. The Greek movement in Cyprus was manifestly conforming to this type of evolution by the time of the outbreak of October 1931.

Whatever the true nature of the Cypriot Greek national movement might be, the history of its 'post-war' activities was a matter of ascertainable fact; and the facts show that these activities passed through two phases. During the thirteen years following the signature of the Armistice between Turkey and the Allied Powers on the 30th October, 1918, the Cypriot Greek nationalists employed the pacific and constitutional methods of protest and petition. In October 1931 they, or their followers, resorted to violence. The change of tactics seems to have been due partly to disappointment at the failure of their long continued and repeated efforts to obtain an open-minded hearing of their case from the British Government and people,[22] but the change did not take place until the abstract and *a priori* desire for union with Greece had been sharpened by a conflict over the control of education in Cyprus and by an important practical difference of opinion and policy, as between the British authorities and the Greek members of the Cyprus Legislative Council, over the public finances—which in Cyprus, as in many other countries, were feeling, in 1931, the strain of the world-wide economic depression.[23]

On the eve of the depression, the economic and social progress which had been achieved in Cyprus under British administration was described in retrospect, by two British officials, in the following terms:

> In 50 years the population of the island has increased by 150,000 persons; the revenue has advanced from £176,000 to about £750,000 and is devoted in its entirety to the public use. Imports and exports have attained a value approximately six times as great as that which they possessed in the first year of the occupation; the production of cereals has trebled; and the fact that the family, which in 1878 supported life on £8 a year, now requires £80 for the same purpose is evidence not merely that the cost of living has augmented but also that the standard has been appreciably raised . . .
>
> A thousand miles of roads traversable by motor-car have replaced the irregular tracks, which formerly were the despair of travellers. A railway has been built. A postal service has been established. All the principal towns have been connected by telegraph; some of them by telephone. The harbour at Famagusta has been enlarged to allow of the entry of steamships, and the ports of Larnaca and Limassol have been improved by the construction of piers, breakwaters, quays and jetties. A regular mail service connects the island with the continent, and Cyprus is included in the itinerary of vessels which under former conditions would have hesitated to approach its shores . . .
>
> The first need of the country was water. Large sums, therefore, were spent upon the construction of reservoirs and channels for irrigation, upon the improvement of existing sources and on the discovery of fresh supplies; and in recent years recourse has been had to sub-artesian borings, which seem destined substantially to increase the quantities of water available for irrigation. With the same purpose of heightening the country's productivity, the forests, valuable not only for

---

[22] 'The policy of memorials for union, delegations to England, local demonstrations with flags and processions, anti-British invective from the press and platforms, and non-co-operation and obstruction in the Legislative Council had come to nothing; and among the extremists in the movement the cry had gone up that they must look in future to deeds rather than words to achieve their object.' (*Cmd.* 4045 of 1932, p. 4.)

[23] The psychological effect of the trade depression is suggested, as an explanation of the progress made by the Cypriot Greek national movement among the Cypriot Greek peasantry in the years 1930 and 1931, in the Governor's dispatch of the 11th February, 1932. (*Op. cit.*, p. 5.)

the timber they produce, but also because they attract rain and preserve in the ground the rain once fallen, have been the object of scientific protection and development. The disastrous process of denudation has been checked and the woods, in danger once of becoming a wilderness, have been converted into a potential source of great wealth . . .

By demonstration and instruction in the method of raising crops and in the care and rearing of fruit-trees, by experimenting with new species, and by combating diseases and pests, the Agricultural Department has sought to increase the quantity, as well as improve the quality, of the island's products. It has established nursery gardens and built stud stables, and it has maintained a veterinary service for the protection of the live stock, whose breeding it has successfully encouraged. In order to relieve the peasant community of part of its burdens, the tithe on produce was abolished; and the Government has endeavoured, by the establishment of an Agricultural Bank and the encouragement of co-operation, to remedy the farmer's present financial distress and lay the foundation of his future prosperity.[24]

Contemplating this record, with some pardonable complacency, as a monument of specifically British handiwork, the British administrators of Cyprus were nonplussed and incensed to see the results either ignored or taken for granted or depreciated by the Cypriots themselves. The truth was that every country which had been extricated from the wreckage of the Ottoman Empire in the course of the nineteenth century had made marked economic and social progress thereafter, irrespective of its political fate. Such progress could be observed not only in ex-Ottoman countries like Cyprus and Tunisia which had passed in 1878 and 1881 respectively under British and French control. It was also marked in Bulgaria and Eastern Rumelia (two ex-Ottoman territories which the Berlin Treaty of 1878 had erected into autonomous states) and in Thessaly (an ex-Ottoman territory which had been annexed to Greece in 1881, three years after Cyprus had been occupied by Her Britannic Majesty). In order to form a really illuminating estimate of the progress of Cyprus under British rule, it would be necessary to institute a comparison with the progress of these other ex-Ottoman territories during, the same fifty years and perhaps also with the progress of Crete, a neighbouring ex-Ottoman island which had become autonomous in 1897 and had secured its long-desired union with Greece in the First Balkan War in 1912. In this place it is only necessary to point out that the progress made in Cyprus, though manifestly creditable in itself, was nothing exceptional or extraordinary.

Nor, on the other hand, was Cyprus at all peculiar among ex-Ottoman countries in having a reverse side of the medal to show. In Cyprus, as almost everywhere throughout the Ottoman World, the evil legacy of the past still displayed itself in the poverty of the agricultural population (notwithstanding the rise which had taken place in the standard of living) and in the extortions of the moneylenders (notwithstanding such enlightened public measures as the establishment of an Agricultural Bank). Moreover, the new economic order brought new evils of its own. For example, the recent development of industrial life in mines and factories infected the Cypriots with the malaise and the sense of oppression which the Industrial Revolution had notoriously evoked elsewhere. These evils began to exert their full psychological effect as soon as the World Depression of 1930–1 had checked and even reversed the general current of progress which had been flowing, off and on, for some fifty years. In these circumstances, the economic depression readily bred political discontent, and nowhere more readily than in Cyprus, where the conflict between Cypriot

---

[24] Sir R. Storrs and B. J. O'Brien, *The Handbook of Cyprus* (London, 1930, Christophers). The whole of the section from which these passages are quoted should be consulted (i.e. pp. 31–7 inclusive).

Greek Nationalism and British Imperialism was a standing cause of political unrest.[25]

It remains to trace the history of this unrest through its pacific into its violent phase.

As regards the numerous memorials which were addressed, during the earlier of these two phases, by Cypriot Greek nationalists to the British Government, it may be sufficient here, by way of illustration, to mention two, to which answers were vouchsafed. A memorial dated the 4th December, 1925, and signed by the Greek elected members of the Cyprus Legislative Council was forwarded by the Governor to the Colonial Office and was answered in the following letter from the Colonial Secretary.

> The Secretary of State[26] in reply desires that the signatories of the memorial be informed that the question of the union of Cyprus to Greece is closed, once and for all, and cannot be re-opened. He regrets that in submitting such a demand the signatories show forgetfulness of the fact that Cyprus has become a Crown Colony . . .
>
> The Secretary of State . . . does not consider that Cyprus has reached a degree of political education such as would justify an immediate extension of constitutional rights.[27]

Another memorial of the same tenor, dated the 20th July, 1929, and likewise signed by the Greek elected members of the Cyprus Legislative Council, was presented to the Secretary of State[28] in London by the Bishop of Kition and two other members who came to England for the purpose. The Secretary of State's reply was embodied in a dispatch of the 28th November, 1929, to the Governor of Cyprus.[29] In this reply, the following were perhaps the most important passages:

> The first request contained in the Memorial is a renewal of the demand that Cyprus should be ceded to Greece. My answer on this point can only be the same as that which successive Secretaries of State have in the past returned to similar demands, namely, that His Majesty's Government are unable to accede to it. This subject, in their view, is definitely closed and cannot profitably be further discussed . . .
>
> The Greek Elected Members put forward certain requests for consideration in the event of the rejection of their major demand for union with Greece. The first of these . . . is the submission that the Island should be granted a form of responsible Government. This is a request which has been given very careful consideration. The conclusion at which I have arrived, not without regret, is that the time has not yet come when it would be to the general advantage of the people of Cyprus to make a trial of a constitutional experiment in this direction.[30] Those institutions already es-

---

[25] The degree and extent of this unrest by the eve of the outbreak of October 1931 can be gauged by the character of the precautionary measures taken by the British Administration in Cyprus, which savoured of the methods of the nineteenth-century Continental European 'police-state.' For example, 'in 1930 (a year of elections) reports of 555 political speeches delivered in villages were received from the police, and 246 in 1931 before the 17th October' (*Cmd.* 4045 of 1932, p. 5, quoted on p. 364 above [of original publication]). There were also an Internal Security Scheme (*op. cit.*, p. 13) and a Defence (Certain British Possessions) Order in Council (*op. cit.*, p. 14) which the outbreak brought into action.

[26] At that time Mr. L. S. Amery.

[27] The full text of the letter from which this extract is taken is published in *The Manchester Guardian* of the 10th April, 1926, under cover of a message from *The Manchester Guardian* correspondent in Rome, who had copied the letter from the Italian press.

[28] At that time Lord Passfield.

[29] This dispatch was communicated to the Greek elected members of the Cyprus Legislative Council and then published in Cyprus. It was also published in England, together with the members' memorial, as a British Parliamentary Paper, *Cmd.* 3477 of 1930.

[30] In this matter, the attitude of the Colonial Office in Downing Street appears to have been less statesmanlike than that of the British authorities in Cyprus itself. According to information received by the writer of this Survey, the Cypriot Greek political leaders were asked more than once by the Governor to propound a considered scheme for the introduction of extended powers of self-government. The Bishop of Kition was reported to have promised on several occasions to submit a scheme but to have left this promise unfulfilled. The inference drawn from these facts by the writer's informant was that the Cypriot Greek nationalist lead-

tablished in the Island which are subject in varying degrees to popular control cannot be said to have attained that reasonable measure of efficiency which should be looked for before any extension of the principle is approved . . .

It is suggested that a Royal Commission should be appointed to inquire into the condition of affairs in Cyprus. This proposal has received my consideration, but after careful reflection I have formed the view that the appointment of such a body would, at the present juncture, be of no real benefit to Cyprus. An inquiry of the character proposed would raise unprofitable issues, and could only distract attention from those more practical matters on which the progress of the Colony depends. There is much to be said for the view that what Cyprus needs at present are fewer occasions for political discussion and more occasions for constructive work.

In addition to the requests for changes, which received these replies, the memorialists had made certain complaints in regard to the existing state of affairs. Their complaints were predominantly financial. They complained of the financial impotence of the Legislative Council, the expensiveness of the British Personnel in the administration, and the diversion of revenues raised in Cyprus for making payments abroad in which the Cypriots had no concern. The third of the financial grievances here ventilated had been the subject of an agreed settlement in 1927; the other two grievances were of the essence of the conflict of 1931.

The history of the diversion of revenues raised in Cyprus went back to the transactions of 1878. In his secret telegram of the 23rd May, 1878, to Mr. Layard, Lord Salisbury had stated that 'as England has no desire to impoverish Porte, she will pay yearly whatever is the present excess of revenue over expenditure in the island.' This was the basis of the provision, cited above,[31] in the Cyprus Convention Annex of the 1st July, 1878; and the five-years' average of the tribute remitted from Cyprus to Constantinople was duly worked out at the figure of £92,799 11s. 3d. per annum. An annual sum of this amount was levied by the British Government upon the revenues of Cyprus from the beginning of the British occupation down to the time of writing; but no remittance was ever made to the Ottoman treasury; for the political crisis through which the Ottoman Empire passed during the years 1875–1881 caused the Ottoman Empire to default on all its financial obligations, including the service of the Ottoman loan of 1855, the interest on which had been guaranteed by the British and French Governments.[32] 'Her Majesty's then Government was advised that "the Cyprus tribute" formed part of the revenues of the Ottoman Empire and could be withheld from the Porte and used for the service of the loan so long as the default lasted.'[33] Accordingly, the British Government proceeded to apply to the interest service of the 1855 loan the required annual amount of £81,752[34] out of the 'Cyprus tribute' and tendered to the Porte the balance only. The Ottoman Government, standing on their dignity, declined to accept this sum of £11,047 11s. 3d. per annum in lieu of the £92,799 11s. 3d. per annum that had been agreed upon; and the British Government retorted by investing the annual balances, with interest, in Consols, as a contribution to the sinking fund of the same loan.[35]

---

ers were unwilling to see any extension of self-government in Cyprus under the British Crown, on the calculation that this would weaken the popular feeling in favour of union with Greece.

[31] On p. 357 [of original publication].

[32] This loan had been raised by Turkey in the European money markets, principally in London and Paris, under the auspices of her allies in the Crimean War, in order to enable her to equip herself with the sinews of war and so increase her effectiveness as a belligerent.

[33] The Secretary of State's Dispatch of the 28th November, 1929, published in *Cmd.* 3477 of 1930, pp. 16–17.

[34] H. C. Luke and D. J. Jardine, *The Handbook of Cyprus* (8th issue: London, 1920, Macmillan), p. 122.

[35] Although the sinking fund, unlike the interest, had not been guaranteed by the British and French Governments.

Meanwhile, the annual remittance abroad of as large a sum as £92,800 proved too heavy a charge for the finances of Cyprus to bear; and from the year 1897 onwards[36] this outgoing was partly offset by an annual grant-in-aid from the Exchequer of the United Kingdom. At first the annual amount of the grant was variable. It was decided year by year through negotiation between the Treasury in Whitehall and the British administration in Cyprus on the basis of the momentary state of the island's finances. This system was inimical to financial progress in Cyprus because it made it impossible for the local Government to calculate their revenues ahead and unprofitable for them to improve their financial position when the improvement was likely to go to the benefit of the Government and taxpayers in Great Britain and not to the benefit of Cyprus itself. In 1910, however, the grant-in-aid was stabilized, as for the year 1911 and subsequent years, at a fixed annual sum of £50,000; and finally, in 1927, as for the year 1928 and thereafter, the British Government offered to raise this regular grant to an amount equal to that of the annual tribute charge—i.e. £92,800 per annum—on condition that Cyprus should contribute a fixed annual sum of £10,000 towards British Imperial Defence. In a written reply to this offer, dated the 27th September, 1927, the twelve Greek and three Turkish elected members of the Cyprus Legislative Council declared that 'the happy answer of the Imperial Government' had 'fulfilled all Cypriot aspirations concerning this burden;' that they 'most willingly' concurred 'in the conditions set forth;' and that they were 'ready to co-operate in the early enactment of the legislation necessary to ratify the decision.'[37] On the 10th October, 1927, an Imperial Defence Appropriation Bill for the payment of £10,000 per annum was duly passed by the Cyprus Legislative Council; and from 1928 onwards the new financial arrangement came into effect.

Therewith, the British Government regarded the question of the tribute as being closed. Under the new arrangement Cyprus, as a part of the British Empire, was certainly less heavily burdened by external charges than she would have been if she had remained a part of Turkey or had become a part of Greece; for, in consideration of her contribution to the service of the Ottoman 1855 loan, she had been exempted, in the financial liquidation of the wars of 1912–18, from being assessed, like other successor states of the Ottoman Empire, with a quota of the Ottoman Debt;[38] and the contribution towards British Imperial Defence, which was the sole charge on the Cyprus Government for external expenses from the year 1928 onwards, represented only about 1.4 per cent. of the Cyprus Budget. On the other hand, from the beginning of the British occupation down to the year 1927 inclusive, the aggregate net tribute paid by Cyprus to relieve the British Government of their liability towards the Ottoman bondholders—i.e. the aggregate excess of all the annual tribute payments over all the annual grants-in-aid—was estimated to have amounted to a sum of about £2,640,000;[39] and this sum represented more than 17 per cent. of the £15,227,350 which was the aggregate revenue raised in Cyprus during the forty-nine years 1879–1927 inclusive.

In regard to the impotence of the Legislative Council, the Greek elected members

---

[36] *The Dominions Office and Colonial Office List*, s.v. Cyprus, Finances.
[37] This reply was published in the *Cyprus Gazette* and was quoted by Lord Passfield in his dispatch of the 28th November, 1929 (*Cmd.* 3477 of 1930, p. 18).
[38] Lord Passfield, *op. cit.*, p. 17.
[39] Memorial from the Greek Elected Members of the Cyprus Legislative Council (in *Cmd.* 3477 of 1930, p. 12).

made the following representation in their memorial of the 20th July, 1929:

Its powers are very limited and where they are a little extended are so much restricted as to annihilate the voice of the whole people of the Island in general and of the large majority in particular. That is to say:

(a) The Legislative Council can introduce no vote, resolution, or law for the appropriation of part of the public revenues or propose a bill imposing a tax without having previously obtained permission from the Governor.[40]

(b) It has no control over the whole of the sums to be appropriated during the voting of the Budget, a great portion of them being beyond its control by virtue of existing Imperial Orders in Council and laws.[41]

(c) It enjoys no substantive participation in the preparation of the Budget, nor is it entitled to exercise any control over the estimates of expenditure.[42]

In general its obtaining rights and privileges are further curtailed by the power reserved to the Governor or the King in the exercise of the prerogative of disallowance[43] and they are completely annihilated by the King's right to legislate for the Colony by Order in Council, not only where the circumstances are such as to call for extraordinary measures, but also in respect of current routine in the service.

We cite the following most recent examples of this latter party [sic]:

(a) The Budget of 1927 rejected by the vote of the elected members of the Legislative Council was nevertheless put into force in its entirety by an Order in Council from the King.[44]

(b) Connected with the Budget and for the purposes of covering a deficiency provided therein a new levy to the sum of £40,000 was also imposed in the same year without the advice and consent of the Legislative Council.[45]

(c) The Penal Law published in the Government Gazette as a draft bill in order to be later introduced into the Legislative Council, as expressly stated in the preamble to the said bill, was imposed as law from London by Royal Order, without its being laid before the Legislative Council and the advice of its members thereon being obtained.[46]

(d) During the last session of the Legislative Council a Pensions Bill as proposed

---

[40] The Governor, of course, represented the Crown, which had retained the right of introducing money-bills in all the Parliaments of the Empire; but whereas, in the United Kingdom and in the other self-governing Dominions, the Crown was represented by a Ministry responsible to the Parliament in which the business was introduced, and subject to dismissal upon receiving a vote of no confidence, the Governor, by whom this prerogative of the Crown was exercised in Cyprus, was responsible not to the Cyprus Legislative Council but to the Colonial Office in Downing Street.—A. J. T.

[41] The appropriation (as distinct from the subsequent allocation) of a considerable portion of the local public revenues by Imperial Orders in Council was of course the rule in British Crown Colonies at the time, though not in the United Kingdom or in the other self-governing Dominions of the British Crown.—A. J. T.

[42] In contrast to the control exercised by such committees as the Public Accounts Committee in the Parliament at Westminster.—A. J. T.

[43] This prerogative was, of course, theoretically still extant in all parts of His Britannic Majesty's Dominions, but in Great Britain (in contrast to Cyprus) it had not been exercised for the past two centuries and a half.—A. J. T.

[44] The elected members of the Council had refused supply on the first reading of the Appropriation Law without discussing the Bill in detail.—A. J. T.

[45] The elected members of the Council had refused to accept the responsibility for this taxation—a common infirmity of legislative bodies whenever these find themselves without effective financial control.—A. J. T.

[46] The Penal Code Bill had been published some ten months and more before the relevant Order in Council was made. At the request of the elected members of the Cyprus Legislative Council, a committee of five members was appointed to examine the bill before introduction. This Committee, however, are stated to have ignored summonses to meet and to have made it clear that they would have nothing to do with the bill. And in these circumstances the new Code was introduced by Order in Council because, in the opinion of the British authorities, a reform of the Cyprus Criminal Code was urgently required.—A.J. T.

by the Government was rejected.[47] The same measure has just been sanctioned from England as law, by means of a Royal Order in Council.[48]

The memorialists went on to point out that while the Legislative Council as a whole was subject to these restrictions upon its powers, the Greek elected members were still further penalized in as much as their united votes were insufficient, by themselves, to secure a majority on the Council, although they represented between them four-fifths of the population of the island. The distribution of seats on the Legislative Council, since its creation in 1882, had in fact been so arranged that the official members and the Turkish members combined should be exactly equal in numbers to the Greek members and therefore superior in voting-power in virtue of the casting vote of the High Commissioner; and this balance was maintained in 1925, when the High Commissioner became Governor and the respective numbers of the Greek and Turkish and official members of the Council were raised from nine and three and six to twelve and three and nine. As between the Greeks and the Turks, the new figures gave the Greeks a representation on the Council in proportion to their strength in the total population. As between the Greeks on the one hand, and the Turks and the English officials on the other, the balance of forces remained unchanged.[49]

In regard to the expensiveness of the English officials, the Greek elected members of the Legislative Council submitted, in their memorial of the 20th July, 1929,[50] that English officials serving in Cyprus had received more lavish treatment than their confrères at home.[51] On the Cyprus estimates for 1931, the total charge for salaries, excluding teachers' salaries, apparently accounted for about 45 per cent. of the whole.[52] Of course the

---

[47] The purpose of this bill was to bring Cyprus into line with other British Colonies in the matter of the treatment of public servants. The unification of pensions throughout the British Colonial Service was a matter of importance for those members of the Service, of British race, who would find themselves transferred from one colony to another in the course of their official career; but this was not a matter of interest to the Cypriots.—A. J. T.

[48] *Cmd.* 3477 of 1930, p. 5.

[49] The Cyprus Legislative Council did not, of course, invariably divide, on all issues, on the lines of Turks plus Englishmen versus Greeks. On any issues, however, in which the question of the union of Cyprus with Greece was directly or indirectly involved, the Turkish elected members of Council could naturally always be relied upon to assist their English official colleagues to outvote their Greek elected compatriots.

[50] In *Cmd.* 3477 of 1930, p. 9.

[51] In 1920–1, when the cost of living was at its 'post-war' peak all over the world, officials in Cyprus had been given a cost-of-living bonus of approximately the same scale as officials in the United Kingdom. Whereas, however, in Great Britain the bonus had been placed on a sliding scale which was governed by a cost-of-living index, in Cyprus the bonus had been permanently consolidated with the basic salary, so that in 1929 the officials in Cyprus were still being paid at the rate of 1920–1, though, according to the memorialists' contention, the cost-of-living index in Cyprus had fallen from 230 in 1920–1 to 130 in 1929 on a norm of 100 representing the level of 1913–14. See the table of official salaries in Cyprus as they actually were in 1929, and as it was alleged that they would have been on the United Kingdom sliding scale, in *op. cit.*, p. 10. The memorialists' figures in regard to the fluctuation in the cost-of-living index in Cyprus were not accepted as correct by the British authorities.

[52] See the figures given by Dr. Z. Rossides in a letter, dated the 28th February, 1931, which was published in *The Manchester Guardian* of the 3rd March, 1931. On these figures, Dr. Rossides worked out the percentage, excluding teachers' salaries, at over 52 per cent., whereas the Under Secretary of State for the Colonies, Dr. Shiels, stated in the House of Commons at Westminster on the 4th February, 1931, in answer to a parliamentary question, that the percentage, *including* teachers' salaries, was between 40 and 50 per cent. According to a special correspondent of *The Times* at Nicosia, in an article published on the 9th December, 1931, the total number of officials (including policemen and schoolmasters) in Cyprus in 1930 was

greater part of the officials to whom these salaries were payable were Cypriots and not Englishmen. The aggregate amount of the salaries drawn by officials of English nationality in Cyprus in the year 1930 appears to have been about £50,000[53]—a figure which represented rather more than 6 per cent. of the total estimates for 1931, and rather less than 14 per cent. of the total charge, in those estimates, for salaries.

The unsatisfied aspirations and unappeased grievances reviewed above were the motive-forces of the Greek nationalist movement in Cyprus and the antecedents to the disturbances of 1931. The two events which actually precipitated these disturbances were the passage of the Elementary Education Law of 1929 and a conflict of wills between the elected Greek representatives on the Cyprus Legislative Council and the British authorities over the Cyprus Budget for 1931.

The main purpose and effect of the Elementary Education Law of 1929[54] was to transfer the control over, and the discipline of, the school-teachers in Cyprus to the British authorities from the hands of those Greek and Turkish bodies—Boards of Education, Town Committees, Village Commissions and Committees of Management—which had previously controlled this as well as other departments of the administration of the island. The ground for this legislative change was that the Greek schools in Cyprus had been used by the Cypriot Greek nationalists as fields for political propaganda, and that the Greek school-teachers who had been unwilling to abuse their position in order to act as propagandists in the nationalist cause had been subjected to illegitimate pressure. There seems to have been much substance in this criticism of the pre-existing system; and it is significant that the bill was passed into law by the aid of three Greek votes on the Legislative Council.[55] Indeed, the Cypriot Greek nationalists frankly declared that they regarded the school-teachers as their missionaries in the cause of Union; and the passage of the new law, which deprived them of their power of subjecting the school-teachers to pressure for this end, was publicly mourned by the Cypriot Greek community as a national calamity, though it was privately greeted with feelings of relief by a number of the schoolmasters concerned.

Yet, however substantial the justification for the passage of this education law may have been, it did not solve the underlying problem, which was inherent in the political situation in Cyprus at the time. So long as the Cypriot Greek National Movement and the British Empire remained in unreconciled and undecided conflict, it was hardly possible to exclude the field of education from the arena of this political struggle; and while the British authorities in Cyprus might perhaps legitimately use their power in order to

---

4,213, and their salaries amounted in the aggregate to £403,209 out of a total expenditure of £800,207 in that year.

[53] The salaries shown in the Dominions Office List and Colonial Office List for 1930 as payable to officials in Cyprus with English names add up to £49,239, if the lower figure is always taken in cases where the list shows a salary as ranging between a lower and an upper limit. The figure thus arrived at is, of course, exclusive of allowances and pensions. In an article published in *The Times* on the 9th December, 1931, a special correspondent at Nicosia states that in 1930 the total number of English officials in Cyprus was 96, and that the aggregate amount of their salaries was £58,572. According to the same authority, one of the telling points in the Cypriot Greek campaign for the union of Cyprus with Greece was the statement that an English district commissioner in Cyprus received as high a salary as the President of the Greek Republic.

[54] The Statute Laws of Cyprus, No.4 of 1929, to amend and consolidate the law relating to the Establishment and Management of Elementary Schools in Cyprus.

[55] These three independent-minded Greek elected members of the Council were respectively an advocate, a merchant and a farmer. None of these was able to stand at the election in 1930.

stop the Greek nationalists from using the local educational system as an instrument of their propaganda among the rising generation of Cypriot Greek children in favour of union with Greece, it was inevitable that the nationalists should resent this action and reasonable that they should feel a certain apprehension lest, in the course of the struggle, the British authorities in Cyprus should sooner or later take advantage of their newly established control over the local teaching body in order to give Greek education in Cyprus a definitely and deliberately denationalizing bias.

This estrangement over the Elementary Education Law of 1929 prepared the way for the open breach over the Budget for 1931.

The estimates for 1931, as presented to the Legislative Council on the 9th December, 1930, showed an estimated expenditure of £801,666 and an estimated revenue of £731,550, involving a deficit of £70,116 on the Budget for the coming year.[56] The Colonial Government proposed to cover this deficit partly from a surplus of £21,185 which was in hand from 1930,[57] and for the rest from the reserve fund of £90,000 which had been accumulated for use in some exceptional calamity (e.g., a plague of locusts or a drought). There was no Estimates Committee of the Legislative Council, but, while the Budget had been in course of preparation, the two leading Greek elected members and one Turkish elected member had been invited to examine the proposed estimates item by item in consultation with the Colonial Secretary. A number of suggestions made by them had been adopted, but they appear to have dealt with small points only and to have refrained from expressing an opinion on major questions. At the opening of the first session of the new Legislative Council, it became clear that no support for additional taxation was forthcoming at the moment from any of the elected members, either Greek or Turkish; and for this reason no proposals for additional taxation were included in the Budget. But in his opening speech on the Budget, on its introduction into the Legislative Council, the Colonial Secretary stated that a committee would be appointed in the early months of 1931, when the financial situation would be clearer, to make a serious investigation into the financial condition of the Colony with a view to making such recommendations as would enable the Budget to be balanced; and on the strength of this undertaking the Turkish elected members agreed to give the Budget their support. The Greek elected members put forward the alternative proposal that the deficit should be covered by economies amounting to £67,003, and that £53,589 out of this total amount should be saved on official salaries.[58] Thereupon, on the 6th December, 1930, the Estimates Bill embodying the

---

[56] If millions are substituted for thousands, the budgetary problem of Cyprus in 1931 will be seen to have been comparable, scale for scale, with that of the United Kingdom in the same year. In Cyprus, likewise, the increase in the estimates was largely accounted for by the development of the social services. In the Cyprus Budget for 1931, the votes for Health, Education, and Agriculture, in the aggregate, were higher by about £90,000 than they had been in 1927. On the other hand, a committee of inquiry had been appointed as early as the beginning of 1930 to investigate possibilities of reduction in the establishment.

[57] This figure was an estimate which proved (to the credit of the finance-officers concerned) to have been an under-estimate. The actual surplus turned out to be £45,753.

[58] See the passages from their public statement to the people of Cyprus, published in the *Messager d'Athènes*, 22nd January, 1931; also the passages from their memorandum to the Secretary of State in Downing Street, published in the same journal, 19th January, 1931. The salaries on which savings were to be made under this proposal did not include those of the schoolmasters, whose salary-bill amounted in the aggregate to £109,098 out of a total salary-bill of £403,209 (see footnote 46 above), though the schoolmasters had all received considerable increases of salary in 1930. The other savings proposed, up to an amount of something over £13,400, seem to have been at least partly illusory. For example, it was proposed to save

Government's proposals was passed, over the heads of the twelve Greek members, by the combined votes of the nine English official members and the three Turkish members, re-inforced by the casting vote of the Governor. Thereafter, on the 4th February, 1931, in the House of Commons at Westminster, the Under-Secretary of State for the Colonies, Dr. Shiels, in answer to a parliamentary question, confirmed the fact that it was proposed to meet the deficit on the Cyprus Budget from the Colony's surplus balances and reserve fund, but announced at the same time that the Governor had appointed a committee to go into the finances of the Colony in order to see whether a saving could not be made. The committee (which was that promised by the Cyprus Government at the moment when the Budget had been introduced) was composed of two English permanent officials (the Treasurer and the Auditor), one Turkish representative (the Delegate of Evqāf), and one Greek member (a merchant by profession) of the Executive Council, and two Greek elected members of the Legislative Council.[59]

On this Budget Committee, the British official members agreed in principle to a temporary levy on official salaries and thereby brought the committee to the verge of signing a unanimous report. The committee did unanimously find in favour of the substi-tution of specific duties for *ad valorem* duties in the customs system; and, apart from the incidental possibility of obtaining an increase of revenue, this proposal might commend itself on its technical merits. In pursuance of a special and unanimous recommendation in this sense which the committee made in April in an interim report, a bill for effecting this change was introduced into the Legislative Council.[60] This bill met with unanimous op-position from the Greek elected members,[61] on the ground that it involved an increase of taxation as well as a change in technical method; and on this occasion the Greek vote was not overborne by a united English and Turkish vote. One Turkish elected member voted with the Greeks, and thus the bill was thrown out on the 28th April, 1931, without the Governor's casting vote coming into play.

Thereafter, on the 19th May, 1931, the Budget Committee presented a majority report signed by the Englishmen and the Turk and a minority report signed by the Greeks.[62] The majority report did not reproduce the Cyprus Government's original plan of drawing upon the reserve fund, which had been embodied in the Estimates Bill and passed through the Legislative Council by the Governor's casting vote on the 6th De-cember, 1930. While still proposing to use the surplus of £21,185 from 1930 towards meeting the deficit of £70,116 on the Budget for 1931, the English official members now proposed, as a next step, to make economies amounting to a reduction of £25,000 on the estimates. When an additional surplus of £24,568 from 1930[63] was taken into the account

---

£7,700 by spending no money on forest utilization, although a revenue of over £11,000 was derived from this source.

[59] The membership of this committee appears to have been as stated in the text, and not as stated by Dr. Shiels in the House of Commons at Westminster, in answer to a parliamentary question, on the 25th Febru-ary, 1931.

[60] Statement by the Governor on the Budget, published in the *Cyprus Gazette* (*Extraordinary*, No.2), 9th September, 1931.

[61] Including one of the two Greek elected members who had served on the Budget Committee, in spite of the fact that he had signed the Committee's interim report. (The other Greek elected member of Council serving on the Budget Committee had been unseated meanwhile, for corruption, on an election petition.)

[62] The texts of both reports are printed in the *Cyprus Gazette, loc. cit.*

[63] For this surplus, see p. 377, above [of original publication].

on the credit side and a payment of £15,000[64] on the Government's guarantee to the Agricultural Bank of Cyprus on the debit side, the net deficit for 1931 stood at £14,363, which was little more than a fifth of the original figure. The signatories of the majority report proposed to cover this residuary deficit by increases of taxation under three heads: first, an incidental gain from substituting specific for *ad valorem* duties in the Customs Tariff (on the lines of the bill which had been thrown out by the Legislative Council on the 28th April); second, an increase in the petrol duty;[65] third, an increase in the wharfage dues. The Greek signatories of the minority report recorded their opinion 'that the stabilization of the Customs Revenue by the conversion of *ad valorem* to specific duties would be desirable;' but they made the proviso that no additional burden should be imposed on the tax-payer; and their proposals for covering the residuary deficit involved no additional taxation and consisted wholly of additional economies. They proposed to save £12,400 by abolishing certain posts and by cutting down travelling expenses and assisted passages. They proposed to obtain a further saving of between £12,000 and £14,000 by making a cut of 10 per cent. on all official salaries above £100 per annum, except on the first £100. On this last proposal the signatories of the majority report put on record the view

> that Government officials share in the common burden of taxation, Government and Municipal, and that they would not demur to a *general* income tax. But to single out a class and to tax it exclusively would be a step for which in our opinion the present position does not offer any justification. We do not consider that the salaries of public officers should alter with periods of prosperity and intervals of depression.

In the light of this majority and minority report from the Budget Committee, and in view of the rejection of the Customs Bill by the Legislative Council, the following measures for balancing the Cyprus Budget for 1931 were taken by the British authorities. The substance of the rejected Customs Bill, together with provisions for increases in the petrol duty and in wharfage dues, was translated into an Order in Council which was made in London on the 11th August, 1931, and was published in Cyprus on the 9th September. On the same date, the Governor published a statement on the Budget in the *Cyprus Gazette*.[66] This statement announced the Government's agreement that the Budget 'must be balanced mainly by economies' and translated this policy into figures. The deficit of £70,116 was to be met by economies amounting to £66,000 on the original estimates of £801,666 and by increased taxation estimated to bring in a net total of £20,533. This new taxation was to be raised on the three heads recommended in the majority report of the Budget Committee and now provided for in the new Order in Council: that is, by increases in the petrol duty and in wharfage dues, and also by an increase in customs receipts incidental to the change from *ad valorem* to specific duties. In the same statement, the Governor also announced economies on official salaries. 'A number of offices hitherto held by British officials' had 'either been left vacant' or would 'be filled by Cypriots;' and from the 1st October, 1931, a temporary charge of 5 per cent. was to be made on all salaries of Government employees above £100 per annum, which was estimated to produce a saving of £10,000 per annum.

---

[64] This was the final figure. The first estimate on this account had been only £7,000.

[65] The introduction of legislation to increase the tax on petrol in Cyprus had been approved by the Secretary of State in Downing Street on the 26th November, 1930; but at the opening of the first session of the newly elected Legislative Council it had been clear that no support for additional taxation was forthcoming at the time from any of the elected members, Greek or Turkish. (See p. 377, above [of original publication].)

[66] *Extraordinary, No.* 2 (1931).

It will be seen that these measures, taken as a whole, represented a compromise between the plan originally put forward, and passed over the heads of the Greek members of the Legislative Council, by the English official members and the Turkish members in December 1930, and the Greek members' counter-proposals. The decisions to leave the reserve fund intact, to cover the deficit mainly by economies, and to reduce the burden of official salaries in general, and of salaries paid to Englishmen in particular, were important concessions to Greek desiderata. On the other hand, the Government were not reducing the salary costs to the extent which the Greeks had desired, and they were not fulfilling the Greek desideratum that the Budget should be balanced without any recourse at all to fresh taxation. It is true that the fresh taxation was not burdensome either in quantity or in kind and that, in conjunction with the new economies, it duly balanced the Cyprus Budget for 1931;[67] but it is also true that the increase in taxation had been imposed on the Cypriot tax-payers, against the vote of the Legislative Council in Cyprus, by a fresh resort to the constitutional short cut of an Order in Council passed in London. The increase of revenue which this Order in Council was estimated to bring in was not much more than twenty thousand pounds sterling. Yet English officials had only to consult the constitutional history of their own country—the classic storehouse of constitutional lore—in order to be reminded that a small tax was capable of producing a large upheaval if an important constitutional principle were involved. To anyone familiar with English history, it would hardly be a matter of surprise that the overriding of the vote of the Cyprus Legislative Council by the Royal Order in Council which was published in Cyprus on the 9th September, 1931, should have been followed by the widespread Cypriot disturbances of the following month. It is true that, in the British Crown Colony system of government, the method of making financial appropriations by Orders in Council, which had been successfully challenged by the Parliament at Westminster some three centuries earlier, was still, in 1931, an ordinary practice, and that nevertheless the British Colonial Empire, taken as a whole, was politically quiescent and contented at this time in the midst of a politically agitated world. There were, however, few British Crown Colonies in which, in 1931, the British connexion was anathema, as it was in Cyprus, to a local national movement; and it was the struggle between Cypriot Greek Nationalism and British Imperialism that brought to life again, in twentieth-century Cyprus, the English constitutional issue which had once produced the English Civil War.

Like many Greek risings at various times and places against Ottoman rule, the Greek rising against British rule in October 1931 in Cyprus[68] was headed by a prelate of the Orthodox Church.[69]

The movement apparently arose out of deliberations, which had begun on the 12th

---

[67] The actual surplus balance at the end of the year 1931 was £23,201. The amount raised, before the end of the calendar year, by new taxation under the Order in Council was £14,274, of which £7,000 was produced by the petrol tax.

[68] The official British account of this affair will be found in a Parliamentary Paper entitled 'Disturbances in Cyprus, 1931' (London, 1932, H.M. Stationery Office, *Cmd.* 4045 of 1932).

[69] On the question whether the Prelates of the Autocephalous Orthodox Church of Cyprus were inspired by disinterested motives in their political activities, it may be remarked that, in the event of a transfer of sovereignty over the island from the British Empire to Greece, the Cypriot Autocephalous Church would automatically become subject to the authority of the Holy Synod of the Greek State, and would lose thereby not only its special ecclesiastical powers but also a part of its property (under the Ecclesiastical Law of Greece, Constitutional Law of 1870, Constitutional Laws of 1929–30).

September, 1931, among the leaders of the Cypriot Greek National Movement, on the question of demonstrating against two recent British official acts: a statement made in the Parliament at Westminster by the Chancellor of the Exchequer on the 8th July to the effect that the accumulated surplus from the payments made from Cyprus revenue as tribute to Turkey under the convention of 1878 had been disposed of for the sinking fund of the Turkish loan guaranteed by Great Britain in 1855,[70] and the Order in Council which had been published in Cyprus on the 9th September, 1931.[71] At this meeting, it was formally resolved (though the resolution was not made public) that, subject to the approval of the Cypriot Greek National Organization, a manifesto should be addressed to the Cypriot people, calling upon them to refuse to pay taxes and to boycott British goods by way of protest.[72] The draft resolution was duly considered on the 3rd October at a joint meeting, held in Nicosia, at the Archbishopric, between the members of the National Organization and the Greek elected members of the Legislative Council. At this meeting there was apparently a difference of opinion not only over the terms of the draft but over a question of political tactics—the proposal being that the manifesto should be read at the opening meeting of the Legislative Council and that the Greek members of the Council should then resign in a body forthwith. Some of those concerned were apparently unwilling to make this personal sacrifice; and the resulting division of counsels remained uncomposed at subsequent meetings on the 10th, 11th, and 17th October.[73] At this stage the initiative was taken by the Metropolitan of Kition (Larnaka), Mgr. Nikódhimos Mylonâs, who was member of the Legislative Council for Lefkara.

At the meeting on the 17th October, the Metropolitan recited to his fellow-members a version of the manifesto which he had drafted himself; and, having obtained their concurrence in principle, he deliberately created a *fait accompli* by publishing his manifesto next day, Sunday, the 18th October, together with a letter addressed to the Governor of Cyprus, Sir Ronald Storrs, in which the Metropolitan conveyed his resignation from the Legislative Council for his own part.[74] The crucial passages in this letter were the following:

> As a deputy I have sworn allegiance perforce to King George. As a prelate and a national leader, I am obliged to-day to recommend to the Cypriots, who are King George's subjects by constraint, the insubmission which is dictated by our violated human rights. Henceforward it will be my duty to go everywhere and summon my compatriots to non-legal resistance against illegitimate authorities and illegal laws . . . We proclaim the union of Cyprus with her mother-country Greece and we declare that we will do all that is humanly possible to give effect to this decision as speedily as possible, in the assurance that God and Justice and Morality will support this struggle of Right against Brute Force.

This step evoked a public protest[75] from eight of Mgr. Mylonâs's colleagues on the Legislative Council; but the Metropolitan had set forces in motion which it was beyond their power to arrest.

---

[70] *Cmd.* 4045 of 1932, p. 2. See also pp. 370–1 of the present volume, above [in original publication].

[71] See p. 380, above [in original publication].

[72] *Cmd.* 4045 of 1932, p. 3.

[73] *Op. cit.*, p. 4.

[74] A full French translation of the text of the manifesto, containing the letter and dated the 17th October, 1931, will be found in the *Messager d'Athènes* of the 26th October, 1931. An extract will be found, in English translation, in *Cmd.* 4045 of 1932, pp. 33–4.

[75] Text, in English translation, in *Cmd.* 4045 of 1932, p. 35.

On Tuesday, the 20th,[76] the Metropolitan of Kition followed up his first gesture by making an inflammatory speech at Limassol.[77] When the news reached the capital of the island, Nicosia, next day, the 21st October, the other Greek members of the Legislative Council found their hands forced. Their decision to resign was announced, a public meeting was summoned by tocsin, and the demonstrators, shouting for Union with Greece and singing the Greek National Anthem, marched, with several of the resigning members of the Legislative Council at their head, to Government House, which they reached after dark when the Governor was at dinner, on the eve of sailing for England. The house was attacked by the mob, and the District Commissioner refrained from reading the Riot Act and ordering the police to shoot until the house had been set on fire. The house was burned with all its contents, though the Governor and his staff escaped injury. Thereupon the movement spread like wildfire among the Greek population throughout the island. At Limassol, the District Commissioner's house was burnt down on the 22nd. At Paphos, an attempt to burn the District Commissioner's house on the 24th was frustrated by the arrival of British troops.

The Governor had telegraphed for military and naval reinforcements on the night of the 21st itself, since 'the permanent garrison consisted of three officers and a hundred and twenty-three men,' and, 'allowing for guards, transport and men in hospital, less than a hundred would be available for parade,' while 'the police were trained and employed almost exclusively in the prevention and detection of crime and were in no sense of the term a military force.'[78] The British Government lost no time in dispatching troops and warships to the spot. On Thursday the 23rd, two British cruisers and two British destroyers arrived at Larnaka, Limassol, Paphos, and Famagusta respectively from the Greek waters of Suda Bay in Crete. On the same day, seven Royal Air Force troop-carrier aeroplanes from Egypt, conveying 150 troops, and one aeroplane from Palestine, arrived at Nicosia. That morning, one of the rioters who had been wounded by the fire of the police at Government House on the 21st died of his wounds; and his funeral, which was attended by the Archbishop of Cyprus, Kýrillos, gave occasion for a further demonstration of Greek national feeling. On the 24th, five persons, including two members of the Legislative Council, were arrested at Nicosia, and on the same day Mgr. Nikódhimos Mylonâs was arrested at Limassol. On the news of the prelate's arrest, there was a riot in Limassol and an attempt at rescue, in which the police again fired on the crowd and a second fatal casualty was inflicted. In the small hours of the morning of the 25th, the six prisoners were conveyed on board a British destroyer. On this latter day, the Union Jack which was flying over the District Commissioner's house at Kyrenia was torn down by a crowd under the leadership of the Bishop of Kyrenia, whose servant hoisted the Greek national flag in the British flag's place, whereafter, during the night of the 25th–26th, the Bishop of Kyrenia was arrested by a party of British troops from Nicosia and was taken to prison in the capital. At Limassol, on the 26th, a crowd adopted Mr. Gandhi's tactics of 'civil disobedience' by gathering salt in contravention of the Salt Laws. There were numerous minor acts of sabotage all over the island, and minor clashes between the Greek population and the gendarmerie and troops, of whom more were arriving. 'There were in all

---

[76] For the events of the 20th and 21st October, 1931, see, besides *Cmd.* 4045 of 1932, pp. 8–13, a first-hand account published in *The Daily Telegraph* of the 2nd November, 1931.

[77] *Résumé*, in English translation, in *Cmd.* 4045 of 1932, p. 35.

[78] *Op. cit.*, p. 13.

some 200 villages in which excitement prevailed and demonstrations were made, but without breach of the law. Less than seventy villages were guilty of destruction of property. Many outrages were the work of small gangs of malefactors or individuals, but no satisfactory distinction' could 'be drawn between communal and individual responsibility for incitement. There' were '598 Greek-Orthodox villages and mixed Orthodox and Turkish villages in the island. Three hundred and eighty-nine of these took no part at all in the disturbances.'[79] The total casualties were six civilians killed, thirty civilians wounded (of whom one died later), and thirty-eight policemen injured, of whom fifteen were Greeks and twenty-three were Turks.[80] Some 400 persons were arrested in all. By the end of the month, the disturbances had virtually ceased and the British armed forces in Cyprus were in complete command of the military situation. The measure of this command is given by the fact that the garrison of British troops in Cyprus, which had consisted of three officers and 123 men on the 21st October, 1931, and which had been reinforced thereafter as recorded above, had been reduced again to the strength of four officers and 175 men by the last day of the calendar year.[81] These figures, taken together with the course of events between those dates, support the British Governor's contention that 'there' was 'no evidence to show that the outbreak was premeditated or prearranged.'[82] On the other hand, the Governor was treading more debatable ground in his further inference that 'the nature of the events disposes also of any suggestion that the upheaval represented a widespread desire on the part of the Greek-Orthodox inhabitants for the transfer of Cyprus to Greece.'[83] The most that can be inferred with any assurance is that, in October 1931, the Cypriot Greeks were not yet in the mood to purchase their political freedom at the price which the Moreot Greeks had been willing to pay in their struggle against Ottoman Imperialism in 1821–9, or the Irish in their struggle against British Imperialism in 1916–21.

The suppression of the rising of October 1931 in Cyprus was followed by punitive measures.

On the 30th October there was published a telegram to the Governor of Cyprus from the Secretary of State for the Colonies in London which contained the following passage:

> You have already taken action against the ringleaders. You have my full support in dealing with them and in any necessary action to put down this sedition or to make it clear to those who have been so unfortunately misled that neither now nor in future will disorder be tolerated. It is obvious that the liberties given under the present constitution have been abused by disloyal political leaders. Accordingly in the general interests of the people of Cyprus His Majesty's Government will have to review, in consultation with you, the whole question of the constitutional future of the island.

At Nicosia, on the 3rd November, it was announced that the six leaders arrested there on the 24th October had now been deported for life; that municipalities were to be held responsible for all damage done by rioters within their jurisdiction; and that the municipality of Nicosia would have to pay £20,000. On the 4th November it was reported that the total number of deaths from the disturbances was now six, and that the number of

---

[79] *Op.cit.*, p. 28.
[80] Telegram of the 14th March, 1932, from the Governor of Cyprus to the Secretary of State for the Colonies at Westminster, printed in *Cmd.* 4045 of 1932, pp. 41–2.
[81] *Cmd.* 4045 of 1932, pp. 13 and 31.
[82] *Op. cit.*, p. 31.
[83] *Op. cit., loc. cit.*

life-sentences of deportation was to be raised from six to ten.[84] On the 12th November, in the House of Commons at Westminster, the Secretary of State for the Colonies, in answer to a parliamentary question, announced that Letters Patent had been approved under which the Legislative Council would cease to exist and power to make laws was granted to the Governor. He added that it would be necessary thereafter to review the whole question of the constitutional future of the island. On the 1st December, 1931, three new laws, enacted by the Governor under the new Letters Patent, were published in the *Cyprus Gazette*. One provided that the Mukhtars (headmen) of the villages should be appointed by the Governor instead of by local election; another that no flags should be flown or displayed without a licence from the Governor; another that no bells should be rung without the permission of the District Commissioner.[85] 'The Reparation Impost Law, implementing the decision that destroyed property should be replaced and repaired at the cost of the responsible towns and villages, was passed on the 21st December. The imposts amounted in all to £34,315 and over 80 per cent. of the total' had been paid by the 11th February, 1932. By the same date, 'more than 2,000 persons' had 'been convicted by the assize and magisterial courts for specific offences connected with the disturbances and' had 'received . . . sentences.'[86]

Meanwhile, the news of the events of October 1931 in Cyprus was arousing manifestations of strong and widespread feeling in Greece; and these repercussions of Cypriot Greek affairs in the independent Greek National State were a new and

---

[84] Ten Cypriots in all were in fact deported: six on the 3rd November, 1931, and four on the 6th; and the announcement that the sentences were life-sentences was made in Cyprus in regard to all ten persons concerned (*Cmd.* 4045 of 1932, p. 30). On the other hand, in the House of Commons at Westminster on the 25th November, 1931, in answer to a parliamentary question whether any of the sentences to deportation were life-sentences, and, if so, how many, and what were the terms of the remaining sentences, the Secretary of State for the Colonies said: 'The deportation orders state that the persons in question must leave the island and remain outside the territory thereafter.'

[85] The motive in the minds of the British authorities in Cyprus, when they drafted the last-mentioned of these three laws (the Statute Laws of Cyprus, No. 18 of 1931), was to guard against the possibility of the church bells being rung again, as they had been rung in October 1931, as a tocsin for summoning the Greek Orthodox population of Cyprus to rise against alien rulers. The new law was not vexatiously administered, and permission to ring bells for and during church services, or as time-signals, or for summoning the children to school, was not withheld when, in compliance with the law, a request was duly filed with the local District Commissioner. In all the towns of the island, however, except one, and in about 20 per cent. of the villages, such requests remained untendered and the bells remained unrung. The fact was that, in the minds of the Cypriots themselves, with their Ottoman background, this law was likely to become invested with a deeper significance. Against this historical background it would signify an assimilation of the British régime in this ex-Ottoman island to the old Ottoman régime by which it had been preceded. Under the Ottoman order, the silencing of the Christian church bells had been one of the symbols of the subjection of the Christian *ra'īyeh* to their Muslim masters; and, since the beginning of the end of the Ottoman Empire, the restoration of the belfries had been one of the outward and visible signs of liberation in one liberated Christian province after another. Some 150 years before the Cypriot rising of 1931, in the generation before the Greek War of Independence, the pealing of the church bells in Orthodox Christian Russia had sounded this note of liberty in the ears of the Ottoman Greek sojourners there.

'The Greeks always longed to go to Russia. There we worked and earned our daily bread, and in time we . . . grew out of being the Turk's *ra'īyeh*. We heard the bells of their churches ringing and gave thanks . . . And when we had satisfied our own souls, we then began to think how to liberate our parents and our brothers and our kinsmen and how to help our dear country to rekindle her own light, as Russia had rekindled hers.' (Khrysanthópoulos, Ph. ['Photákos']: *Memoirs* (Athens, 1899, Sakellários), pp. 16–17.)

[86] *Cmd.* 4045 of 1932, p. 30.

not unimportant international aspect of the Cyprus question.

So long as the old and bitter feud between the Greek and Turkish peoples was in progress, there had been little response in Greece to Cypriot Greek irredentism—partly because the free Greeks felt (no doubt rightly) that their kinsmen under British rule in Cyprus were well off by comparison with the far larger number of 'unredeemed' Greeks who were under Turkish rule elsewhere; partly because it had been believed (as it turned out, wrongly) by Greeks in Cyprus and in Greece alike that the British had no intention of occupying Cyprus permanently and that the island was certain to become united with Greece sooner or later.[87] By the time of the Cyprus disturbances of October 1931, the situation had changed. The Graeco-Turkish national feud had been suddenly and unexpectedly brought to an end by the comprehensive Graeco-Turkish settlement of 1930—an act of statesmanship which was accompanied by a *détente* in the popular feeling between the Greek and Turkish peoples.[88] The Greeks no longer looked forward to enlarging the borders of Greece by further acquisitions of territory from Turkey. The residual Greek minority in Turkey and Turkish minority in Greece were insignificant in numbers; they balanced one another; and their respective interests were now safeguarded in precise agreements between the Greek and Turkish Governments. In this new situation, the only considerable communities of still 'unredeemed' Greeks were to be found, not under Turkish rule in Thrace or in Anatolia, but under Italian rule in the Dodecanese and under British rule in Cyprus. Moreover, in this 'post-war' period, the British Government, like the Italian Government, had declared—repeatedly and emphatically—a determination to retain in their permanent possession, as an integral part of their dominions, the Greek *terra irredenta* which was under its rule. In these circumstances, it was natural that the Cypriot Greek movement for the union of Cyprus with Greece should attract to itself those sympathies in Greece for 'unredeemed' Greeks which had previously been absorbed by the 'unredeemed' Greeks under Turkish rule.

This concentration upon Cyprus of national interest and feeling in Greece became manifest in the repercussions which were produced by the news from Cyprus in October 1931. There was a sharp conflict between the popular impulse to express pro-Cypriot and anti-British sentiments, and the Government's policy—laid down by Monsieur Venizelos—of preserving a scrupulously and sincerely 'correct' attitude in regard to a matter which was juridically a foreign affair wherein Greece had no official concern.

As early as the 23rd October, Monsieur Venizelos enunciated his policy, with characteristic clarity and vigour, in the following statement to the press:

> As I have declared many times, there is no Cypriot question between the Greek Government and the British Government. That question is between the British Government and the people of Cyprus. Up till now, the Cypriots have carried on their campaign by means of memorials, addresses, meetings, and protests, that is to say by means which the liberal minded British consider absolutely lawful. To-day, unfortunately, according to the information in the press, criminal excesses have taken place, such as attacks on soldiers and police and the burning of Government House at Nicosia. Faced by excesses of that kind, British tolerance comes to an end and a strict application of the law begins.
>
> I can only express my profound regret for these excesses. The promoters of the movement certainly did not wish for them, but they ought to have known that if they pushed things too far the moment would come when they would be no longer masters of the situation.
>
> If the Greek press would listen to me, I should advise it to condemn these excesses, from

---

[87] On this point, see pp.360–1, above [in original publication].

[88] For an account of this settlement, see the *Survey for 1930*, Part II B, section (iii).

which no good can come. No sensible man can imagine that excesses of this kind will force Great Britain to satisfy the national aspirations of the Greeks of Cyprus.

These words were accompanied by action; for, at the first news of the outbreak in Cyprus, the Greek Government recalled to Athens the Greek Consul, Monsieur Kyrou, who was stationed in the island. Already, in September, the transfer of this particular official to another post had been decided upon by the authorities in Athens—apparently on the ground that he had been allowing his personal sympathies for the Greek nationalist movement in Cyprus (he was of Cypriot origin himself) to deflect him from his duty of conforming to the 'correct' attitude of his home Government. His summary recall to Athens, which followed, anticipated the issue in London of a Royal Warrant revoking his *exequatur*.

Meanwhile, as the news of the events in Cyprus continued to arrive in Greece, Monsieur Venizelos found increasing difficulty in restraining manifestations of popular feeling. His advice was not followed by the press, and the press campaign which ensued was accompanied by demonstrations. In Athens, an intended demonstration of students was quashed by a veto from the authorities; but at Salonika, on the 28th October, an attempt, by a body of students, to demonstrate in front of the British Consulate was only checked by the intervention of troops as well as police. On the 31st October, the Greek National Union of Students addressed an appeal, on behalf of the Cypriots, to student organizations all over the world;[89] and on the same date the Holy Synod at Athens passed a vote of sympathy for the Orthodox Greek prelates and people of Cyprus.[90] Simultaneously, a Cyprus Committee was constituted at Athens under the chairmanship of an ex-President of the Greek Republic, Admiral Koundouriotis.[91] On the 30th October it had been announced in the press that a *requiem* service for the souls of the Cypriots who had lost their lives in the disturbances was to be held in the church of St. Constantine in Athens on Sunday the 1st November. Thereupon, on the 31st October, Monsieur Venizelos addressed a communication on this subject to the people of Athens, and to the councils of the professional, urban, working-men's and ex-service men's organizations, from which the following passages may be quoted:

> Considering that the proposed organization of an open-air meeting of this kind in the centre of the city would not serve the general interests of the country, I have had orders issued to the competent authorities to prevent this manifestation from taking place. Consequently, a crowd will not be permitted to assemble in front of a church situated in the city.
>
> No one, of course, wishes or has the right to prohibit manifestations of the opinions of the different popular groups so long as they do not assume the character of open-air demonstrations likely to give rise to excesses—which, as a general rule, are carried very much farther than is intended even by those who provoke them.
>
> Moreover, I desire to make known to all citizens that the Government, in fulfilment of an elementary duty, will never allow persons who are engaged in political or national struggles outside the frontiers of Greece to attempt, by means of intrigues inside the country, to create friction between Greece and the states of which they are nationals, and with which it is imperative, in the general interest of the country, that relations of an absolutely friendly and harmonious character should be maintained.
>
> Those fractions of the national family which are to be found outside the frontiers of Greece cannot be permitted to put obstacles in the way of the national policy, which can be determined only by the citizens of the country itself, in exercise of their sovereign rights. And the opin-

---

[89] Text in *Le Messager d'Athènes*, 31st October, 1931.

[90] Text *ibid.*, 1st November, 1931.

[91] The text of a declaration, dated the 30th October, 1931, by the newly constituted committee will be found *ibidem*.

ion of the citizens is represented by the constitutional powers—that is to-day by the Government and to-morrow by the legislative bodies which assemble on the 15th November.

Not to recognize these principles would be equivalent to a political anarchy unworthy of a serious nation.

In consequence of this communication, the *requiem* service on the 1st November was held outside Athens, at Amarousi. Thereafter, on the 3rd November, manifestos were issued by the chamber of Commerce and by the business community in Athens;[92] on the 4th, a manifesto was issued by the Association of Newspaper Editors;[93] and on the 5th the Municipal Council of Athens, at a special meeting, passed a vote of sympathy with Cyprus. There were further demonstrations in Athens on Armistice Day, the 11th November, which was celebrated as 'Cyprus Day' in Greece in 1931. On the eve of these latter demonstrations, on the 10th, Monsieur Venizelos issued a further appeal for restraint, which he addressed particularly to the press and to the Cyprus Committee. He reminded them that the maintenance of friendly relations with Great Britain had been the stable policy of Greece since the beginning of her independence, and he pronounced that those who jeopardized these friendly relations were insane. Thereafter, on the 18th November, 1931, Monsieur Venizelos reasserted the same points in a speech in the Greek Chamber (Βουλή).

This was not the first occasion on which Monsieur Venizelos, as Prime Minister of Greece, had boldly flown in the face of Greek national sentiment by insisting upon a policy of 'correctness' in an international situation in which the question of Greek national unification was involved. Some twenty years earlier, in the spring of 1912, on the eve of his first general election since he had been called to office in Athens, Monsieur Venizelos had similarly checked a similar agitation for the union with Greece of Crete: another ex-Ottoman island in which the majority of the population consisted of Orthodox Christian Greeks, one of whom was Monsieur Venizelos himself. On that occasion, the Cretan statesman's courageous and sagacious policy had quickly borne fruit, for before the year was out Monsieur Venizelos had won a sweeping victory in the Greek elections and had seen Crete reunited with Greece upon the outbreak of the First Balkan War. On this analogy, it might be surmised that, in the autumn of 1931, he was working more effectively through his policy of restraint than the majority of his countrymen were working through their campaign of protest towards that union of Cyprus with Greece which all Greeks had at heart. Indeed, there were certain passages in Monsieur Venizelos's speech in the Chamber on the 18th November, 1931, which suggested that the latest chapter in the history of Cyprus might, after all, have a happy ending.

I feel it my duty, addressing myself to the Greek islanders, to explain to them that if the Great Powers,[94] whose subjects they happen to be, maintain that material interests of theirs are dependent on the continuance of the island's occupation, there is no power which could alter their attitude. It is only if Great Britain were to be convinced either that Cyprus is of no more use to her or that the strategic advantages derived from the occupation of the island could be secured to her by the retention of a small part of it—only then would there be any possibility of the islanders' nationalistic demand meeting with a favourable reception, and this on the additional condition that the relations of the population with the Sovereign Power were sufficiently smooth to avoid giving the impression that Great Britain has yielded to violence . . .

If Great Britain likes to regard the question as a closed question, it cannot be but closed. Yet, after addressing myself to the Cypriot people and speaking to them in rather a hard and pain-

---

[92] Texts in *Le Messager d'Athènes*, 3rd November, 1931.

[93] Text *ibid.*, 4th November, 1931.

[94] In using the plural, Monsieur Venizelos was apparently referring to Italy, in respect of the Dodecanese, as well as to Great Britain in respect of Cyprus.—A. J. T.

ful manner, I thought I was equally justified in adding that the question of the realization of the Cypriot demands is not a closed question in my estimation.

Of one thing I am certain; the violent agitations in Cyprus cannot promote the Cypriot cause. We cannot hope for such a noble gesture on the part of the British Government in recognition of the Cypriots' demands so long as such a gesture may be misunderstood abroad as due to pressure.

An Historical Note on the 'Greekness' of Cyprus

In the conflict between the British Government and the Cypriot Greek nationalists over the political future of Cyprus, one of the chief controversial questions was that of the extent and the degree to which a desire for political separation from the British Empire and for political union with the Republic of Greece was entertained by the living generation of Cypriots whose mother-tongue was Greek and whose religion was Greek Orthodox Christianity. Though this was a question of fact, the facts here in question were not easy to ascertain with exactitude because they were facts of a psychological order.[95] There was, however, another and quite distinct question of fact which had been imported into the controversy: the question whether the Greek-speaking Orthodox Christian Cypriots were historically true Greeks in the same sense as the contemporary Greeks of Greece (i.e. the Greek-speaking Orthodox Christian inhabitants of territories which, at this time, belonged politically to the Greek Republic). This second question was perhaps somewhat academic as compared with the first from the standpoint of the current political issue. On the other hand, it was an easier question to answer with precision, because the facts here in question were not psychological but material. The question resolved itself into two concrete inquiries: At what date did Greek become the prevalent language in Cyprus? And was the Greek-speaking population of Cyprus of the same racial origin as, or of different racial origin from, the Greek-speaking population of territories which, in A.D. 1931, were under the Greek national flag?

On the former point we have the evidence of Ancient Greek inscriptions in Cyprus, of the geographical distribution of Ancient Greek dialects, and of Assyrian and Egyptian and Hittite historical records. On the latter point we can obtain indirect light from our evidence on the former point.

The earliest Greek inscriptions in Cyprus are conveyed not in the ordinary Greek alphabet (which was borrowed from the Phoenician) but in a peculiar local syllabary (which appears to have been adapted from one of the scripts current in Crete in the pre-Hellenic or Minoan Age). The Greek inscriptions conveyed in this syllabary which have been discovered by modern archaeologists come from every part of Cyprus, with a preponderance of finds in the west (especially at Paphos) and in the interior (especially at Idalion and Golgoi). The inference is that the form of Greek employed in these inscriptions was the prevalent language in Cyprus at the time when the inscriptions were cut; and the archaeologists attribute them to the fifth and fourth centuries B.C.[96]

The evidence for the prevalence of the Greek language in Cyprus is carried back rather more than two centuries farther than this by an official record of a King of Assyria. In 673 B.C., 'the kings of Cyprus, nine Greeks and one Phoenician, tendered their homage' to Esarhaddon. 'They were: Aigisthos of Idalion, Pythagoras of Chytroi, Keisos or

---

[95] On this, see pp. 363–5, above [in original publication].

[96] See A. Thumb, *Handbuch der Griechischen Dialekte* (Heidelberg, 1909, Winter), p. vii (a table of the syllabary) and pp. 279–96.

Kissos of Salamis, Etewandros of Paphos, Heraios of Soloi, Damasos of Kourion, Admetos of Tamassos, Onesagoras of Ledra, Pytheas of Nure (Aphrodision), and Damusi (the only Phoenician) of Kartikhadasti (Kition?) . . . The fact of only a single Phoenician king appearing in Cyprus at this time is significant: the Phoenicians never had much power in the island, which was always predominantly Greek, as it is to this day.'[97]

If we now inquire how long before the year 673 B.C. the then already attested prevalence of the Greek language in Cyprus had actually been established, a general study of the dialect-map of the Ancient Greek language shows that the introduction of the ancient Cypriot dialect of Greek into Cyprus must have been prior to the last convulsion (the so-called Dorian invasion) in the *Völkerwanderung* which intervened (*c.* 1425–1125 B.C.) between the end of Minoan history and the beginning of Hellenic. This evidence from the dialect-map has been well summarized as follows:

'No two dialects, not even Attic and Ionic, belong together more obviously than do those of Arcadia and the distant Cyprus. They share in a number of notable peculiarities which are unknown elsewhere. This is to be accounted for by the fact that Cyprus was colonized, not necessarily or probably from Arcadia itself, as tradition states, but from the Peloponnesian coast, at a time when its speech was like that which in Arcadia survived the Doric migration. This group represents beyond question the pre-Doric speech of most of the Peloponnese.'[98]

At what stage of the *Völkerwanderung* of *c.* 1425–1125 B.C. did this ancient Greek colonization of Cyprus take place? Contemporary Egyptian records show that the *Völkerwanderung* took the form of a series of successive waves of migration. Archaeological evidence shows that one of the earliest of these waves deposited in Cyprus a population uprooted from the Aegean area. Was this first wave of immigration into Cyprus from the Aegean already a Greek wave? Or did the Greek wave not come till towards the end of the migration period? The latter view used to be held by scholars. Mr. H. R. Hall, for example, in a work published in 1913 which has already been cited, dates the Greek colonization of Cyprus at the turn of the thirteenth and twelfth centuries B.C.

'A mixed body of Peloponnesians, Ionians, Kythnians, Arcadians, and Laconians took ship across the sea and appeared in the midst of the probably non-Greek Minoan colonists of Cyprus, who had established themselves there some two centuries before. These second colonists from Greece brought with them a Peloponnesian dialect of Greek, which thenceforth became the language of the island.'[99]

Since the passage just quoted was written, the new evidence derived from Hittite records of the second millennium B.C. has led scholars to assign higher dates to the first appearance of Greeks, and of the Greek language, first in the Aegean, then along the south coast of Anatolia, and finally in Cyprus. As the latest authoritative expression of opinion on this matter, we may take the second edition of the second volume of Eduard Meyer's *Geschichte des Altertums*. In the first instalment of this edition of this volume, which was published in 1928, Meyer dates the Greek colonization of Cyprus immediately after 1400 B.C. on the archaeological evidence, and adds that 'the archaeological finds bear out the evidence afforded by language, by the cult of Apollo Amyklos, and by the

---

[97] H. R. Hall, The Ancient History of the Near East (first edition, London, 1913, Methuen), p.496, text and footnote.
[98] C. D. Buck, *An Introduction to the study of the Greek Dialects* (Boston, 1910, Ginn), p. 6.
[99] Hall, *op. cit.* pp. 68–9.

name of the town Lakedaimon in the interior of the island. The name of the Achaeans was also preserved in Cyprus in several contexts . . . The intimate relation (*enge Verbindung*) in which the island has stood to the Aegean World since a high antiquity comes out in the fact that the Dove-Goddess, whose cult and image we have come across in Crete and Mycenae, is identified with the great goddess of Cyprus and is called after the island: "Cypris," "Cyprogeneia."'[100]

In the second instalment of the same edition of the same volume, which was published posthumously in 1931, Meyer remarks that the Greek colonists came to Cyprus before the Phoenician: the Greeks, towards the end of the Mycenaean Age, the Phoenicians not until the eleventh century B.C. 'The contrast between the Greek and the Phoenician colonization comes out very sharply. The Phoenicians occupy two points on the coast as stations for trading with the indigenous population; on the other hand, the Greeks not only occupied almost the whole of the coastline of the island but also colonized the great plain in the interior and from there made themselves masters of the copper-workings of Idalium and Tamassos.'[101] The two colonies which the Phoenicians succeeded in planting in Cyprus were Kition and Lapethos; the pre-Phoenician and pre-Greek population of Cyprus survived unhellenized down to Classical times in one place and one only: Amathus. The whole of the rest of the island was hellenized by the Greek colonists whose advent in Cyprus is to be dated, on the latest authoritative view, as early as the fourteenth century B.C.

This testimony from scholars is weighty, because in their minds, when they were forming their opinions, the question of the 'Greekness' of Cyprus was a purely scientific and academic question, and they gave their answers without any thought of their bearing upon current political controversies.

D. The Greek Press and Cyprus, June-July 1932

The Right Honourable   British Legation,
Sir John Simon, G.C.S.I, K.C.V.O   Athens,
etc., etc., etc.   July 9th, 1932.

Sir,

With reference to my despatch No. 291 of June 15th, I have the honour to inform you that the debate in the House of Commons on July 1st has provoked a fresh outburst of unfriendly comment in the Athens press. "Hestia" describes His Majesty's Government as being deceived by the "lying reports" of Sir Ronald Storrs and still completely in ignorance as to the true situation in Cyprus, "Ethnos" suggests that the administration of Church property by the British "may serve to swell the indemnity due to Sir Ronald Storrs for his collection of antiquities consisting of stolen objects." Another government paper "Phone tou Laou" says that those who hoped that with the departure of Sir Ronald Storrs the tyranny over the Cypriots would cease, made a mistake. The new Governor, it continues, is putting into effect restrictions against men of science and prominent citizens. This "policy of revenge" the paper says, is infamous and is unfortunately tolerated

---

[100] Meyer, *op. cit.*, pp. 552–5.
[101] *Op. cit.*, pp. 8–7.

by a Prime Minister who comes from the working classes and who a few years ago promised at Berne to labour for the free government of the peoples.

I have transmitted a copy of this despatch to His Majesty's High Commissioner at Cyprus.

I have the honour to be,
with the highest respect,
Sir
Your most obedient,
humble Servant,
Patrick Ramsay

The Right Honourable
Sir John Simon, G.C.S.I., K.C.V.O.
etc., etc., etc.

British Legation,
Athens,
June 15, 1932.

Sir,

With reference to my despatch No. 273 of June 7th regarding the question of Cyprus, I have the honour to inform you that the departure of Sir Ronald Storrs from that colony has been seized by the Greek press as a further opportunity to abuse him.

2. "Hestia" (anti-Venizelist but in relation with Monsieur Michalakopoulos) remarks that the Secretary of State for the Colonies evidently considers that an African colony is better suited to the administrative capacities shown by Sir Ronald Storrs in the "great Greek island," the "evil governor" embarked surrounded by an especially strong police force to suppress any hostile manifestations, this "anti-British Governor" has left the prisons of the island overflowing, he has obtained as many pounds sterling as he could in reparations, and Cypriots will always remember the manner in which he showed his interest in the island by pillaging its monuments to fill his famous collection. The article closes with an expression of hope that Sir Reginald Stubbs will keep the example of his predecessor before him in order to avoid it.

3. "Politia" (Royalist) says that public opinion in Great Britain does not understand the state of affairs in Cyprus and hopes that the authorities in London will soon realize that the solution of this problem is to grant a real constitution to the Cypriots, to permit the repatriation of the exiles and the return of the prelates in the immediate future and to cease regarding the Cypriots as a coloured tribe. "Eleftheron Vema" (Venizelist) publishes a telegram from Nicosia reporting an official communiqué issued by the Colonial Secretary regarding an interview between Sir Ronald Storrs and the Archbishop of Cyprus, which is stated to have been most cordial and to have closed with an announcement by the Governor that the Bishop of Paphos was free to return to Cyprus.

4. I have transmitted a copy of this despatch to the acting Governor of Cyprus.

I have the honour to be,
with the highest respect,
Sir
Your most obedient,
humble Servant,
Patrick Ramsay

IV. Amendment of the Criminal Code, June 1932 (CO 67/245/9)

A. A Law Further to Amend the Criminal Code, 8 June 1932

THE STATUTE LAWS OF CYPRUS
No. 34 of 1932.
A LAW FURTHER TO AMEND THE CRIMINAL CODE.

Ronald Storrs
Governor.

8ᵗʰ June, 1932.

Be it enacted by His Excellency the Governor and Commander-in-Chief of the Colony of Cyprus as follows:–

1. This Law may be cited as the Cyprus Criminal Code Order-in-Council, 1928, (Amendment) Law, 1932, and shall be read as one with the Cyprus Criminal Code Order-in-Council, 1928, as amended by the Cyprus Criminal Code Order-In-Council, 1928, Amendment Law, 1931, (hereinafter collectively referred to as "the Criminal Code"), and the Criminal Code and Law may together be cited as the Cyprus Criminal Code, 1928 to 1932.

2. Section 50 of the Criminal Code is hereby repealed and the following substituted therefor:-

50. For the purpose of the last preceding section a seditious intention is an intention—

(1) to bring into hatred or contempt or to excite disaffection against the person of His Majesty, his heirs or successors or the Government of the Colony as by law established, or

(2) to bring about a change in the sovereignty of the colony, or

(3) to excite His Majesty's subject or inhabitants of the Colony to attempt to procure the alteration, otherwise than by lawful means, of any other matter in the Colony as by law established, or

(4) to bring into hatred or contempt or to excite disaffection against the administration of justice in the Colony, or

(5) to raise discontent or disaffection amongst His Majesty's subjects or inhabitants of the Colony, or

(6) to promote feelings of ill will and hostility between different classes of the population of the Colony:

Provided that it shall be lawful for any person:-

(a) to endeavour in good faith to show that His Majesty has been misled or mistaken in any of his measures; or

(b) to point out in good faith errors or defects in the government or constitution of the Colony as by law established or in legislation or in the administration of justice, with a view to the reformation of such errors or defects; or

(c) to persuade in good faith His Majesty's subjects, or inhabitants of the Colony to attempt to procure by lawful means the alteration of any matter in the Colony as by law established other than that referred to in paragraph (2) of this section, or

(d) to point out in good faith, with a view to their removal any matters which are producing or have a tendency to produce feelings of ill will and enmity between different classes of the population of the Colony."

8th *June*, 1932.

H. Henniker-Heaton,
Colonial Secretary.

B. British Commentary

I attach an extract from a minute by Mr. Bushe with marginal comments by Mr. Parkinson on the case of M. Lanitis, who was recommended for deportation on account of his "union with Greece" activities.

The main amendment which the Governor proposes has the affect of splitting up the definition of "seditious intention" contained in Section 50 of the Criminal Code into a number of sub-sections, and of bringing in a new one which defines as a seditious intention an intention "to bring about a change in the sovereignty of the Colony."

There can be no doubt that the time has now come when this legislation is necessary if we are to restore firm rule in Cyprus. The only doubtful point appears to be whether the wording suggested by the Governor would have the desired effect, i.e., of making illegal the activities of the unionists. In view of past experience with the Cyprus Courts, it would appear that it is of paramount importance that there should be no doubt about this. This, however, is a matter on which the Legal Advisers will ? advise. As regards the procedure in amending an Order in Council by a local Ordinance, I presume that this is all right, see Section 364 of the Criminal Code Order in Council which gives the Governor power to alter or amend the Order. Now that the Legislative Council has ceased to exist, the Governor will no doubt be in order in making the amendments himself.

It would appear that in Section 2 Sub-section (1), (4), the words "or to excite disaffection against" should be inserted after the word "contempt."

The amendment provided for in Section 2 Sub-section (d) is ? a matter for the Legal Advisers on which no departmental observations seem necessary.

Chamberlain

The most important provision of this Bill is that it brings within the definition of a seditious intention an intention to bring about a change in the sovereignty of the Colony. It is clearly essential that some such provision should be enacted in order to enable the local Government to repress the movement for union with Greece. Mr. Duncan advises that there are no legal difficulties, and I do not see that the wording can be improved. It is certainly better that the wording should be in general terms rather than expressly refer to Greece.

It may be noted that the Governor expects violent opposition, but is quite prepared to face the consequences. I recommend that the draft Bill should be approved subject to the amendment suggested by Mr. Chamberlain.

CRD 8/3

V. Letter from R. Storrs, 9 June 1932 (CO 67/247/10)

SECRET.

The Right Honourable   Government House,
Sir Philip Cunliffe-Lister, G.B.E., P.C., M.P.,   Nicosia, 9th June, 1932.
Secretary of State for the Colonies.

Sir,

      I have the honour to submit a report briefly summarising the political developments that have taken place in the Colony of Cyprus since the end of the year 1926. It had been my intention and hope to have concentrated exclusively upon forward and intensive economic development, but politics have been increasingly thrust upon me and upon the attention of His Majesty's Government by the exigencies of a situation resulting from a prolonged epoch characterised by periodical declarations of policy unaccompanied by the local means to enable its effective adoption or maintenance. Economic and social development, while highly agreeable to and appreciated by the masses, did not commend itself to local politicians for the simple reason that, by suggesting an alternative to Enosis, it diverted the limelight from themselves and their cause. From the beginning there were signs that no degree of progress would induce these irreconcilables to abandon their theory or practice. Nevertheless, looking back over the past five and a half years and taking into account the circumstances in which I found myself placed, I am aware of no general principle of policy that I would reverse or modify if I had to begin again, least of all that of attempted legislative and social co-operation with the inhabitants of the country. The opportunity of friendly collaboration was, especially during the first period, extended to the elected representatives of the people. That they should have proved incapable of embracing or appreciating it is no disparagement of the offer, though its contumacious and finally seditious rejection has forced upon Government the adoption of other methods.

      2. On my first landing at Famagusta I was greeted by the Mayor with an address of welcome containing an allusion to Union and bound up in the blue and white colours of Greece, and Greek flags were abundantly flown as I drove through Nicosia. This I was informed by the Commissioner and Police to be quite a normal procedure, and therefore, not wishing to create an incident on my arrival, I accepted it without comment. It was, as I found later, indicative of the tolerance with which the whole movement for Union was traditionally treated by past Governments. Neither the Annexation of Cyprus in 1914 nor its formal constitution as a Crown Colony in 1925 had been utilized by the Government or allowed by the propagandists to affect the movement in any way whatever.

      3. Anxious to investigate rural conditions and to see things for myself I visited in my first two and a half years all the cities, townships and some two hundred villages in the Colony. At about half of these I was greeted by Greek flags, with frequent allusions by schoolmasters to the national aspirations. At the Pan-Cypria or annual Greek-Orthodox Cypriot Sports Meeting the whole of the stadium was, according to tradition, decorated with Greek flags, and the first time that the Union Jack was hoisted there was on the occasion of my attendance in 1927. Greek Independence Day was the signal for nationalistic church services with Te Deums throughout the Colony, and for processions and meetings in the various stadia, at which fiery, though never, it would seem, legally

seditious harangues were pronounced to excited but orderly crowds. The difficulties involved in taking a strong line with such agitators are exemplified in paragraph 7 of my Secret despatch of February 12th, 1931. I confined myself at first to reversing the decision of one of my predecessors by directing that the six Commissioners should fly the Union Jack on their offices and residences.

4. My experiences in Egypt and Palestine have I hope not predisposed me against a certain measure of toleration, but the condition of things I found in this British Colony was such as I could hardly believe to be realised by His Majesty's Government, and I therefore addressed to the Secretary of State a secret despatch of the 18th January, 1928, describing the circumstances in which a British Governor was placed and asking for confirmation or criticism of the attitude I was adopting. My reason for desiring to obtain a decision on this important issue was that the alternative appeared to be either to accept the present anomalous and almost humiliating tradition, or, by ceasing visits and inspections, to sever relations with the people, thus playing into the hands of the politicians, who, by the development of the Agricultural Bank and the multiplying of Co-operative Credit Societies, began to feel, and indeed stated in the Athenian Press, that they were losing grip with those they had hitherto influenced, their only remaining leverage being the Church and the educational machine. I suggested that a remedy might lie in the modification of the scholastic curriculum, should the Government be in a position to assume financial responsibility. Mr. Amery conveyed to me his entire endorsement and approval of my policy and attitude, and adopted my suggestion that I should tackle the educational problem. Meanwhile the action of His Majesty's Government in accepting my proposals for settling the Tribute question had by now made available, after the framing and testing of the 1928 Budget, sufficient funds to make at least a beginning in acquiring control of the machine, which I accordingly proceeded to do, resuming the charge later upon my recovery from the severe illness which laid me low in 1928; and, by convincing three Greek Orthodox members of the Legislative Council of the rottenness of the existing system and the necessity for Government intervention, was able to pass the 1929 Education Bill, under which the appointment, promotion, transfer, and dismissal of school-teachers passed from the political committees to the Government. This measure was decisive as a final rupture of friendly relations between Government and the extreme politicians, on whose part it was henceforth a question of war to the knife undisguised. Not one of the three above members was able to present himself at the 1930 elections. In the Athenian Press I became, instead of the distinguished Phil-Hellene who had "abolished the Tribute," the Imperialistic Dictator: in the local Press I was lampooned as the man who had "assassinated Hellenic education." The politicians were, in my opinion, correct in their diagnosis of the situation, for the 1929 Law was the thin end of a wedge, which time and gradually applied pressure would have driven home between themselves and their aspirations.

5. Meanwhile the existing Constitution, always difficult, had, through constant and increasing obstruction, become unworkable. During my illness the Greek members walked out of the Chamber sooner than vote the Estimates, and recourse had to be taken on more than one occasion to Orders in Council. In 1929 I therefore informed the Secretary of State that in my opinion there must be a change in the Constitution, urged that it should be amended forthwith and submitted concrete proposals for an alternative. I discussed the matter with him in person and would, I think, have obtained some result, but for the General Elections of 1929 which compelled His Majesty's Government to defer

their decision. As the Government was not returned to power I was compelled to take the matter up again with their successors, and in 1930 renewed the quest with Lord Passfield, who evinced a sympathetic knowledge of the situation, but appeared to be in favour of something more in the nature of the Donoughmore Constitution. While fully realizing the difficulty of resuming or curtailing constitutional liberties once accorded, I had to make it clear that if the only change to be introduced gave an increased measure of demagogic control, we had better remain as we were. Nothing was therefore done to amend the Constitution.

6. Even now, by the maintenance of a sympathetic and above all of a patient attitude, it was possible to carry on so long as the three Turkish Moslem members could be depended on to vote with the Government. Unfortunately the Turkish Consul, Assaf Bey, a strong Nationalist and Kemalist, had succeeded in creating a small but active element of opposition to the loyal majority. I discovered his intrigues and reported them to His Majesty's Government who caused his recall, but not before he had so influenced the Turkish electorate that one of the three members returned could no longer be counted upon to support the Government. This completely upset the balance of power. The Greek Orthodox members were quick to perceive their advantage and to follow it up. The Government was thus placed in a position of absolute dependence upon an obstructive, unreasonable and determinedly hostile majority, counting upon and assisted by the dead weight of opposition and detraction continuously (and as a rule not illegally) applied by the schools, the Press, pulpit and platform of Enosis propaganda. The criticism followed familiar lines, and was consistent only in being always destructive. If the policy was conservative, 'nothing was being done': if forward, it became 'squander-mania.' If limited to physical or practical development, it was derided as 'materialistic': if cultural, by lectures, Museum or a Public Library, characterised as the 'imposition of unwanted luxuries to the exclusion of vital necessities.' Any course of action adopted *proprio motu* by the local Government was 'ill-considered.' But any previous consultation of specialist advice in order to insure the best results was invariably saluted as 'the plague of experts.' Such congenial arguments against the attitude of 'the foreign ruler' were indeed annually for a few weeks discredited by my speech delivered at the opening of the Legislative Council, when past progress and future programme were surveyed in some detail and placed in the hands of every Mukhtar and Policeman in the language of his village for broadcasting on the morrow of delivery. Efforts were also made through periodical announcements arid such organs as the Agricultural and Forest Journal to bring home the truth to those most concerned in learning it, but in the absence of special Press regulations or the dubious and costly expedient of an organ subsidised by the Government it was not possible to insure that the public should be adequately protected from the constant and calculated pressure of calumny and abuse.

7. About this moment matters were complicated by the removal of the correct (and appropriately named) Greek Consul, Mr. Inglessis, and the appointment of the Cypriot-descended Mr. Alexander Kyrou. It was not long before intelligence reached me of his political activities, of which I immediately notified His Majesty's Government, expressing the opinion that British prestige was seriously endangered by the association of this official with disloyal manifestations. The evidence, however, which it was possible to obtain proved insufficient to justify diplomatic action, but it was suggested, in consultation with the Department, that I should interview Mr. Venizelos on the occasion of his visit to England last July. Mr. Venizelos, while emphasising his own entire correctness

and neutrality and that of his Government, admitted that he could not always rely upon his agents, and promised that Mr. Kyrou should be withdrawn from Cyprus by the end of August, 1931. The course of events after that date is fully set out in my despatch No. 80 of February 11th.

8. I have been assisted by your public approval and support during and since the disturbances, and I would further record my appreciation of the manner in which the Department has refrained from imposing upon me doctrinaire or conventional instructions, has left the initiative to me, and has accepted and adopted the majority of my suggestions for specific action as well as for general policy.

9. In conclusion I beg to add that, although I would not have chosen the recent process of events, which has indeed resulted in some inconvenience to myself, yet as a British Governor and in the interests of Cyprus as a British Colony, I would not have the results otherwise. I believe that I have devoted to Cyprus not less of zeal and of sympathy than my predecessors, and that to my successor (to whom this brief but documented survey may perhaps prove useful) I am bequeathing a clearer and more regular situation than that which I inherited.

I have the honour to be,
Sir,
Your most obedient,
humble Servant,
Ronald Storrs
Governor.

VI. Enosis Appeal from Greece and the Greek Angle, 1932 (CO 67/244/8,9)

A. Appeal of the Central Committee for Cyprus

APPEAL
OF THE CENTRAL COMMITTEE FOR CYPRUS

At this moment, when the people of Cyprus are struggling for their liberties and sacrificing their all upon the altar of the Fatherland, we feel it to be our duty to declare that the whole Greek race is watching this manly effort with admiration and fraternal solicitude.

The people of free Greece are not forgetful of the strong bonds of gratitude and sincere friendship, which bind them to Britain, one of the Powers, which once guaranteed Greek independence. But they believe that the liberal traditions of the British nation demand the satisfaction of the legitimate national aspirations of an island—Greek by race, language and sentiment—which Great Britain 53 years ago took over as a mere inanimate pledge from another Power, an alien conqueror of the island.

For this reason the undersigned have met this day and formed a Committee of fifty members, for the sole purpose of enlightening by every means the public opinion of the civilized world, and especially that of the great British nation, as to the imperishable human rights, on which the Greek nation bases its plea, that the people of Cyprus be permitted to determine their own destinies.

We believe that, in so doing, we are but fulfilling an elementary duty of our race to our sorely-tried brethren of Cyprus. And we venture to trust that our effort, which but reflects the sentiments of the nation, shall not be in vain.

Long live Greek Cyprus!

Athens, 30 October 1931.

PAUL CONDOURIOTIS, President

A. Canaris, Vice-President   S. Loverdhos, treasurer
Th. Ypsilantis, Vice-President   Ph. Dragoumis, secretary general

D. Acrivos	M. Gheorgandas	J. Papaflessas
S. Agapitos	A. Grivas	G. Pesmazoglou
N. Alivizatos	D. Hadziscos	Th. Petimezas
M. Averoff	T. Iliopoulos	Th. Petracopoulos
A. Benakis	A. Kyriakidhis	P. Pierracos-Mavromichalis
A. Botsaris	N. Levidhis	J. Rallis
G. Capodistrias	P. Mavromichalis	N. Rangavis
A. Christomanos	C. Mazarakis-Aenian	J. Theotokis
C. Codzias	P. Mazarakis	D. Tombazis-Mavrocordhatos
A. Corizis	M. P. Melas	S. Tricoupis
A. Criezis	G. Metaxas	J. Tsamadhos
J. Damverghis	A. Miaoulis	A. Valaoritis
E. Deliyannis	P. Nirvanas	G. Vassiliadhis
S. Evghenidhis	C. Palamas	C. Voulgaris
A. Frandzis	D. Papadhiamandopoulos	A. P. Zaimis

B. The Cypriot Question from the Greek Angle, 21 November 1932 (CO 67/244/9)

SECRET
Mr. Clauson,   21/11/32
Colonial Office

The Cypriot Question from the Greek Angle.

Below is a report from our representative in Greece dated 19th October, 1932, which summarizes up to that date the results of his enquiries, since the Cyprus outbreak of 1931, into the Greek connexions with Cypriot national organizations:

General.

(1) Since the outbreak of disorder in Cyprus in the autumn of 1931 one of our principal objectives in Greece has been to follow the activity of the partisans of the Enosis movement, estimate the importance of Greek moral and financial help, discover to what extent Greek official personages were helping the movement in an underhand manner and find out all possible details about individuals connected with the movement who are domiciled in Greece.

(2) The underground machinations and personal jealousies of the more prominent "Enosis" leaders in Cyprus, which led to the outbreak, were soon unveiled, thanks to information from Cypriot sources in Greece. The flamboyant outburst of Greek sympathy for their oppressed brethren, which looked ugly on the surface last November and December, was regarded in the light of knowledge and experience of local conditions, as a passing phase. The reported remittance of cash in large quantities for the support of the movement was generally deprecated and the main tenour of reports indicated that the Greeks would soon find some other preoccupations which would touch them more closely and would help to quench their facile enthusiasm for meddling in other people's affairs.

(3) The progress of events has justified these opinions and estimates. The Greek financial crisis developed space and therefore the tumult and the shouting about Cyprus is moribund, if not already dead. The main centre of pro-Enosis propaganda has now shifted to the U.S.A. and the U.K. In the former country the Greek organisations, the Ahepa and the Gapa, are being milked to supply funds, etc., for the propagation of the sentimental vapourings about Cyprus, which seem to appeal to some sections of American thought. This is under the direction of an organization known as the K.E.O. which is mentioned again below. In the U.K. the Cypriot deportees have been detected in the prosecution of unholy amours with persons of very doubtful political morals and there is evidence to show that Communist partisans have been trying to hook them for their own purposes. The return to Greece of some of the original deportees from Cyprus gave rise to reasonable suspicions that Greek officials either at home or abroad had been giving facilities with the unofficial left hand unbeknown to the official right hand. Some information on this point is given in later paragraphs.

(4) At present, as far as it is possible to foresee, the pro-Enosis movement in Greece has declined to the point of being almost negligible. It has recently been discovered from more than one source that the more notorious propagandists have tied themselves up with party politics, in that they have coquetted with one political party with the object of playing it off, for their own special purposes, against another; i.e. having had little encouragement from the Liberals, they are now extracting specious promises of support from the Popular Party, if and when the latter party is in a position to implement them. It would appear that some date after the Greek Kalends is likely to see the realisation of their hopes.

Summary of recent Enquiries.

(5) The following is a summary of the results of the recent enquiries which have been conducted:

(a)   Individuals connected with the movement in Greece.

Enquiries concerning persons in Greece alleged to be active in pro-Enosis propaganda have produced much information, of which a summary covering more important points is as follows:

Names.	Information obtained.
J. Kpryzis	Sub-Governor of the National Bank of Greece and member of the famous committee of 45 organized under the presidency of Admiral Koundouriotis for propaganda work in favour of Cypriot aspirations last autumn.

"Eleftheriades"	This is believed to be Juvenalios Eleftheriades, an archimandrite who is a professor at the high school in Famagusta.
Giannis	Almost certainly Ioannis Ioannides, a doctor. Brother of the Deputy for Nicosia, Georgios Hajipavlou. This person has been very prominent in the direction of the pro-Enosis movement in Greece and also one of the protagonists in the formation of the Cypriot Political Club of Athens. He has also been present at all the public or other meetings in favour of the Cypriot cause. His address, Tsakaloff 3, Athens, has been confirmed.
Ioannides	Another man whose Christian name is Stylianos. He is a law student originally from Paphos and is President of the Cypriot Students' Brotherhood. He takes an active part in any propaganda on the Cyprus question. He is a "bad hat" who lives on the credulity and generosity of pro-Cypriot enthusiasts. Since August last he has been seen almost permanently in the company of Kolokassides and Tsangarides, the Cypriot deportees who got back to Greece from London in a suspicious manner.
Argyrios	This is Argyrios Argyrides, a schoolmaster in Macedonia, who came originally from Pallouriotissa near Nicosia.

(b) The Cypriot Students' Brotherhood in Greece, which is always to be found in the foreground of any propaganda activity is directed by the following officers and prominent members:

Stylianos Herakleous Ioannides—President. Law student, origin Paphos.
Kyriakos Karamanos—Secretary. Student of Philology. Origin Limassol.
Georgios Fessas—Treasurer. Medical Student. Origin Paphos.
Simeon Kassianides—Member of Committee. Medical Student. Origin Kornos.
Nico Themistocleous—Member. Medical Student. Origin Nicosia.
Paskhalis Paskhalides—Medical Student. Origin Proasteio.
Kostas Aghiomanitis—Medical Student.
Petros Nikolaides—Medical Student. Origin Kythraia.
Kostas Mouskis—Medical Student. Origin Nicosia.
Takis Evangelides—Medical Student. Origin Nicosia.
Mikis Pierides—Medical Student. Origin Nicosia.
Kypros Theophanides—Medical Student. Origin Nicosia.
Georgios Tsangarides—Medical Student. Origin Nicosia.

(c) The direction of Enosis propaganda appears now to be taking a new form. The recent arrival in Greece of one Rediades, who is the correspondent in London of the Athens newspaper, "Politeia," and his association with Cypriot deportees, Theophanis Tsangarides and Theodoros Kolokassides, led to enquiries as to their doings. Nothing is known in Greece concerning Rediades' contacts and occupations in London, but his paper, owned and edited by one Nocoloudis, gives pride of place to Enosis propaganda news.

(d) It has been learned from more than one source that the organisation of pro-Enosis propaganda has now been taken over by a triumvirate composed of Tsangarides, Kolokassides and Stylianos Ioannides, with Rediades as foreign correspondent and liaison officer for England and the U.S.A. The executive machinery is to be supplied by the Cypriot Brotherhood which has passed under the control of this triumvirate, and probably the newspaper "Politeia" will be pressed into service for broadcasting the information, articles, etc., which are being sent out of Cyprus through third or fourth parties. Rediades is to arrange for the adequate distribution of this material in England and the U.S.A. and is to send copies of all relevant publications in those countries to the triumvirate in Greece a toutes fins utiles.

(e) How far Greek officialdom has clandestinely helped the Cypriot malcontents and propagandists since the outbreak last autumn has not been satisfactorily established. It is persistently asserted by some sources that officials of the Greek M.F.A. have been most helpful to the Enosis propagandists and there is much presumptive evidence to bear this out, but it has been found impossible to produce concrete proof of the direct complicity of individuals in a conspiracy directly opposed to the declared policy of the Prime Minister. The strong rumours affecting the late Consul-General in Cyprus, Kyrou, his subsequent removal, the close relations between the newspaper "Estia," owned and directed by the brother Kyrou, who are proteges of Nikhalakopoules, the reported intention to appoint the late Consul-General to an important consular post in the U.S.A., are all very significant facts. On the other hand, the recent resignation of Archilaos Kyrou from the honorary presidency of the Cypriot Brotherhood, since it has fallen under the control of the triumvirate mentioned above, appears to show that official circles are now becoming more circumspect over the Cyprus question. The return of Tsangarides and Kolokassides to Greece was facilitated, according to information obtained, by the left-handed help of officials. Tsangarides' brother, the cavalry colonel, is said to have approached Venizelos personally on this matter, but, getting no help, he wrote to Sophokles Venizelos in Paris, who arranged the matter through the Military Attaché and the Consul in Paris.

(f) The very latest development, which is but a few days old, is the beginning of a schism in the ranks of the pro-Cypriots due, it is stated to fear of the methods to be employed by the triumvirate and to the fact that they are meddling in Greek party politics. Neutral or anti-Enosis Cypriots in Greece have been threatened with violence by minions of the new organisation and the word has gone round among them that an armed "Cheka" of Enosis bravos has been formed to do them hurt. The alleged understanding between the pro-Enosis organisation and the Popular Party has roused all the Venizelists.

(6) Taking all the factors, including the present political and financial difficulties of Greece, into consideration, there is small danger in asserting that the seed of the Enosis movement in Greece is now falling on rather stony ground.

VII. Dispatch of H. R. Palmer, 19 June 1934 (CO 67/254/6)

A. Letter of H. R. Palmer, 19 June 1934

The Right Honourable   Government House
Sir Philip Cunliffe-Lister, G.B.E., P.C., M.P.,   Nicosia, 19th June, 1934.
Secretary of State for the Colonies.

Sir,

     With reference to Sir R. E. Stubbe's confidential telegram of the 24th. Of March, 1933, and subsequent correspondence relative to the objections to granting the bishop of Kitium and Mr. George Hadjipavlou passports valid for Greece, I have the honour to state that I am informed that the latter gentleman arrived in Athens on the 4th or 5th of June and is now residing there.

     2. I assume that Mr. Hadjipavlou obtained clandestine entry into Greece in the same manner as the deportees Theophanis Tsangarides Colocassides to whom reference was made in the Foreign Office enclosure to your despatch No. 332 of the 4th of August, 1932.

     3. I would be glad if the attention of the Greek Government can be drawn to this matter, if the British Minster in Athens confirms the report of Mr. Hadjipavlou's presence there. It is to be apprehended that this deportee will associate himself with and considerably add to the forces of the Cypriot faction in Athens which is led by the Bishop of Kyrenia. I attach a copy of a recent report on which reliance can be placed, setting forth the present position of the Enosis movement in Athens. I have little reason to doubt that the advent of Mr. Hadjipavlou will strengthen the extremists who advocate the methods of terrorism.

I have, etc.,
H. R. Palmer.
Governor.

B. Enosis Movement in Athens, 12 May 1934

Criminal Investigation Department,
Nicosia, 12th May, 1934.

SECRET.
Intelligence report (Summary)
10.5.34–12.5.34.

Enosis.

     The protagonists of the Enosis Movement in Athens have been particularly active amongst the Cypriot students recently.

     An organization named the "Society of Friends of Cyprus" was formed in Athens early in 1934. Its object is to accomplish the Union of Cyprus with Greece. Its methods are extremist and terrorism is openly advocated.

     The Bishop of Kyrenia and Savvas Loizides (both deportees) are the guiding spirits of the movement.

     Achilleas Kyrou, editor of the Athens newspaper "Estia" has opposite views and advocates pacifist methods. As a result there is a divergence of opinion in the ranks of the Cypriot students in Athens. The majority are of the same opinion as A. Kyrou.

The members of the Cyprus National Bureau and the Society of Friends of Cyprus are identical.

The Cyprus National Bureau receives its funds from the Great committee which is presided over by Admiral Condouriotes. However it is not thought that the Great Committee necessarily approves of the methods advocated by the Society of Friends of Cyprus.

C. Newspaper Extract, 14 February 1934

"Hestia" of 14th February, 1934.

The end of a petty tyrant

Information from England announces that Sir R. Storrs, Governor of Northern Rhodesia and ex-Governor of Cyprus, has resigned for reasons of health.

The career of a higher British official, who was extremely ambitious and who looked upon his post in Cyprus as the beginning of a splendid career which should raise him to the highest posts in the British Empire, thus comes to an end on the most inglorious and lamentable manner. This man made the mistake of thinking that, with a view to his advancement, he might employ in the 20th century the medieval methods of the Venetian and Frankish petty tyrants, but in this way he succeeded only in provoking the hatred and indignation of a population infinitely superior to his own civilisation and culture.

The pity is that the methods and systems, which Sir R. Storrs introduced into Cyprus, and which led him first to an insignificant African colony and then to retirement at the age of 49, are still being maintained by England in Cyprus.

Chapter 5
Prelude to the Struggle: 1935–1950

The fifth and final chapter in this compendium opens with a memorandum from the Colonial Office that assesses the history of British administration of Cyprus up to 1935. With the outbreak of hostilities in World War II, Enosis activities re-emerged. Governor Palmer tells us that pro-enosis groups began to re-appear in 1937, in spite of legislation that had been passed in 1932 defining as sedition any efforts to alter the sovereignty of the Island. Various minutes and letters indicate that the Enosis movement was active throughout the war, and that the German government played a role in encouraging it. By 1943 activities led Governor Woolley to propose repressive measures that his superiors in London thought excessive and ill-advised. Correspondence in 1944 illustrates the quite different perspectives and sympathies of the Foreign Office and those of the Colonial Office (CO 67/319/5). Mr. Battershill's minute to Mr. Acheson on 14/8/44 provides an unusual social analysis of the Enosis leadership. The last two documents take us up to the plebiscite of 1950. The Enosis campaign of the 1950's is thoroughly documented and chronicled, hence the decision to end the record at that point. It is perhaps both ironic and appropriate that the volume ends with the sentence, "The view of H.M.G. is that it is essential that full sovereignty should be maintained in Cyprus and that the less the question of union with Greece is discussed the better."

I. British Policy in Cyprus, September 1935 (CO 67/259/10)

CONFIDENTIAL.

BRITISH POLICY IN CYPRUS.
MEMORANDUM BY COLONIAL OFFICE.

1. Cyprus at present is being governed on the principle of benevolent autocracy. The forms of representative government which formerly existed have been superseded by a strict Crown Colony system. The legislative and administrative power is vested solely in the Governor. Following on the riots of 1931, stringent measures have been adopted for the preservation of public order and to restrict the activities and propaganda of the

secessionist group who favour the union of the Island with Greece. A strict censorship and press law is in operation. The flying of the Greek flag is prohibited. Assemblies, meetings and procession are severely regulated.

2. There is good ground for considering that this firm government is welcomed by the population as a whole and that the Island is in a better and more contented condition than it has been for many years. This result has been achieved by the systematic pursuit by the Cyprus Government of a policy carefully worked out and based, not on *a priori* principles but on the objective fact of the local situation. The explanation of this policy and of the necessity for its adoption must be sought in the historical background against which it has been framed. This background is indicated in the succeeding paragraphs.

3. The key-note of the British administration of Cyprus from the occupation in 1878 until the riots of 1931 was liberty rather than efficiency. A wide measure of self-government was bestowed upon the islanders. The action of the central Government was directed to the maintenance of law and order and the proper administration of justice rather than to the development of material resources and the amelioration of social conditions. It is true that some improvements were made in the latter direction: and the Island, the time of the annexation in 1914, showed great advance upon its derelict condition in 1878. A road system had been provided: harbours had been improved: and a railway had been built. Regular mail, post and telegraphic services had been established. The spread of education had been assisted by grants from Government. But there was nevertheless little of the activity in administrative and economic development which is now a feature of the British colonial system. Direct Government action moved within a limited scope and intruded little into the ordinary life of the people. This easy-going system was, no doubt, in harmony with the general spirit of the times: but in the case of Cyprus there were local and particular reasons for it.

4. Up to the outbreak of war with Turkey in November, 1914, Cyprus was in the position of a leased territory. It was occupied and administered by Great Britain, but sovereignty over it resided in the Sultan. The British tenure was, therefore, far from definite and permanent. The Cyprus Convention of 1878 had indeed contained a clause under which, in certain circumstances, the Island was to be evacuated by Great Britain: in which event its administration would have reverted to the Ottoman Empire of which it was still an integral portion. There was in these conditions no permanent incentive either to the British Government to improve the administration or to British capital to assist in development. The public interest in Cyprus, which had been provoked by the occupation of 1878, had soon subsided. The occupation of Egypt in 1881 was considered to have deprived the Island of the value at first attributed to it as a strategic point on the route to the Far East. The Island was then no longer regarded as a necessary base for naval and military operations in the Eastern Mediterranean: and its original significance from the standpoint of Imperial defence was diminished by the establishment of a British garrison in Egypt and of British control over the Suez Canal. After 1878, therefore, the Island quickly receded from the main stage of events on to which for a brief period it had been introduced by Lord Beaconsfield at the Congress of Berlin.

5. The political institutions conferred upon Cyprus by Great Britain were not designed to stimulate governmental activity. In 1882 a Legislative Council based upon liberal conceptions was established. It comprised the Governor and twelve elected and six official members. In later years the size of the Council was varied but the balance be-

tween the elected and the official members remained the same. The Constitution, therefore, placed the legislative power in the hands of an unofficial majority. This feature dominated the situation in Cyprus for 49 years until, following upon the riots in the autumn of 1931, the Constitution of 1882 was abolished. The Executive Government during these years was in a permanent minority in the legislative Council. In this situation it had to discharge as best it could the duty of carrying on the administration: it could not resign and hand over this duty to others. The unofficial majority formed a permanent and irresponsible opposition whose criticisms of the Government were not sobered by any prospect of being called to power. The Government could only carry its measures through the Council by playing off the Greek-speaking against the Turkish-speaking element among the elected members and from time to time, when a serious deadlock occurred, by resort to an Imperial Order-in-Council. Governmental machinery of this fragile character could be run only on a low current. As was to be expected from the characteristics and history of the islanders, the talents of the elected members were more fitted for petty politics and intrigue than for the constructive work of government. The British Administration was, therefore, forced to consider its measures in the light not so much of their administrative merits as of "political considerations," often of a retrograde nature. The subordinate institutions of the Island reflected the character and defects of the central body. They tended, that is to say, rather to give play to the principle of control by an elected oligarch, than to secure an efficient and progressive administration. The schools were under the control of boards upon which the local politicians were in a majority: and the important field of education was thrown open to the influences of petty intrigue and factious irredentist propaganda. The Municipal Councils which administered the affairs of the chief towns were constituted on the same principle and placed in the control of popularly elected councillors. Gross corruption was rampant in all these elected bodies.

6. There can be little doubt that the Constitution of 1882 was quite unsuited to the character and requirements of the islanders. It was imposed on them at a period when in the outside world there was much faith in the efficacy of representative institutions, regardless of the environment in which they were planted. The Constitution did not grow organically out of the Island's past. Cyprus had been ruled by foreign masters during practically the whole of its recorded history: and had at the time of the British occupation been under Turkish rule for over three hundred years. Such a history was not calculated to prepare the soil of Cyprus for the healthy germination of representative institutions on the Anglo-Saxon model. The qualities of character which had been developed in the Cypriots were not those which fit a people for the responsible conduct of its affairs.

7. Before the war the defects and abuses of this system had little more than local significance. If the Cypriots were deprived of many of the advantages of material progress, they enjoyed a large measure of liberty and freedom from disturbances either from within or from without. At the same time the drift of ideas and ideals was away from British affinities and sympathies. The annexation to the British Empire in November, 1914, though it brought many legal and formal changes, had no substantial effect on the outlook and life of the Island. During the war it was not possible to do more than to continue the old policy and attend to the bare essentials of administration. The Island made money out of the war, remained peaceful and secure and experienced none of the vicissitudes which the war brought to neighbouring countries. The islanders escaped the obligation of compulsory military service. They enjoyed a sound currency and were not called

upon to bear the heavy direct taxation which was a feature of other fiscal systems. In the years immediately following the war, there were few innovations in the policy pursued by the British Administration. The general dislocation and depression in the outside world disturbed the Island's trade, and there was little money available for reforms or the development of Cyprus from an imperial point of view.

8. As the Island emerged from the post-war period, it became apparent that new ideas were at work. It may be said broadly that these ideas were moving towards two objectives, one of which was economic and the other political. These ideas came from different sources, the one from the British Government and the other from the Greek-speaking politicians: and evidence of disharmony between them soon became obvious. On the economic side the Government began a policy of development and improvement. The Island was now a British colony. Throughout the Colonial Empire after the war there began a policy of vigorous economic development with a view to stimulating the production of primary, and particularly agricultural, products. This was accompanied by attempts to improve and systematize administrative machinery in a manner which signalized the much greater interest which was being taken by Great Britain in her overseas possessions. In the general improvement of personnel and machinery was reflected the specialisation and standardization which, at the time, were showing themselves in the world generally. Cyprus naturally came within the range of these forces. The Government, changing the old policy, embarked upon a regime of which the goal was efficiency. Simultaneously, on the political side, the movement for union with Greece broke into unrestrained activity. This feature also reflected the general tendencies in the outside world. The theories regarding self-determination of small nations and the nationalistic tendencies which resulted from the war inflamed and embittered a political movement in Cyprus which, although it had long been present, had on the whole been amiable and academic.

9. The movement for union with Greece ("Enosis") is a basic political factor in the Cyprus situation. Like most nationalistic movements it is complex and paradoxical and the motives behind it are extremely mixed. In some measure it originated among the Cypriots in a wish to find reputable ancestry in the Homeric Greeks, and to emphasise the Byzantine connection of the Cypriot Church with the Emperor Zeno as a solace against Turkish oppression. There is thus among certain but relatively small elements of the population a genuine idealistic desire for union with political Greece and a belief in the connection of Cyprus with the great Greek tradition of learning and art which has supplied spiritual nutriment to the whole of western civilization. A more wide-spread and concrete consideration is the idea existing among ecclesiastics and politicians, who have in the past had great weight with the local community, that their material and personal interests would be better served by union with Greece than with Great Britain. The movement, owing to the friendly tolerance of the British authorities for many years, has not always been marked by hostility to the British. Claptrap phrases regarding Byron and Gladstone and the liberal tradition have been the common stock-in-trade of the local politicians. It has even been suggested that England might hand the Island over to Greece and at the same time maintain a naval base there and undertake to protect it from aggression by any other foreign power. The cession of the Ionian Islands to Greece in 1864 after 49 years of protectorate lent support to the belief that England with her liberal tradition might, as a friendly gesture towards Greece and the Greek-speaking Cypriots, assist them

in fulfilling these aspirations which it must be added owe their dissemination very largely to the absence of any form of British propaganda to counteract them.

On the other hand, the political passion engendered by the movement has from time to time torn aside these amiable fictions. And the disturbances 1931, in which Government House was burned down, mark the highest pitch of the antagonism. The real cause for its persistence and intensity undoubtedly lies in the attitude and intransigence of the local Orthodox Church. This factor of the Church is essential to any understanding of philhellenism in Cyprus. The influence of the church among the Cypriots has been and still is very great. It is notorious that the church is corrupt through and through. The village priests are ignorant peasants and often do not understand the language of their liturgy. It is not an exaggeration to say that the priest is often the worst man in the village. The revenues of the monasteries and sees are more often than not directed to the support of the concubines and illegitimate off-spring of the monks and bishops. The church is a scandalously bad landlord. But, in spite of these facts, it has, owing to the strength of its material position as the largest landlord, a strong influence in the affairs of the country. The reason for this is largely historical. In Turkish times the Archbishop was the only spokesman of the Greek people with the authorities and the ecclesiastical hierarchy were in a great degree used by the Turkish Governor as the machinery through which to deal with the people, collect taxes and generally govern the Island. The church thus acquired great influence which has persisted.

The spread of British ideas meant the termination of the political power of the church: hence in their hatred of England rather than of their love of Greece the leaders of the church have used the "Enosis" movement in the hope that, if it is successful, they will be reinstated in their former position of authority with its many opportunities for personal power and profit. The argument, which from time to time has been put forward that there is a real connection, either geographical or historical, between political Greece of today and Cyprus, is extremely thin. It is very doubtful whether the Greek-speaking Cypriots can be said to be of the Greek race. The many nations which have passed over the island from antiquity onwards have left their mark upon it and ethnologically there is no question that the Cypriots are of very mixed provenance.

10. The clash between the Government and the "Enosis" movement led to increasing difficulties from 1926 onwards. The Government in its attempt to introduce a more progressive administration had to get its measures through the Legislative Council. The unofficial members were not slow to exploit their powerful position on the Council for political purposes. The Government first attempted to meet opposition with conciliation. In every administrative department a good deal of deference necessarily had to be paid to the views and suggestions of the elected members to the extent of gravely impairing efficiency, and conniving at "log-rolling." Their services were freely employed upon Committees in the endeavour, by bringing them face to face with administrative problems, to enlist them on the side of constructive action. Important posts in the Government Service were given to Cypriots. Great toleration was shown to expressions of philhellenistic feeling: and the unrestricted display of the Greek flag was a regular feature of the Island. But this policy of conciliation appeared only to encourage the opposition of the politicians to British rule. In November, 1926, the elected members rejected the local budget by a unanimous vote as a protest against the continuance of the payment which Cyprus as a succession state of the Ottoman Empire was making for the benefit of the

bondholder of the Ottoman public debt. In order to keep the machinery of government working, the necessary legislative measures had to be taken by an Imperial Order-in Council. At the same time the British Government made a substantial gesture of conciliation. It agreed to take over the burden of the Cyprus contribution towards the Ottoman Public Debt Charge. This amounted to £92,800 a year. Formerly the Island had received a grant-in-aid from the Imperial Treasury of £50,000 a year to assist it in meeting this obligation. The remaining £42,800 a year it had to find from its own revenues. The concession made in 1927 by the British Government was however subject to the condition that Cyprus should contribute £10,000 a year towards the cost of Imperial defence and nothing was said about the balance amounting to about £600,000, that Cyprus had paid between 1914 and 1926. The net annual gain to the revenue of Cyprus from this arrangement from 1927 onwards was therefore £32, 800 a year.

11. In spite of this concession, however, opinion in Cyprus considered that the British Government should have assumed the whole liability since 1914, and the situation continued to deteriorate. Further overriding Orders-in-Council were necessary in order to carry on the government. The Parliamentary Under Secretary of State for the Colonies on visiting the Island in 1930 was met with lavish displays of the Greek flag and the occasion was taken to make demonstrations in favour of union with Greece. There was a growing disposition among the philhellenist extremists to resort to deeds rather than words to achieve their objective. In 1931 the campaign of abuse and invective against the British administration became increasingly strong. About this time it was seen that the old Archbishop had not long to live and the Bishops of Kitium and Kyrenia, with a view to the succession, entered upon a competition for popular favour by outbidding each other in seditious speeches and actions in support of union with Greece. The supporters of the movement, who were mostly lawyers, schoolmasters and priests, directed their campaign towards removing the apathy of the villagers in the cause of union. Speeches were every where delivered against the Government. Social clubs and athletic organisations were exploited on behalf of the union movement and it became increasingly apparent that the attempts at conciliation and a liberal policy had had the opposite effect from that which was intended. The agitation came to a head when, in October, 1931, the Greek elected members resigned their membership of the legislative Council. The Bishop of Kitium, the firebrand of the movement, around whom the agitation centred, became an open advocate of violence and illegal processes and made a speech in which he was reported to have spoken as follows:–

> "For the benefit of this country we must not obey their laws.
> Do not be afraid because England has a fleet. We must all try for union
> and, if necessary, let our blood flow."

A few days after this utterance an undisciplined crowd burned down Government House and the whole Island for some days was in a state of revolt. These events are chronicled in detail in the annexed Command Paper, to which reference is invited, and it is not necessary to recapitulate them here in detail.

12. The situation was speedily re-established by the advent of His Majesty's ships, and of troops and aircraft from Egypt. It was made plain to the islanders that however liberal the British Government might have been in its internal policy, recourse to violence would not be tolerated. The ringleaders of the revolt, including the Bishops of Kitium and Kyrenia, were deported and have not since been allowed to return to the Is-

land. As soon as the prestige of the Government was re-affirmed, a series of drastic measures were adopted to restore and maintain order and suppress seditionist agitation. Letters Patent were issued on the 12th November revoking the Constitution of 1882 and abolishing the Legislative Council. The supreme legislative and executive authority was placed in the hands of the Governor. The Defence Order-in-Council, which had been proclaimed upon the outbreak of the disturbances, conferred drastic powers upon the Government. A strict censorship was established and a Press Law was passed which deprived the press of its former liberties. Amendments were made to the Criminal Code, reinforcing the law with regard to sedition. An important step was taken in prohibiting the display of the Greek flag which had for so long been a singular feature in the outward aspect of a British Colony. A levy for reparations was made upon the communities within whose borders damage had been done in the course of the disturbances. Municipal elections, which gave an opportunity for political agitation, were abolished and close control was established by Government over the affairs of the Municipalities.

13. The Government at the same time proceeded with a number of measures for the development and better administration of the Island. Sir Ralph Oakden, an experienced Indian Civil Servant was appointed to visit Cyprus as Financial Commissioner and to report upon its finances and economic resources. The Secretary of State's Agricultural Adviser also paid a visit to the Island to assist in the formulation of schemes of agricultural improvement. As a result, a number of schemes are about to be carried into effect which should prove a material contribution to this important department of the Island's life. The police were reorganised. New measures were taken for the care of the unique antiquities which the Island possesses. Sir George Hill, the Director of the British Museum, and Sir Charles Peers, a former President of the Society of Antiquaries, visited the Island and issued reports as to the measures which should be taken. An unofficial committee, called the Cyprus Committee was formed in England to raise funds for the work and create interest in it in this country. Steps were taken for the enactment of a new Antiquities Law. The educational system in the Island is also being thoroughly reformed. Elementary education, which was formerly largely under the control of unofficial committees, is now under the direct control of Government. An antiquated curriculum has been reformed and steps are being taken to include in it the teaching of English. The secondary schools, which were formerly nuclei of philhellenist propaganda, are being brought more closely under Government control. New measures are being taken for the training of teachers and the whole system is being improved and brought into conformity with modern needs.

14. The results of this combination of firmness and activity on the part of the Government have been excellent. There seems no doubt that the people of the Island welcome the new state of affairs and are happier and more contented than they have ever been under British rule. It has been brought home to them that they are British subjects and that the British Government has no intention of permitting any change in that status. The trend which is being given to education and flying of the Union flag instead of the Greek flag all help to show that disloyalty will not be tolerated. The firm rule of the Government makes a definite appeal to oriental mentality which expects a government to govern. The striking demonstrations of loyalty which occurred on the occasion of the recent Silver Jubilee mark the great change of spirit which has taken place since 1931. It is now realised that Cyprus is an integral part of His Majesty's Empire, and that there is not,

and will not, be any intention of handing it over to foreign power: but it is clear that nothing less than a sustained and uncompromising assertion of British ascendancy is required in order to counter the irredentist influences which threaten the development of the Island as a British Colony.

September, 1935.

II. Letter of H. R. Palmer, 4 June 1938 (CO 67/291/3)

The Right Honourable   Government House
Malcom MacDonald, P.C., M.P.,   Nicosia, 4th June, 1938.
Secretary of State for the Colonies

Sir,

I have the honour to refer to my secret (2) despatch of the 20th May, 1938, forwarding copies of extracts from Police Intelligence Reports on the subject of Nationalistic activities in Cyprus, and to inform you that the movements to which those extracts refer must be regarded as symptomatic of a definite tendency manifested in several directions and on numerous occasions recently towards a revival of pro-Enosis activity by the small but noisy section of agitators who have been in opposition to the policy of the Government of Cyprus during the last two years, and possibly by other external influences.

2. This local opposition, which was to a large extent inspired and guided by Mr. D. N. Dimitriou of Larnaca, culminated last year in an abortive attempt to form political associations in the principal towns of the Island and in the journey to England of the *soi-disant* deputation consisting of Messrs. Dimitriou, J. C. Clerides, and G. S. Vassiliades, for the purpose of representing to the Secretary of State certain aspects of the policy of this Government with which they appear to have supposed the Secretary of State to be unacquainted. Reference to these matters is contained in my secret despatch of the 18th June, 1937, and a note of an interview with Mr. G. S. Vassiliades which took place at the Colonial Office on the 27th July, 1937, was forwarded to me under Mr. Dawe's demi-official letter of the 29th July, 1937.

3. The reply to Mr. Vassiliades, as recorded in the above-mentioned note, was clear and unequivocal and the publication in Cyprus of the statement authorised in your predecessor's secret telegram No. 91 of the 27th July, 1937, to the effect that the Secretary of State fully supported the policy which the Government was pursuing and that there was no prospect whatever of any constitutional change in Cyprus had a steadying and salutary effect on the general situation. I had indeed been led to hope that Mr. Dimitriou and his friends, realising the hopelessness of their position, had decided to address themselves to less controversial and more constructive pursuits. It appears from recent events, however, that this hope was premature.

4. I observe that Mr. Vassiliades stated in his interview at the Colonial Office that "their movement was distinct from the movement for Enosis." It was in the guise of loyal British subjects earnestly desiring opportunities for further co-operation within the framework of the Empire that the members of the deputation came forward to put their case. But the professions of these gentlemen cannot unfortunately be accepted at their face value; and must be judged in the light of the activities which have engaged them and their associates both before their departure and after their return. It is in fact evident that

there is no appreciable difference between the political outlook of Messrs. Clerides and Vassiliades, and that of the Bishop of Kyrenia and the Locum Tenens. The latter, it may be mentioned, has only recently forbidden any service to be held on His Majesty's Birthday, June 9th, in the Greek Orthodox Churches. He has had the Bishop's House at Paphos painted in the Greek Colours, blue and white, and has stated he would welcome Martyrdom de luxe, i.e. deportation, if it were accompanied by a 'pension.'

5. Without however, recapitulating past events, which are sufficiently described in relevant despatches in detail, it may not be inappropriate if I refer to a recent case in which Messrs. Vassiliades and Clerides have been directly concerned, together with a Limassol advocate, Lefkos Zenon, a nephew of an ex-Mayor of Limassol, of scandalous and unsavoury reputation, and a bitter enemy of the present Mayor of Limassol and those associated with him on his Municipal Council. A libel action was recently instituted at Limassol against the Governor in his personal capacity in which Messrs. Vassiliades and Clerides appeared with Mr. Lefkos Zenon for the plaintiff. Subsequently a statement attributed to Mr. Clerides as legal adviser to the Archbishopric concerning the attitude of the Locum Tenens of the Archiepiscopal See towards the communications recently addressed to the latter in accordance with instructions conveyed in your predecessor's secret despatch of the 14th May, and in reply to the Locum Tenens Petition forwarded in my despatch of the 7th January, was to the effect that "The Locum Tenens will not take any steps towards an election, and if an Archbishop is elected by force of legislation, as was done in 1908, he will not be recognised by the Church of Cyprus."

6. Particulars of the libel action mentioned in the preceding paragraph were reported briefly to Mr. Acheson in my demi-official letter of the 27th May. A writ of summons was filled by a certain Joannis Kyriakides, an old man of nearly 90 years, a retired advocate of Limassol and sometime member of the Legislative Council, claiming damages for libel alleged to be contained in a preface, signed by myself as Governor, to a pamphlet entitled "The Criminal Activities of the Hassanpoulia," printed at the Government Printing Office, Nicosia. The son of this Ioannis Kyriakides, Pheidias Kyriakides was gravely compromised in the Limassol riots of 1931, and, though the fact was unknown to the Governor, Ioannis Kyriakides was closely associated with Ali Chelabi, the last of the Hassanpoulia. A copy of this publication was forwarded to your predecessor, and to the Legal Adviser, Sir Grattan Bushe, by myself personally. The District Court at Limassol, on the 2nd June, granted an application to set aside the writ of summons on the grounds that the document was an official publication and as such absolutely privileged under the Civil Wrongs Law, 1932.

7. There is abundant evidence that this action stated to be instituted by this decrepit old man, was not made in good faith, but was part of a deliberate attempt to undermine the authority of Government by means of a personal attack against the representative of the Crown and at the same time to threaten the position of the Mayors of Nicosia and Limassol; of Cypriot members of the Executive and Advisory Councils, and other loyal local advisers of Government. Thus, in the first place, no steps were taken, as is customary in actions of this nature, to approach the defendant with a request for an explanation or apology. Secondly, a letter written by Mr. Vassiliades to one Phanos Ioannides, a notorious agitator now in London, came into my hands a few days after the writ was filed. I enclose a copy of this document, which is sufficiently indicative of the motives by which Mr. Vassiliades and his friends have been actuated. Finally, it is not with-

out significance that the three advocates acting for the plaintiff in this case should have come forward from three different districts in the Island: and all the parties must have been well aware that the Governor was unaware that Mr. Kyriakides was a member of Legislative Council forty years ago, and even of his existence.

8. Mr. Clerides, who conducted the case in Court on behalf of the plaintiff, is, as has been mentioned, also the advocate employed by the Archiepiscopal See. Concerning Mr. Lefkos Zenon, of Limassol, I may add that he is notorious for his pro-Enosis sentiments. A speech made by him on the occasion of the recent Pan-Cyprian sports at Famagusta, expressed the hope that "athleticism and hope will remain under the blue sky of Greece"—an obvious reference to Enosis.

9. But apart altogether from this particular sequence of events, I think it advisable to invite your attention to a recrudescence of pro-Turkish sentiment which has appeared over a period of some months, and particularly during the last few weeks in the newspapers "Soz" and "Ses," which are published in Turkish, and are frequently inspired by Turkish nationalistic influences. The former of these two organs gave considerable space to an appeal of a political character made on behalf of sufferers in the recent earthquake in Asia Minor which was sponsored by the Locum Tenens shortly after his detention at Paphos for political reasons. The articles which appeared praised the Locum Tenens in extravagant terms for his initiative on behalf of the Turkish sufferers and drew attention to the absence of any official appeal by the Department of the Evcaf. This tendency for Greek and Turkish nationalistic influences to join hands in an anti-Government campaign is a comparatively recent development which illustrates the diversity of the channels through which the current of nationalistic feeling is capable of being fostered. An artificial propagandist exuberance and lack of restraint is at the present time being exhibited in connection with the forthcoming visit to Cyprus of the Turkish Naval Training Vessel "Hamadiye" by these newspapers.

10. Another factor which complicates the situation and constitutes an embarrassment to the Government of Cyprus is the continued existence in Greece of certain elements and tendencies of a pro-Enosis character. You are aware from correspondence ending with my secret despatch of the 13th of May of difficulties continually being encountered in connection with the grant by the Greek Government of pensions to Cypriot school teachers. I have now received information from local sources to the effect that a Law will shortly come into operation in Greece dealing with the pensions for Greek doctors in Egypt, and that it is hoped by certain Cypriot Greek doctors here that this measure will be made applicable to them also. This report has not been confirmed, and I refer to it, not in order to suggest that the Greek Government has in contemplation any measures that might be embarrassing to the Government of Cyprus, but as indicative of the existence of propaganda from this quarter which is inimical to the good administration of the people of Cyprus as loyal subjects of the Empire. Further evidence of the "Enosis" movement in Greece is contained in a despatch written by Mr. Hopkinson from Athens on the 19th of May to the Secretary of State for Foreign Affairs, on the subject of the enlistment in what is known as the "National Youth Organization" in Greece of a Cypriot British subject. There is also, now, in Athens a party known as the "National Cypriot Youth," headed by the deportee Bishop of Kyrenia, which is reported to have been formed to combat the spread of Anglophil sentiments in Greece.

11. One more aspect of present-day problems in Cyprus deserves mention; the growth, observed in recent weeks, of so-called labour movements resulting in petty strikes, mainly of a vexatious or frivolous character which it is believed have been inspired to some extent by external communistic influences. I do not suggest that these movements, which have, where necessary, been satisfactorily settled by the intervention of the District Commissioner, have any direct connection with the nationalistic manifestations which I have described in the preceding paragraphs of this despatch, but it is patent that any considerable unrest among those employed in industry might provide a fertile opportunity for exploitation by "politicians" and would undoubtedly be so exploited were those who are insistent for the grant of liberal institutions in a position to gain any measure of influence or power.

12. The only conclusion which can be drawn from this brief survey of the present political situation is that the "Enosis" feeling constitutes an undercurrent in Cyprus which only time, education, and propaganda, coupled with the continuation of firm administration on District lines by Commissioners possessing qualities of tact, experience and sympathy, can eradicate. That the great majority of the people in Cyprus have a loyal and sincere sentimental attachment to the British ideal and especially to the persons of His Majesty and the Royal Family has been amply demonstrated on recent occasions of National mourning or rejoicing, as well as during the visit to Cyprus of Her Royal Highness, the Princess Royal. On the other hand, it has equally been shown that any incident in which Hellenistic feelings can be appealed to is capable of provoking a wide-spread and dangerous response among the populace in urban areas which is still too easily influenced and aroused by a nationalistic cry. Examples of such mass emotion were provided so recently as last year by the visit to Cyprus of Prince Andrew of Greece and the display by the Greek wrestler Jim Londos, to which my secret despatch of the 16th June, 1937 refers.

13. My conclusion is that the present system of administration in the Island which ensures an adequate and continuous local surveillance and control by Commissioners of those political manoeuvers which might threaten or jeopardize good order and peaceful progress in the community must be maintained, reinforced, and strengthened in such a way as to place the authority and prestige of the District Administrations on a permanent and unshakable basis. At the same time, a firm resistance must be maintained to any movement directed to securing "democratic rights" or "electoral privileges" which, if granted, could only lead to immediate and complete deterioration of the administrative situation and to the reflexion of open-voiced sedition and Enosis politics. To any suggestion that in the present state of political tension in the Mediterranean, some concession to the Cypriot nuclei of political unrest in this Island, by giving them greater opportunity for self-expression might be politic and wise, I would reply that such reasoning is quite foreign and inappropriate to the peculiar mentality and conditions of Cyprus; that in point of fact, what the agitators represent to be the wish of the bulk of the people, is not their wish at all; and that, unless we are to run the risk of Cypriot politics becoming a serious factor of permanent embarrassment in our foreign relations in the Levant, we must continue to govern Cyprus firmly, in the same manner in which it has been governed for the past seven years, while making the utmost use of the many Cypriot Councils, Advisory, District, Municipal and others, which now exist, and in which Cypriot opinion is fully and adequately represented.

I have the honour to be,
Sir,
Your most obedient, humble Servant,
H. R. Palmer
Governor

III. Petition from Greece for Enosis, 8 October 1938 (CO 67/282/16)

A. Petition

The Right Honorable Neville Chamberlain,   Athens, 8 October, 1938.
President of the Cabinet Council,
London.

Sir,

The Cypriots residing in Athens have followed with breathless anxiety the recent grave crisis in the affairs of Europe, in which the world's peace trembled in the balance. They shared in the universal relief over the happy outcome of that crisis and in the admiration of Your Excellency's splendid and successful effort for the maintenance of peace, which, as the eminent Prime Minister of Canada said, proved you to be one of great peacemakers of history.

In the course of your effort, for which you have won the lasting gratitude of the wives and mothers of the whole world, you uttered words, which have found a profound echo in every Cypriot's heart. You declared solemnly that to men, who appreciate the great boon of liberty, life without liberty was not worth living. In the House of Commons you declared that Britain could not repudiate the principle of the self determination of nations, which she had proclaimed at the close of the World War, even if that principle now presented itself under more unfavourable conditions. You proclaimed principles of a lofty and generous civilization, which could not fail to touch deeply the people of Cyprus, with their long and desperate struggle for liberty.

We are confident, Sir, that we voice the sentiments of our fellow-Cypriots, in expressing the ardent hope that you personally will give friendly and sympathetic consideration to the Cypriote question in behalf of which we have made so many appeals, thus far without success. We feel sure that you will consent to consider the application of the noble principles enunciated by you to the people of Cyprus, who will repay you with their lasting gratitude.

With the deepest respect
For the Cypriote Fraternity of Athens:
For the Society of Cypriots settled in Greece:
For the Cypriots Youth Association:
For the Cypriote Political Union:
For the Cypriote Labour Union of Athens:

Central Cypriote Office
Paparrigopoulou 3,
Athens.

B. British Commentary

The petition enclosed in the F.O. letter is from the Cypriot community in Greece, asking the PM to allow the principle of self-determination to be applied to Cyprus. It is rather a piece of opportunism by politicians than a plea for the redress of a genuine grievance by people who have some sort of claim on HMG. The F.O. do not wish to acknowledge it & this would probably be the best way to prevent cheap recrimination.

The F.O. in the covering letter at No. 6 say that this is a matter which concerns us rather than them; this would tend rather to throw the onus of ignoring the petition on to the Colonial Office.

The Registry & the Precedents Section have been unable to find any precedents which might indicate the usual action to take in a case like this. On the one hand, it seems that this petition should be ignored as an attempt to create trouble by committing HMG to a definite course of action—it was a garbled enough version of the petition that got through to the German news agencies. On the other hand, it is not desirable that the C.O. should lay itself open in any way to the accusation that it will not listen to petitions.

Under the circumstances perhaps the case could be met by an S.O. letter from Mr. Acheson to Sir A. Noble saying that he feels that the conduct of the Cypriots in Athens, in petitioning for a plebiscite in Cyprus, is a matter that concerns the F.O. & Greece rather than the C.O. and Cyprus, and that he consequently has no comment to make on the F.O. letter of 22 October at No. 6. A copy of this letter, together with No. 6 & enclosure might be sent L/F to Governor for reference.

R. W. Barlow 11/11/38.

IV. Statement for Enosis, January–March 1939 (CO 67/303/12)
A. Introduction

Mr. Emilianides, who has recently been released from internment following the 1931 riots, is now agitating again, and the copy of his speech at No. 1 contains all the familiar arguments advanced by his type in favour of the restoration of the conditions which gave political agitators their opportunity.

R. W. Barlow
2/3/39

The real interest in this, and the reason why it is forwarded, is that the re-emergence of Emilianides is a result of the recent press articles in this country, and the questions in Parliament, suggesting that Cyprus should have a more Liberal form of Government. Sir Richmond Palmer's view, of course, is that any movement towards more Liberal institutions, and in particular towards elections, will revive once more the Enosis agitation in Cyprus, and he has forwarded this extract to show that one of the first results of the representations which have been appearing in the press here has been to encourage a notorious Enosis leader who had abandoned politics to return to them. It is not without significance.

Acheson 3/3/39

Extract From Press Officer's Report dated the 23rd. January, 1939.

ANEXARTITOS (22.1.49):

Advocate A Emilianides, the Cyprus "hommes de letters," reverts to politics.

Advocate A. Emilianides of Nicosia, who was Secretary to the "National Organization of Cyprus" until the 1931 disturbances and has, since his release from internment in the Island following the riots, confined the whole of his spare time and energy to literary pursuits, is again in the political pulpit preaching politics. His first sermon which appeared in yesterday morning's "Anexartitos" is being translated and will be submitted to you in due course.

B. "Criteria on Political Maturity," A. Emilianides, 22 January 1939

OFFICE OF THE
PRESS OFFICER
CYPRUS, 24th January, 1939.

SECRET

Hon. Colonial Secretary,

I have the honour to submit the following translation, in duplicate, of the leading article in "Anexartitos" of 22nd January, 1939, written by Achilleas Emilianides, as promised in my report numbered as above of the 23rd January, 1939:–

CRITERIA ON POLITICAL MATURITY
by ACHILLEAS EMILIANIDES

The accusation which has often been made against the inhabitants of this historic country that they lack political maturity is easy and extempore. An accusation which is untenable and incorrect, frivolous and slanderous, because during the 60 years of British administration a Cypriot was never given the opportunity to try his political merit and faculty.

The argument of the so-called political liberties up to 1931 might perhaps be advanced again frivolously, and it is now the opportunity to clarify this question once for all.

The constitutional régime which had been in operation up to 1931 was nothing but a sham situation which, instead of helping the development of political faculty and bring into notice the great Cypriot leaders, it served to pulverize them in the dim atmosphere of the Legislative Council. The Cypriot politician, the politician of that epoch who was elected after so much trouble and sacrifices had no power at all. In the eyes of the people he was their agent, their legislator and the man who made promises and undertook responsibilities on behalf of his constituents. On entering, however, the Legislative Council's Chamber he realized at once that he had no other power but to make suggestions which were not listened to, propose amendments to draft laws which it was not intended to apply, vote against measures which, in spite of the manifested will of the majority, would have been brought into operation by an Order or by a casting vote. How then was it possible for Cypriot efforts to operate and fructify within such a frame?

That system has already been condemned by many, even by a distinguished professor of Edinburgh University who wrote about Cyprus in the English Review "United Empire." But let also this be noted: When the constitution was amended in 1925 it was not the large electoral area but the smaller area which had been taken as a basis and this was done in order that a Member of the Legislative Council may be bound to and look after the interests of only a specified number of constituents instead of being the representative of Cyprus and take upon himself the care of all its interests.

Let us now come to the method of holding the election and we shall see that it is the system which is again to blame and bears all the responsibility for this wretchedness. Instead of having electoral centres in every village and hold the elections on Sundays, the voters were obliged to travel dozens of miles to find the polling station.

Is then a people politically immature when demanding the settlement of this anomalous and sham situation and struggles against that system which assisted corruption?

Have the people ever been asked to express their opinion or even when not asked to do so, they did express their views in a definite manner, have they been listened to until to-day?

Various arguments have been advanced from time to time which have never been taken into consideration. Even lately, in order to disturb again the atmosphere, the Cypriot politicians who lived ignored for nearly 8 years were accused of philo-fascist sentiments.

No such nonsense and slander has ever been uttered against a people and its politicians.

In this country where the population is 5/6 Greek it always existed a deep appreciation of, and attachment to, the good and lofty liberal principles which the British politician proclaim in the House of Commons. And, exactly because we are Greeks we were taught and learned in our schools to love England as a protector and friend of the Greek nation. In our reading books there were pages regarding Byron, Canning, Gladstone and Queen Victoria.

But we were prohibited to use these reading books and we were recently told by official mouth that political liberties are not suitable for all people and that the Cypriots do not require such liberties. And when the Cypriots protested and said that they believed in the principles which British politicians have undeviatingly proclaimed, they were ordered to keep silent.

It is worth while declaring once more that in spite of all the disappointments which they have experienced the Cypriots in general and each one separately still believe in the British liberal principle and that they hate the Fascist systems as strangling the elements of man's liberties. Everybody has watched with agony the tragedy of unfortunate Ethiopia, and hundreds of Cypriots—the present members of the British Legion—fought on the side of the allies for the lofty ideals of liberty, as it was then said.

It is an easy matter for any one to make an accusation for lack of political maturity. The accused, the pseudonym signatory and those who hold the same views must first examine whether they themselves are politically mature.

A. K. EMILIANIDES.

H. McLaughlan.
Press Officer.

V. "Greater Greece" Movement, 27 May 1941 (CO 67/315/19)

A. "Greater Greece" Movement, 27 May 1941

Colonial Office,
Downing Street, S.W. 1,
27th May, 1941.

Dear Nichols,

I enclose for your information a copy of a memorandum on the "Greater Greece" movement prepared by Battershill, with a copy of his covering letter. A good deal, of course, has happened since the memorandum was written, and local opinion has undergone some change.

A. Mayhew

Memorandum

The idea of a Greater Greece and of Greek Imperialism in the Mediterranean has formed the subject of speculation in Cyprus ever since Greek resistance to Italy proved successful. These speculations have recently been stimulated by an article by Mr. Compton Mackenzie in "Reynolds News." The article itself has not reached Cyprus but according to quotations from it in the Athenian newspapers which have arrived here, the author suggests that Great Britain should declare her decision to cede Cyprus to Greece; guarantee the restoration of the Dodecanese to Greece; give Greece a share in the control of the Suez Canal and ask her to undertake the mandate in Libya.

Cypriot vernacular papers have noticed this.

The <u>Neos Kypriakos Phylax</u> first printed a summary of the article without comment under bold front-page headlines—"English writer supports the creation of strong Greece. Recommends a declaration that Cyprus and the Dodecanese will be ceded to Greece." Later it reproduced a commentary upon the article from the Athenian review "Nike" which reads

> "For the English writer the question of the return of Cyprus and the
> Dodecanese to the bosom of their mother-country does not even arise;
> in this instance it is not a matter of territorial adjustment. Cyprus and
> the Dodecanese will naturally re-enter the organism to which they
> have never ceased to belong. They are Hellenic countries and Hellenic
> they will remain."

(The words "return" and "re-enter" when applied to Cyprus are somewhat significant!) This is probably the most uncompromising expression of Enosis politics which has appeared in the Cyprus press for many years.

The <u>Eleftheria</u> commented on Mr. Mackenzie's article in very carefully worded terms, mentioning that Greater Greece could again make contributions to civilization if she were again given the opportunity hand in hand with England of attaining her former glory, and suggesting the foundation of a new order in the Eastern Mediterranean.

Some examples of opinion on this subject seen in the censorship or expressed orally are given below. Letters continue to come from Greece mentioning Enosis aspirations:

    (a) A leading politician of Larnaca is of opinion that when Italy is destroyed Britain will offer Cyprus to Greece and then the Mayors and the Archbishop will be appointed by Greece (on which grounds he recommends postponement of municipal elections).

    (b) A Cypriot volunteer in the Greek Army writes of the creation of a Greater Greece "which according to the declarations of English politicians will surely include our native land Cyprus."

    (c) A Greek subject recently employed in Cyprus with a mining company and now in Athens writes to a lawyer in Nicosia "I hope that with the triumphs on the Albanian front, England understands that she will render a great service to her own interests to create after the war a Great Greece ruling the Mediterranean and including Cyprus. Consequently we shall see then what we shall do about mining business."

    (d) A domestic servant told his employer, an English administrative officer, that an acquaintance of his had warned him to tell his master to begin packing his bags as in two months time Italy will be defeated and Greece will be in Cyprus.

It is somewhat significant that Germany is never mentioned as an enemy of Greece or as a possible factor in the immediate situation in the eastern Mediterranean. Cypriot opinion has been quite definite that Italy is the enemy of Greece and that Germany will never attack Greece. There are no immediate signs that that opinion has undergone any change even though at the time of writing this memorandum German troops have been on the Greek frontier for some days.

The idea that the end of the war will see the "return" of Cyprus to the bosom of "Mother Greece" is not a new one. A year ago it was being sedulously fostered by the German broadcasts in Greek. These were no doubt mainly directed to Greece in order to discourage the Anglophil attitude of that country with stories of British oppression of Greek Cyprus. At the same time these broadcasts succeeded in engendering in a large number of Cypriots the belief that in return for Greek co-operation a victorious Germany would cede Cyprus to Greece. German propaganda has been silent on that topic for many months and as long as Greece remains Germany's potential, if not actual, enemy it will doubtless so remain.

B. British Commentary, May 1941

All this is prior in date to the Greek collapse. It remains to be seen whether there will ever be an independent Greece again, to say nothing of a "Greater Greece ruling the Mediterranean including Cyprus."

Initialed 19/5/41

VI. Dispatch from C. C. Woolley, 9 June 1943 (CO 67/319)

A. Letter from C. C. Woolley, 9 June 1943

The Right Honourable
Oliver F. G. Stanley, P.C., M.C., M.P.,
Secretary of State for the Colonies.

Government House,
Nicosia, 9th June, 1943.

Sir,

I have the honour to enclose for your information a copy of a memorandum which I have had prepared on the present situation in regard to the agitation among the Greek-speaking population of this colony for union with Greece.

2. You will no doubt have gathered from the spate of telegrams sent to England by various politicians, clubs and political organisations, following the municipal elections of the 21st March 1943 and the debate on Cyprus in the House of Lords on the 31st March, that there has been a pronounced and widespread recrudescence of Enosis agitation here, which up to the present shows little sign of abating.

3. Apart from the above telegrams, other manifestations have been:–

1) Telegrams in the same strain to the Greek and American Governments.

2) Articles and letters almost daily in all the Greek newspapers, advocating union with Greece.

3) Enosis was the main plank in the platform of all national candidates at the recent municipal elections and so popular was the cry that their AKEL opponents were obliged openly to identify themselves with the cause or lose a large measure of popular support. After the elections, the first act of all the Greek members of the municipalities was to send telegrams to England advocating union.

4) Agitation by the Locum Tenens, who, Sunday after Sunday, preaches enosis and is now endeavouring to form a pan-Cypriot council for the prosecution of the national cause. He is receiving active support from AKEL, which in a recent manifesto has declared that union with Greece will be its principal aim after Fascism is defeated.

5) The Mayor of Nicosia and his friends, who are at present at loggerheads with both the Locum Tenens and AKEL and decline to co-operate with them, have issued a separate manifesto calling for support of a united pan-Cypriot front for promotion of the island's national cause.

6) Permits for meetings of a non-political character have been abused in several instances, the meetings ending in demands for union.

7) At the recent annual Flower Carnival in Nicosia, attended by the Mayor and the Greek Consul, there were enosis displays and tableaux. One of these symbolically proclaimed that the Cypriots prefer the rags of their mother to the gold of their foster-mother. The Greek national anthem only was sung, and Greek flags only were flown. (I should mention here that this Government has no fault to find with the Greek Consul, who, in somewhat embarrassing circumstances, has up to the present invariably maintained an attitude of scrupulous correctitude, which, indeed, does nothing to endear him to the more fanatical Cypriot nationalists).

8) Attempted demonstrations, which were easily suppressed, in Famagusta and Nicosia by students and schoolboys carrying flags and shouting "Enosis."

4. I wish to make clear that up to the present there have been no disorders of any kind, and the agitation has been pro-Greek rather than anti-British in character, though there is perhaps an under-current of anti-British feeling. The immediate aim of the agitators is to prepare the way by intensified propaganda, both at home and abroad, for a united demand by the entire Greek-speaking population in the Colony for union after the war. Nor would it appear that at the moment the temper of the people is such that disturbances are likely to occur, but the situation is unquestionably deteriorating and its potential dangers must not be under-estimated. Indeed, it is the opinion of some of the Government's official and unofficial advisers who were here at the time that the situation already resembles that immediately preceding the 1931 riots.

5. Advantage is being taken of the tolerance shown and latitude given by the Government since Greece entered the war, and it is reasonably certain that if the present agitation is allowed to go on unchecked it is bound, sooner or later, to lead to trouble requiring force to suppress it. The political situation must be looked at against the psychological background of a volatile, unstable and sentimental Mediterranean people, whose acts are governed by emotion, not reason. It is here that the danger lies. The movement tends to undermine the authority of the Government, bringing it into contempt and making administration of the country increasingly difficult. The loyal elements, both in the Government service and outside, are discouraged, while the Turkish community in particular is becoming restive and apprehensive and is forming its own "self-defensive" organizations. This development accentuates racial animosity. Doubts as to our intentions, which unimpeded displays of Hellenic "patriotism" arouse, are throwing this usually loyal minority into the hands of Turkish nationalist politicians who preach that it must look to Turkey and not to Britain for inspiration and protection. It must be supposed, too, that the apprehensions of the Turkish community do not pass altogether unnoticed in Ankara.

6. There is only one satisfactory answer to this question, namely a definite pronouncement by His Majesty's Government as to the future of Cyprus. As such an announcement is impracticable in present circumstances, it remains to be considered what action can and should be taken to minimize the dangers to which this agitation is giving rise. I am naturally anxious that any action taken should not precipitate a situation more serious than it is at present or one that it is designed to avoid. Disturbances, or even active non-cooperation by the people, at the present time would not only be unfortunate in themselves but also in the repercussions which they would have abroad. At the same time it is my view, which is shared by my advisers, that in the interests of law and order the present agitation should not be allowed to continue and that some unmistakable indication should be given to the public that the law must be respected. Unless this is done the movement will gather strength and there can be no question that as soon as the restraint imposed by the war and by the presence of large bodies of British troops in the country is removed, there will be trouble. It may come even during the war: for example, if the Greek Government returns to Athens, we must be prepared for hysterical local reactions which, like those that marked the entry of Greece into the war in 1940, it will be neither possible nor politic to suppress.

7. With these considerations in mind and to prevent the situation from getting out of hand I would recommend in the first place that I should be authorized to announce, with reference to recent representations which have been received by His Majesty's Gov-

ernment from various bodies in Cyprus, that, as stated in December 1941, the question of the transfer of Cyprus to Greece is not under consideration by His Majesty's Government.

I further feel bound to recommend that the following executive action should be taken:–

(a) all telegrams and other correspondence to addressees abroad advocating union should be stopped in censorship and their publication in the local press prohibited. All incoming correspondence of a similar nature should also be stopped.

(b) all applications for permits to hold processions or meetings to advocate union with Greece should without exception be refused. As reported in my telegram no. 226 such an application made on behalf of Mr. Servas, Mayor of Limassol, has already been refused and I have since refused similar applications for meetings at Famagusta and Paphos.

(c) where permission given for meetings of a non-political character is abused by references to enosis, any further applications by the same persons to hold meetings should be refused.

(d) should any associations such as those contemplated by the Locum Tenens and the Mayor of Nicosia be formed for the express purpose of advocating a change in the sovereignty of the Colony, they should be prohibited from holding meetings.

(e) the local Greek press should be warned that further agitation in their columns for union with Greece can no longer be permitted and that disregard of this warning will render them liable to action under the Criminal Code and the Newspapers, Books and Printing Press Law.

8. While it is impossible to say with certainty what the reaction will be to these steps, it is my belief that they will have the desired effect and that there will be no serious repercussions. Any public protests which may result will be tempered to some extent if the repeal of certain provisions of the Church Laws of 1937 is simultaneously announced. On the latter subject I am addressing you separately in this mail.

9. I would add that I have consulted my Executive Council and the senior Administrative Officers on this matter and they are unanimously of opinion that the measures proposed in this despatch are called for and should be taken without delay.

I have the honour to be,
Sir,
Your most obedient,
humble Servant,
C. C. Woolley
Governor.

B. Memorandum on "Enosis," May 1943

Memorandum by the Cyprus Secretariat.

May, 1943.

"ENOSIS."

Without attempting any detailed survey of the origins of the Enosis movement it is worth recalling that it is no new development. The community of language and religion with the people of Greece and the desire to exchange the humble reputation of the Cypriot for the reflected glory of Ancient Hellas had already created a problem before the British occupation 65 years ago. If since then it has gathered strength this is less through dissatisfaction with the results of British administration of the island than through the belief that a Greek administration would be more sympathetic and cheaper. Such sentiments are often dormant but they are always liable to be played upon by politicians—which they were with serious consequences in 1931. In the sequel to those disturbances the outward paraphernalia of the enosis movement disappeared but its roots were not cut.

2. In the pre-war period, though the activities of Cypriot politicians were for the most part directed toward securing for themselves a larger say in the administration of the Colony, signs were not wanting to show that the feeling of kinship with the Greeks was unchanged; indeed, with the continuous contacts with Greece which improved communications (including broadcasting) provided, it could not have been otherwise. The Church too, retaining something of the political leadership which the Turkish administration had recognized and being jealous of the prospective ascendancy of secular politicians, tended to counter the movement to secure political liberties by cultivating and championing "national" instincts. It was by pandering to such instincts that the Locum Tenens with an eye on the Archiepiscopal throne, sought to retain his popular following, and it was' his preaching of enosis doctrine which led to his restriction to Paphos for a year on two occasions. Symptomatic of this attitude of the Church is that prayers were and are regularly said for the King of the Hellenes in all Orthodox churches.

3. On the outbreak of the present war the agitation for the grant of political privileges subsided, but at the instigation of the Locum Tenens, then rusticated to Paphos, the Church adopted a non-co-operative attitude reflecting the neutrality of Greece. The preaching of tendentious sermons continued, and movements which tended to keep Greek nationalist sentiment alive and to discourage the growth of a patriotic interest in the progress of British war activities were surreptitiously fostered. The press, which had only lately been released from strict control, gained boldness during the first year of the war and its insistence on the Hellenic character of Cypriots was a feature of a recrudescence of enosist activities in the Spring of 1940. Further support for the cause of enosis of a most undesirable character was forthcoming at this time in the Greek broadcasts from Berlin. But for all this enosis remained very much in the background and interest in it was largely academic up to the time of Italy's attack upon Greece.

4. The decision of Greece to resist the violation of her territory inspired spontaneous demonstrations of enthusiasm in Cyprus: processions carrying Union Jacks and Greek flags paraded the streets and for many days a spirit of exaltation prevailed. These demonstrations were perfectly friendly and indeed were partly inspired by satisfaction at the union of British and Greek arms against the common foe; the Locum Tenens himself proclaimed that all differences with the Government were ended. But the Greek successes in Albania and the prospect of Greece wresting the Dodecanese from a prostrated Italy seemed to some enthusiasts to pave the way for the inclusion of Cyprus in the Greek Kingdom and thus the "sacred struggle of mother Greece" became identified with the

239

cause of "enosis." General Metaxas himself said "we cannot leave those who belong to our race in foreign hands." Meanwhile Greek exploits were lauded in the press to the exclusion of other war news, funds to aid Greece were opened; an abortive effort to raise volunteers for the Greek Army was made and Greek Independence Day on 25th March 1941 was celebrated with exceptionally extravagant vociferation.

All this was cited as proof of the Hellenism of Cypriots through which they would qualify for inclusion in the Greater Greece which some English writers advocated.

5. The disillusionment which followed the occupation of Greece by the Axis was intense, and under threat of the invasion of Cyprus enosis was for the time being forgotten. The desire for enosis, always difficult to assess, had none the less been strengthened by the valour of Greek resistance, for the Cypriot was more than ever wishful to share the Greek name to which such glamour had accrued. On the other hand the alliance of Britain and Greece in the war, by dissolving the restraints imposed in previous years on such manifestations as the flying of Greek flags, provided the politicians with effective means for playing on nationalistic sentiment whenever the occasion offered.

6. In the autumn of 1941 the advocates of enosis took heart from the apparent adoption of their cause by the Greek premier who at a public banquet in London, which was attended by British politicians and officials, said he visualized the expansion of Greece after the war to include various territories including Cyprus. This statement was publicized by the B.B.C.; it was the starting point for much exuberance in the Cyprus Greek press, which represented it as a clear promise of union with Greece, and it was acclaimed in numerous congratulatory telegrams sent to Mr. Tsouderos at the instigation of nationalist politicians. Such was the resulting excitement and such the anxiety of the Moslems that an official statement, authorized by His Majesty's Government, to the effect that the cession of Cyprus to Greece was not under consideration was published on 2nd December 1941. But this did not dispel the belief that the Greek Government was not only in favour of enosis but was prepared openly to support it. Indeed Mr. Tsouderos, in replying to his congratulators, expressed confidence in the settlement of the Cyprus question after the war in accordance with the principles of freedom and justice—a catchphrase which has seen much service in Cyprus before and since.

7. The next revival of enosis agitation had purely local origins. The year 1942 saw a steady gathering of strength on the part of the Labour element which was not unconnected with the general consensus of opinion that the Red Army looked like a winner. The Nationalist politicians, who broadly speaking represent local vested interests, were disturbed by this development and particularly by the demand of Labour for constitutional liberties: these politicians feared their own eclipse by Labour in elected bodies. Their reply was the old cry "enosis or nothing." In a series of able and effective articles the leading Greek newspaper "Eleftheria" proclaimed this as the orthodox enosis faith and castigated those who were demanding mere political liberties unconnected with the union of Cyprus and Greece.

8. The antipathy which the nationalist politicians felt and still feel for organized Labour was not based solely on class difference. On the entry of Greece into the war the trade unions had failed to co-operate in the various "patriotic" activities. The most they would do was to collect funds to aid Greek air raid victims since this was not contrary to the habit of boycotting the "imperialist" war—a habit which they had learnt from non-belligerent Russia. For this "anti-Hellenic" policy the unions were much criticized and

some resignations ensued. After the German attack on Russia had brought the Soviet Union into the Allied camp, AKEL (the new "anti-fascist" Labour Party) decided, however, to embrace the cause of enosis in order to widen its appeal. But the party's opponents remained unconvinced of any change of heart; nor have they been appeased by the efforts of AKEL to prove the depth of its follower's patriotic sentiments by celebrating such occasions as Greek Independence Day and the anniversary of the Italian attack upon Greece. Meanwhile the nationalist politicians and press continued to reiterate their faith that enosis would follow Allied victory, as night the day, and this was sustained by the encouragement it occasionally received from Greek sources.

Such was the approach to enosis from the two opposing directions when in the wave of political activity prior to the municipal elections in March, 1943 the time honoured practice of appealing to the emotional Cypriot by beating the enosis drum once more brought the subject to the forefront of the political arena.

9. "National" parties contested the elections in each of the five District towns where there was a poll. Enosis was the one positive feature of their programme and the abuse of Labour opponents was always coloured by the assumption that these, with their pro-Russia bias, were traitors to the national cause. To this there came the answer from the Labour camp (which provided the only opposition in all towns except Paphos) that the workers were no less loyal to the "national aspirations" than the nationalists ding-dong combats ensued in which the candidates vied with one another in the extravagance of their enosis speeches. And when the issue was decided the new mayors, nationalists and AKEL-ites alike, all promised faithfully to work to the goal of enosis. The celebration of Greek Independence Day, which happened to follow six days later, gave them an early opportunity of proving their worth as patrons of enosis; and so the torrent of seditious and inflammatory oratory flowed on. The populace, reacting speedily to the stimulus, paraded in the streets singing national songs and marked the climax of their church services with shouts of "Zito Enosis!" in towns and villages alike.

10. Hardly had this excitement abated when the first news of the debate on Cyprus in the House of Lords came through. The nationalist press lost no time in trumpeting that the Under-Secretary of State's references to the prospects of self-governing institutions left the Cypriots cold, seeing that their one and only aspiration was "complete national restoration as a member of the Greek family." The news that Lord Faringdon had ridiculed the Cypriots' alleged loyalty to the Greek Crown added fuel to the fire. The Labour newspapers were not slow to follow suit and, led by the Mayor of Nicosia, the politicians clubs and organizations throughout the country signified their Hellenic patriotism by sending telegraphic protests to the Prime Minister of England. One hundred and seventy odd of these messages were sent. Some enthusiasts also hastened to reassure the Greek Premier that they remained loyal to the enosis cause notwithstanding all the talk in London about self-government and their messages were acknowledged "with appreciation."

11. Other factors which have contributed to sustain enosis propaganda at a high level were the knowledge that there are well known people in Britain who are sympathetic to the conception of a Greater Greece—such as Mr. Compton Mackenzie whose full-blooded championship of enosis has been fully reported in Cyprus—; and the efforts of nationalist politicians to close their ranks following the successes of Labour in the municipal elections. The foundations of future trouble have been laid in the establishment of new

nationalist organizations in several centres. The main object of these is to combat AKEL but their methods will undoubtedly include the persistent reiteration of enosis claims.

12. In enosis politics the attitude of the Locum Tenens of the Archiepiscopal See has always to be reckoned with. He has lately been flirting with AKEL, whom he cannot be supposed to love, and has praised its "national activity." In spite of criticism of this unnatural alliance he has stuck to his guns, stressing the need for the unity of all classes and parties if the goal is to be reached. Bishop Leontios' attitude has been vigorously defended by the Labour press and his supposed rapprochement with AKEL is a useful point to make in answering critics of the Party's communistic proclivities.

The Locum Tenens' ambition to establish an island-wide organization covering all existing nationalist, Labour and rural groups to promote the enosis cause is not yet within sight of achievement, for despite their common cries of enosis the rift between Labour and their opponents has been widened by the municipal election campaigns. Indeed, the antipathy between the two camps is such that the untutored observer might be excused for supposing that enosis was in issue between them rather than between the Greek Cypriots and His Majesty's Government.

13. It may be argued that this state of affairs is not unsatisfactory from the Government's view point, and indeed there are other factors which might suggest that the present agitation, though it will not subside, will not rise above its present level. Labour is not sincere in its adherence to the enosis cause (the persecution of so-called communists in Greece before the war has not been forgotten); the mercantile community has a lively appreciation—though of course it would not admit this—of the benefits bestowed by the £ sterling and a British passport; the well-to-do as a whole realize that after the war Greece will be burdened with a costly task of reconstruction and they fear that their place in the Panhellenic Paradise may be that of paying guests; the refugees, who for the most part come from the poorer strata of Greek society, have not been the best advertisement for Greek administration; there is an uncomfortable feeling that the Greek tendency to despise Cypriots will be accentuated by the islanders' indifferent contribution to the war effort; and last but not least there is the restraining influence of the presence of a strong garrison in the island.

14. In face of all these considerations one might reasonably expect that the present storm would blow itself out and be followed by only occasional gusts of fluctuating intensity; and with the advent of the hot weather—normally the close season for political excitements—it might legitimately be concluded that there is little reason to apprehend seriously untoward developments in the immediate future. But unfortunately logic and reason do not mould the course of political events in Cyprus for the Cypriot is essentially the creature of his emotions and self-control is not the strongest of his characteristics. It cannot be disputed that as regards "national aspirations" the emotional temperature has been steadily rising. It has received stimulus from both English and Greek sources and the excitable unthinking mob in every town and the ignorant peasantry in every village have been re-infected. So long as the tolerance which has been shewn up to now is allowed to continue the atmosphere will be combustible. There are several directions from which the spark might be struck which will ignite this inflammable material and precipitate a conflagration. There is the animosity between the worshippers of Greece and Russia, there are the outraged feelings of the Turkish minority (one-fifth of the population) at the prospect of their abandonment to the "revengeful Greeks," and it is not impossible

that the flagrance and persistence of Cypriot disloyalty may some time try the patience and good humour of our own soldiers too far. Among a people of so mercurial a temperament as the Cypriots it is impossible to predict where and when an explosion might occur. But it would be folly to deny that a point has been reached where there is danger of an explosion if some precautions are not taken.

15. The alternative to continuing to run this risk of disturbance by pursuing a policy of *laisser aller*, is to take the steps which the law provides to stop the seditious activities which inflame separatist sentiment and bring the Government and the law into contempt, and to make it plain that these activities will not be tolerated in future. It is not unreasonable to suppose that the bulk of the population would acquiesce, as they did in the past when firm action was taken against enosis agitation (for example, when the Locum Tenens was rusticated to Paphos). What the Government sacrificed in popularity it would gain in respect.

16. Continued inaction by the Government will be construed as timidity and weakness of which full advantage will be taken by the irresponsible elements. It may even be construed as an indication that His Majesty's Government is inwardly disposed to cede Cyprus to Greece after the war. The agitation would thus gather further strength. Economic difficulties and unemployment problems following the completion of defence works are likely to add to the difficulties of the situation. Moreover it is important to bear in mind that Greece may be re-occupied some time before the end of the war and even if active Greek support for the enosis cause is not forthcoming the influence of radio and the newspapers from Athens will once more play upon local sentiment and a much more serious situation may easily develop then.

In the meantime, quite apart from the incessant embarrassments caused to the administration by the obligation to turn a blind eye daily to active sedition and the interference with orderly government which this agitation imposes, the perpetual cry of "enosis or nothing" will stultify, as it did before in 1931, every effort of progress which the Government may attempt or the people desire.

C. Extract from Bulletin, October 1943

SECRET

EXTRACT FROM ISSUE NO. 2 OF OVERSEAS SECURITY AND SHIPPING INTELLIGENCE BULLETIN, DATED OCTOBER, 1943.

SECURITY INTELLIGENCE

13. Enosis

During the last 30 years the demand for Enosis, meaning Union (with Greece implied), has been the burning question in Cyprus politics. The majority of the Orthodox Christian community, asserting their right to self-determination, which to their mind has been reaffirmed by the terms of the Atlantic Charter, urge that in view of the identity of their speech, religion and (although this is a moot point) descent, Britain should hand over the island to the Mother Country as she did the Ionian Islands. The offer of Cyprus to Greece in 1915 in return for her entry into the war appears to them to indicate that Britain has acknowledged the relationship and is not indisposed to consider parting with the Colony. Assurances that it is the policy of H.M.G. in time to make Cyprus a self-governing Colony within the Empire do nothing to diminish the demand. The barrage of telegrams protesting against the Duke of Devonshire's recent statement on Cyprus in the House of Lords repeated in unequivocal terms that the sole aspiration of Orthodox-Christian Cypriots is Enosis.

The prospect of self-governing exercises little attraction for this people who have been subject to foreign races almost since the beginning of history. Imbued with a marked inferiority complex, their one ambition is to share the traditions and prestige of a nation with which they feel they have some affinity. They prefer to be treated as foundling children by Greece than even as independent members of an alien commonwealth which although rich and powerful has no emotional appeal. The political liberties, which are demanded until the end of the war permits the realisation of Enosis, are sought mainly in order that the campaign for Enosis may thereafter be more effectively prosecuted.

Previous to 1821 Greece had been like Cyprus part of the Ottoman Empire, and there was little traffic between the two. On Greece declaring her independence however, intercourse increased, encouraged by the Church, and Athens became among other things the centre to which Cypriot-Greeks went for higher education.

The assumption by Britain of the administration of the Island from Turkey was hailed with delight, mainly because of the untold wealth which it was thought association with the Empire would bring. The liberal constitution introduced by Gladstone in 1880 was also well received. As however prospects of a Golden Era vanished and the British officials showed little disposition to mingle with the inhabitants on equal terms, enthusiasm flagged, and as European peoples became nation-conscious, the Enosis movement began.

It did not however acquire momentum until the Balkan war of 1912, when a number of Cypriots, including members of well-known families served with the Greek forces. But as until the Annexation of 1914 Cyprus remained Ottoman territory the demand for Enosis could not be too rigorously pressed as it was realised that the ultimate control of the destiny of Cyprus lay with Turkey, and not with Britain.

After 1924 when British possession was formally recognised in the Treaty of Lausanne, there remained no apparent obstacle to Britain giving expression to her traditional benevolence to smaller powers and Enosis propaganda became more vocal. Speeches advocating Enosis became a stock feature of any gathering, political or social, while streets and buildings were draped with Greek flags on the slightest pretext.

The disturbances of 1931 were the culmination of a rivalry between political factions to demonstrate their "patriotism" (Hellenic) although discontent with the local administration also played a part. Afterwards Enosis propaganda was squashed with a heavy hand during what the Enosists call "the 10 years dictatorship." As the Colony began to enjoy a period of unprecedented prosperity and the population became absorbed in money-making to the exclusion of politics, the movement might but for the war have been stifled.

With the diminution of private trading after 1939, however, attention reverted to political issues, and the Italian attack on Greece in 1940 furnished the opportunity for Enosis leaders to fan the smouldering embers. The local Government could scarcely take exception to the celebration of an Ally's feats of arms in Albania, and the Greek flags which had lain in mothballs since 1931 were hoisted again. Enosis propaganda appears as Cyprus' contribution to the war effort.

When Greece fell in 1941 but continued fighting and the liberation of Europe became the battle-cry of the Allies, the local orators claimed that no more worthy tribute could be paid to her services to the cause than the inclusion of Cyprus in Greater Hellas. That they themselves should contribute practical support to Greece has rarely been hinted, and the hint has always been coldly received and studiously disregarded. Since 1941 recruiting for overseas service has been at a low ebb and appeals for funds for Greek charities have been poorly answered, while the interest shown in the first refugees quickly evaporated.

The Enosis movement should not be construed as necessarily anti-British. Britain's long-standing friendship with Greece is keenly appreciated, Byron, Canning and Codrington being local heroes, and the appeal for Enosis is to her reputation for fair play which stands high. Among a people afflicted with xenophobia the individual Englishman is well received. The local administration's periods of popularity have admittedly been few, but that arises from the necessity of keeping a tight grip on a people not naturally amenable to law and order.

(Extract from Security Summary—Middle East No. 135)

D. British Commentary

Mr.Law's suggestion was that the Cyprus Government should stop through the censorship "any telegrams from Enosists to the Greek Government."

The Governor does not define exactly what he suggests. But reading the letter and enclosure together it seems that he has in mind stopping through the censorship all letters and telegrams to and from Cyprus from and to foreign countries on Governments which are calculated to encourage Enosis sentiment: and forbidding the publication of such communications in the Cyprus newspapers.

This step is, I imagine, quite likely to be raised in the House, if it is approved, and of course it is capable of being raised in an embarrassing form, if, for example, a message which is ostensibly one of congratulation or greeting to the Greek King or Prime Minister on the occasion of some Greek anniversary or festival is stopped on account of the usual Enosis twist.

If the Governor's proposal is adopted, is it to be extended to communications to and from this country? I should see no objection to that, although I imagine communications to and from Members of Parliament must be exempted . . .

There is however another issue. The emergence of a political party pledged to Enosis, logical though it is in itself, is a challenge to the Government. It constitutes a defiance of the law (being an unlawful association under the Cyprus Criminal Code Section 61(b)), all the more significant in Cypriot eyes because it would not have been tolerated or even contemplated a few years ago. If the party becomes a live well-organised political body it is capable of giving great impetus to the Enosis movement in Cyprus, which has hitherto had no organisation behind it and has been kept before the public rather by spasmodic activities of the Locum Tenens and a few other individuals than anything else. Even if the party is not allowed to hold public meetings to advocate Enosis, it could still do much to give strength and coherence to the movement. The Governor is as No. 20 shows anxious about the situation caused by the revival of Enosist activities and is proposing to address the Secretary of State officially about it. But he does not suggest that anything should be done to prevent the foundation of this illegal body, feeling perhaps that such action might do more harm than good in view of the potential reactions in Cyprus or in Parliament here. On the other hand it will he very much more difficult to take action against it, if and when it has succeeded (as it may) in organising itself into a strong political party with wide popular support.

A. B. Acheson 11/6

While I agree that it is most desirable to be "tough" with these Enosists and to strengthen the Governor's hands I am far from convinced that his proposal is calculated to achieve his object.

2. The fact that such messages were being held in Cyprus would become known and in any case it would be necessary to give instructions openly to the Press not to publish such messages. Protests to individuals in London would be made and the matter would almost certainly be raised in Parliament where, though there would be little sympathy for the Enosists, much play would be made regarding freedom of the individual and freedom of the press. We could hardly stop Enosist communications going to President Roosevelt and so the ban would apply almost solely to the Greek Government which might ask why it had been singled out for this treatment. There is a good answer but would H.M.G. wish to state it in terms?

3. Apart from the difficulties at this end would the proposal have any real effect in damping down Enosis? I do not think it would. The main effect would be to stop some of the more open signs of Enosis and while this would be to the good it would not go far; for the Cypriot is wily enough to take other measures for keeping alive this sentiment.

4. I have the greatest sympathy with the Government whose position is a difficult one and I agree with his view that unless something is done fairly soon there may be trouble. He is addressing S.S. officially on this subject and I suggest we should await that despatch sending him in the meanwhile a telegram draft marked A.

Initialed 24/6

Mr. Acheson.

I should explain to you, and have explained to the Secretary of State, that para. 2 of this letter probably refers to a conversation between the Principal concerned in the Foreign Office and myself. The suggestion was made to me that probably the best thing would be for the Governor of Cyprus to stop any telegrams issuing from Cyprus to the Greek Prime Minister or other members of the Greek Government. I replied that it was not so much the telegrams from Cyprus which gave cause for embarrassment as the replies which were returned to them, and that I could well imagine that there might be difficulties if the Governor were to impose a ban on any outgoing messages to members of the Greek Government on such an occasion as yesterday. I said that I also thought that there might well be repercussions in Parliament if action of the kind contemplated was, in fact, taken by the Governor. I certainly did <u>not</u> say that it would <u>not be possible</u> to do what the F.O. suggested.

Initialed
26.3.43.

I have discussed this letter with Sir Charles Woolley. He was rather attracted by the suggestion that telegrams conveying Enosist sentiments to members of the Greek Government should be held up in the censorship. But he would like to consider it with his advisers in Cyprus. The absence of the normal replies would lead to enquiries. If the enquirers are informed that the telegrams had been held up by the Censors there may be political reactions locally which would be more objectionable than the reactions to which the current arrangements give rise, particularly if members of the Greek Government can be persuaded to send colourless answers to such telegrams.

Initialed 30/3

Sir G. Gater.

I have delayed this owing to pre-occupations with Palestine affairs.

The Governor's despatch and enclosure No. 22 in this file which should be read with his despatch No. 9 in 90129/3 shows that a more serious state of affairs exists in Cyprus now than was the case when he was here earlier in the year. This is largely due to the holding of municipal elections, to the passions aroused locally by the debate on Cyprus in the House of Lords, and to the fact that the war is receding from Cyprus.

The red light is clearly showing and the situation seems to be moving towards the position in 1931 just before the riots.

It had been hoped when Sir C. Woolley was here that we could hold the position until the end of the war when the fate of Cyprus will be finally decided; but I am beginning to doubt whether we can maintain this attitude without risk of serious trouble.

The Governor's suggestions are contained in paragraph 7 of his despatch. It follows from my minute of 24th June that I do not think his proposals at (a) and (e) of paragraph 7 would achieve much locally while they would be likely to raise difficulties at this end. I have in mind the possibility of some statement on the Palestine model which would not go to the extent of compromising the post war settlement but which would suggest that speculations of this kind should now cease as they are harmful to the war effort.

Mr. Shaw is coming to England and I suggest that this should be kept for discussion with him. Before his arrival I will have a draft statement and other suggestions ready for consideration.

Initialed 5/7

VII. Dispatch from A. B. Wright, 5 December 1949 (CO 67/352/2)

<u>TO THE SECRETARY OF STATE FOR THE COLONIES</u>

<u>FROM CYPRUS </u>(Sir A. Wright)
5th December, 1949.

IMMEDIATE
Secret

Consideration of possible developments in the "plebiscite" affair reported in my secret telegram No. 586 leads me to address the following representations to you in connection with the telegraphic correspondence about Enosis and the Greek Government.

2. About one week before the plebiscite movement was reported, I learnt that Ethnarchy was contemplating extension of propaganda campaign in two stages as follows.

First, a plebiscite to be carried out in the churches. Second, formal election (in accordance with local procedure of electing archbishop) of persons (? to go) to Greece to represent Greek people of Cyprus in Parliamentary Chamber in Athens in imitation of historic coup adopted for Crete.

3. Now that adoption of first stage of the campaign (though without mention of churches) has been announced by Ethnarchy possibility that it may proceed to second stage cannot be ignored. One local Greek paper has this morning announced intention of Ethnarchy that plebiscite should be immediately followed by "declaration of union" and election of deputies to the Greek Chamber. "Declaration of union" is a familiar phrase locally as having been used as signal for outbreak of disturbances in 1931.

4. Certain aspects of this possibility may have important bearing on attitude of Greek Government towards Cyprus. If locally elected Cypriots were to go to Greece and request admission to Chamber, Greek Government would no doubt have to ensure that admission was refused and the general tenor of British Ambassador's advice suggests that resulting popular and press clamour in Greece would bring fall of Greek Government or resignation of responsible Ministers. It seems, therefore that eventuality of Prime Minister's resignation would be rendered more and no less probable by refraining now from effective action. Without sustained hope of influential support from Greece, Ethnarchy would hardly proceed with proposed campaign. Campaign is, however, well timed in view of impending elections in Greece.

5. Possibility (outlined in next paragraph) that local Communist Party may become partners in the campaign described above might induce Greek Government not only to bring to an end the situation already complained of but positively advise Ethnarchy (through channels at its disposal) to abandon campaign.

6. In the interest of a common front on Enosis question A.K.E.L. party through medium of E.A.S. has announced . . . is prepared on certain conditions to back with all its power plebiscite proclaimed by Ethnarchy. Meanwhile it will continue collection of signatures for memorial to United Nations. One of the conditions is that delegates representative of all parties should be chosen to raise Cyprus question with United Nations. Whether or not United Front was achieved, A.K.E.L. would doubtless exploit situation to utmost of its ability in order both to promote internal disorder and to attract external interference on international plane.

7. I am satisfied that large majority of the Greek population here view proposed plebiscite with misgiving if not with fear, but it would not openly be opposed and any attempt by this Government to prevent it would be ill advised. Should, however, movement proceed to second stage, widespread excitement would be engendered for A.K.E.L. to

exploit and it would be imprudent to ignore possibility of situation (in) which only course to prevent serious disorder would be to proclaim Defence Order in Council full powers.

8. All such developments may be avoided if Greek Government could now be induced to dissociate itself from Enosis campaign and to make clear to the people in Cyprus that it was doing so in a genuine desire to cooperate with the British Government and without any reservation.

9. I will inform you of any significant advance in the above reported movement. If the plebiscite is proceeded with I should be disposed to issue pronouncement of the Government's intentions towards any undesirable developments (paragraph 7 above) and including repetition of His Majesty's Government's policy towards status of Cyprus. I would consult you about its terms.

VIII. Visit of Cyprus Ethnarchy Delegation to the United States, 1950 (CO 67/370/4)

CONFIDENTIAL

Visits of Cyprus Ethnarchy Delegation to the United States.

The "plebiscite" held in Cyprus on the 15th of January, 1950 and throughout the following week resulted, as expected, in an overwhelmingly large vote in favour of union with Greece (Enosis). It is estimated that about 96% of the Greek population of the Island signed. (One fifth of the population is Turkish and is strongly opposed to Enosis.)

2. The reactions of the Cyprus Communist Party and the Cyprus Church was in each case to send a delegation to bring this result to the notice of countries likely to be interested. The communist delegation first came to London, where they attracted little attention and were refused an interview by the S. of S. for the colonies. Since then they have been travelling round the capitals of Eastern Europe. They have been following the line that union with Greece cannot be hoped for while the "monarcho-Fascist puppet government" in Athens continues in existence under the thumb of the Anglo-American Imperialists: consequently the cause of the Cypriots is identical with the cause of the enslaved Greek workers. Cyprus is a useful card in the Communist hand, both on account of its strategic importance and on account of its potentialities as a source of friction between the British, Greek and Turkish governments.

3. The Church, or Ethnarchy, Delegation, which has consistently refused to have anything to do with its rival, started off by visiting Athens where it remained for several weeks. The Government of General Plastiras maintained upon the whole, a correct attitude. After General Plastiras had interviewed the Delegation a communiqué was issued stating that:

> "As regards the Greek Government, the latter intends to treat the question of Cyprus within the framework of its relations with the great power which is its friend and ally as soon as it considers that the time is propitious for a favourable settlement."

4. In general however the Delegation had considerable success in Athens. The Speaker of the Chamber accepted a volume containing plebiscite signatures and large and enthusiastic meetings in favour of union were held. More important, the Archbishop of Athens took the cause up and it appears that the machinery of the Greek Orthodox

Church is now well engaged in the Enosis campaign. This will doubtless have repercussions among the Greeks and Cypriots in the United States.

5. In August the Ethnarchy Delegation went on to London where they attempted, without success, to see the Prime Minister, the Secretary of State for the Colonies and the Archbishop of Canterbury. In refusing to receive the Delegation the Secretary of State for the Colonies wrote to its leader, the Bishop of Kyrenia, that while he would have been glad to see the Bishop in other circumstances he considered that no useful purpose would be served by his receiving the Delegation which he was leading since the views of H.M.G. on the subject he proposed to raise had already been made clear on a number of occasions.

6. Meanwhile both the Communist Delegation and the Ethnarchy Delegation have stated that they would bring the Cyprus question before the U.N.O. They have in fact missed their opportunity as regards the forthcoming session; but it does not follow that they will let the plan drop.

7. The view of H.M.G. is that it is essential that full sovereignty should be maintained in Cyprus and that the less the question of union with Greece is discussed the better.

Index